The Tenth Justice

The Insanity Defense and the Trial of John W. Hinckley, Jr.

THE
TENTH JUSTICE

THE SOLICITOR GENERAL
AND THE RULE OF LAW

BY

LINCOLN CAPLAN

ALFRED A. KNOPF · NEW YORK

1987

THIS IS A BORZOI BOOK
PUBLISHED BY ALFRED A. KNOPF, INC.

Grateful acknowledgment is made to the following for
permission to reprint previously published material: *Thomas
Barr:* Excerpts from "Statement by the Lawyers' Committee
for Civil Rights Under Law," June 4, 1985, by Thomas Barr
et al. Reprinted by permission of Thomas Barr. *Archibald
Cox:* Excerpts from the lecture "Storm Over the Supreme
Court," given at Hunter College in 1985. Reprinted by
permission. *Harvard Law School Library:* Excerpt from a
Memorandum dated March 8, 1933, by Felix Frankfurter, from
the Felix Frankfurter Papers, Harvard Law School Library.
Reprinted by permission.

Portions of this book originally appeared in *The New Yorker.*

Library of Congress Cataloging-in-Publication Data

Caplan, Lincoln.
The tenth justice.

Bibliography: p.
Includes index.
1. United States. Solicitor General. 2. Government
attorneys—United States. 3. Rule of law—United
States. I. Title.
KF8793.C36 1987   347.73'16   87-45342
ISBN 0-394-55523-6   347.30716

For Susan

Contents

Solicitors General
of the United States

Name	Term	President
Benjamin H. Bristow	October 1870–November 1872	Grant
Samuel F. Phillips	November 1872–May 1885	Grant
John Goode	May 1885–August 1886	Cleveland
George A. Jenks	July 1886–May 1889	Cleveland
Orlow W. Chapman	May 1889–January 1890	Harrison
William Howard Taft	February 1890–March 1892	Harrison
Charles H. Aldrich	March 1892–May 1893	Harrison
Lawrence Maxwell, Jr.	April 1893–January 1895	Cleveland
Holmes Conrad	February 1895–July 1897	Cleveland
John K. Richards	July 1897–March 1903	McKinley
Henry M. Hoyt	February 1903–March 1909	Roosevelt
Lloyd Wheaton Bowers	April 1909–September 1910	Taft
Frederick W. Lehmann	December 1910–July 1912	Taft
William Marshall Bullitt	July 1912–March 1913	Taft
John William Davis	August 1913–November 1918	Wilson
Alexander C. King	November 1918–May 1920	Wilson
William L. Frierson	June 1920–June 1921	Wilson
James M. Beck	June 1921–June 1925	Harding
William D. Mitchell	June 1925–March 1929	Coolidge
Charles Evans Hughes, Jr.	May 1929–April 1930	Hoover
Thomas D. Thacher	March 1930–May 1933	Hoover
James Crawford Biggs	May 1933–March 1935	Roosevelt
Stanley Reed	March 1935–January 1938	Roosevelt
Robert H. Jackson	March 1938–January 1940	Roosevelt
Francis Biddle	January 1940–September 1941	Roosevelt
Charles Fahy	November 1941–September 1945	Roosevelt
J. Howard McGrath	October 1945–October 1946	Truman

Name	Term	President
Philip B. Perlman	July 1947–August 1952	Truman
Walter J. Cummings, Jr.	December 1952–March 1953	Truman
Simon E. Soboloff	February 1954–July 1956	Eisenhower
J. Lee Rankin	August 1956–January 1961	Eisenhower
Archibald Cox	January 1961–July 1965	Kennedy
Thurgood Marshall	August 1965–August 1967	Johnson
Erwin N. Griswold	October 1967–June 1973	Johnson
Robert H. Bork	June 1973–January 1977	Nixon
Wade H. McCree	March 1977–August 1981	Carter
Rex Lee	August 1981–June 1985	Reagan
Charles Fried	October 1985–	Reagan

The Tenth Justice

I

The Tenth Justice

THE UNITED STATES takes pride in its commitment to the rule of law, and during this century the individual who has best represented this dedication may be a little-known figure called the Solicitor General. The nation's constitutional government is distinguished by its need for the consent of the governed, and the law is the compact between the people and their representatives. Of all the nation's public officials, including the Attorney General and the Justices of the Supreme Court, the Solicitor General is the only one required by statute to be "learned in the law."[1] Although he serves in the Department of Justice, and his title, like the Attorney General's, is displayed in large bronze letters on the facade of the Department's building, he also has permanent chambers in the Supreme Court. The fact that he keeps offices at these two distinct institutions underscores his special role. The Solicitor General's principal task is to represent the Executive Branch of the government in the Supreme Court, and when he takes the lectern before the Justices, his status is clear. With his assistants and other lawyers for the government, the Solicitor General is among the last attorneys to carry on the custom of arguing at the Court in formal garb of striped pants, dark vest, and tails. The Justices expect the substance of his remarks to be distinguished as well. They count on him to look beyond the government's narrow interests. They rely on him to help guide them to the right result in the case at hand, and to pay close attention to the case's impact on the law.[2]

Because of what Justice Lewis Powell has described as the Solicitor's "dual responsibility"[3] to both the Judicial and the Executive Branch, he is sometimes called the Tenth Justice.[4] Although he operates in a sphere of government that is invisible to almost all citizens, his influence is undeniable. Some parts of it are not hard to measure. During the 1983 Term of the Supreme Court, of the 3,878 petitions for writs of certiorari (the form in which most parties ask the Court to review a case) submitted by lawyers across the country, the Justices granted only 3 percent. Of petitions from the Solicitor General, they approved 79 percent, or almost four out of five. Whenever the government supported a petition as amicus curiae, or friend of the Court, in a case where it was not directly involved, the chances that the Court would approve the petition rose from 2 percent to 78 percent—up thirty-nine times. The Solicitor General, unlike the ordinary legal counsel, appeared to have almost a standing invitation to come to the Court, and was able to bring along most advocates he sponsored. Once he arrived before the Court, he was even more effective. Of the 262 cases the Justices considered that Term, the government took part in 150. The Solicitor General (or SG, as he is called) won 83 percent of his cases outright and partial victories in another 2 percent, for an exceptional overall success rate of 85 percent.[5]

While the SG's performance has only rarely reached this level,[6] it has been remarkably better than the record of nongovernmental attorneys in almost every year since the SG became the government's chief lawyer and began to do what most people assume falls naturally to the Attorney General. Until 1853, the Attorney General's was a part-time job. He had a smaller salary than the other members of the President's Cabinet, and was expected to supplement his income through the cases that he attracted in private practice because of his office. The government's modest amount of legal business was then managed by lawyers who did not work for the Attorney General, and its court appearances in civil suits were dealt with by a Solicitor in the Department of the Treasury.[7]

In the mid-nineteenth century, as the country grew, the volume of official legal work expanded and became more than the government could handle. Private attorneys then took on the public's cases. But their judgments about the law were sometimes at odds with the government's, and their fees were high. As dissatisfaction with this arrangement spread, a congressional panel known as the Joint Committee on Retrenchment recommended that a Ministry of Justice be established to save money and consolidate the government's legal work under one master. The legislators also realized that the Attorney General was increasingly preoccupied with management and politics, and had little time for the intricacies of courtroom law.

In 1870, when Congress created the Justice Department, it drew on the model of Treasury's Solicitor and directed that "there shall be . . . an officer learned in the law, to assist the Attorney-General in the performance of his duties, to be called the solicitor-general. . . ."[8] Congressman Thomas Jenckes, a Republican from Rhode Island who sponsored the bill establishing the office, explained: "We propose to have a man of sufficient learning, ability, and experience that he can be sent to New Orleans or to New York, or into any court wherever the government has any interest in litigation, and there present the case of the United States as it should be presented."[9] Though early SGs tried occasional cases before juries (the first Solicitor was Benjamin Bristow, who had made his reputation prosecuting the Ku Klux Klan),[10] the people in the office have for many years concentrated on the government's appeals, especially to the Supreme Court.

In 1986, the Justice Department had 5,107 attorneys.[11] The SG's office had only twenty-three, the size of a small law firm. The Solicitor's team has always been relatively tiny, but within the Executive Branch the SG has played a powerful and almost judicial role consistent with his standing as the Tenth Justice. For every petition the SG sends to the Supreme Court, he rejects five from federal agencies with grievances they want the Justices to settle.[12] Often he spurns an agency's request because he thinks it is wrong about the law. (A Solicitor General once wrote, "Government lawyers, like those in general practice, may experience that marvelous adjustment of perspective which often comes to the most ardent advocate when he loses—that is, the realization that he really should have lost.")[13] Even if he thinks the agency is right, the SG is not easily persuaded to allow an appeal. As the then Associate Justice William Rehnquist noted with approval in a 1984 opinion, "The Solicitor General considers a variety of factors, such as the limited resources of the government and the crowded dockets of the courts, before authorizing an appeal." [14] If the facts of a case that the government has lost are so unusual as to give it little weight as a precedent, or if there is general agreement among the dozen regional U.S. Courts of Appeals about the law under scrutiny, the SG will usually accept the defeat.

Lawyers on the Solicitor's team prefer to talk about the cases they present to the Supreme Court, but they spend half their time sifting through proposed appeals from trial-court rulings against the government. [15] In a speech at the University of Oklahoma, one Solicitor General bragged, "If the district court in Oklahoma City makes a decision which the United States Attorney doesn't like, he may well tell the press, 'I am going to appeal.' When I see those statements in the press, I say to myself, 'Yes, he is going to appeal if I say he can.' But sometimes I don't." [16] The SG and his staff have a reputation for stinginess, and the trait matters because they are in effect a court of last resort. By screening cases that they believe are not ready for hearing by the Courts of Appeals or the Supreme Court, the Solicitor General and his aides help assure that judges rule on those the SG does consider ripe for appeal.

The SG's influence at the Supreme Court is even more striking than his authority within the Executive Branch. He does not sit beside the Justices on the bench, but he stands in place of them when he decides which cases should be taken to the Court. For all its dominance, the Supreme Court is a relatively passive institution: the Justices must wait for litigants to raise issues before they can address them. And they rely on the Solicitor General more than anyone else to help choose and present the most pressing matters for review. Not long before he died, in 1985, retired Justice Potter Stewart said that he and his colleagues regarded the SG as a "traffic cop," acting to control the flow of cases to the Court. [17]

It was William Howard Taft, a former SG himself, who, as Chief Justice, made the Solicitor so essential to the Justices on this count. Taft believed that citizens were entitled to one appeal, not two—the appeal they could take from a trial in federal court to a Circuit Court should end the government's duty to provide a safeguard against an unfair ruling in the lower court. [18] In 1925, he helped guide through Congress a law known as the Judges' Bill, which ended the Justices' duty to take almost every case appealed to them, and increased their discretion to select the cases they wanted to hear and let others rest as lower courts had decided. Once empowered to pick most of its cases, the Court relied on the SG to guide the choice.

The influence of the Solicitor at the Court goes beyond helping the Justices set their docket. The Justices also turn to the SG for help on legal problems that appear especially vexing, and two or three dozen times a year they invite him and his office to submit briefs in cases where the government is not a party.[19] In these cases especially, the Justices regard him as a counselor to the Court.[20] But in every case in which he participates, the Justices expect him to take a long view. The Solicitor General advises the Court about the meaning of federal statutes as well as about the Constitution, so his judgments regularly affect the work of the Legislature as much as the Executive and the Judiciary. Lawyers who have worked in the SG's office like to say that the Solicitor General avoids a conflict between his duty to the Executive Branch, on the one hand, and his respect for the Congress or his deference to the Judiciary, on the other, through a higher loyalty to the law.[21]

For many generations before the Reagan era, in both Democratic and Republican administrations, the Solicitor General more often than not met the standards of a model public servant— discreet, able, trustworthy. Most took him for granted. During the first six years of the present Administration, however, the role of the Solicitor General was transformed. The transformation went considerably beyond the normal, unexceptional differences in policy and approach that can naturally be expected to occur from one SG to the next. Instead, far-reaching changes were pushed through by Presidential Counsellor–turned–Attorney General Edwin Meese and Assistant Attorney General William Bradford Reynolds, two of the Administration's most powerful and controversial officials; the changes were resisted by Rex Lee, the Administration's first SG, who has since returned to private practice and to the teaching of law at Brigham Young University; they have been carried out by Lee's successor, the present Solicitor General, Charles Fried; and they are at the center of many of the deep, near-seismic reforms that the Reagan Administration has tried to bring about in American law.

II

Lore

IN A CORRIDOR on the fifth floor of the Justice Department, where the lawyers in the SG's office work, photographs of thirty-six of the thirty-eight men who have served as Solicitor General hang in a kind of gallery. Aside from one in color and a sepia-toned print whose border seems tinged with gold, the photos are black-and-white. Like the reputation of the archetypical SG, the subjects of the pictures appear direct, upright, and somehow eccentric. Almost half wear mustaches. None is a woman, and two— Supreme Court Justice Thurgood Marshall and former appeals court judge Wade McCree—are black. Their average tenure has been three years.

Except for a few articles in law reviews, occasional mentions in books about other legal topics, and speeches by Solicitors reprinted in bar journals, little has been written about the SG. The history of the Solicitor General is passed on among the small circle of lawyers who know about it—usually by moving down the line of men pictured in the gallery and telling stories of what they and their teams contributed to the office. The stories are then retold to a new SG or lawyer in the office so he will know the tradition he's expected to uphold.[1]

By most accounts, John W. Davis, who was SG from 1913 through 1918, was one of the truly distinguished Solicitors. He was then appointed Ambassador to Great Britain (in 1918), and ran for President (in 1924), but while he was SG he made the job more prestigious than the Attorney General's.[2] As soon as Davis began his first argument before the Supreme Court as Solicitor General, Chief Justice Edward White sighed in relief: the government's brief was in good hands. As SG, Davis often took long walks with the Chief Justice, who used the chance to remind Davis about the Court's reliance on him. White generally did not say much about himself, but one day he stopped, planted his feet, and said, "You know, Mr. Davis, I'm not an educated man. Everything I get I've got to get through my ears. If you say that something happened in 1898, and the next time you say it happened in 1888, why Sir, it's just as if you'd stuck a knife in me!"[3]

Thomas Thacher, SG from 1930 through 1933, perfected a technique that became an insider's signal of the Solicitor's views. Thacher had given up one judgeship to take the job, and subsequently filled another judgeship, and, perhaps because of his judicial temperament, he was reluctant to sign briefs whose legal validity he doubted; but he was also unwilling, on the other hand, to withhold from the Supreme Court arguments he could not fully discredit. In close cases, he decided, he would sign the government's brief, but tag on a disclaimer that became known among the SG's lawyers as "tying a tin can." "The foregoing is presented as the position of the Internal Revenue Service," the brief would clatter, letting the Justices know it was not the Solicitor General's view. Since the Court rarely subscribes to the arguments of a brief from any part of the government without the SG's sponsorship, the judgment that Thacher (and, later, others) expressed by tying a tin can was usually decisive.[4]

One of the SG's more distinctive practices is known as "confessing error." If a private attorney wins a case he thinks he should have lost in a lower federal court, he is likely to accept his victory in diplomatic silence. But when the government wins on grounds that strike the Solicitor General as unjust, he may "confess error" and recommend that the Supreme Court overturn the flawed decision. Most confessions of error involve criminal convictions, and happen for a range of reasons: a jury was selected unfairly; a judge gave faulty instructions to the jury before asking its members to reach a verdict; there was scant evidence supporting the verdict.

Confessions of error please almost no one but the SG and the defendant, who goes free. The government lawyers who have tried the case feel betrayed. The judge whose decision the SG wants overturned thinks the rug has been pulled out from under him by a double-dealing government. Judge Learned Hand sometimes complained, "It's bad enough to have the Supreme Court reverse you, but I will be damned if I will be reversed by some Solicitor General."[5] Some current members of the Supreme Court—Chief Justice Rehnquist and Justice Byron White, in particular—clearly dislike the practice, and browbeat the SG when he steps up to confess.[6] Rehnquist has urged his colleagues that they should not "respond in Pavlovian fashion"[7] when the SG confesses error, but should instead make their own ruling on the case.

But Archibald Cox, who was SG from 1961 to 1965 and who ranks with Davis and former Supreme Court Justice Robert Jackson as one of the three most respected Solicitors, has expressed a stalwart's faith in the practice of confessing error. "It tests the strength of our belief that the office has a peculiar responsibility to the Court," he told the Chicago Bar Association in 1962, during his tenure as Solicitor.[8] "It affects the way all our other cases are presented. If we are willing to take a somewhat disinterested and wholly candid position even when it means surrendering a victory, then all our other cases will be presented with a greater degree of restraint, with a greater degree of candor, and with a longer view, perhaps, than otherwise." The view expressed by Cox was originally endorsed in 1942 by the Supreme Court, in an opinion that declared, "The public trust reposed in the law enforcement officers of the Government requires that they be quick to confess error when, in their opinion, a miscarriage of justice may result from their remaining silent."[9]

The best-known instance of a Solicitor General acting with candor and disinterest, to use Cox's terms, occurred in 1955, when Senator Joseph McCarthy was just past his heyday and the influence of McCarthyism was still heavy. Someone accused John Peters, a physician, of disloyalty to the United States and membership in the Communist Party. Peters was a senior professor of medicine at Yale University, and had advised the Surgeon General for years as a consultant. The government found Peters innocent of the charges in eight separate hearings held over four years, but he was eventually judged unfit for government service by an agency known as the Loyalty Review Board.[10] The board relied on confidential informers and would not let Peters know the identities of, or cross-examine, these witnesses. He claimed he had a constitutional right to confront them and to rebut the charges they made against him. At every stage of the board's hearings against him, the only evidence publicly introduced was favorable testimony from an ex-president of Yale, a distinguished federal judge, and others in the doctor's corner. The case against him was based on secret testimony—as the chairman of the review board put it, on "evidence given by confidential informants not disclosed" to Peters.[11]

The Solicitor General was Simon Sobeloff, who held the post from 1954 to 1956. When Peters appealed, Sobeloff concluded that it would do no one any good for the Justice Department to oppose him in the Supreme Court. With the encouragement of Attorney General Herbert Brownell, Jr.,[12] the SG set out narrow grounds for siding with the doctor. As Sobeloff indicated, the case had "far-reaching importance."[13] It was bad for Peters to be kept in the dark about his accusers, but it was worse that the members of the Loyalty Review Board, acting as judges, were also ignorant about the identities and, therefore, the reliability of some of the informants. The SG called this "well-nigh indefensible," and concluded, "The President recently said in his State of the Union Message: 'We shall continue to ferret out and to destroy communist subversion. We shall, in the process, carefully preserve our traditions and the basic rights of every American citizen.' Now is the time, and this case the appropriate occasion, I believe, for showing the country that the Administration is as firmly pledged to the second sentence as the first."[14]

Brownell asked other senior officials at the Justice Department to consider Sobeloff's argument. FBI Director J. Edgar Hoover strongly disapproved, and Brownell rejected the Solicitor General's proposal.[15] Sobeloff decided his only option was to withhold the SG's backing from the government's case. He refused to sign the government's brief or to argue its merits before the Supreme Court, and another Justice Department official took over the case. The Court ruled against the government and for Peters, though the Justices did not address the major constitutional question.

Outside the Court's rarefied circle, the idea of refusing to represent the government may sound like the gesture of a prima donna.
If you do not like what the government stands for, why not quit?
The answer lies in the SG's responsibility to the Court as well as
the Executive, and, because of that, Sobeloff's decision set a standard of integrity for SGs to come. It also cost him considerably.
Prior to Sobeloff's taking his stand, he had been promised a seat
on the Court of Appeals for the District of Columbia, perhaps as
a step to the Supreme Court. ("Every time Sobeloff comes to see
me," said Justice Felix Frankfurter, "I feel as if he's taking my
temperature.")[16] Not long afterward, a seat on the appeals court
came open, but Sobeloff was passed over in favor of the man who
had taken on the Peters case for the government—Warren Burger.
Burger made his name as a conservative foil to the liberal majority
of the D.C. Circuit, and later was appointed Chief Justice of the
United States. Sobeloff eventually filled a seat on the federal Court
of Appeals in Maryland.

Had Sobeloff gone on to the Supreme Court, he would have
been one of a handful of SGs who have subsequently won such
appointment. They include William Howard Taft, Stanley Reed,
Robert Jackson, and Thurgood Marshall. Lloyd Wheaton Bowers
would have been in this group, but he died before President Taft
was able to appoint him.[17] (As of this writing, Robert Bork has
been nominated to the Court, and, if confirmed, he will join this
select company.) With such other distinguished figures as Archibald Cox, the first Watergate Special Prosecutor, the SGs-
turned-Justices lead a pantheon of highly respected lawyers who
have served in the SG's office and gone on to positions of wide
esteem in the law. Many of the more prominent former SGs may
have become judges in part because the SG's office itself has a
judicial cast.[18] A young law professor who hopes to work there
said, "It's the only spot, besides a judgeship, where your job is to
figure out what *you* think is the right answer for the law and then
to present your argument to the highest court in the land."[19]

The post itself gets a lot of deference from members of the bar,
whatever their station. In 1940, Frank Murphy, an experienced and
vain politician then freshly appointed to the Supreme Court, asked
a clerk if any member of that bench had ever held as many important public offices as Murphy himself. "Well, there was Taft," the

clerk answered. "He was Solicitor General, he was a Circuit Court judge, he was president of the Philippines Commission, he was Secretary of War, he was President of the United States, and, of course, he was Chief Justice." Crestfallen, the new Justice asked, "He was Solicitor General, too?"[20]

Not all the stories about the SG's office make dignified heroes of their subject. From 1933 to 1935, a North Carolina trial lawyer named J. Crawford Biggs was Solicitor. One Justice referred to him as "Serjeant Buzfuz," after the Dickens character whom Biggs seemed to resemble.[21] In the eyes of an attorney who worked for him in the SG's office, Biggs was "kindly, honest, and gentle, and just unqualified for the job."[22] After the new man's first Term as SG, the Justices sent word to President Roosevelt that Biggs should be forbidden to argue again if the Administration wanted to win any cases before the Court.[23]

Part of the blame for Biggs's appointment can be laid on Felix Frankfurter. Then a professor at Harvard Law School, he had declined Franklin Roosevelt's offer of the post. "I was lunching with Mr. Justice Holmes on March 8, 1933, the occasion of his ninety-second birthday," Frankfurter wrote in a memo to himself,[24] when he was summoned to see the President. "I want you to be Solicitor General," Roosevelt told him. "This took me completely off my feet," Frankfurter reported, but he apparently recovered quickly. "If you don't mind my saying so," he told the President, "I think I know the demands of that office perhaps more completely than there is reason for you knowing them. I have known about the work of that office almost from the time that I left the Law School. It is exciting and profoundly important professional work. But if a man is to be Solicitor General, he must make up his mind that it will absorb sixteen hours of the day." Frankfurter added, "It is my genuine conviction—I am sure it is so—that I can do more to be of use to you by staying in Cambridge than by becoming Solicitor General."

After Frankfurter convinced Roosevelt he could serve the New Deal better from Harvard than from the Justice Department ("Felix is a stubborn pig!" FDR grumbled,[25] but the President did not hold it against Frankfurter, and eventually appointed him to the Supreme Court), the professor suggested that Roosevelt name Dean Acheson instead. Acheson was a partner in a leading Washington law firm now known as Covington & Burling and a former law clerk to Justice Holmes. As one former Solicitor put it, "He was well qualified, would have been a fine SG, and would doubtless have gone on to the Supreme Court." [26] But Roosevelt could not appoint him: Acheson's father was Episcopal Bishop of Connecticut, and had refused to grant a divorce to Homer Cummings, blocking Cummings from a third marriage in the church. Cummings was by then Roosevelt's Attorney General, and he vetoed Acheson. Roosevelt threw up his hands and said, "Well, get me somebody!" [27] And in place of Acheson, who later became a distinguished Secretary of State, Cummings and the President chose J. Crawford Biggs.

Biggs was not the only ill-chosen SG. J. Howard McGrath, the Solicitor from 1945 to 1946, distinguished himself by leaving his duties almost completely to his assistants. [28] He had been appointed for political reasons, [29] and he was the only SG to argue no cases at all before the Supreme Court while he held the title. [30] He was elevated to Attorney General after a year as Solicitor, but he fell into shady dealings, and was charged with covering up the abuses of some cronies. He resigned. [31]

Walter Cummings, Jr. (no relation to Homer), [32] also became Solicitor General for reasons besides pure merit. His tenure officially began in December 1952, in Harry Truman's last full month as President, and it lasted ninety days, until soon after Dwight Eisenhower was sworn in—the shortest stint ever for an SG. In the SG's office and at the Supreme Court, the thirty-six-year-old Cummings was known as the "boy wonder." The word was he had been brought back from private practice to become Solicitor (he had already spent six years as an assistant to the SG) because his father, the chairman of a big Chicago bank, had guaranteed some loans for Truman's 1948 campaign. [33] ("That's the first I've heard of it," Cummings said when he was asked about this.) Whatever the story, Cummings later proved himself. After practicing law for the next decade, he was appointed to the U.S. Court of Appeals for the Seventh Circuit, in Chicago, where he now sits regularly on a three-judge panel composed entirely of alumni from the SG's office.

Because of the stellar quality of his aides, boasted Francis Biddle, who was Solicitor in 1940 and 1941, "My assistants could draw rings around most of their contemporaries in private practice." He went on, "The Solicitor General's office was small, compact, and easily managed, with a tradition that excluded hacks and enlisted men of marked ability, all of them young."[34] Biddle and others relied on gifted lawyers, some of whom backed up three, four, or five SGs, and then moved on to more visible assignments. Not long before Biddle's time, when Stanley Reed was Solicitor General (from 1935 to 1938), the assistants included perhaps the most talented lawyers who ever worked in the office. Among them were Edward Ennis, who became head of the American Civil Liberties Union; Warner Gardner, later a well-regarded Washington lawyer at his firm of Shea & Gardner; Henry Hart, who earned a reputation as a pioneering scholar for his inquiries into federal law and the legal process; Alger Hiss, the central figure in a perjury trial of the nineteen-fifties, before his rise and fall; Charles Horsky, eventually a senior partner at Covington & Burling; Harold Leventhal, later an influential member of the U.S. Court of Appeals for the District of Columbia; and Charles Wyzanski, who made his mark as a strong-willed federal trial judge in Boston.

Onetime lawyers in the SG's office tend to be proud and even sentimental about their service, showing off the collections of quill pens they have picked up from counsel's table at their arguments in the Supreme Court. (Before every argument at the Court, a bailiff lays out on both counsels' tables writing quills like the ones originally used by Chief Justice John Marshall, and lawyers are welcome to take them as souvenirs.)[35] Though his former aides sometimes confess that Reed was the only SG to faint before the Supreme Court in the middle of one of his own arguments,[36] they treasure a picture of the Reed gang of assistants, decked out in double-breasted suits with formal vests, as a prized keepsake.

Biggs was firmly propped up by Erwin Griswold, and McGrath by Paul Freund, a former law clerk to Justice Louis Brandeis and aide to Reed. Both Griswold and Freund confirmed their youthful promise by later accomplishments. Griswold became dean of the Harvard Law School and, after twenty-one years in charge, returned to the Justice Department as Solicitor General from 1967 to 1973, under Presidents Lyndon Johnson and Richard Nixon. Freund became a great constitutional scholar and the editor of a definitive history of the Supreme Court. Outside academic circles, he is sometimes recognized as the man who turned down President John F. Kennedy's offer of the Solicitor Generalship. Freund's work on the history of the Court had just begun when the offer came, after the election in 1960, and he felt he should not abandon his new venture. "I'd rather make history than write it,"[37] Kennedy told Freund, probably not knowing that Freund had already made some history as McGrath's stand-in.

During his time in the SG's office, Freund once made a memorable argument for the government in a minor case. By the time he was supposed to speak, the Justices had said everything he had planned to, in their harsh questions to his opposing counsel. Freund rose and said, "May it please the Court, there is a typographical error on page ten of our brief," which he corrected. "If there are no questions, the government rests." The Justices looked surprised but then pleased, and gave the United States a unanimous decision. For years afterward, Felix Frankfurter told friends about Freund's moment, "Since I've been on the Court, I've heard learned arguments, I've heard powerful arguments, I've heard eloquent arguments. But I've heard only one *perfect* argument."[38]

The aide who guided the SG's office while Walter Cummings carried the title was Robert Stern. He never became as well known as Griswold or Freund, even in legal circles, but he may have achieved as much influence. There are many books written by former Solicitors or by lawyers on the SG's staff ("This manuscript was originally written in odd intervals between arguments in Court as Solicitor General," Robert Jackson wrote in the introduction to his book *The Struggle for Judicial Supremacy*),[39] and not all are good. James Beck (SG from 1921 to 1925) was a reactionary man, whose trademark in oral argument before the Supreme Court was quoting liberally from Shakespeare. ("I hope to God Mrs. Beck likes Shakespeare!" Justice Holmes muttered at the close of one of Beck's arguments, loudly enough for many in the courtroom to hear.)[40] Beck also wrote a primer called *The Constitution of the United States,* which a leading constitutional scholar of the time, Thomas Reed Powell, mocked in the *New Republic*. "The new book which Mr. Beck has written about the Constitution is a very different kind of book," he observed. "You can read it without thinking."[41]

In 1950, Stern co-authored with Eugene Gressman, professor

of law at the University of North Carolina, a book titled *Supreme Court Practice*, which answered a need of many attorneys—and of the Court. Now in its sixth edition, and co-authored as well by a former Deputy Solicitor General named Stephen M. Shapiro, the tome (1,030 pages long, and sold for ninety-five dollars in 1986) is accurately billed as offering "everything that a lawyer should want to know in prosecuting or defending a case in the Supreme Court." [42] On its endpapers the volume includes floor plans of the Supreme Court building, so lawyers who use the book can find their way from the checkroom or the lawyers' lounge on the first floor to the Clerk's office and the cafeteria on the floor below, or to the Library on the third floor. Since the book was first published, the Justices have sometimes taken suggestions for changes in the Court's procedures that are made in one edition and adopted them as official rules reported in the next. [43]

Erwin Griswold is now the patriarch of the extended SG family. His memory of office lore stretches back to 1929, when, at the age of twenty-five, he first joined the four other lawyers then on staff, and it covers almost half the history of the Solicitor General. Many other lawyers, who once worked there or still do, have memories that help define the SG's tradition as well. "If there is a secret handshake," said David Strauss, a former assistant to the Solicitor General and now an assistant professor at the University of Chicago Law School, "it is that there is a way of being a good government lawyer, with the government's interests in mind. There is a feeling of unity, and it's never stronger than when you know you have differences of opinion about policy, but are bound in your commitment to keep the barbarians at bay, to maintain the integrity of the law." [44] Solicitor General Frederick Lehmann once declared in a brief confessing error for the government, "The United States wins its point whenever justice is done its citizens in the courts." His declaration was carved into the rotunda of the Attorney General's office at the Department of Justice as a reminder to all his visitors, and it is a motto of the SG. [45]

In the terms of the Solicitor's office, it has been important for the SG to be "independent" in order to fulfill his duty to both the Executive Branch and the Supreme Court, and to help the courts do justice. Former SG Francis Biddle crystallized the theory of independence in his memoir titled *In Brief Authority*. [46] The SG, he wrote, "is responsible neither to the man who appointed him"—that is, the President—"nor to his immediate superior in the hierarchy of administration"—the Attorney General. "The total responsibility is his, and his guide is only the ethic of his law profession framed in the ambience of his experience and judgment. And he represents the most powerful client in the world. Nor are there any of the drawbacks that usually go with public work, no political compromises, no shifts and substitutes, no cunning deviations, no considerations of expediency," Biddle wrote. "The Solicitor General has no master to serve except his country."

Biddle's words describe an ideal that has never been entirely fulfilled. Not even he questioned that the Solicitor General works for the Attorney General and serves at the pleasure of the President.[47] He understood that the word "independent" does not mean the SG should be free to argue points of view that regularly diverge from the administration's. The Executive Branch is in some sense the SG's client, and within the bounds of the law the SG must strive to represent its interests as they change from one administration to the next. In any case, he is not likely to disagree often or by much, because a President will not appoint—and certainly will not keep—a Solicitor who does not share his vision of the law.

Nonetheless, by tradition, and because of his responsibilities to the Court, an SG must be free to reach his own carefully reasoned conclusions about the proper answer to a question of law, without second-guessing or insistence that his legal advice regularly conform to the politics of the administration he represents. An SG must have the independence to exercise his craft as a lawyer on behalf of the institution of government, without being a mouthpiece for the President. To a remarkable degree, as each Solicitor General has placed his own stamp on the job, he and his staff have often made arguments to the Supreme Court as if they had no greater authority to satisfy within the government than the SG himself and the traditions of the office. The government has profited from this standard, and, according to lawyers who represent the government and those who regularly oppose it, so has the rest of the country.[48]

III

The SG and
the Supreme Court

THE RELATIONSHIP BETWEEN the Supreme Court and
the SG's office has long been more intimate than anyone at either
place likes to acknowledge. From the nineteen-twenties, and possibly before, through the early seventies, once a Solicitor General
was confirmed by the Senate, he began his tenure by paying his
respects to the Court and formally calling on each of the Justices. [1]
As an old SG hand put it, "They impressed on the Solicitor
General their reliance on the accuracy and trustworthiness of the
government's briefs, and their expectation of high quality. They
put the fear of the Lord in a new SG, and he would come back
to the office determined that the highest standards would be met." [2]
During the first visit of one new SG, Justice Frankfurter gave him
detailed instructions to pass on to the lawyers in the SG's office:
one should keep his voice up during arguments, another shouldn't
talk so much, and a third was hopelessly dull and should not be
allowed to argue at all. Paul Freund said, "It doesn't take a sledge-
hammer to make an impression when a member of the Court says
something to the Solicitor General."

The Justices also, then and now, have kept up with the lawyers
in the SG's office while they are on active duty. In 1985, one Justice
told about attending lunches with the assistants and the deputies,
though not with the SG himself, and laughed, adding, "That
should make the hair stand up on the backs of the necks of private
attorneys when they hear about it." [3] He explained, "The first time
I was asked to go, I raised the invitation with one of my colleagues.
'Anything wrong with this?' I said. 'Hell, no!' he told me. 'It's
been going on for years.' I know the private bar may wonder about

the propriety of this sort of lunch, but if they don't have confidence in us, I don't know what to say." After the Justice spoke, a deputy in the SG's office was asked, "When was the last time you had lunch with a Supreme Court Justice?" He said, "Last Tuesday." [4]

During the fifties, when Felix Frankfurter was on the Supreme Court and a number of his younger friends, including a former law clerk, were in the SG's office, he began to meet regularly with the SG's lawyers. [5] The group invited other Justices to lunch as well, and since then, a few times a year, the SG's staff gets together with a Justice to sort through administrative details (whether the Court should retain its current limits on the number of pages allowed in briefs, for example) [6] and to talk. Occasionally, a Justice will give the lawyers a thought about an aspect of their duties before the Court that spurs them to try doing better at it. Justice Rehnquist once told the group that even a terrible oral argument was useful to the Justices, because it was the one event requiring all nine members of the bench to focus on a case at the same time. He sent back some lawyers thinking that they should prepare more conscientiously for oral arguments. [7]

The unusual private ties between the Supreme Court and the SG's office are matched by their close public dealings. Whenever a member of the Court dies, the SG is asked to call a meeting of the Supreme Court bar to honor the Justice. [8] Lawyers in the SG's office say this duty makes the Solicitor the president of the Court bar. [9] (He isn't, because there is no such post.) [10] The Justices also call on former Solicitors for help in special Court projects. Until the late thirties, for instance, there was no uniform code of civil procedure for use in federal courts; in the absence of common guidelines, each federal court used the rules of the state where it sat. This practice yielded a disarray of rulings by federal judges, and half the appeals in the federal courts were about the weblike details of procedure. Chief Justice Charles Evans Hughes appointed a commission headed by ex-SG William Mitchell to devise some uniform rules, and the Justices accepted eighty-six of the group's eighty-eight recommendations. [11]

The Justices also give the SG special dispensations in Court. In the Supreme Court's rules, the Solicitor is one of the few lawyers allowed to file a brief as a friend of the Court without the permission of the parties to the suit.[12] The SG is also the only amicus regularly given time to argue his case before the Court. Unless he abuses the privilege, the SG is the sole advocate to whom the Justices regularly grant requests for extensions of time to file papers with the Court.[13] The special treatment for the Solicitor is most visible to outsiders in the SG's briefs themselves. Until 1980, the Court allowed private law firms to pick their own colors for the covers of their briefs, and attorneys worked hard to distinguish themselves in the minds of the Justices by the colors they chose. (In a case about fishing rights, the Puget Sound Gillnetters Association filed briefs in salmon pink.) The rules of the Court now assign the colors that lawyers are supposed to use for covers of documents submitted to the Justices, according to the document's role in a case: petitions for writs of certiorari must be white; responses to petitions light orange; appellants' briefs on the merits light blue. One exception to the new rule was permitted: the SG's filings, and no other party's, were to be bound in gray, regardless of the government's role in the case. The exception was a concession to the SG's office, which had filed briefs clad in gray for so long that the government's submissions are still called gray briefs. But some years before the SG's office had switched to tan. The messenger service that runs twice a day between the Justice Department and the Supreme Court carries only tan-covered filings from the SG's office.[14]

Stern, Gressman, and Shapiro's *Supreme Court Practice* explains most of the Court's procedures, including the ones that favor the SG, but there is a practice engaged in by almost no one but the SG's office that the book doesn't mention. It's called "lodging," which is not a standard procedure. At the office of the Clerk of the Supreme Court, it is generally used to refer to the ordinary practitioners' technique of dropping off at the Court certain materials that are part of the record in a case coming up for review. The documents would reach the Court soon enough through regular channels, but on the chance the Justices or their law clerks want to start studying the case right away, one of the parties lodges the papers (e.g., part of the trial transcript or a key piece of evidence) with the Clerk.[15]

For the SG's office, lodging means something different: a case runs through a trial and an appeal, and it arrives at the Supreme Court; the SG's team considers the merits of the case, and finds a document (an annual report from Congress, a study from a government agency) that, while not in the trial record, sheds light on the government's argument; the SG's lawyers "lodge" the goods with the Clerk (they do it one or two dozen times a year)[16] and inform the Justices that the materials are there in case they want to examine the papers. This runs contrary to the rule that appeals courts cannot consider evidence that has not been presented to the trial court below.

A deputy clerk who was asked which Supreme Court rule permits lodging replied, "There is no rule. It's just a practice."[17] He went on, "Any lawyer can lodge documents with the Court, as long as the material qualifies as the kind of background the Justices could take judicial notice of and refer to in their opinions as generally known facts." But only the SG's office regularly lodges papers that are not part of the record. Most lawyers don't know about the practice, because it's not in the Court's rules. And, as one former assistant to the SG put it, "It rarely happens that private lawyers lodge material; they've usually been with the case a long time and have already brought forth their best stuff."[18] The SG's office, by contrast, always takes a fresh look at a case. "The truth," the ex-assistant went on, "is that the time the SG's office has to review cases when they are in the lower courts is minuscule. Until we get to the nitty-gritty of preparing a Supreme Court argument, we don't give it our best. But then we do." A Deputy Solicitor added, "We're not entitled to make a new argument in the Supreme Court, but if we think of a way to make the old argument better, we sure try."[19]

In 1975, Solicitor General Robert Bork was planning to file an amicus brief supporting the death penalty in a case pending before the Court.[20] One of the arguments raised by opponents of the death penalty is that it does not deter criminals, so it cannot fulfill a basic function of criminal law. The lawyers in the SG's office who were working on the case didn't have much besides logic on which to rely in their rebuttal of this claim, but late one night the deputy in charge was unwinding in front of his TV, and he caught the end of a debate about the death penalty on a talk show. [21] One of the participants mentioned an unpublished study by Isaac Ehrlich, an economist at the University of Chicago, which went a step beyond any of the well-known work in the field. [22] Ehrlich claimed that each additional execution of a convicted murderer might save eight lives, because that many potential offenders would be deterred from committing murder. The deputy tracked down Ehrlich and asked if he could see the study (it was called "The Deterrent Effect of Capital Punishment: A Question of Life and Death") for possible use in the SG's brief. The SG lodged the study with the Supreme Court.

One lawyer opposing the SG's office in the death-penalty case was David Kendall, now a partner in the Washington law firm of Williams & Connolly. When the SG's office called him to report about the government's plan to lodge the Ehrlich study with the Supreme Court, Kendall said, "I went through the roof. It wasn't even published, it was full of arcane mathematics, and it was indigestible to the average reader. And the copy they lodged was a dim Xerox. The whole business was an outrage." To Kendall, the study failed to meet the Supreme Court's standard because it did not qualify as general knowledge. Since the majority opinion of the Supreme Court did not rely on the study, however, it also appeared to have little to do with the outcome of the case. "As far as I'm concerned," Kendall said, "it was a low blow without lasting consequences." [23]

But the case nicely framed the lodging question. "This is an adversary system," Kendall said. "Just because the SG has what he thinks is the best available information doesn't mean he can put it into the record for the Supreme Court to consider. You don't have safeguards at that stage. The Supreme Court is not a trial court. Letting the other side know about new material doesn't cure the central vice. You can't cross-examine the preparer of a report lodged with the Court, so lodging ends up being a tool for the government to wrest some advantage for itself. They can ask agencies to prepare authoritative-sounding material that is not necessarily reliable and the opponent is caught on the horns of a dilemma: he doesn't want to be seen as overreacting, so he doesn't want to file a motion to strike the stuff that's been lodged with the

Court; but he doesn't have a real opportunity to respond to the substance. The result is that lodging is a subversion of the process for finding facts, and there's not much a private lawyer can do about it.

"In the Supreme Court," he went on, "the SG's office is the home team. They are always up there, and whether or not you assume they have right and truth on their side because they are the government, it's an adversary system. Both sides in the conflict compete under fair and noble rules, under which justice is done when there is the fullest airing of facts and arguments by both sides. The government is the government, and should be fully respected. The SG's office serves as a buffer between the Judiciary and the Executive Branch. But it isn't a benign and altruistic referee guiding every step of the law. Otherwise, there'd be no need for lawsuits."

Most contests in which the SG's office lodges fresh documents draw no special notice from the Supreme Court. But occasionally the Justices have broken their silence about this unorthodox procedure. In a case about drug trafficking, Justice Byron White all but thanked the SG's office in a footnote for the documents that it had lodged.[24] In 1985, Justice John Paul Stevens got off what lawyers in the SG's office considered a barbed footnote about lodging. Writing for his colleagues in a majority opinion, Stevens held for the SG in a case about a cutback in food stamps, but he did not like the government's use of little-known facts to shore up its argument.[25] Another Justice said, "Some years ago, we had a case about avocadoes up here, in which the question was whether a California statute setting the amount of oil in an avocado was superseded by a federal law. The record was meager, so I sent my law clerk down to the Agriculture Department to find some stuff. Our feeling was it's not so important what facts you use to decide it as what principle you rely on, but you should gather the best information that you can. The SG knows this and argues that if the Court thinks this way, why shouldn't the SG? That's the sort of thing that sometimes causes eyes to pop."[26]

Lodging and other practices that favor the Solicitor General point up the exceptional terms that sometimes govern dealings between the Supreme Court and the SG's office: the Solicitor

General plays by different rules because he represents the United States. If the SG's office owes a special duty to the Court, and the Justices hold the SG's lawyers to a higher standard of craft, why shouldn't the Court give those lawyers some extra scope?

The most amazing episode of intimacy between the SG's office and the Supreme Court took place in the early fifties.[27] An assistant named Philip Elman was in charge of civil-rights cases for the office through the reigns of five SGs. He was later appointed a member of the Federal Trade Commission, and was for many years a professor at the Georgetown University Law Center. "It may sound sentimental and corny in these very cynical days," he recalled in 1983 for Columbia University's Oral History Project, "but we took it for granted, without making any big fuss over it or being self-righteous, that our job was to do justice, to treat people fairly and not give a damn what anyone thought." Elman helped formulate the government's position and write its amicus brief in a landmark case in which the Supreme Court struck down restrictions that prevented blacks from buying property, and he wrote other briefs calling for desegregation of dining cars on trains, of law schools, and of graduate schools. When it came to asking the Supreme Court to outlaw segregation in public schools, Solicitor General Philip Perlman drew the line. He would not let the government argue that an 1896 case called Plessy v. Ferguson,[28] upholding the doctrine of separate-but-equal, should be overturned.

Like other assistants who worked for the SG during and after the New Deal, Elman joined the office with the encouragement of Felix Frankfurter. In the days when Justices had only one clerk (most Justices now hire four), Elman had been Frankfurter's. As Elman told the story, the two became close friends, and the Justice influenced his former aide's view of history. "The entire length of our relationship from 1941 to 1965, when he died," Elman said, "the Justice and I would talk on the phone a good deal. He would call me almost every Sunday night at home. He would have gone through the Sunday papers, and after dinner he liked to talk, or 'schmooze,' as he would say. We'd have a long, relaxed, gossipy conversation for an hour and a half sometimes." With "certain unspoken restrictions," according to Elman ("we never discussed a case that I had argued"), they seemed to talk about almost everything. Frankfurter's colleagues (he referred to them in code—Robert Jackson, for example, was Jamestown, the town in upstate New York he came from, and Stanley Reed was the "chamer," meaning "ass" or "fool" in Yiddish) were a favorite topic.

"And along came the first of the kind of miracles that Frankfurter was waiting for," Elman reported. J. Howard McGrath, who had moved from the SG's quarters to the Attorney General's during the Truman Administration, and was Perlman's boss, resigned after he was accused of corruption. President Truman replaced him with a former congressman and federal judge named James McGranery. "McGranery, to put it as simply as I can," Elman recalled, "was a kind of nut." McGranery and Perlman didn't get along, and the Solicitor General quit as soon as he could. Robert Stern became Acting SG, and he and Elman went to see the new Attorney General. Elman: "We told McGranery, who hated Perlman, who had been very happy to see him go, that Perlman, even though the Department had consistently taken the position that Plessy was wrong and should be overruled, had refused to participate as amicus in the pending school segregation cases. We told him the Department of Justice should stick to its position and file an amicus brief in the Court. McGranery's immediate response was, 'You're right, boys. Go ahead and write a brief.'

"So that's how we happened to file the first brief in Brown v. Board of Education in December 1952, signed by McGranery as Attorney General and by me. . . . We were the first to suggest . . . that if the Court should hold that racial segregation in schools is unconstitutional, it should give district courts a reasonable period of time to work out the details and timing of implementation of the decision. In other words, 'with all deliberate speed.' " For Elman, "This first brief we filed in December 1952 is the one thing I'm proudest of in my whole career."

The Supreme Court's embrace of the "deliberate speed" formula is often criticized on the ground that it gave Southern states an excuse for avoiding compliance with the Court's ruling. But, according to Elman, the government would not have filed a brief without this formula, and the government's participation in the first Brown case was crucial, because it signaled to the Justices that the Executive Branch was ready to enforce a call for desegregation of public schools. Elman has commented about this proposal that "it was entirely unprincipled, it was just plain wrong as a matter of constitutional law, to suggest that someone whose personal constitutional rights were being violated should be denied relief." And yet, in his view, it became a rallying point for the Supreme Court, a notion that ultimately helped the Justices reach a unanimous decision.

Where did this idea come from? "Not from Frankfurter," Elman says, before seeming to contradict himself: "But it did grow out of my many conversations with him over a period of many months. He told me what he thought, what the other Justices were telling him they thought. I knew from him what their positions were. If the issue was inescapably presented in yes-or-no terms, he could not count five votes on the Court to overrule Plessy." Hugo Black, for example, the former Alabama senator who was counted as a vote to overturn the precedent, warned his colleagues what the change would mean. "The Klan is going to ride again," he prophesied. "This will be the end of liberalism in the South."

The Supreme Court heard arguments on Brown during the 1952 Term, but could not reach a decision. "There's no question that the grand strategist in all this inside the Court was F.F.," Elman has said of Frankfurter. "He was writing memos to his colleagues and having his clerk, Alex Bickel"—who later became a renowned professor at Yale Law School—"do research into the legislative history of the Fourteenth Amendment, the results of which he then circulated to the Court. To use the Yiddish word that Frankfurter used all the time, he was the *Kochleffel*. It means cooking spoon, stirring things up; the man stirring everything up inside the Court was Frankfurter. They couldn't decide the cases, they didn't know what to do with them, they had no majority, and they hadn't even taken a formal vote, because they didn't want to harden anybody's position. So in the summer of 1953 before they adjourned, they set the cases down for reargument: they asked five questions of the parties, and they invited the Attorney General of the United States and the attorneys general of all the states requiring or authorizing segregation to file briefs and present oral argument."

McGranery had by then been replaced by Herbert Brownell,

Jr., as Attorney General. After the Supreme Court's order for reargument, Brownell called a meeting to decide how the government should respond to the Court's invitation. Elman and Robert Stern, as Acting SG, considered the invitation "the equivalent of a royal command," as it would be today. But others among the AG's advisers (including Warren Burger) said that Brownell was free to accept or refuse the offer, and recommended that he stand clear of a case which was certain to set off tremors in the South. Brownell's opening move was to shift responsibility for the case from the SG's office to his own, and ask J. Lee Rankin to oversee the project.

"Some time later," Elman has said, "I think much later—I remember writing a letter to Frankfurter during the summer telling him that nothing, absolutely nothing, was going on in the Department of Justice—Rankin called me into his office and said that he had gotten the green light from Brownell. I'm sure Brownell had talked to Eisenhower about it. The feeling we all had at the time was that Eisenhower would not be sympathetic to the idea, because he was known to believe that public education was something for the states, the federal government should stay out of it, and this problem was the Court's and not his as President. So I give Brownell and Rankin the most credit for the Eisenhower Administration's decision to participate."

Elman was relieved of his other duties in the SG's office, and put in charge of writing the government's brief. When he finished, Rankin read it and made no changes. Over a period of weeks, when he had free time, Brownell called Elman in, and the assistant and the Attorney General went over the brief. They "would sit there and he would read it," Elman said, "and if there was something he didn't understand or agree with, he would stop and ask me to explain, or justify it. We did a little rewriting in his office."

At the close of the summer, before the government filed its brief, Chief Justice Fred Vinson died. He was a onetime senator from Kentucky whose reluctance to confront the issue raised in Brown was well known. When Frankfurter had tabulated votes for and against overturning Plessy, Vinson's was one the Justice marked as a no. As Elman tells it, "Frankfurter was then in New England where he spent the summer. The Justices all came back to Washington to attend the funeral services. I met Frankfurter, I think at Union Station, and he was in high spirits. I shouldn't really report all this, but this is history and, as he used to say, history has its claims."

Elman: "Frankfurter said to me, 'I'm in mourning,' sarcastically. What he meant was that Vinson's departure from the Court was going to remove the roadblock in Brown. As long as Vinson was Chief Justice, they could never get unanimity or anything close to it. If Vinson dissented, Reed would surely join him, Tom Clark probably would too, and Jackson would write that the issue should be left to Congress. Anyway, Frankfurter happily said to me, 'I'm in mourning.' And, with that viselike grip of his, he grabbed me by the arm and, looking me straight in the eye, said, 'Phil, this is the first solid piece of evidence I've ever had that there really is a God.' "

Although it was never publicly announced, Earl Warren had been slated to become Solicitor General until Vinson died.[29] Instead, President Eisenhower appointed him to replace Vinson as Chief Justice and, in December 1953, Brown v. Board of Education was reargued. Among the lawyers who presented views for or against overruling Plessy v. Ferguson were three Solicitors General, though none was then in office.[30] John W. Davis, at the age of eighty, and three and a half decades past his tenure as SG, made an emotional speech on behalf of separate-but-equal education that brought tears to his own eyes (and, because it endorsed segregation, also tarnished his reputation).[31] Thurgood Marshall, more than a decade before his time as Solicitor, presented part of the NAACP Legal Defense Fund's argument. J. Lee Rankin argued for the government. Though Rankin went on to do his share of advocacy when he became SG two and a half years later, the argument in Brown was his first before the Justices.

In his oral history, Philip Elman spells out his running debate with Felix Frankfurter about the most convincing argument for the government to make on the merits of the Brown case. He was also asked what he thought about possible charges that these discussions with the Justice were improper—that, at a minimum, they gave the government an unfair advantage because opposing lawyers could not rebut Elman's presentation to the Justice.

(While concurring in the view that Elman had exaggerated "both his own role and the Court's reliance on his arguments," a *New York Times* editorial called the Elman-Frankfurter collaboration "deeply disturbing" and "unethical.")[32] To put the question in perspective, imagine the uproar if word got out that, of the two dissenters in the Court's landmark decision on abortion, Roe v. Wade[33]—Justice (now Chief Justice) William Rehnquist and Justice Byron White—one had held regular conversations with one of his ex-law clerks working in the SG's office about a case dealing with that issue.

"Yes," Elman has observed, "I suppose there's a point there. I don't have any easy, snappy response to that. In Brown, I didn't consider myself a lawyer for a litigant. I considered it a cause that transcended ordinary notions about propriety in a litigation. This was not a litigation in the usual sense. I don't defend my discussions with Frankfurter; I just did what I thought was right, and I'm sure he didn't give it much thought. I regarded myself, in the literal sense, as an amicus curiae." He added, "Brown v. Board of Education, which we fully discussed, was an extraordinary case, and the ordinary rules didn't apply. In that case I knew everything, or at least he gave me the impression that I knew everything, that was going on at the Court. He told me about what was said in conference and who said it. The constitutional issue went to the heart of what kind of country we are, what kind of Constitution and Supreme Court we have: whether, almost a century after the Fourteenth Amendment was adopted, the Court could find the wisdom and courage to hold that the amendment meant what it said, that black people could no longer be singled out and treated differently because of their color, that in everything it did, government had to be color-blind.

"As I look back now, I can see myself in Brown v. Board of Education as having been his junior partner, or law clerk emeritus, in helping him work out the best solution for the toughest problem to come before the Court in this century."

In May of 1954, in a unanimous decision, the Supreme Court outlawed segregation in public schools.[34] The Justices retained jurisdiction of the case to decide how their order should be implemented, and the government's separate brief on this question contained a detail that emphasized how unusual the case really was. The government again offered the Elman "deliberate-speed" proposal: the timetable for desegregation should be flexible, and, rather than the Supreme Court, the district courts should oversee the process because they were closer to local conditions which might dictate a faster or slower pace. "It must be recognized that racial segregation in public schools is not a separate and distinct phenomenon," the draft brief lectured. "The Court's decision in these cases has outlawed a social institution which has existed for a long time in many areas throughout the country. . . ."

At this point in the final brief, there was an extraordinary addition. In a small, wiry hand, Dwight Eisenhower filled the margin and top of the galleys for the draft with a long comment to bolster an already strong expression of concern about the decision to abandon the separate-but-equal doctrine in favor of equal opportunity and integration of the races. It was wholly unprecedented for a Solicitor General to bring the proofs of any brief to a President for approval. Elman recounted, "I punctuated and put his language in more readable form. These are Eisenhower's sentences, edited by me. Where I wrote that the Court had outlawed a social institution that had existed for a long time in many areas throughout the country, he added this language (as cleaned up by me): '[Segregation is] an institution, it may be noted, which during its existence not only has had the sanction of decisions of this Court but has been fervently supported by great numbers of people as justifiable on legal and moral grounds. The Court's holding in the present cases that segregation is a denial of constitutional rights involved an express recognition of the importance of psychological and emotional factors; the impact of segregation upon children, the Court found, can so affect their entire lives as to preclude their full enjoyment of constitutional rights. In similar fashion, psychological and emotional factors are involved—and must be met with understanding and good will—in the alterations that must now take place in order to bring about compliance with the Court's decision.'[35]

"As I look at it now, thirty years later," Elman said, "I'm astonished at the liberties that I, a young lawyer in the Solicitor General's office, felt free to take with the language of the President of the United States, which he wasn't going to have an opportunity to change, because it went from me to the printer. It shows the degree of what seems to me now astonishing self-confidence, or even arrogance, I had at the time. Anyway, it was the first and only instance I know of in which the President of the United States was coauthor of a brief in the Supreme Court. I think the point he made was a valid one. I wish I had thought of it first."

IV

"Independence"

THE TIES BETWEEN the Solicitor General and the Supreme Court confound the textbook notion of checks and balances exercised by each branch of government on the others, but the question of the SG's independence within the Executive Branch has been a more riveting concern to lawyers in the SG's office. Solicitors in every Democratic and Republican Administration since the nineteen-sixties have pondered this question.[1] The SGs have treated "independence" as a paradox. They recognize that they serve at the pleasure of the President, and often put the word in quotation marks. Yet they have considered it a fundamental requirement of the office of Solicitor.

Erwin Griswold was a moderate Republican when he was appointed SG by a Democrat, Lyndon Johnson, in 1967. His hobby had been the SG's office since 1929, when he first went to work there. Like William Mitchell, who was widely respected as the Democratic SG for the Republican Coolidge Administration in the twenties,[2] Griswold was praised as a worthy and nonpartisan appointment. Although his style of arguing in the Supreme Court was occasionally a stubborn one ("He's like the U.S.S. Griswold," said one Justice. "Questions from us just bounce off him harmlessly as he cruises through his speech"),[3] and he upset some Democrats in the Justice Department by taking a less aggressive stance in favor of civil rights than they wished,[4] he proved to be a good, fair-minded Solicitor.

After Johnson left office, the Nixon Administration kept him on as SG. Nixon's men thought the ex-dean of Harvard Law School added a conspicuous touch of class to the Justice Department,[5] and (except for William Rehnquist, then an Assistant At-

torney General, who refused to stand on ceremony)[6] senior officials at the department always called him Dean. Griswold had a
courtly and formidable Midwestern manner, and he believed in
protocol. Recognizing that he worked for the Attorney General
and the President, he tried to keep the Republicans as happy with
his advocacy as he had the Democrats.[7] He did not fully succeed.

In 1971, the Nixon Executive Branch forced the Supreme Court
to rule on one of the great clashes between the government and
the press in American history: the Pentagon papers dispute.[8] Before the fight became a lawsuit, Griswold counseled privately that
the government should not sue a number of newspapers that had
published parts of the Defense Department's classified history of
the Vietnam War. Attorney General John Mitchell didn't ask his
opinion. After the Nixon White House decided to sue the offenders, the case rose quickly to the Supreme Court and Griswold took
charge. The brief he eventually filed angered defenders of the press
by its assertion that publication of the papers could cause "immediate and irreparable harm to the security of the United States."[9]
But, according to Sanford Ungar in *The Papers and the Papers,*
Griswold's judgments behind closed doors belied this view. Calcu-
lating that it would take him six weeks to read through the forty-
seven volumes of the Pentagon papers and make up his own mind
about the nature of their contents, Griswold called in officials from
the Defense Department and other agencies to identify for him
items in the papers that, if published, would in their view threaten
national security. He concluded that, except in about a dozen
instances, the government should stop objecting to publication of
the history, because the only harm that would come of it was
political embarrassment. The Supreme Court refused to enjoin
publication of any part of the papers.[10]

In other cases, Griswold drew a sharper line between his own
and the Administration's views about what was legal. Following
the example of Simon Sobeloff, who fifteen years earlier had
refused to argue for the government, Griswold declined in two
cases dealing with national security and the draft; he believed the
Nixon Administration was seeking more authority for the Executive Branch than the laws in question allowed. Since the Supreme
Court was not likely to rule in the government's favor, he thought
that he would diminish his credibility with the Justices if he made

the claims that the Executive Branch wanted him to press. (In 1985, when he was asked why he believed this, Griswold said, "I've dealt with the Court for fifty-odd years, so it was perfectly obvious.") [11] Griswold also presented views about civil rights that, while sometimes too moderate for the Johnson Administration, were often too liberal for Nixon's.

The last straw for Griswold may have been his role in an antitrust case, in which he bridled at a direct order from Richard Nixon. [12] The United States had brought suit against the conglomerate then known as International Telephone & Telegraph, or ITT, on the theory that one of the firm's mergers had violated federal laws. The government lost in the lower courts and the SG's office decided it should take the case to the Supreme Court, to ensure that the lower-court ruling did not become a precedent hindering other challenges to conglomerate mergers. "I think this is a very hard case," Griswold wrote in an internal memo, "but it is an important one and Antitrust wants to go ahead, and it is in the public interest, I think, that we should learn more about what the law is in this area." [13]

Richard Nixon also thought ITT was an important case. From the Oval Office, one day in the spring of 1971, with his tape system on, Nixon called Richard Kleindienst, who, as Deputy AG, was running the Justice Department. [14] "The IT and T thing—stay the hell out of it," Nixon said. "I know all the legal things, Dick, you don't have to spell out the legal—That's right. That's right. Don't file the brief. Your—my order is to drop the God damn thing. Is that clear?" Nixon may have been interested in the case because of his taste for questions of economics—conglomerate mergers were then a major business story. It was more likely that the President had given his personal attention to the lawsuit because, as Jack Anderson reported, ITT had promised to contribute $400,000 to the Republican National Committee and the Nixon Administration for the 1972 Republican Convention if the Administration would settle the suit. [15]

Minutes after Nixon phoned him, Richard Kleindienst called Griswold into his office and asked about the status of the ITT case. The SG informed the Acting Attorney General that the government had one day left before the deadline for filing its brief at the Supreme Court. Kleindienst told him to ask the Court for a month's extension, while they figured out how to persuade the President to let the Justice Department resolve the case on legal grounds.[16] Looking back fourteen years later, Griswold said, "I would have resigned if we hadn't been able to work out the differences, because it was a direct political interference, without any professional justification. But we worked everything out, and the case got settled properly."[17] (The case also contributed to Kleindienst's downfall. A year after he officially replaced John Mitchell as Attorney General in 1972, Kleindienst resigned and pleaded guilty to having perjured himself before the Senate about the ITT affair. "I was not interfered with by anybody at the White House,"[18] he had sworn before the facts came to light.)

After Richard Nixon was reelected in 1972, Nixon unilaterally announced Griswold's resignation as Solicitor General. "I was approaching sixty-nine years old," Griswold recalled in 1985, "and had been in the office for six years, and it was entirely up to him to decide what he wanted to. But Mr. Nixon decided without telling me. I heard it from a friend who had heard it over the radio. It would have been courteous if the President had at least sent me a note, or called me over to thank me, but he didn't do either of those things. I'm rather proud of the fact that the only commission I have as Solicitor General was signed by Lyndon Johnson."[19]

THE NIXON ADMINISTRATION appointed Robert Bork to replace Griswold as Solicitor General. The President and Bork agreed about the threat to the Republic posed by what Bork called the "Imperial Judiciary." Bork was concerned about the "tyranny of the minority" (of judges, among others) and the transformation of the Supreme Court into a "naked power organ."[20] Though Bork was making a name for himself in constitutional law, and held a professorship in constitutional law at Yale Law School (the same chair William Howard Taft had filled in the early years of this century),[21] he was better known as an antitrust scholar. He had attended the University of Chicago Law School during the rise of the conservative, free-market movement in economics labeled the Chicago School. Chicago was the first university to hire an economist on a law-school faculty, and Edward Levi, who was then law-school dean and later became Attorney General under

Gerald Ford, taught an antitrust course with economist Aaron Director in which they used economic theory to rebut the law's traditional antitrust doctrine. [22] Bork recalled, "A lot of us who took the antitrust course or the economics course underwent what can only be called a religious conversion. It changed our view of the entire world." [23] He made his reputation by arguing that antitrust policies meant to spur economic efficiency often did just the opposite. [24]

At the end of the first Nixon term, Bork was invited to Camp David, where the President asked him to be SG. He had caught Nixon's attention while helping the Administration devise limits to propose to Congress on busing as a tool of school desegregation. [25] "Nixon gave me a remarkably thoughtful lecture about judicial restraint," Bork said in 1985. [26] "It was a good lecture. I could have delivered a better one, but then I'd been teaching for a long time. I had met him once before, in a meeting about busing where I happened to say that the only way the government could support a piece of pending legislation was by relying on a case called Katzenbach v. Morgan, which gave the Congress broad power to define the contents of constitutional provisions. I said, 'You don't want to do that. It's corrupt constitutional law.' Nixon turned and said, 'I believe that, but I didn't know there was a constitutional law professor in the country who did.' I suppose that first meeting was where they got the idea of making me Solicitor General."

Unlike Erwin Griswold, Bork avoided political run-ins with the Nixon Administration, which was increasingly preoccupied with Watergate during his tenure as SG. Bork, who has a beard like Rasputin's and a reputation for brilliance, was appointed by President Reagan to the U.S. Court of Appeals for the District of Columbia in 1982. Before his 1987 nomination to the Supreme Court made him famous, Bork was already a name on legal trivia quizzes. He became one after Attorney General Elliot Richardson and Deputy Attorney General William Ruckelshaus resigned rather than comply with Richard Nixon's order to fire Archibald Cox as Watergate Special Prosecutor in October of 1973. [27] ("If you really are determined to get rid of Cox," Ruckelshaus told Nixon's men, "I think Bork may be your man.") [28] As the next official in line to succeed the Attorney General, Solicitor General Bork believed it was his duty to end the confrontation between Nixon and Cox over the Watergate inquiry. If he himself were also to resign, Bork thought, Nixon would appoint someone from outside the Justice Department as the new Attorney General, probably from the White House staff, and the department would be crippled by a mass resignation of angry career attorneys. Since, unlike Richardson and Ruckelshaus, Bork had made no personal commitment not to fire Cox, he decided to carry out the President's order. He also signed a commitment to abolish the Special Prosecutor's office, and did so. The American people, however, overwhelmingly condemned the Cox firing (Western Union delivered over 150,000 telegrams to Washington in the two days immediately following, and many telegrams to Congress said simply, "Impeach Nixon"), and the Nixon Administration realized that it needed to defuse this response. Bork agreed. Despite his personal belief that ongoing Watergate inquiries by the Justice Department and the U.S. Attorney in Washington made a special prosecutor unnecessary, with the concurrence of the White House (and perhaps at its direction) he appointed Leon Jaworski to succeed Cox.

During the two months after Richardson's and Ruckelshaus's departures, Bork functioned as both Attorney General and Solicitor. He relied heavily on his Deputy SGs, until William Saxbe became Attorney General in January of 1974. When Bork focused again on the SG's work, he regularly acted on the philosophy that won him the job. He worked on the Supreme Court brief that urged the Justices to permit state laws to impose the death penalty, and in other major cases he also presented conservative views. Living with what he called the tension between legal principle and political expediency, Bork regularly found means to carry the Administration's message to the Court.[29] He was a more enthusiastic advocate of Nixon's legal notions than Griswold had been (and, in the process, drove away one assistant who believed that the former Yale professor had compromised the integrity of the SG's judgment about the law),[30] and he was equally forthright about making arguments favored by Ford.

Bork also showed commitment to the legal standards of the office. During his confirmation hearings for the Solicitorship, one senator had asked whether he would argue his own highly unconventional views about antitrust law or more mainstream interpretations. [31] He promised to defer to others in the Justice Department about the government's positions, and he did. In most instances, Daniel Friedman (now a federal judge, and then a Deputy SG) decided what to argue in antitrust. [32]

In February of 1975, Bork's former teacher and longtime friend Edward Levi was appointed Attorney General. Bork consulted with Levi about cases that might cause a stir. [33] He spent days considering whether to try persuading the Supreme Court to hear a challenge to mandatory school busing in Boston after a petition for certiorari was filed by one of the parties. He believed that busing had been used as a tool of desegregation more often than the Justices had intended when they first ruled that it was legal for courts to order busing as a last resort, [34] and that the Justices ought to remind lower-court judges that busing was only one of the possible remedies for discrimination. This was the policy of the Ford Administration, but after lengthy discussions in which the President participated, the treatment of the case was left for the Justice Department to decide, and Bork was convinced by the Attorney General and others not to enter the case. [35] (The Supreme Court denied cert., and the Boston busing plan stood.) [36]

Like Erwin Griswold, who chose not to file an amicus brief in Roe v. Wade, Bork felt no need to register an opinion for the government about each major social issue. He believed the SG's job was to represent the long-term interests of the government as much as the policies of the current Administration. Sympathetic to a Republican law-and-order view of criminal law, he nonetheless confessed error in some criminal cases. Adopting a stance like Griswold's, he refused to make oral arguments in cases he considered "fatuous." Bork mocked the tradition of the SG ("Everybody talked about it as a place where the lore was very arcane and celestial music played," he said, "so I called myself Der Meister Shyster"), [37] but he accommodated himself to it. "The SG's job is the chief purely legal job in the government," he observed in 1975. "So far, in my experience, he's been quite independent." [38]

NOT LONG AFTER Wade McCree succeeded Bork as SG, in 1977, under the Carter Administration, a case came along that put the SG's independence to a severe test. Called Regents of the University of California v. Bakke,[39] it came to stand in some lawyers' minds for the proposition that, in the final analysis, it is proper for the President and his aides to intervene at will in the affairs of the SG and to dictate the government's legal positions in the Supreme Court.[40] In fact, the case helped persuade Griffin Bell, who was the first Attorney General of the Carter Administration, of the opposite.

Allan Paul Bakke was a white engineer who wanted to attend the University of California Medical School at Davis. After his interview at Davis, a faculty member called him "a well-qualified candidate for admissions whose main hardship is the unavoidable fact that he is now 33."[41] On the medical school's admissions scale, Bakke received 468 points out of a possible 500. Earlier in the year, a rating of 470 had won automatic entry. Bakke had delayed completing his application because his mother had been ill, and by the time he filed, there were few places left in the class. He was not admitted.

Bakke applied again the next year, and was again rejected, and he filed a suit in state court, protesting his rejection. The core of his complaint was that the medical school's policy of reserving sixteen of the hundred places in its entering class for blacks, American Indians, Chicanos, and Asian Americans deprived him of his right to equal protection of the law under the Fourteenth Amendment to the Constitution. At trial, Bakke won a partial victory. (The judge ruled that the medical school had violated the Constitution by establishing a quota for admissions, but did not order Davis to admit Bakke, because Bakke had not proved he would have been admitted if the special admissions program did not exist.) On appeal to the California Supreme Court, he won again. According to Justice Stanley Mosk, who wrote the court's opinion, the Davis program violated the constitutional rights of white applicants "because it afford[ed] preference on the basis of race to persons who, by the University's own standards, [were] not as qualified for the study of medicine as non-minority applicants denied admission." In dissent, Justice Matthew Tobriner wrote an opinion that was longer than the majority's. In Tobriner's mind, the main value promoted by the Fourteenth Amendment was

racial integration. The Davis program sought that end. He regret-
ted that a remedy for the "inequalities flowing from past discrimination will inevitably result in some detriment to nonminorities,"
but as long as the remedy was "adopted in good faith to promote
integration" by using a racial classification related to that goal, the
court should uphold the program. [42]

When the Bakke case rose to the United States Supreme Court,
the federal government was not a party and the Justices did not
ask the SG to submit an amicus brief giving an opinion on the law.
But the government kept watch on the case. Drew Days, who was
the first black to head the Civil Rights Division of the Justice
Department, believed that it raised "very serious questions" [43]
about the validity of a wide variety of federal regulations dealing
with education, employment, and other areas of social policy. He
recommended that the Solicitor General enter the case as a friend
of the Court and throw his weight against Bakke, and behind the
University of California, in favor of affirmative action.

On the way to the Solicitor General, the recommendation
from Days made an important stop. The assistant to the SG assigned to the case was Frank Easterbrook. In the small circle of
Supreme Court–watchers, he was known both for his superb academic record at the University of Chicago Law School and for his
conservative legal views. (In 1985, when Easterbrook was thirty-
six, President Reagan appointed him to the U.S. Court of Appeals
for the Seventh Circuit, in Chicago.) Easterbrook was the first
official with a voice in the Bakke case who argued that the U.S.
government should submit a friend of the Court brief on behalf of
Bakke and against the University of California. [44]

At Davis, Easterbrook argued, there was no proof that the
medical school had previously engaged in racial discrimination
that might justify giving members of minority groups some current advantage in the admissions process to put them on an equal
footing with other candidates. And it was not enough to show that
blacks and other minorities had been discriminated against generally in society. Otherwise, he reasoned, "benign" discrimination
like the kind practiced by Davis was not benign. As far as Allan
Bakke was concerned, "he might as well have been black and
turned away on account of race." Easterbrook believed the U.S.

government could not endorse the Davis program, because it provided "gross over-compensation to minority applicants."[45]

Wade McCree was the first black elected to serve as a city judge in Detroit. He was a judge on the United States Court of Appeals for the Sixth Circuit before becoming Solicitor General, and he regularly served as an envoy of the black community to establishment councils. During the summer of 1977 (the first summer of the Carter Administration and of McCree at the Justice Department), the SG had been drawn into a dispute about another case.[46] He didn't pay attention to Bakke until August, not long before the brief in the Supreme Court was due. By then, the President had given a press conference at which he said that the government's position in the case would stand as a symbol of the new Administration's commitment to affirmative action. At the close of his statement about the case, he added, "I might say that the Secretary of HEW and the Attorney General, who are lawyers—and I am not—will prepare our position."[47]

President Carter omitted the Solicitor General from the list of lawyers preparing the government's brief, but McCree was in the thick of it. By late summer, when lawyers in the government said "Bakke," they referred to the fight over prestige and policy within the Executive Branch that had developed about the case.[48] The Justice Department was divided into two camps, one represented by Drew Days and the Civil Rights Division and the other by Frank Easterbrook. The memo by Easterbrook was approved by Lawrence Wallace, the Deputy SG in charge of civil-rights cases, and was turned into a draft brief.[49]

Just before Labor Day in 1977, the draft was leaked to *The New York Times* and a story about it caught the attention of Joseph Califano, the Secretary of Health, Education, and Welfare. He got hold of the brief. In his memoirs, *Governing America*, Califano related, "On the morning of September 6, I called Griffin Bell to complain about the brief. He suggested that I meet with Solicitor General Wade McCree. That meeting, the next day, was deeply disturbing."[50] Califano went on, "McCree, who is black and had been a judge before being appointed Solicitor General, sat with two bright young white holdovers from the Nixon Administration. They did not disguise their distaste for affirmative action. . . ."

The two "young white holdovers from the Nixon Administration" were Lawrence Wallace and Frank Easterbrook. (Wallace was hired in 1969 by Erwin Griswold, and Easterbrook in 1974 by Robert Bork.) At the meeting, according to Califano, one of the two younger men said he thought it was impossible to write a brief that approved a special admissions policy for the Davis medical school.

Califano: " 'Like hell it's impossible,' I said. 'I don't have any problem writing it. A lot of people in this country have worked for years to try to get equality for blacks, to develop affirmative action programs, to remedy past discrimination. We're not going to have that work thrown out the window by a couple of young lawyers.' "

Califano urged President Carter to play an active role in reshaping the Justice Department brief. In a memo to the President, marked *"Confidential"* and signed "From Joe Califano," he opened, "The draft Justice Department brief in the Bakke case is bad law, and pernicious social policy." Uncertain whether Carter would read the whole memo, Califano sent with it a handwritten note for the President's eyes only.

The second paragraph of the note read: "The brief-writing process (indeed the whole consultation process) has been so closely held—dominated through this past week by two holdover lawyers in the A.G.'s office—that even I, with a Department as deeply involved as any in the govt., with a legal background, with a presidential press statement that I would be involved, first got wind of the brief's existence in a *N.Y. Times* article over Labor Day weekend."

In the first paragraph, Califano warned: "I believe you will make the most serious mistake of your administration in domestic policy to date if you permit the Justice Department to file the *Bakke* brief in the form I read it and under present circumstances."[51]

Before Califano's memo reached the President, White House aides had already focused on the draft of the Bakke brief. Attorney General Bell told his view of the aides' involvement in his memoirs, *Taking Care of the Law.* "After a good deal of writing and rewriting McCree gave me the initial draft," he said. "I then made perhaps the biggest mistake with regard to the power centers at the

White House." [52] He took a copy of the draft when he went to see President Carter to talk about the government's position, and the President gave the copy to his counsel, Robert Lipshutz. The brief circulated to Stuart Eizenstat, the President's chief adviser on domestic policy, and other members of the staff. While the facts of the Bakke case made it a poor vehicle for a full endorsement of affirmative action by the Administration, [53] the President's aides decided anything less would amount to disapproval.

In a joint memo to the President, Eizenstat and Lipshutz contended, "The brief which the government files in the Bakke case will not simply be a legal document. Rather, it will be seen as a statement of this Administration's policy on an issue—affirmative action—which is an integral part of large numbers of Federal programs." They wanted the government to file a brief with more pronounced advocacy. "In a fundamental sense," they judged, "the brief is, in its own word, too 'dispassionate.' " [54]

On a cover page, Carter wrote:

Stu—Bob

I agree:

a) Strong affirmative action
b) no *rigid* quotas
Remanding may be ill advised—
Jump into drafting process—
                                        J.C.

On September 12, which was the day of a Cabinet meeting, the *Times* carried a story about the Justice Department brief that reflected little of the White House deliberations. The headline read, "CARTER SAID TO BACK BAR TO RACE QUOTAS." [55] According to Califano's memoir, "That did it. I decided to raise the issue at the cabinet meeting." Andrew Young, now mayor of Atlanta, then U.S. Ambassador to the United Nations, spoke before Califano at the meeting. Young, a black who had been one of Martin Luther King, Jr.'s chief aides during the civil-rights movement, reported that the anti-quota position of the government's draft brief was seen by the civil-rights community as a "betrayal." [56] The late Patricia Roberts Harris, a black who was then

Secretary of Housing and Urban Development and a former dean of the Howard University Law School, complained that the brief was of "poor legal quality." Califano cautioned that the Bakke brief should be done "meticulously, as thousands will go over it." [57] Bell explained that Wade McCree was still working on the brief and that the President would have the chance to review it before the Justice Department submitted it to the Supreme Court. To Eizenstat, the process was now finally working as it was supposed to. [58]

Bell did not agree. He announced to the Cabinet that he doubted he would "circulate any more briefs in the future." [59] The Bakke case had taught him a lesson, and he now had a better understanding of his responsibilities as Attorney General. He had resigned from a seat on the United States Court of Appeals for the Fifth Circuit to join the Cabinet, and he believed the Justice Department should be as free from political meddling as a courthouse. The word "independent" recurred in his comments about the ideal character of the department. As in its use to describe the position of the Solicitor General, the word had a special meaning. The Attorney General recognized his duty, and the SG's, to the President. He didn't believe it was his prerogative to make government policy without regard to Administration aims. But he thought the commotion about the Bakke case had lowered the quality of the government's brief and threatened to turn it into a statement of partisan policy rather than law. [60] Bell had arrived at the view expressed later, in 1986, by Chief Justice Rehnquist: "I don't think the White House is well served by having a Solicitor General come to the Court and read the legal equivalent of a press release." [61]

How Bell acted on his commitment to the independence of the Justice Department and, in turn, to the independence of the Solicitor General during the Bakke negotiations would have surprised the President's aides if they had known about it. After a quarrelsome meeting with Eizenstat, Lipshutz, and Vice-President Walter Mondale at the White House, the Attorney General made an executive decision. As he put it in his memoirs, "Riding back to the Department of Justice, I instructed Adamson"—Terrence Adamson, one of his assistants—"not to tell McCree of the meeting or the Vice-President's comments." [62] The pressure on

McCree was "heavy enough without adding the weight of one of the White House's centers of power," and Bell decided to shelter the SG.

At the Justice Department, McCree was known for his diplomatic skills and his off-the-cuff limericks. When protectors of wildlife successfully sued the would-be builders of a dam that threatened to destroy the breeding ground of a small fish called the snail darter, the case eventually arrived in the SG's office.[63] McCree wrote:

> "Who can surpass the snail darter?
> The fish that would not be a martyr.
> It stymied the dam,
> Near the place where it swam,
> Can you think of a fish any smarter?"[64]

In 1985, McCree recalled Bakke well. "I knew Bell was taking a lot of heat on the case. The papers would speculate about it, and you know what a gossip mill Washington is. I was slow to get into the case myself, because I had another to attend to, but by the end of the summer I was in it. The Solicitor General, you may know, gives everyone with a stake in a case a chance to be heard. That is, before filing a brief, he meets with government people and others who want to be heard on the legal issues. Secretary Califano came over and made a big pitch, and we heard him out. At one point he got fairly exercised and talked about how he had dedicated his life to fighting for equal rights. When he accused Larry Wallace of undercutting the rights of blacks, Larry got all hot and said, 'Well, *some* lawyers in this room have been making a half million dollars a year representing Coca-Cola and other big corporations'—referring to what Califano pulled down before he entered government—'while the rest of us have been working in the government on behalf of civil rights.' Pat Harris, over at Housing and Urban Development, called me about this and said, 'You know, I've been black for a long time, and I know what it's like to be discriminated against.' I said, 'Pat, I've been black for longer than you have.' She said, 'I'm not just talking about biological years.' I said, 'Neither am I.' "[65]

He went on, "I talked regularly with the Attorney General

about Bakke, but I never received, directly or indirectly, a statement that the White House wanted me to do this or that. I suspect Bell did. I didn't know it at the time. But whatever directions he received he didn't transmit to me as an order. Which says to me that he wasn't *told* to tell me, because I'm certain he would have. Bell is too well disciplined a person. If the President had said, 'Tell McCree to do thus and so,' I'm sure Bell would have."

According to Bell's assistant Terrence Adamson, Bell and Adamson set up a system to handle outsiders' comments on Bakke. It worked like this: Bell told Adamson to field all suggestions about Bakke from the White House. Instead of passing them on to McCree, he was to collect them in a drawer. From time to time, Bell and Adamson would talk with McCree and others in the Justice Department about the brief. They would pass on suggestions, whether from the White House or the Attorney General, without saying who made which ones. The ideas had to succeed on their own without the advantage of sponsorship from a high office. They did not arrive on Oval Office stationery, or even on the Attorney General's, and the brief-writers were free to incorporate or reject the comments. From Bell's point of view, instead of writing what the President's aides believed they were "instructing," the Solicitor General was insulated from their direct pressure, so he could think through the law with the help of others in the Justice Department and then tell the White House what he thought the law allowed. Despite Califano's fear that McCree would be controlled by Easterbrook, the Solicitor General knew about and shared the President's belief in affirmative action. [66] But he was free to choose the argument he thought best in this case. He decided to argue that, instead of supporting Allan Bakke, the government should recommend that the Supreme Court remand the case to California so the state court could decide whether the Davis program qualified as legitimate affirmative action. [67]

When the Supreme Court handed down its decision the following June, Justice Lewis Powell began for the Court: "We speak today with a notable lack of unanimity. I will try to explain how we divided. It may not be self-evident." [68] There were six separate opinions, and enough variety in the Justices' approaches for every government faction in the Bakke fight to find cause for vindication. On the one hand, the Court ordered the University of California to admit Bakke. It found the Davis program unconstitutional, because, on the basis of race alone, the program "totally foreclosed" opportunities for people like Bakke to compete in the special admissions program. On the other hand, Justice Powell's opinion, explaining his decisive swing vote, plainly acknowledged the value of affirmative action. An opinion by Justice William Brennan pleased the government's civil-rights lawyers, because it favored affirmative-action programs on terms those lawyers had recommended. According to Califano, who also focused on Brennan's opinion, "Our arguments and persistence had made a difference. Although I was sorry to have ruffled the feelings of Bell and McCree, both of whom I liked, they could be soothed." [69]

FROM THE VANTAGE of the Solicitor General, however, the most important document to come out of the Bakke case was issued soon after the government had filed its brief with the Supreme Court and long before the Justices issued their decision. It was dated September 29, 1977, and entitled "Memorandum for the Attorney General Re: The Role of the Solicitor General." [70] Signed by the Assistant Attorney General for the Office of Legal Counsel, John Harmon, the memo was researched by Miles Foy, a former law clerk to Judge Bell. [71] It had been prompted by a controversy over the snail-darter case, memorialized by Wade McCree in his limerick, but the paper spoke directly to issues raised by Bakke. The clash between the President's legal and political advisers had moved the AG's lawyers to put their judgments on paper.

"The purpose of this memorandum," it began, "is to discuss (1) the institutional relationship between the Attorney General and the Solicitor General, and (2) the role that each should play in formulating and presenting the Government's position in litigation before the Supreme Court." [72]

The memo settled the first issue quickly. "The short of the matter," it concluded, "is that under our law the Attorney General has the power and the right to 'conduct and argue' the Government's case in any court of the United States"—and the Solicitor General worked for the AG. But the answer to the second issue lurked in tradition as much as law, and it was harder to pin down. The SG had enjoyed "independence" within the Justice Department and within the Executive Branch. He was not "bound" by the views of his "clients" within the government, and he was free to confess error, rewrite briefs, and turn down requests for petitions to the Supreme Court for four reasons: "The Solicitor General must coordinate conflicting views within the Executive Branch; he must protect the Court by presenting meritorious claims in a straightforward and professional manner and by screening out unmeritorious ones; he must assist in the orderly development of decisional law, and he must 'do justice'—that is, he must discharge his office in accordance with law and ensure that improper concerns do not influence the presentation of the Government's case in the Supreme Court."

Why couldn't the Attorney General do the same? Because his political responsibilities might "cloud a clear vision of what the law requires." In the memo's words, "For this reason alone, in our view, the tradition of the 'independent' Solicitor General is a wise tradition." In the small number of cases that arose amidst political controversy, the Attorney General could strengthen the SG's independence by taking responsibility for the final judgment on the government's position and shielding the SG from political pressure. By preserving the Solicitor General's independence, the Attorney General enhanced the SG's ability to serve as "an officer learned in the law."

The memo closed by addressing the most difficult question: "How does one identify the 'rare instances' in which intervention by the Attorney General may be justifiable?" According to the Attorney General's aides, it was not enough that the Attorney General disagreed with the SG over a question of law. If the SG had made a mistake, the Supreme Court could correct him. If the Court upheld him, "then all the better, for his legal judgment and not that of his superiors was correct. . . . In either case," the paper stated, "the potential benefit of intervention is usually outweighed, in our view, by the mischief inherent in it."

About legal judgments, it was settled—the SG should be independent. "But if 'law' does not provide a clear answer to the question presented by the case before him, we think there is no reason to suppose that he, of all the officers in the Executive

Branch, should have the final responsibility for deciding what, as a matter of policy, the interests of the Government, the parties, or the Nation may require. To our knowledge, no Solicitor General has adopted a contrary view." So decisions about policy should be made by the Attorney General. "But the Attorney General and the President should trust the judgment of the Solicitor General not only in determining questions of law but also in distinguishing between questions of law and questions of policy. If the independent legal advice of the Solicitor General is to be preserved, it should normally be the Solicitor General who decides when to seek the advice of the Attorney General or the President in a given case."

The upshot of the Bakke case turned out to be this, the first official statement about the role of the Solicitor General in the century-old history of the office. In May of 1977, at the start of the Carter Administration, Erwin Griswold had written a letter of alarm to the Attorney General. [73] Griffin Bell had added to the hierarchy of the Justice Department an Associate Attorney General, to join the Deputy AG as one of two senior administrators. As a consequence, the Solicitor General slipped to fourth place in rank in the department—whereas he had started in 1870 in second place, with prestige almost equal to the Attorney General's. "I am concerned lest the office of the Solicitor General will be downgraded," Griswold wrote, fearing that the office would lose its authority as the government's "principal spokesman" before the Supreme Court as it gave up rank.

The memo about the role of the SG, written four months later, suggested that Griswold need not have worried about the significance of the Solicitor's loss of seniority. Commissioned by an Attorney General who was concerned about the impact on legal opinions of the process by which they were made, it was an endorsement of the SG's independence from the Attorney General and the White House by an office with a reputation for scholarship and impartiality. The Office of Legal Counsel articulated why the Solicitor General's independence was necessary if the government was to maintain and offer to the Supreme Court "a clear vision of what the law requires."

V

The Bob Jones
Case

THE FIRST PUBLIC sign of change in the Solicitor General's office under the Reagan Administration came during February 1982, in a footnote within a brief filed by the office in the Supreme Court. "This brief sets forth the position of the United States on both questions presented," the note stated about a case called Bob Jones University v. U.S. "The Acting Solicitor General fully subscribes to the position set forth on question number two, only."[1]

When the Bob Jones brief was filed, Lawrence Wallace was Acting Solicitor General. Rex Lee, who had been sworn in as SG seven months before, had once represented the Mormon church when it faced a problem like Bob Jones's and, to avoid the appearance of a conflict of interest, he had taken himself off the case.[2] Wallace is otherwise the senior Deputy Solicitor and, perhaps more self-consciously than anyone who works for the SG, he considers it his duty to maintain the traditions of the office.[3] When the Justices of the Supreme Court present the Court's new opinions, as they regularly do in an austere ceremony, he is often the only lawyer for the government who attends. He sits at counsel's table in front of the Justices, to signify that whatever the Court's judgment, the government is prepared to comply. At the SG's office, he minds everyone's business. This includes the minor details of submissions to the Court that he does not make. As Wallace explains it, Justice William O. Douglas once told him how much he appreciated that even the SG's footnotes could be relied on: unlike the notes of some other lawyers, the SG's squarely supported the propositions for which they were cited.[4] The moral is that Wallace feels compelled to hold the whole office to that high standard.

The story about Justice Douglas's comment is no parable. It is common for Wallace to quote a talk with a Justice as authority for one of his maxims about the Solicitor General's office. Wallace had been editor-in-chief of the *Columbia Law Review*, an associate at Covington & Burling, a law clerk to Justice Hugo Black, and a professor at the Duke University School of Law, and, by the start of the Reagan Administration, he had been with the SG's office for thirteen years. At forty-nine, he had argued about 65 cases before the Supreme Court,[5] more than anyone else then in the government. (As of 1987, the only living advocate who had argued more cases was Erwin Griswold; his 117 put him second among twentieth-century lawyers, behind John W. Davis [140 cases], and fourth on the Supreme Court's all-time list, behind Davis, Daniel Webster [between 185 and 200], and a little-known lawyer named Walter Jones, who, between 1801 and 1850, argued 317.)[6]

Wallace knew that his footnote in the Bob Jones brief was likely to draw close attention. The disclaimer (he called it "dropping a footnote" instead of "tying a tin can") was not as extreme as Simon Sobeloff's refusal to sign the government's brief in the Peters case a generation before, but it was a strong alternative.

In some public-relations material, Bob Jones described itself as "the world's most unusual university."[7] Located in Greenville, South Carolina, the school gives "special emphasis to the Christian religion and the ethics revealed in the Holy scriptures."[8] The Reverend Billy Graham started there as a student, but transferred away because the school's ultra-fundamentalism proved too much for him.[9] In 1982, in its regular programs for those in kindergarten through graduate school, Bob Jones had approximately sixty-three hundred students.[10] In its smaller Institute of Christian Service, taught exclusively by "born again" Christians, the university had students from more than a hundred denominations, who came to learn Christian character and the principles of the Bible.[11] "The institution does not permit dancing, card playing, the use of tobacco, movie going, and other such forms of indulgences in which worldly young people often engage," a judge wrote about the university, "and no young man may walk a girl on campus unless both of them have a legitimate reason for going in the same direction."[12] During the 1980 Presidential campaign, Ronald Reagan gave a speech at Bob Jones, and called the school a "great institution."[13]

Along with another institution called Goldsboro Christian Schools, in Goldsboro, North Carolina, the university was before the Supreme Court because of its admissions policy against blacks. For most of its history, the school had excluded them. School leaders believed from their reading of Scripture that God intended the races to live separately, and they ran the university accordingly.[14] In 1970, the Internal Revenue Service ruled that Bob Jones no longer qualified for tax-exempt status because of this segregationist policy, so the school changed it. Blacks could be accepted if they were married to other blacks, or if they promised not to date or marry outside their race. After the new policy took effect, Bob Jones enrolled five blacks. By the time of the Supreme Court case, a decade later, the number of blacks attending the school was less than a dozen, making the ratio of whites to blacks about 550 to one.[15]

From the vantage point of the Solicitor General's office, the legal issue in the Bob Jones case was routine. It was a tax question.[16] After the Supreme Court called for desegregation of public schools in Brown v. Board of Education, "segregation academies" sprang up through the South. The Civil Rights Act of 1964 outlawed direct government aid to these private, whites-only schools, but the law said nothing about indirect subsidies through tax exemptions. The academies claimed to be exempt from federal tax as educational institutions under an often used section of the tax code. For a few years, the IRS excused the schools from paying Social Security, income, and other taxes, and allowed their benefactors to deduct from their own taxes the contributions they made to the schools, but by 1970, when about four hundred thousand Southern children were attending "seg academies," the agency decided to alter its stance. Doing "what we thought the law compelled us to,"[17] IRS Commissioner Randolph Thrower said later, the Nixon Administration notified about five thousand schools that it would read the tax code a new way. To qualify for a tax exemption, schools had to be charitable in the broadest sense. They could not serve ends at odds with public policy. In the case of Bob

Jones University, the IRS revoked the school's exemption, on the grounds that its admissions policy contradicted the nation's commitment to halt racial discrimination.

At trial, Bob Jones won its suit against the IRS. The presiding federal district judge ruled that the university qualified for an exemption as a religious institution, despite its admissions practices. The IRS won on appeal, when the Court of Appeals rejected the lower court's "simplistic reading" of the law.[18] The university asked the Supreme Court to review the case, and Lawrence Wallace responded with another type of action peculiar to the office of Solicitor General: he "acquiesced." He agreed that the school's petition should be heard, though he opposed it on the merits. The case had drawn unusual attention from political officials in the Reagan Administration, and Wallace believed he could dampen the interest with this partial concession.[19] Like the longtime tax lawyers advising him, Wallace had no doubt the government had properly won its appeal, because the IRS ruling had been backed by the President when it was made and was amply supported by the Constitution, Supreme Court rulings, and subsequent acts of Congress.[20] But, instead of recommending that the government oppose the school's petition to the Supreme Court, which would have reduced the university's chances of being heard to about one in a hundred, he agreed that the Justices should take the case, on the grounds that many schools might be affected by the case and that the bar needed guidance from the Supreme Court.

Not long after Wallace submitted the SG's acquiescence, Congressman Trent Lott, a Republican from Mississippi, sent letters around the government protesting the Wallace position that the Court of Appeals should be upheld. His missive went to the President, the Attorney General, the Commissioner of the IRS, and Solicitor General Rex Lee. "The last time I read the Constitution," he declared, "it provided that the *Congress* is to make the laws—not appointed officials."[21] The phrase "appointed officials" covered members of the Executive Branch (including the IRS) and the Judicial Branch. Because the Court of Appeals in the Bob Jones case had upheld the IRS reading of the tax code, Lott and his supporters thought the judges were as remiss as the tax officials. One of Lott's supporters in this venture was Senator Strom Thurmond, a Republican from South Carolina, who became chairman of the Senate Judiciary Committee after the Republicans gained control of the Senate in 1980, and who sat on the board of trustees of Bob Jones University.[22] Like the President, Thurmond and Lott were foes of "judicial activism." In the words of a Justice Department memo prompted by Lott's letter, any court that read the law in a way that was not "clearly mandated by statute or the Constitution" had engaged in "judicial activism and policy-making."[23]

The group within the Justice Department that rallied to reverse Wallace's position on the merits became known as "the Bob Jones team." The senior member was Edward Schmults, the Deputy Attorney General and the department's second-ranking official. The team included William Bradford Reynolds, Assistant Attorney General for Civil Rights; Charles Cooper, his assistant; Carolyn Kuhl, an aide to Attorney General William French Smith; and Bruce Fein, an aide to Schmults.

The Reagan Administration's interest in the case bubbled up from the middle ranks. After Wallace took his stance, Fein wrote a paper arguing that the case deserved the Attorney General's special attention. In his words, "The IRS did not have the authority under the law to promulgate those regulations, and the obligation of the [Justice] Department was to go by what the law actually says instead of going the other way because it makes us feel good. One of the problems we've had in the last twenty years is 'feel good law.' " Kuhl found some campaign material saying that candidate Reagan had opposed "the IRS's attempt to remove the tax-exempt status of private schools by administrative fiat"[24] and that the 1980 Republican platform pledged to "halt the unconstitutional regulatory vendetta launched by Mr. Carter's IRS Commissioner against independent schools"—even though it was President Nixon's commissioner who, with Nixon's approval, had begun what the platform called a vendetta.

Reynolds might have been expected to show concern about the reaction of blacks to the Fein position, since, as head of the Civil Rights Division, he was responsible for enforcing laws passed to protect the rights of minorities. Instead, he agreed there was nothing in the tax code to deny tax-exempt status to Bob Jones University. During the first year of the Reagan Administration, the Justice Department had been criticized in the right-wing press for showing disloyalty to the President's social program by not pressing it hard enough. To senior officials like Reynolds and Schmults, other lawyers in the department observed, the Bob Jones case seemed to present a chance to improve the record.[25]

Trent Lott's letter was summarized in the President's log of congressional mail as urging the President "to intervene in this particular case." President Reagan scrawled in the margin, "I think we should." Some of the President's advisers believed the shift contemplated by the Bob Jones team was no more than an about-face on a policy of the Carter Administration, and they approved. Not long afterward, Michael Deaver, one of the President's initial triumvirate of senior advisers, said, "I just heard that it was a reversal of Carter policy and at that point I tuned out."[26] The Bob Jones team held a series of meetings about the case, excluded Wallace from them, and encouraged him to continue drafting a brief for the government as he saw fit; by the time Wallace was invited to take part in a review of the Justice Department's options, the team had already convinced Attorney General William French Smith to overrule the Acting Solicitor General.[27]

To lawyers in the SG's office, which sometimes displays its skills by presenting conflicting sides of a case with equal weight, the Bob Jones team's position was indefensible. First, they believed that it was wrong on the law. For a decade, the IRS had applied the tax law in keeping with the commitment to halt discrimination. Congress had considered amending the tax code thirteen times since then, each time deciding it was not necessary to clarify the law because the IRS was already reading it properly. The Supreme Court summarily upheld this position in 1971.[28]

Next, the change didn't appear to serve the Administration's interests. If the President's followers wanted to make a statement about the appropriate division of responsibility under the Constitution for making, enforcing, and interpreting the law, a case that required the Administration to endorse racism while doing so was an ill-chosen vehicle. Bradford Reynolds defended himself in 1985 by declaring that "neither I nor the Administration ever favored granting tax-exempt status to racially discriminatory private schools," [29] but that was the instant effect of their judgment that the statute in question permitted no other reading. Though the crux of the Administration's theory may have been based on an earnestly held principle—that the doctrine on which the IRS based its decision to revoke tax exemptions in 1970 had no obvious limits—it was not convincing. The Administration asked: If Bob Jones no longer qualifies for an exemption because its exclusion of blacks violates public policy to end racial discrimination, what about schools that admit only women? Can't they be said to violate public policy against discrimination based on sex? [30] But the IRS had made no move to expand the doctrine along these lines, and there was solid evidence that Congress had approved the agency's special concern about race. Tied to this divisive issue, the Administration's position came off as a construction of lawyers whose insensitivity seemed willful.

Finally, the reversal took no account of the perspective of the Supreme Court. Reagan aides treated the flip-flop in position, from the brief acquiescing to the brief on the merits, as if it were a natural course of events. Yet the move had no serious precedent. The credibility of the Solicitor General had been built up, among other ways, by close inquiry into the case at hand and then by maintaining a consistent position about it before the Justices. [31] The Attorney General's decision meant a rejection of the brief that Wallace had submitted four months before, when he recommended that the Justices take the case. "I had the responsibility to represent the United States in the Supreme Court," Wallace said. "It was my case. I can't remember another occasion during my 14 years in office when we've changed position in a case after taking a position with the Supreme Court." [32]

After the Administration's new stance was announced, the views of the Reagan Administration were widely seen as an endorsement of racism. "THE REWARDING OF BIAS," the Los Angeles *Times* called the government's new stance. "HYPOCRITICAL TAX CHANGE MEANS RACISM WILL PAY," judged the Tallahassee *Democrat*. "TAX-EXEMPT HATE," *The New York Times* summed up. [33] White House aides tried to convince reporters that the President had not guided the decision to overrule IRS policy in the case, [34] but at a press conference President Reagan rejected this cover. He was asked by ABC's Sam Donaldson, "Are you responsible for the original decision, or did your staff put something over on you?" The President replied, "Sam, no one put anything over on me. No, Sam, the buck stops at my desk." He requested, "Judge us [by] how well we recover and solve the situation."[35]

In the wake of the public outcry, the President's aides tried to make their judgment sound coherent, and declared that Congress should take responsibility by amending the IRS code to forbid tax exemptions to schools like Bob Jones. Backpedaling from Southerners like Strom Thurmond, who argued that the case had to do with "religious and private civil rights," the President repeated the logic of his 1980 platform: the only reason for his Administration's new policy was to keep the IRS from governing by "administrative fiat." As the President summed up the extreme position of his lawyers, "There was no basis in the law for what they"—that is, the IRS—"were doing."[36] Under the heading "Just a Little More Tax-Exempt Hate," the *Times* articulated a common response in an editorial: "Until Congress passes the law, Mr. Reagan insists that the Internal Revenue Service begin granting such exemptions. Whatever his preference in this case, therefore, he persists in signaling that his Administration will acquiesce in discrimination wherever and for as long as it can."[37]

The proposal for Congress to provide a bailout and settle the issue went nowhere, because many members appeared to believe there was no "problem" to fix. Under other circumstances, they might have taken the opportunity to clear up an ambiguous detail of the tax code. Now they felt manipulated by a government trying to get Congress to cover up the Executive Branch's gaffe. William Brodhead, a Democratic Congressman from Michigan, told witnesses for the Administration that testimony they had given about their proposal was "the shabbiest, most unbelievable bunch of crap I've heard since I've been here."[38]

The Acting SG's role in the case sparked a final bit of drama over submission of the Administration's brief. The Bob Jones team wanted Wallace to sign it, making it look like business as usual; Bruce Fein threatened to have Wallace disciplined[39]—lawyers in the SG's office say fired—if Wallace did not cooperate; Wallace proposed that Edward Schmults, the Deputy AG, sign the brief on behalf of the Attorney General; and Schmults called Rex Lee, who was out in Utah giving a legal seminar, to get Wallace to sign the brief. Lee calmed everyone down ("The Bob Jones team realized they couldn't chop off the head of the senior Deputy Solicitor and not have the Washington *Post* on their backs for weeks after," observed a lawyer involved with the case),[40] and urged a compromise. Wallace signed, and "dropped" his footnote.

Around this time, Wallace received a personal letter from Marvin Frankel, a former federal judge who is now a lawyer in private practice. It was one of a dozen well-wishing notes or calls that the deputy received in response to his footnote.[41] "With the semi-proprietary interest of an SG alumnus (1952–1956)," the judge wrote,[42] "I have watched your career from afar with approval and admiration. Not being a writer of fan letters, I haven't found occasion to share these sentiments with you. Now, however, I'm prompted to report directly my special applause for your sound and courageous stance on the IRS-racial discrimination business. I'm sure the decision to take this position was not reached lightly or without anguish. Recognizing the personal cost to you, I want you to know that some of us out here appreciate your contribution to principle and public decency."

A year and a quarter later, the Supreme Court gave Wallace a public vindication. "Given the stress and anguish of the history and efforts to escape from the shackles of the 'separate but equal' doctrine of Plessy v. Ferguson," the Court stated about the 1896 decision, "it cannot be said that educational institutions that, for whatever reason, practice racial discrimination, are institutions exercising 'beneficial and stabilizing influences in community life,' or should be encouraged by having all taxpayers share in their support by way of special tax status." The Executive, Legislative, and Judicial Branches had long agreed on this interpretation of public policy, a majority of the Court went on, and the IRS couldn't "blissfully ignore what all three branches of the federal government had declared." Signed by Chief Justice Warren Burger, a consistent conservative, the Court's opinion stated that "there can no longer be any doubt that racial discrimination in education violates deeply accepted views of elementary justice."[43]

With William Rehnquist dissenting, the Justices ruled eight to one in favor of the IRS.

After the Bob Jones decision was handed down, the White House adopted the view that the media were responsible for damage to the Administration caused by its handling of the case because reporters had misrepresented the story. Bradford Reynolds assigned blame to the Supreme Court and to blacks as well. Taking the Court's reference to the Plessy case out of context, he said, "I believe that one factor in their decisional process was that this was an extremely controversial issue that had been played in the media and understood by the public only in terms of the segregation of schools. The Court, I think, wanted to be sure whichever way they decided it, that this wasn't going to be pinned on them as another Plessy v. Ferguson." Reynolds also commented, "Bob Jones was and will remain an albatross for us, particularly out in the black community. When the press blatantly labeled our actions as racist, the large majority of the black community—which don't have the kind of education that would permit them to sort through the legal issues—came away with the attitude, 'Gee, they must have people in there that really are racist!' "[44]

A summary of the Administration's views was included in a study of the event by the Kennedy School of Government at Harvard University. The chronicle of the Bob Jones case concluded that, despite "widespread unhappiness over the way the case had been handled, the controversy was not of serious personal consequence for any official. No one got fired, transferred or disciplined because of Bob Jones; indeed a number of officials who played leading roles in the drama were promoted."[45]

Lawrence Wallace became an unrecorded casualty of the case. He had for many years handled the government's civil-rights cases. It was known as a controversial area, but he had an idea how to keep in-house disagreements in check. He expressed it with a nautical metaphor. When the government's opinions heeled to the left, as they had during the Carter Administration, the SG's recommendations should shift to the right, like ballast against the keel of a boat. And when the prevailing views went off on the opposite tack, the SG's recommendations should move accordingly, to provide balance, maintain continuity, and keep the government as upright as possible.[46]

During his fourteen-year tenure, Wallace had worked for four SGs and five Administrations, with the Republicans outnumbering the Democrats three to one (the SGs) and three to two (the Administrations). He considered himself a civil servant with a duty to the government, and although he regularly miffed both Democratic and Republican political appointees by toning down their partisan contentions, he had succeeded until the Reagan Administration by employing this notion of counterpoise. "Larry was right about every major civil-rights case in which he participated, from the day he arrived in the Justice Department," said Brian Landsberg, who until 1986 was the senior career attorney in the appellate section of the Civil Rights Division; "and he is an awesomely talented lawyer."[47]

In his letter to Wallace, Marvin Frankel had concluded, "I would hope that neither this good action or anything else will require you to need specific support from colleagues like me. But I ask you to record my availability if and when you think I might be of any use. Meanwhile, accept my respectful cheers and gratitude. And my confident wishes and expectations for your continued distinction at the top of our shared profession." Wallace didn't call on Frankel for assistance, but he might have. After the Bob Jones case, Wallace was relieved of all responsibility for civil-rights cases.[48] Though he remained a Deputy Solicitor, he was treated by Reagan loyalists like a whistle-blower who had to be kept away from any sensitive assignment.

The support of Warren Burger in the Bob Jones decision actually hurt Wallace in the eyes of the Reagan team. By the time the Chief Justice handed down his opinion for the Court, Wallace had been singled out by top appointees at the Justice Department as the cause of things gone wrong in the case. If it hadn't been for Wallace's footnote, the case would have come out differently[49]— and, for them, the judgment of the Supreme Court confirmed this. Though Wallace considered it his duty to protect the President from the zeal of his political appointees, he was accused of disloyalty. The lesson of the Bob Jones case for the Bob Jones team was that if other cases arose in which the Solicitor General had to disqualify himself, the President would not be able to tolerate having Wallace in charge.[50] Toward the end of the Carter Administration, the day Benjamin Civiletti was sworn in as Attorney

General to replace Griffin Bell at the Justice Department, a young lawyer had found Wallace in his office instead of at the ceremony. "I've seen Administrations come and go," the Deputy Solicitor General told her with misplaced confidence, "and they've never made much difference to my work." [51]

Wallace's ouster was consistent with the theory that the Bob Jones dispute resulted from his inability to get along with Bradford Reynolds and other top civil-rights attorneys appointed by the Reagan Administration. Since Wallace is a large man, with a habit of flicking his hands in the air like a conductor, he brings out the mimic in many lawyers at the Justice Department who have dealt with him. The aping is sometimes meant as affection, but Wallace's manner can be fussy and he may have simply rubbed Reynolds the wrong way. "Larry put himself in the way of a lot of trouble," said one of his colleagues in the SG's office. [52]

The nature and timing of Wallace's replacement suggested why another analysis of Bob Jones was more accurate: a political appointee took his place at the start of 1983, five months before the Supreme Court ruled on the case. For the first time in the history of the SG's office, the Reagan Administration appointed a Counselor to the Solicitor General and Deputy Solicitor General, who became known as the political deputy. The reason given for the new post was plausible: the SG should be backed up by a second lieutenant of the President's so that when the Solicitor had to remove himself from a case, as Rex Lee did in Bob Jones, he could defer to a manager whom the Administration trusted. [53] But the appointment of the political deputy was the first hard evidence of how the relationships, first, between the SG's office and the rest of the Justice Department, and then between the SG's office and the Supreme Court, were being transformed by the Reagan Administration.

The new man was Paul Bator, a conservative legal scholar from Harvard Law School. A *summa cum laude* graduate of Princeton and of Harvard Law School, where he presided at the *Law Review,* he had clerked for Justice John Harlan, an outstanding conservative jurist. Bator was widely respected as a co-author of the second edition of a definitive volume about the workings of federal law known as Hart and Wechsler, after the two original authors who created a new field of legal study in the nineteen-fifties and who also served in the SG's office. Bator's finicky style challenged the mandarins in the SG's office to meet a new standard. "Once you've served in the office," he said, "you're hooked. It's like opera singers who perform at La Scala."⁵⁴

In keeping with the Reagan Administration, one of Bator's favorite themes was judicial restraint. "More precisely," he instructed, "we want our federal judges to do *two* things—both hard. We want them to be bold, to be fearless, in exercising the power they legitimately possess, to rule without timidity where the law requires them to rule, and damn the consequences. But we ask another thing, too, one that may be harder. We ask that they be scrupulous *not* to rule, *not* to act, to leave the exercise of power to others, where the law does not justify judicial intervention." Bator illustrated his understanding of the choice by quoting Romantic poetry. He said, "Shelley's 'Adonais' asks: 'Of what scene are we actors, of what the spectators?' To intervene everywhere is bad; never to intervene is bad; is there a concept of the judge's role that solves—or, more accurately, dissolves—the antinomy?" He found it in *"interpretation,"* and, comparing a judge to Arturo Toscanini conducting Beethoven, or Vladimir Horowitz playing Brahms, he declared that the judge's responsibility was to interpret the law in a "spirit of obedience."⁵⁵

Bator had his own views about what he was meant to do as political deputy. He said in 1985, "It was rather clear from the situation what was needed. They were not looking for someone who would give the office a political trashing. If someone was put in there whom the office regarded as incompetent or as merely political, who was not a fine lawyer or a person of distinction— that would have been inappropriate. I think that the office and the Solicitor General himself thought that I was an ideal solution. In a soft and general way, I was sympathetic to the Administration, certainly in the area of constitutional law. But basically I'm an apolitical person. I'm a professor, I'm an academic, I believe in academic integrity. I've always stood for very severe professional standards. The SG's lawyers felt that I would have credibility vis-à-vis the political people, while being sensitive to concerns of tradition, continuity, and integrity, and the Administration types felt that I would be a more sympathetic ear to their concerns than Larry and some of the others."[56]

Arguing like lawyers to soften the impact of their decision reorganizing the SG's office, Reagan officials cited the precedent of a political appointment made during the Nixon Administration.[57] Jewel Lafontant had made a speech to second the nomination of Richard Nixon at the 1960 Republican Convention, the year that Kennedy defeated Nixon, and she eventually served as a representative to the United Nations during the first Nixon term.[58] As a "three-fer" (she was young, female, and black—a symbol of Nixon's needed support from three groups), she was then named a Deputy Solicitor in the SG's office.[59]

Paul Bator bore no resemblance to Lafontant, and his mission was completely different. Whereas Lafontant was expected to perform like other lawyers in the SG's office, Bator had a new charter. He was brought in as a monitor, by an Administration that did not trust the counsel of the Solicitor General's career attorneys.

"You must remember that the tradition of independence has always been within the context of an underlying responsibility running from the Solicitor General to the Attorney General, and from the Attorney General to the President," Bator explained in 1985, oversimplifying and, by emphasis, contradicting the understanding of the Solicitor Generalship expressed by the Office of Legal Counsel at the time of Bakke. "It has never been *real* independence."[60]

VI

Judicial Restraint

DURING THE SUMMER of 1913, when William Howard Taft left the Presidency and moved to Connecticut to teach constitutional law at Yale Law School, he read every case in which the Supreme Court had interpreted the Constitution.[1] Today, even a scholar whose energy and talents matched Taft's couldn't begin to make his way in a summer's time through the volumes of Supreme Court decisions on constitutional law. Professors say the law has been "constitutionalized,"[2] meaning that many aspects of social life once the province of politics, like abortion and school prayer, have been dealt with by the Supreme Court as matters of constitutional law.

This phenomenon is part of a broader change in the role of courts in the United States. During the Carter Administration, the Justice Department commissioned a bipartisan group of lawyers, judges, and scholars to prepare a report on the topic.[3] This 1984 study confirmed that in the past generation the number of cases in federal courts had dramatically increased. The number in state courts dwarfed those in federal courts—roughly, 100 million a year versus 250,000—but on the basis of cases per capita both showed a significant increase. At the turn of the century, there were 19 cases filed in federal court for every 100,000 people; in 1980, there were 80, or more than four times as many.[4]

The most prominent change noted by the study was in "major constitutional reform." Beginning with the Supreme Court's landmark opinion in Brown v. Board of Education, in 1954, the Justices "taught in a dramatic and visible way that when other institutions fail to respond, constitutional claims can be vindicated in Ameri-

can courts." Congress contributed to this change by being "prolific in recognizing new claims and entitlements" and passing
"dozens of major statutes" to protect civil rights, the environment,
and a wide range of other social interests. The change in courts
that caused the most concern was the redefinition by judges of the
role of federal courts. [5]

The controversy centered mainly on the courts' treatment of
lawsuits brought to reform public institutions like schools, prisons,
hospitals, and police departments. Instead of simply forbidding
unlawful actions or awarding damages for wrongs, which was
their historical function, the courts gradually took to telling the
Executive Branch, states, and local governments what to do and
how—what Archibald Cox called "an unprecedented judicial un-
dertaking." The traditional notion that judges should serve as
referees in disputes between parties was challenged by a new breed
of activist lawyer and a new concept of the activist judge, in which
courts guided the parties to shape a solution to a problem—as the
study on the role of courts described it, "to take on social grievances left festering by indecisive political institutions." This idea
had not always worked well, the commission acknowledged, but
it was successful enough to warrant serious discussion. Contrary
to the view that courts had usurped power from other branches of
government, for example, the report judged that they had "helped
to energize them." Instead of weakening public confidence in
courts, "judicial decrees ha[d] arguably increased respect for the
judiciary in general." In fact, the report concluded with a flourish,
courts had stirred a "deep and durable demand for justice in our
society." They assured the vindication of rights that otherwise
would have gone unprotected. [6]

When the Reagan Administration came to power, it expressed
a much less tolerant view of this expansion in the role of courts.
Among lawyers who once brought suits to reform institutions like
schools and prisons, there was a growing nucleus who recognized
problems associated with policymaking by courts. [7] Was it fair that
a small group of attorneys could take it on themselves to direct
social change simply by filing a lawsuit? Was it right that the
prospects for change could turn on whether the attorneys drew a
sympathetic judge? Even if they did, and the judge, through the

cumbersome mechanism of a trial, was able to learn what he needed to know to order reforms, could he manage alone something as complex as a school system or a prison?

The Reagan Administration explored none of these questions in detail. Its conclusions about the expanding role of courts were categorical and wholly negative. In remarks before the Federal Legal Council in October of 1981, Attorney General William French Smith declared, "We believe that the groundswell of conservatism evidenced by the 1980 election makes this an especially appropriate time to urge upon the courts more principled bases that would diminish judicial activism. History teaches us that the courts are not unaffected by major public change in political attitudes."[8]

The Attorney General went on to identify three ways the Administration would press the courts to retreat from "policymaking": by limiting the matters they considered to narrowly defined cases or controversies as opposed to cases that raised general problems; by resisting the "multiplication" of constitutional rights; and by cutting back on the "extravagant use" of injunctions and remedies to right social wrongs. Smith called this agenda a commitment to "judicial restraint"—what he termed "the importance of judicial restraint to the constitutional principle of separation of powers." Having said what the Administration would do, Smith then tried to dampen criticism before it arose. He assured his audience that although the Administration would lobby the courts to be constrained, it would not fail to enforce the law of the land, even if the new officials "disagreed" with the statutes or court rulings in question. He said, "No one should doubt that this Administration's adherence to the Constitutional principle of separation of powers will exact from us the same degree of obedience and moderation that we will urge upon the courts."[9]

Smith made a point of emphasizing that the Administration would take its legal views "all the way to the Supreme Court,"[10] and that the Solicitor General was already looking for cases that would be good vehicles for the trip. The Administration had tried to select a man who was right for the job, and from its point of view Rex Lee appeared to be a fitting choice as Solicitor General. The dean of Brigham Young University's J. Reuben Clark Law

School and a Mormon, Lee had graduated first in his class from the University of Chicago Law School, clerked for Justice Byron White, and served in the Ford Administration as Assistant Attorney General in charge of the Civil Division.[11] In two compact volumes (*A Lawyer Looks at the Constitution* and *A Lawyer Looks at the Equal Rights Amendment*),[12] he had shown an ability to articulate conservative legal ideas in plain terms.

The first book made some lawyers in the SG's office nervous, because its survey of constitutional law struck them as simplistic.[13] (Chapter 1, paragraph 1: "The Philadelphia summer of 1787 was unusually hot and humid. For the fifty-five delegates gathered to deliberate as a Constitutional Convention, there were problems more serious than the unpleasant weather.")[14] They wondered how a mind tuned to this level would deal with the nuances of Supreme Court practice.

The second provoked another concern. No one knew what the Equal Rights Amendment would mean for constitutional law, the author argued, but, whatever its impact, the objective could be reached in better, more flexible ways than amending the Constitution. (The ERA was defeated in 1982. It had been a divisive subject since it was proposed in 1972.) At Lee's confirmation hearings before the Senate Judiciary Committee, Eleanor Smeal, president of the National Organization for Women, described his ERA writing as "a mass of error, omission, and distortion unworthy of a candidate for the position of Solicitor General of the United States."[15] She tied his "significant bias" against, or "extreme insensitivity" to, equal rights for women to his "close association" with a conservative public-interest law group called the Mountain States Legal Foundation and to some of his actions as dean at the Brigham Young law school which Smeal found objectionable. As a board member of the foundation when it was directed by James Watt (who later became Ronald Reagan's first and often combative Secretary of the Interior), Lee had supported lawsuits that were, in the words of Joseph Coors, its onetime chairman, designed to "meet the challenges made by the extreme environmentalists, no-growth advocates, and excessive government." The group had also opposed the latest congressional extension of the period for ratifying the ERA. Until his nomination, Lee had also been the founding and only dean of the law school. "During his

tenure," Smeal contended, "he demonstrated no serious commitment to (or concern with) the involvement or advancement of
women in his profession."[16] Only 16 percent of the students at J.
Reuben Clark Law School were women, as opposed to the national average of 33 percent; there was only one woman member
on the twenty-five-person faculty, for 4 percent of the total, versus
10 percent on average at law faculties across the country. The
opposition from liberal lawyers and feminists that was stirred by
Lee's background and books endeared him to Reagan supporters.

A lawyer who worked for him in the SG's office observed,
"You meet Rex Lee, and you think, Huck Finn."[17] Lee is a tall,
slim, boyish-looking man, with slick brown hair and a slight stut-
ter. His manner is open and winning. He was forty-six when the
Reagan Administration chose him to be SG. "I had heard they had
a list of candidates for the job," Lee recalled in 1985, "and after I
had an interview in March of 1981, the phone call came that April,
two days after the Boston Marathon. I was about to go back home,
after running pretty well—three hours and seven and a half minutes, which is a good time for me. I will remember Mr. Smith's
sentence throughout this life and the next. He simply said, 'We
would like to have you come and join this Administration as the
Solicitor General.' "[18]

If one goes by the numbers, Lee's four years as SG were
extremely successful. In one year, the government won a higher
percentage of its cases in the Supreme Court than in any Term
since the Justice Department began keeping modern statistics, in
1955,[19] and in the other three it did almost as well; it consistently
persuaded the Court to review a high share of the government's
lower-court losses; and, as a friend of the Court, it played a part
in helping resolve major cases to which it was not a party. During
one of those four years, Lee's record in persuading the Supreme
Court to overturn the Ninth Circuit, which is now considered the
country's most liberal Court of Appeals, was phenomenal. In the
1983 Term, the Supreme Court reversed the Ninth Circuit in
twenty-seven out of twenty-nine cases. The Justices reviewed
fourteen of those cases in part because Lee asked them to—he had
filed twice as many petitions from rulings of that circuit as he had
from the next highest circuit on the list.[20]

As things turned out, this record of accomplishment was not

Lee's legacy. In the SG's office, the cases that marked his tenure were like Bob Jones. They were known as "agenda cases." [21] Whether they were the vehicles William French Smith had in mind when he outlined the Reagan Administration's campaign for judicial restraint, they came to represent the President's efforts in the Supreme Court while Lee was SG. The core of the President's social agenda was identified in his speeches and in key planks of the Republican National Platform: against mandatory busing as a tool of school desegregation; in favor of voluntary prayer in public schools; against the constitutional right to abortion; against affirmative action for admission to schools or hiring in jobs to remedy past discrimination against minorities; in favor of cutting back on the legal rights of individuals accused of committing crimes. [22]

In his writings before he became Solicitor General, Lee had adopted each of these positions; and in his early days as SG he spread the word that too many people with too many causes had access to the federal courts, and too many fundamental rights were available for them to assert. [23] At the end of his second year as SG, Rex Lee viewed the Reagan agenda in a new light: he described it to the Los Angeles *Times* as "an albatross around my neck." [24]

Lee's unhappiness with what he called the "enormous pressure" on him to push the Supreme Court "too far too fast" [25] had a lot to do with the difference between his concept of the law and the one prevailing within the Reagan Administration. A key part of the disagreement focused on the meaning of judicial restraint. Since the start of the Republic, the great debate in American law has centered on the proper scope of the power of unelected federal judges. The Constitution makes no mention of the Supreme Court's power to rule on the lawfulness of acts of Congress and the President, but legal scholars and Congress have long agreed that the Court must have that authority, which is ultimately derived from the Constitution. In his starched, imperious style, Learned Hand once lectured that the power of judicial review was "not a logical deduction from the structure of the Constitution but only a practical condition upon its successful operation." He went on, "Without some arbiter whose decision should be final the whole system would have collapsed." [26] Alexander Hamilton expressed the same idea in Number 78 of the *Federalist Papers*, and this power of review has been a tenet of the American system of law since 1803, when Chief Justice John Marshall, in Marbury v. Madison, declared, "It is emphatically the province and duty of the judicial department to say what the law is." [27]

Yet many disagree about the proper bounds of judges' review, and the main opposing views among legal theorists reflect a deep conflict about the role of courts in the American version of democracy. One side sees judicial review as a simple but crucial part of a system of checks and balances whose distinction comes from its ability to protect the freedom of minorities from the tyranny of the majority. Adherents of this notion, sometimes known as "political jurisprudence," have won wide support for the idea that courts are inevitably engaged in politics, and that judicial review is a basic function of a democratic government. [28] ("Few accusations against the Supreme Court are made with more heat and answered with less candor than that it makes political decisions," Robert Jackson once wrote. "Of course, the line between political science and legal science is not fixed and varies with one's definition of his terms. Any decision that declares the law under which a people must live or which affects the powers of their institutions is in a very real sense political.") [29]

The other side sees review by judges as what Alexander Bickel called "a deviant institution" whose existence contradicts the "distinguishing characteristic" [30] of American government—rule by the majority. From this vantage, judicial review—hardly a democratic process—appears to undermine the ultimate freedom, the freedom of the majority to govern. Its scope must be sharply limited.

To ease the tension between the fact of judicial review and the majoritarian roots of American government, lawyers and judges from the second school have promoted a philosophy of judicial restraint. A classic scholarly statement of the philosophy was made in 1893 by James Bradley Thayer, a Harvard Law School professor. [31] He used the notion that judicial review is undemocratic to create a guiding stricture, urging that judges restrict their findings of unconstitutionality to laws that can't fulfill any legitimate purpose. He translated a theory about the Constitution's limits on the role of courts into a practical rule.

In the first decades of this century, Justices Oliver Wendell Holmes and Louis Brandeis articulated this theme when they dissented from Supreme Court rulings that struck down social legislation viewed by the conservative majority as anti-business. A generation later, Justices Felix Frankfurter and John Harlan and federal judges like Learned Hand built on the theories of Thayer, Holmes, and others, with memorable lines of explanation: "The Constitution is not a panacea of every blot on the public welfare, nor should this Court, ordained as a judicial body, be thought of as a general haven for reform movements," Harlan maintained. [32] Courts shouldn't serve as "superlegislatures" nor judges as "a bevy of Platonic Guardians," wrote Hand. [33] "There is not under our Constitution a judicial remedy for every political mischief, for every undesirable exercise of legislative power," Frankfurter declared. "The Framers carefully and with deliberate forethought refused so to enthrone the judiciary." [34]

The judges who best articulated the philosophy of restraint were also gifted legal craftsmen, and they constructed modern canons for the courts to follow, to limit the scope of judicial review. The Supreme Court and other federal courts should defer when possible, they said, to the judgments of democratically elected bodies, from the Congress down to local school boards. Since the states are the foundation of the Union, and the Constitution draws its power from them, the courts should defer to state and local over federal authority. Exercising passive virtues, the judges went on, courts should decide no case unnecessarily. When they do rule, they should do it on the narrowest possible grounds. Except in unusual instances, they should keep the law consistent and avoid rash decisions by closely following precedent. Judges should carefully interpret all sources of law, including cases, statutes, and the Constitution itself, and they should not read into a case or law provisions that are not there. With these canons, the theory of judicial restraint became a force for legal conservatism—helping judges conserve their authority for use in the gradual evolution of the law. [35]

Legal doctrine is shaped by circumstances, and judicial restraint became a preoccupation in the law during the constitutional crisis of the nineteen-thirties. When Franklin Roosevelt came to the Presidency, [36] the Supreme Court was controlled by

Willis Van Devanter, James McReynolds, George Sutherland, and Pierce Butler, a quartet of conservative Justices known as the Four Horsemen. While Roosevelt's government was likely to win the backing of Louis Brandeis, Harlan Stone, and Benjamin Cardozo in Court arguments, losing the vote of either Owen Roberts or Charles Evans Hughes (whose son gave up the Solicitor General-ship after only a year, so his father could become Chief Justice) [37] had instant consequences: it meant that whatever statute in the President's program of social and economic revival was under examination would be overturned. In the spring of 1935, when the Depression remained severe, Roberts joined the conservatives to strike down several pieces of important New Deal legislation. And on a day known by historians as Black Monday, the Justices unanimously outlawed a key piece of legislation called the National Industrial Recovery Act. The pattern continued through the next year. Justice Stone wrote, "We finished the Term of Court yesterday, I think in many ways one of the most disastrous in its history." [38]

In retrospect, most scholars agree that the Supreme Court overreached itself to break down the legal foundations of the New Deal. With no other recourse at the time, Roosevelt proposed his audacious Court-packing scheme to remake the courts and overcome this roadblock. If a judge or Justice did not retire or resign within six months after his seventieth birthday, the President proposed to add a new judge to the same bench. He could appoint up to forty-four new lower-court judges. Since there were six Justices near or over seventy, the plan would also give Roosevelt the authority to choose a half-dozen new ones almost immediately and control the High Court.

For half a year, the proposal caused a national furor. The President was accused of perverting the Constitution, showing disrespect for the Judiciary, and pretending that his scheme was prompted by an aging bench of Justices when it was really motivated by their judgments against the New Deal. In Congress, where the President had strong allies, there was also a sustained debate about Roosevelt's plan. When the plan was officially presented to the members in February 1937, Vice-President John Nance Garner held his nose and pointed thumbs down. [39]

The next month, Owen Roberts settled the question. Perhaps

responding to the Court-packing threat, he voted for a minimum-wage law that was hard to distinguish from one he had voted against not long before, and swung the Court in favor of the Roosevelt-backed law. The Court never overturned another piece of New Deal business regulation, and the Roosevelt scheme died in Congress. By 1941, Roosevelt had appointed seven Supreme Court Justices to fill vacancies that occurred naturally over time,[40] and any need for his questionable scheme was past.

To prevent a reprise of the crisis and to keep their power in check, judges who were sympathetic to the liberal aims of the New Deal embraced the conservative doctrine of restraint. Because of the eminence of the judges who led this movement, the canons of restraint that they developed came to be associated with objective standards of good lawyering more than with a particular philosophy. The craftsmanship of these judges provided a ready and persuasive answer to the charge made by members of another compelling movement, known as Legal Realism, which developed during the twenties and thirties. The realists contended that court-made law was based only on the personal views of judges and not on any neutral principles of law.

Possibly the most influential contribution to legal scholarship after the critique of realism or the canons of restraint was another attempt to state neutral principles for lawyers and judges. It consisted of a set of teaching materials for law students, and its conclusions were so quickly accepted as common wisdom that lawyers usually fail to credit them at all. Called "The Legal Process: Basic Problems in the Making and Application of Law," the materials were put together by Henry Hart, the onetime assistant to the Solicitor General who is better known for co-authoring the innovative volume on federal courts referred to as Hart and Wechsler, and by a young Harvard Law School colleague of his named Albert Sacks, who later became the law school's dean. They were assembled in the fifties, distributed to students at Harvard and other major law schools in mimeographed form, and never published as a book.[41] Though the 1,417 pages of legal-process materials can't be reduced to a nutshell, and they summarized generally held notions as much as presenting new ideas, they did better than any law-school casebook in telling what it meant to "think like a lawyer." Karl Llewellyn, of the University of Chicago Law School, said the cardinal mistake made by law students was to think that because there is no right answer in the law, every answer is equally correct.[42] Dealing almost exclusively with court decisions interpreting statutes rather than the Constitution, the legal-process materials gave lawyers guidelines for addressing legal problems when the law itself dictated no answers.

Instead of worrying about the outcome of cases, the materials focused heavily on "process"—which institutions in the law are most competent to decide what. Is a controversy about fact or law, and should a jury or a judge resolve it? If a court is faced with a question about the meaning of a statute, should it require evidence of individual legislators' intentions to clear up the ambiguity, or should it look at the purpose of the law and interpret it by making sure the application in the case at hand squares with that general purpose? The materials were criticized for overemphasizing process at the expense of substance, and for ignoring the outcome of cases, on the theory that big corporations and others with money and status are more likely to control the process than the poor and the powerless, and to get what they want. The authors were chastised for operating on unreal assumptions—for instance, that laws passed by legislatures reflect a consensus from which a common purpose can be gleaned, instead of compromises between antagonistic groups that defy neat understanding by a judge.

Yet, like the writings of Frankfurter and the other respected promoters of judicial restraint, the legal-process materials came to stand for the essence of good lawyering. They called for a mixture of close analysis and common sense, and favored careful argument, attention to facts and to precedent, and written documentation. They put a premium on step-by-step decisions and intellectual honesty—on gradualism, continuity, and measured change in the law. These are the qualities singled out by lawyers when they describe the virtues of the SG's office. In the paradoxical ways of the law, they make far more persuasive the government's occasional calls for novel legal doctrine to accommodate sweeping social change.

When Rex Lee was Solicitor General, he used the word "restraint" in two senses.[43] On the one hand, like supporters of judi-

cial restraint who hailed from previous generations, he believed
that the philosophy of a limited role for the courts was best fulfilled
by observing the canons that had been constructed. He concurred
with the understanding of separation of powers expressed by William French Smith, but he thought the philosophy only took on
life through conservative legal practices. On the other hand, he
admired the careful and intelligent craftsmanship of the lawyers in
the SG's office, and recognized how much they relied on restraint
in their lawyering before the Supreme Court. He believed in the
principles that they followed. The government should only raise
issues that are ready for decision by the Court. If it appears as a
friend of the Court, it should not raise issues that no party to the
suit has brought up. If it discovers a precedent cutting against the
argument it is making to the Justices, the government has a duty
to let the Court know about the case. The "restraint traditionally
exercised by Solicitors General" had a measurable value, Lee
judged, because "the single most important factor contributing to
the success of a President's litigating objectives is the preservation
of the Solicitor General's unique standing with the Supreme
Court." [44] As he told the Los Angeles *Times,* "the positions taken
by the Solicitor General for years have carried special weight with
the Supreme Court because they are regarded as representing not
merely the political views of the Administration but the broad
interests of the nation. One of the most important jobs I have is
protecting the tradition of John W. Davis, Robert H. Jackson,
Charles Fahy, and Thurgood Marshall." [45]

The idea of judicial restraint embraced by the Reagan Administration was notably different from the traditional view
adopted by Lee and others. It was distilled by Judge Richard
Posner, of the U.S. Court of Appeals for the Seventh Circuit in
Chicago. "I believe judicial restraint refers to a policy of reducing
the power of the federal courts vis-à-vis the other branches of
government," he stated in 1985 at a symposium on the courts
sponsored by a conservative organization called the Manhattan
Institute for Policy Research. "It is not a policy of standing by
whatever has been done. If it is that, it would constitute an irresist-
ible engine of judicial activism." [46] By Posner's logic, if believers
in the new substantive version of restraint applied the old-style
standards, they would end up extending decisions of the "activ-

ist"—that is, liberal—judges they opposed. To undo the damage of these judges, Reagan's judicial appointees had to be unrestrained in the traditional sense and his lawyers had to urge unrestrained positions. Posner distinguished between his philosophy of judicial restraint and the techniques of judging that should be used to enact it; he argued that judges had to abandon restraint in the latter to put the former into practice. Frankfurter and others had warned that judges should be reluctant to expand their power. Posner urged that judges dramatically cut it back. In place of restraint, he counseled what might be called "judicial retrenchment," and, along with other Reagan judicial appointees like Robert Bork and Antonin Scalia, he acted on that philosophy.

In a 1985 book called *The Federal Courts,* Posner recognized an astonishing implication of his theory. He volunteered that his definition would make it "restrained" to overturn one of the most important precedents in American law. In Marbury v. Madison, Chief Justice Marshall affirmed the power of the Supreme Court to hold acts of Congress unconstitutional. He set forth a rationale for an essential aspect of judicial review. "A decision overruling Marbury v. Madison would be pretty wild stuff," Posner wrote, "but it would be self-restrained in my terminology because it would reduce the power of the federal courts vis-à-vis the other organs of government." [47] Rarely has the term "restraint" been used to signify anything so far from its standard legal meaning.

As one step in his first-rank training (Yale College, *summa cum laude;* Harvard Law School, where he was president of the *Law Review;* a clerkship for Justice William Brennan), Posner, too, had worked as a young lawyer in the SG's office. [48] He was a favorite of the Reagan Administration years before he provided it with a rationale for its new notion of judicial restraint. The most controversial legal scholar of the late seventies and early eighties, he has done more than anyone to create the movement known as Law and Economics. Building on the work of Robert Bork and others at the University of Chicago, the movement holds that the conservative free-market economics promoted by Adam Smith and current followers of his like Milton Friedman, is the best guide to human behavior under law, and to prescribing what the law should be. Law and Economics is considered by many (overlooking the contribution of "The Legal Process") the most influential legal movement in the past half-century. It directly squares with the Reagan vision of economics. [49]

In over a hundred articles, fourteen textbooks, book reviews, testimony before Congress and federal agencies, speeches, law-school classes at the University of Chicago, where Posner taught, and, eventually, in appellate opinions after President Reagan appointed him to the Court of Appeals in 1981, the prolific Posner has urged to a widening audience that the life of the law is really economics. As George Priest, of the Yale Law School, put it, "Posner achieved for the law Einstein's dream for physics: a unified theory." [50] One of Posner's recommendations, formulated in collaboration with an associate, Elisabeth Landes, was to abolish adoption agencies and legalize the sale of babies to the highest bidder. He argued that the high cost of foster care and the growth of a black market in healthy infants demonstrated both the failure of government regulation and the promise of unfettered exchange. [51]

That particular idea has not been accepted, but Posner's Law and Economics views have helped to change how many lawyers do their work. Instead of concentrating on the reasoning that defines a legal doctrine, many lawyers and legal scholars now analyze a law's purpose and impact in terms of economics. Where almost any law does not follow the logic of economics, they insist it should. The wide popularity of this view has helped ease the impact of the Reagan Administration's approach to the law: it has given new currency to a focus on social results instead of legal reasoning. Posner has a gift for provocation and he once sharpened the edge of his radical ideas by delivering them with a paraphrase of Oliver Wendell Holmes. "I hate 'justice,'" Posner said. "The word is meaningless. If it's used in a judicial opinion, it's used to obscure the grounds. I think we could do without it." [52]

The Administration's notion of judicial restraint has often been presented as a call for results, and not for a shift in legal philosophy. In an interview in the Los Angeles Times in June of 1986, for example, President Reagan seemed to turn the definition of judicial restraint upside down once again, when he explained that "restraint" meant achieving in the courts what Congress had refused to do for the Administration. "Well," said the President, "you have found that Congress has been unwilling to deal with these problems that we brought up." A reporter told the President that one of his senior aides, Patrick Buchanan, had said, "If you got two appointments to the Supreme Court it could make more difference on your social agenda in achieving it than twenty years in Congress." The reporter asked, "Do you agree with that?" The President replied, "Yes."[53] In a speech to the Knights of Columbus not long afterward, he made a similar point. He predicted, "In many areas—abortion, crime, pornography, and others—progress will take place when the federal judiciary is made up of judges who believe in law and order and a strict interpretation of the Constitution."[54]

Ronald Reagan equated support for his social agenda with support for judicial restraint, and so did his advocates. Bruce Fein, the member of the Bob Jones team who often wrote articles and appeared on TV to popularize the Administration's legal views, contended that "judges wedded to the doctrine of judicial restraint" were judges "who reject the idea underlying the Supreme Court's decrees on abortion, school prayer, civil rights and criminal law: that the judicial power of interpretation is not confined to carrying out the intent of our constitutional authors."[55] According to *Benchmark*, a New Right journal, the principle of "restraint" demanded that judges not "impose alien values upon the American people, enlarge the rights of criminals, impede Federalism and the restoration of States' Rights, or further the cause of abortion."[56]

The Fein and *Benchmark* lists strayed from the line laid down by Richard Posner, and they had little to do with the tenets established by Frankfurter, Harlan, and others. They also identified the cases in which Rex Lee encountered what he called "enormous pressure" to forsake his commitment to the canons of restraint and the traditional restrained practices of the SG's office, and to campaign for the Administration's agenda in the Supreme Court.[57] During the first year of the Reagan Administration, Lee sometimes brushed aside initiatives from low- and middle-level political officials at various government agencies who were eager for the SG to append an idea to a government brief, even if it had little bearing on the case at hand. ("Rex rarely entertained these juvenile right-wing fantasies," said one former lawyer in the SG's office.)[58]

When, however, the Administration began to press for legal

changes that would enact the beliefs at the core of the President's social agenda, the story changed dramatically. Contradicting Lee's sense of his responsibilities, Bruce Fein told the *Wall Street Journal* that the SG "shouldn't be abashed about urging the Court to overrule decisions and making speeches criticizing the Court." For the sake of a version of judicial restraint that was unrestrained, Fein urged the SG to proceed aggressively as well. Dismissing the idea of an independent SG, he insisted, "My conception of the office of Solicitor General is that it should be a foremost promoter of the policies of the President before the Court." The *Journal* made clear its understanding that Fein was speaking for the Administration. [59]

Besides recasting the idea of judicial restraint without admitting the liberties they were taking, the President's lawyers based their radical legal strategy on an unsupported premise. Like William French Smith, the lawyers used the President's victory at the polls in 1980 as a mandate for the Reagan social agenda. In fact, as Thomas Ferguson and Joel Rogers pointed out in the *Atlantic Monthly* in 1986, [60] the American public was steadfast in rejecting central parts of the Reagan agenda. Only a third of those who originally voted for the President agreed with his views about abortion, according to a Los Angeles *Times* poll. By 1984, NBC News reported that two-thirds of the voters believed abortion should be legal and that the decision should be "left to the woman and her physician." At the end of the Carter Administration, Louis Harris found, only 45 percent of the public agreed that affirmative-action programs were necessary if women and minorities were to get their share of jobs and higher education and break the historic cycle of discrimination against them. By the second year of the Reagan Administration, the number had jumped to 57 percent, and by 1985, 71 percent. As Ferguson and Rogers reported, "Here, too, the movement of public opinion has been directly opposite to the movement in public policy." The numbers revealed that the campaign to turn the President's agenda into law was fueled not by a wave of American opinion but by the personal beliefs of the President and his followers.

VII

The Shadow
Solicitor

THE PRESSURE ON Rex Lee to promote the Reagan agenda
came mostly from William Bradford Reynolds, Assistant Attorney
General for Civil Rights. At first glance, he seemed an unlikely
antagonist. Reynolds is an ascetic-looking man, with thinning
blond hair, a well-defined forehead, and rimless glasses that frame
his clear gray eyes. A graduate of Yale College and Vanderbilt
School of Law, where he was second in his class and editor-in-
chief of the *Law Review,* he had practiced law with a conventional
Washington firm;[1] though he later downplayed the overture,[2] his
moderate leanings were suggested when he expressed a serious
interest, never realized, in running the Antitrust Division of the
Justice Department during the Carter Administration.[3] Reynolds
had also worked for three and a half years as an assistant to the
Solicitor General under the Nixon Administration. While at the
SG's office, he argued eleven cases before the Supreme Court and
wrote the briefs in forty.[4] He was known as a good soldier.

Reynolds had no special preparation for the post of Assistant
Attorney General for Civil Rights. As the Reagan Administration
began to make its appointments, Reynolds's first job choice was
the post of chief of the Attorney General's Office of Legal Counsel,[5] which had issued the paper about the role of the Solicitor
General. When, however, other candidates for the civil-rights job
proved too controversial,[6] Reynolds was named to the position
because he had good credentials and the unblemished appeal of a
moderate. It was the understanding of lawyers in the Civil Rights
Division that he secured the appointment by promising to lead the
Reagan Administration's attack on school busing and affirmative

action,[7] but his prior record gave no hint of his future zeal as a promoter of the President's agenda.

Soon after the Administration took office, Reynolds made good his pledge about busing.[8] The case involved the schools in Seattle. The city's school board had taken a lead from the Supreme Court in an earlier case, and had voluntarily approved a plan to use mandatory busing as part of a remedy for segregation in the schools. When the voters of Washington passed a referendum to ban busing, the school board challenged the legality of the referendum. Under the Carter Administration, the Justice Department had supported the school board's successful defense of the plan. The Reagan team arrived the year the case rose to the Supreme Court, and Reynolds recommended that the Administration switch sides. Rex Lee concurred. The Justices, however, rebuffed the government's new position and upheld the busing plan.

Reynolds appeared to overlook some basic facts about busing. Like others in the Reagan Administration, he seemed to treat mandatory busing as a social menace that had to be stopped before it touched many more communities. In reality, in the United States at the time half the children went to school by bus, and less than 7 percent were bused as part of a desegregation plan. While busing indirectly helped increase segregation rather than diminish it in cities like Boston where whites fled to the suburbs, more students were bused to segregated schools (public, private, and parochial) than to integrated ones, and most of this busing was done at public expense.[9]

Even in the places where mandatory busing was used to help desegregate schools, the story was different from that told by the Reagan Administration. In a speech in Charlotte, North Carolina, President Reagan declared that the Democrats "favor busing that takes innocent children out of the neighborhood school and makes them pawns in a social experiment that nobody wants. And we've found out that it failed."[10] The President picked the wrong audience for this comment.[11] The schools in the area known as Charlotte-Mecklenburg were the first in the nation to be integrated under a court order for busing. According to the Charlotte *Observer*, the area's "proudest achievement" in the previous twenty years was its "fully integrated school system." An editorial directed at the President said, "It would have been quite appropriate and very much appreciated if you had noted that accomplishment, which any president might hold up as a model to the rest of the country. Instead, you said something quite different, an unwelcome reminder of some ugly emotions and unfounded fears that this community confronted and conquered more than a decade ago." [12]

Not long after the Supreme Court decided the Seattle case, Reynolds went to Capitol Hill to testify on the Administration's civil-rights policies. He was asked by Carl Stern of NBC News whether the White House had applied any pressure on the Justice Department to drop its support of school busing in Seattle. Reynolds said no. [13]

"No pressure from the White House as to the Administration's view?" Stern continued.

"Absolutely none," Reynolds answered.

Stern then showed Reynolds a copy of a memo he had obtained that had gone from Lyn Nofziger, a political aide in the White House, to Reynolds and three others.

"I enclose for your perusal a letter to me of August 4 from Ken Eikenberry, the Attorney General for the State of Washington, and a longtime Reagan worker and supporter," Nofziger had written.

"Not surprisingly, he, like 99.9 percent of the people who have supported Ronald Reagan in the past, is at odds with mandatory school busing—as I think we all are. Surely, if we are going to change the direction of this country, mandatory school busing is a good place to make changes—as I thought we would do because I thought that was what the President wanted.

"I do hope we can give Mr. Eikenberry's problems a careful look."

Stern asked Reynolds about the memo: "You believe it doesn't contain a White House view?"

"It may contain Lyn Nofziger's view. I don't think I read it as a . . ."

"What does it say on the top of this letter?"

"You can read the letter."

"It says 'The White House.' "

The letter confirmed what lawyers at the Justice Department and in the civil-rights community had suspected: in major cases like those on the Reagan agenda, Reynolds formed his legal opinions with the President's political goals in mind. He took his cues from the White House, and was rewarded with its strong support.

One lawyer, who dealt with Reynolds on behalf of the SG's office and who was sympathetic to his aims, observed, "Brad, whom I like and admire in many ways, is also very fearsome because he is so rigid. Once he takes a position, he is a bit of a bully and very hard to deal with. He's incredibly willful. Sometimes he's the most charming, delightful, sophisticated person, and then, when he gets into the mode of someone who's got to have his way, he's impossible. He's totally domineering. The most important thing about Brad Reynolds is not to think of him as political. He isn't even an ideologue, though many people think so. In some ways, he's a seventeenth-century lawyer. He gets ideas into his head that this is the way the law is, and then, by God, it's like that. He thinks of the law as a very formal set of syllogisms." [14]

An early incident at the Civil Rights Division showed that Reynolds's dealings with lawyers who challenged him were sometimes as rigid as his thinking about the law. In July 1981, he received a memo from Robert D'Agostino, one of his aides. It was about a desegregation case in Yonkers, New York. D'Agostino offered a critique of a letter from the Justice Department to the Superintendent of Schools in Yonkers detailing why the department had sued the school system. [15] "Paragraph four," he wrote, "states that blacks were 'improperly classified as emotionally disturbed.' Why improperly? And by what evidence does Justice presume to impose their views on who is or who is not emotionally disturbed (presumably disruptive in the classroom)? Justice's position is that unless equal proportions of blacks and whites are classified as emotionally disturbed, the law violates the civil rights statutes or the Constitution. What hogwash. *Blacks, because of their family, cultural and economic background, are more disruptive in the classroom on the average.* " (Italics added.)

Not long after, over a hundred government civil-rights lawyers—more than half of those working for him—sent Reynolds a petition: "The undersigned Civil Rights Division attorneys wish to express our profound concern with the unsupported assumptions and sweeping generalizations" in the D'Agostino memo. "We believe that those assumptions and generalizations—particularly those regarding the impact of family, cultural and economic background on the behavior of black children—as well as the pejorative use of historically emotional code words such as 'racial mixing' are antithetical to the recent pronouncement of Attorney General Smith that the Justice Department 'will not permit any of our citizens to be stigmatized by government as the result of their race,' and reflect a shocking insensitivity to and lack of understanding of the principles which form the very basis for this Division's existence. As attorneys who share the Attorney General's stated commitment to 'vigorously enforce the Nation's civil rights laws,' we petition the leadership of this Department to repudiate the racially offensive statements" in the memo.[16]

Reynolds called a meeting of the lawyers who had signed the petition. Instead of disavowing or downplaying the words of his aide, however, he angrily scolded those who had circulated the petition and called them "unprofessional"[17] for taking the matter public. Minor as it may seem, this clash between Reynolds and the career attorneys in the Civil Rights Division over the D'Agostino memo was a forewarning of the Assistant Attorney General's frequent and explosive disputes with the office of the Solicitor General. The fights that Reynolds picked with the SG's office about the Administration's filings in the Supreme Court unleashed considerably more of his fury because so much was at stake.[18]

Reynolds exercised his will in a wide range of cases, but those dealing with affirmative action provided model examples.[19]

THE DAY RONALD REAGAN replaced Jimmy Carter as President, the status of blacks and other minorities in America was not instantly transformed. The discriminatory conditions that Carter Administration lawyers for and against affirmative action had agreed were the backdrop for the Bakke case could be found in other cases. Once the overarching challenge of establishing legal equality among people of different races was met during the sixties, every President from Lyndon Johnson through Jimmy Carter recognized that legal equality for people of different races did not assure them equality of opportunity. In executive orders of the President, in statutes passed by Congress, and in decisions of the Supreme Court, each branch of the government reached a conclusion stated by Justice Harry Blackmun in the Bakke case. "In order to get beyond racism, we must first take account of race," the Justice wrote. "There is no other way. And in order to treat some persons equally, we must treat them differently." [20]

In recent years, there has been caustic disagreement among scholars about the meaning of social data on blacks and other minorities. [21] Some believe that the gap between white and black prosperity is closing, and, measured over several generations, it is certainly true. Others see a drop in discrimination by whites against blacks, yet no real progress in closing the prosperity gap, and they worry that many blacks lack the ability to compete with whites. They hold that blacks must escape from dependence on special favors, like public subsidies and affirmative action, and prove their worth in the working world. In either case, disparities exist that lead some people to consider affirmative action necessary.

According to a National Urban League report titled "The State of Black America 1986," as the American economy marched briskly on during the middle years of the Reagan Administration, "black Americans slipped further and further to the rear of the parade." [22] The black unemployment rate held steady at three times the white, the proportion of blacks living in poverty was three times the proportion of whites (and four times for children), and, as the Census Bureau reported, blacks owned on average less than one-tenth the property and material wealth that whites did. The facts that had for a generation buttressed laws in favor of affirmative action were, if anything, more dispiriting in the Reagan Administration, because the country had failed to improve them in any dramatic way. [23]

Reynolds claimed to follow a simple principle: not only should society be color-blind, but the Constitution is color-blind as well, and, with the federal civil-rights laws, it requires "individual equality of opportunity." [24] Where individuals prove they have been victims of discrimination, the wrongs should be righted. The victims should be made whole, one at a time. Whatever the burdens of race handed down to current generations from the past, the Constitution does not allow favoring people of one race over another, even if the purpose is to help them achieve the same opportunities as others in society. To Reynolds, this philosophy represented an alternative to civil-rights "orthodoxy." In the old days, government and other lawyers had sought and courts had permitted what Reynolds called "mandatory busing to achieve racial balance in schools; hiring, promotion, and even layoff quotas to guarantee equal race and sex proportionality in the work place; and manipulation of electoral systems to assure racially proportionate success in elections." Reynolds referred to the goal of this orthodoxy as "equal results," not "equal opportunity," and observed that its supporters believed in treating people as "fungible representatives of some group" instead of "unique individuals." He compared using affirmative action for blacks to treating people suffering from alcoholism with liquor. [25] He described the results of the traditional approach to civil rights as a "racial spoils system." [26]

To make sure his version of affirmative action would be presented, Reynolds often chose to disagree with the Solicitor General about tactics when he had no difference of opinion over the desirable outcome of a case. [27] Reynolds was consulted by the SG just as prior civil-rights chiefs had been by previous Solicitors, but that did not satisfy him. He tried to usurp the role of the SG. In a 1983 case about layoffs from the Boston Fire Department, the question was whether, when layoffs were necessary, the Civil Rights Act of 1964 allowed the department to retain blacks hired in an affirmative-action program and lay off white firemen with seniority. [28] The assistant to the SG who worked on the case was a young former law professor named Carter Phillips, who had once clerked for Chief Justice Warren Burger. "I'm not a flaming liberal" is how Phillips described himself. [29] He agreed with Reynolds that Title VII, the part of the Civil Rights Act at issue, protected the white firemen with seniority. As a sports-minded lawyer in the office remembered, "The only question for the SG to decide, in Rex's words, was, 'Do you go for a touchdown, and make the case for seniority over affirmative action?' Or, 'Is this the case where the government should seek a big victory in cutting back affirmative action, so you go for the Super Bowl?' "[30]

According to Phillips's reading, the legislative history of Title VII indicated that the law permitted no affirmative action when a public agency like the fire department was deciding who should get laid off. Retaining less senior blacks when layoffs were required would amount to applying an illegal quota, because all the firefighters whose jobs were in jeopardy had proved themselves and the fairest basis for distinction among them was seniority. Affirmative action in promotions, on the other hand, was easier to justify as a tool of opportunity, and, in hiring, easier still. Since one section of the statute dealt with layoffs and another with hiring and promotions, it seemed sensible to devote the government's brief to the question about layoffs, which was now before the Court, and leave aside any discussion of affirmative action in hiring, which wasn't. "One of the traditions in the SG's office," said the lawyer familiar with the case, "is that we don't hide the ball. We try to be full and frank in making our arguments, to give the whole picture, and we didn't have room to do that about affirmative action in general."[31]

Reynolds would not accept Phillips's view. He insisted that his own deputy, Charles Cooper, from the Bob Jones team, write an alternative brief.[32] For ten days, Reynolds led a move to transform the SG's brief into a broadside on quotas as a form of affirmative action. When Rex Lee sided with his assistant, Reynolds went over Lee's head to Attorney General William French Smith. (This was a tactic known to lawyers in the Justice Department as "running to the AG," which Reynolds often used and which, to some government lawyers, reflected his disdain for the SG's independence.) As if Phillips's decision not to submit a brief that argued against *all* quotas were a sign of weakness, Reynolds called him "that quota lover!" in a meeting with the Attorney General.[33] Smith told Lee and Reynolds to resolve their differences. At Lee's instruction, Phillips did his best to incorporate the Reynolds point of view in a rewritten brief. Not long afterward, the case became moot when the Massachusetts legislature passed a law reinstating all the firefighters who had been laid off, but the effort to protect the SG's diminished independence still had costs.[34]

The struggle over the Boston affair went unnoticed outside the Justice Department, but a case much like it the next Term drew wide attention. [35] Carl Stotts was a middle-aged black firefighter who had been one of the original dozen blacks hired by the Memphis Fire Department in 1955. Memphis has a population of 650,000 people, about half white and half black. By 1976, the city had hired 1,863 white firefighters and 94 blacks: the ratio was about eighteen to one. Blacks were rarely promoted, and after years of being passed over, Carl Stotts decided to do something about it. He brought a lawsuit in 1977, and he won. The city of Memphis settled out of court. Until the racial makeup of the fire department reflected the balance of whites and blacks in Memphis, the city agreed to a goal of making blacks 50 percent of new firefighters hired, and 20 percent of those promoted.

A second Stotts case was before the Supreme Court in 1984. [36] It arose out of unexpected circumstances. In 1981, a year after the settlement in the first case, cutbacks in the federal budget forced Memphis to lay off firefighters. [37] Twenty-two drivers of firetrucks had to be furloughed; nine of them were black. Seventeen lieutenants had to be demoted; fifteen of them were black. Three captains had to be stripped of their rank; two of them were black. The contract between the city and the firefighters' union ordained that last hired should be first fired. Even though officers had not been promoted solely according to seniority (otherwise more blacks would have been officers), the union insisted that the city protect the "senior" firefighters when it decided whom to lay off. Carl Stotts filed suit and won the early rounds of his second lawsuit against this policy.

Although the Memphis case raised the same issues as the one from Boston, which Rex Lee had steered Carter Phillips to resolve by focusing on the issue of affirmative action in layoffs, Reynolds insisted on reopening the question in the Memphis brief. He tried again to have the SG make a more general case against affirmative action. Reynolds and Phillips ended up in shouting matches along the corridor between the Civil Rights Division and the SG's office. One of the Solicitor's assistants familiar with the case said, "Working on an agenda case, you knew life would be pretty unpleasant." He added, "If Brad had shown the same enthusiasm in defending the civil rights of minorities as he did in attacking them, I would have no problem with him. But even in the instances when he came out on the side of the minority communities, he did it grudgingly, and he was always looking for a way out."[38] The Supreme Court ruled against Stotts on the question of layoffs, but the Justices made no ruling on the original settlement between Memphis and Stotts for hiring and promoting black firefighters, and it remained in effect with the force of law.[39]

In these and other disagreements between Reynolds and the Solicitor General's office, the issues at stake were often the sort of technicalities that cause passionate divisions among lawyers and bafflement for almost everyone else. To civil-rights lawyers, no struggle is more important than convincing a court to use an "effects" standard, as opposed to "intent," when interpreting a law that requires an individual to prove his rights have been violated.[40] It can spell the difference between winning and losing. If the court finds that the law calls for an intent test, it is unusually difficult to prove that a defendant has discriminated, because motives are hard to pin down. In some suits brought by blacks, this is tantamount to proving the charge that a defendant is a racist. To Reynolds, urging an intent test was consistent with his philosophy of equal opportunity: an individual who had been wronged ought to be able to prove his antagonist's intent to discriminate.[41] An effects test would let a class of people recover even if no one had consciously meant to injure them, so it would confer benefits on individuals who could not show they had been personally discriminated against.

Reynolds weighed in heavily on an intent/effects case called Guardians Association v. Civil Service Commission (best known as Guardians), which went to the Supreme Court in 1983.[42] It posed the question whether in the Civil Rights Act of 1964 the ban on discrimination by any institution receiving funds from the government required the plaintiffs to prove the defendants intended to discriminate, or simply to prove the effects of the defendants' actions. The plaintiffs were blacks and Hispanics on the New York City police force who claimed that written exams used to make appointments to the force discriminated against minorities. Applicants were appointed in order of their test results, and the plaintiffs had been hired after whites who scored higher.

Congress had not chosen between the two tests, and had delegated to federal agencies the power to interpret the section of Title VI of the Civil Rights Act, the law at issue. Lawyers in the SG's office wondered how the government could argue that it favored an intent test. [43] The standard was difficult to meet, it violated the law's spirit, and it contradicted hundreds of long-standing rules made by federal agencies, which almost uniformly relied on an effects test. It contradicted the standard designated by many other laws that were modeled on Title VI as well, and it was not practical. Government inspectors could rarely put witnesses under oath to increase the reliability of statements about intent. Even if they could, an inspector who might find evidence of discrimination under the less stringent effects test was likely to doubt whether the evidence met the more demanding test of intent.

Without consulting any of the agencies whose inspection procedures would be implicated—a breach of tradition for the Civil Rights Division—Reynolds pressured the SG to back the intent test. He was vehement, and he transformed the government's choice between favoring the effects test or the intent test into a choice between backing the intent test or filing no brief at all. [44]

"In Guardians," explained a veteran in the SG's office, "Reynolds pressed a line that showed the Administration's lack of commitment to the rule of law. In that case, rules of every federal agency were implicated. Reynolds and other Reagan folks urged a view that would have had a huge impact on all these rules, because they wanted the Court to hold that the law dealt only with intentional discrimination, all else being innocent. Reynolds refused to talk with the affected agencies, and he disregarded the canon saying that an entrenched interpretation of the law by agencies—a long-standing practice—is what federal courts defer to unless they have a very compelling reason not to. In this case, the canon was supported by the fact that Congress had approved the government's understanding of the law through subsequent decisions to fund the fight against discrimination. The Supreme Court rejected the line that Reynolds pushed, but there were four dissenters who went with his view and said the law should be interpreted more narrowly. What was disturbing about the dissent is that the Court never got the impression from the SG's office of how deeply entrenched the broader interpretation of the law really was throughout the government—the five-to-four vote, inviting challenge, might have been six to three, or even seven to two, if the Solicitor General had been allowed to play his usual role and inform the Justices about the workings of the law. Guardians was the only major civil-rights case in the last ten years where the Department of Justice sat out. Guardians was as big a scandal as Bob Jones, and no one outside the government noticed." [45]

In the roster of cases where Reynolds squared off against the SG's office, the fight in 1985 over Vasquez v. Hillery was especially instructive of how Reynolds pursued policy at the cost of lawyerly restraint. [46] On the surface, nothing happened. Inside the government, however, dealings about the case between the SG's office and Reynolds became a stressful trial. [47]

The case arose from the following events. In 1962, a black man, Booker T. Hillery, was indicted for murder by a grand jury in Kings County, California. [48] ("Did I understand you to say that this crime occurred in *1962*?" Chief Justice Warren Burger asked when the case was argued before the Supreme Court in 1985.) [49] Hillery asked the local court to quash his indictment, on grounds that blacks had been systematically excluded from the grand jury. Even though the judge responsible for impaneling the jury, Meredith Wingrove, admitted he had never appointed a black to a grand jury in the six years he had been on the bench, and that, in looking for "the better type of our citizens" for the jury, he had never found a black "that the court feels would make a proper Grand Juror," he also said that he had once tried to find a black for a jury but recalled that the number of blacks in Kings County in 1962 was only around 5 percent of the total population.

After the defendant was convicted and sentenced to death, his case followed many steps. They took sixteen years, which the defendant spent in prison. In May of 1978, after Hillery's appeals in state court ran out, he filed a petition for habeas corpus in federal court. (Habeas corpus is a writ used by prisoners who believe they are illegally confined, and often goes to a federal judge with a claim that the prisoner has been wronged in state court.) Hillery claimed that he had been denied equal protection of the law because blacks had been systematically excluded from the Kings County grand jury. Another five years, and the court granted Hillery's petition, overturning his twenty-one-year-old conviction for murder.

"For over 100 years," the district court observed, "it has been held that a criminal conviction cannot stand if it is based on an indictment returned by a grand jury from which members of an identifiable group to which [the defendant] belongs have been excluded because of their race."[50]

Among evidence heard by the judge, an expert on statistics testified that if the grand juries empaneled in Kings County between 1900 and 1962 had been picked by chance, the probability that no black would have been included was fifty-seven in a hundred billion. The judge thought this analysis might be too sweeping, so he narrowed his sights to the by now seven-year period when Judge Wingrove, the only superior court judge in the county, selected juries. The chance that no black would ever be selected was two in a thousand.[51] The Court of Appeals upheld the ruling.

In the Civil Rights Division at the Justice Department, Walter Barnett, a career attorney then in charge of the appellate section, recommended to Reynolds that the government stay out of the case in the Supreme Court. The main question for the Justices, he wrote, was "whether racial discrimination in state grand jury selection can be challenged on federal habeas corpus where there were no infirmities, in jury selection or otherwise, at the trial."[52] Since the Court had considered the same question in 1979, not many years before, and five current Justices, or a majority of the Court, had accepted the position that the government urged as a friend of the Court in that case, Barnett argued that the "repetition of our previous argument would be superfluous." The Criminal Division of the Justice Department, with the main responsibility for the new case, agreed, because a recent statute called the Jury Selection and Service Act had virtually eliminated the central issue in the Hillery case by outlawing the sort of discrimination under review by the Supreme Court.[53] Even if the constitutional basis for the Hillery decision was reversed, the statute left ample grounds for similar lawsuits. As a prosecutor, the United States had nothing to gain by taking part in the case.

Reynolds disagreed, and presented the Hillery case as a paradigm of the kind the Reagan Administration should pursue, to cut back on the use of the "dramatically and unduly expanded"[54] doctrine of habeas corpus, preserve the "finality" of state criminal judgments, and limit access to the federal courts. He wrote, "Even if we would otherwise be inclined to stay out of this case, I believe we have a special responsibility to the Court to participate." The brief filed by the government in the previous case "contained the same fundamental analytical flaws as the decision ultimately rendered" and the government was "obliged to correct this mistake by now urging the Court to adopt a rational approach to the problem of grand jury discrimination." He went on, "I do not believe that we properly carry out our responsibilities to either the judicial or executive branch of government by automatically giving preclusive effect to the analysis contained in our earlier filings. *This is particularly true in the civil rights context where, to say the least, we have not slavishly adhered to the constitutional reasoning advanced by prior Administrations.*" (Italics added.)

"This is the way this guy thinks with mirrors," said a lawyer in the SG's office who was familiar with the case. "He takes the standard logic of government lawyers before the Supreme Court and reverses it."[55]

Joshua Schwartz was the assistant to the SG on the case. "While it is undoubtedly necessary and proper for the government to alter its position on important issues of law from time to time in a democratic nation," Schwartz conceded in a memo to the SG, "the Supreme Court's willingness to allow us to do this freely is intimately related to its conviction that we exercise a very high level of self-restraint in our dealings with the Court." He cited a Supreme Court opinion praising this trait of the Solicitor General's, and continued, "The government as a whole accordingly has a vital interest in reserving the kind of change of position that would be involved here for cases in which there are compelling federal governmental interests that must be served and where no other party can be counted upon to make the arguments that we could make. This is not such a case." With drama and a touch of deadpan, he closed, "I think it important to note that the argument on the merits simply isn't as open and shut as the memos from OLP"—a division of the Justice Department called the Office of Legal Policy, which was known for its New Right political cast and had concurred with Reynolds—"and Civil Rights suggest. To file a brief supporting the state would be to ask the Court to discard 100 years of precedent regarding practices that have been thought by Justices adhering to a wide variety of viewpoints to impair the integrity of the judicial process. I do not see a sufficient justification for the United States to file such a brief."[56]

The precedent Schwartz had in mind was an 1880 case in which the Supreme Court said that deliberate exclusion of blacks from a grand jury "is practically a brand upon them, affixed by the law, an assertion of their inferiority, and a stimulant to that race prejudice which is an impediment to securing to individuals of the race that equal justice which the law aims to secure to all others."[57] In more than a dozen cases since then, the Justices had rejected the Reynolds notion that a conviction should stand despite racial discrimination in the selection of a grand jury, and Rex Lee agreed with his assistant that the government should not challenge this line of precedent. Lee couched his judgment in terms that radiated sympathy to the President's agenda. "The most significant issues the Court will consider next term involve some aspect of racial discrimination," he wrote, "and all of these cases are central to the Administration's objectives. The Court is likely to be closely divided on all these issues. In the interest of success in these cases we must not do anything to imply that we are opposed to elimination of racial discrimination in jury selection or broader contexts."[58] Reynolds asked the Attorney General to overrule Lee, but the recently sworn-in Edwin Meese did not. In January of 1986, for a majority of the Supreme Court, Justice Thurgood Marshall wrote an opinion supporting the SG's judgment. About the view urged by Reynolds and argued in the Court by lawyers for the warden of a prison in California, Marshall echoed the lower-court judge and sounded the theme struck by Joshua Schwartz. "Our acceptance of this theory would require abandonment of more than a century of consistent precedent," Marshall wrote, and he concluded, "the need for such a rule is as compelling today as it was at its inception."[59]

THE FIGHT OVER Vasquez v. Hillery was one of the many disputes between Reynolds and the SG's office that stayed private during Rex Lee's tenure, and spared Reynolds the burden of public scrutiny. Though Reynolds regularly brought pressure to bear on Lee and the SG's office, the only dispute between Reynolds and Lee that went public was about one of a series of appeals known as the religion cases. It was this dispute that led ultimately to Lee's resignation as SG. [60]

The religion cases took on the urgency of the President's agenda when one (Lynch v. Donnelly) raised the question whether the city of Pawtucket, Rhode Island, had violated the Establishment Clause of the First Amendment by sponsoring a nativity scene as part of its annual Christmas display. [61] At Lee's request, Paul Bator took charge of the case. Bator's junior partner was Michael McConnell, a young lawyer in the SG's office who now teaches at the University of Chicago Law School. [62] Bator and McConnell saw it as an opportunity to challenge the wisdom of the Supreme Court's three-part test for determining whether government involvement with religion was constitutional. According to Lemon v. Kurtzman, decided in 1971, government involvement with religion is permissible only if it has: a secular purpose; a primary effect that neither enhances nor inhibits religion; and no entanglement between the institutions of government and religion. [63] To the lower courts, sponsoring a crèche as part of Pawtucket's Christmas celebration enhanced religion by giving it the city's seal of approval, so it was unconstitutional. [64] To Bator, this was a wooden reading of the First Amendment.

The core of the government's brief was a recommendation that the Supreme Court reconsider the Lemon test. "We suggest," it said, "that the three-part test . . . results in analytic overkill when applied to the type of government action under consideration here." Applying it to the annual sponsorship of a crèche by a city "tempts courts to engage in hypocrisy." "It should not be necessary," the brief observed, "for a court to assert that the traditional religious references that fill American official life have lost all religious significance in order to uphold them. This Court's sessions are opened by the traditional cry, 'God save the United States and this honorable Court.' Are we to say that the constitutional *validity* of this plea *depends* on it being wholly perfunctory, a piece of meaningless boilerplate?" The crux of the Bator-

McConnell idea was accommodation of religion—and accommodation between the conflicting injunctions of the First Amendment's Establishment Clause ("Congress shall make no law respecting an establishment of religion") and its Free Exercise Clause ("or prohibiting the free exercise thereof"). They urged that Pawtucket be allowed to include "a small nativity scene as part of an elaborate annual display connected with the celebration of Christmas." [65] To the consternation of old-line civil libertarians and the satisfaction of the Reagan Administration, the Supreme Court agreed. [66]

Some lawyers in the Justice Department considered the "accommodation" theory quite radical, [67] since it rejected the ideal of a separation between church and state celebrated by decades of active Supreme Court precedents. [68] These lawyers considered the theory more useful as a symbol of the Reagan Administration's commitment to promoting religion in American life than as a tool of law, because it appeared to justify almost any government support of religion that stopped short of outright endorsement of a specific sect. The Supreme Court had not in fact endorsed the concept. To reach the result favored by the government, it applied the Lemon test.

But the "accommodation" theory did not represent the most extreme point of view in the debate on this issue. A New Right organization called the Center for Judicial Studies gathered some of the more vociferous extremists and published their views in *Benchmark*, a bimonthly journal.

The masthead of *Benchmark* provided a key for understanding its influence during the Reagan Administration. [69] In 1984, the journal's book-review editor was Gary McDowell, who then took a leave of absence to join the Justice Department and run the staff that drafted the Attorney General's speeches. In 1985, the journal's Supreme Court editor was Bruce Fein, the former Associate Deputy Attorney General and member of the Bob Jones team. A dozen other editors and contributors either worked for the Reagan Justice Department or, when its point of view was considered too far out for a government official to present, carried its message to the public as friends of the Administration. [70]

The journal and the center were founded by James McClellan,

a former aide to Senator Jesse Helms, the Republican from North Carolina, and a former chief counsel to the Senate Judiciary Committee. McClellan also edited *Benchmark*. According to him, the purpose of the center and the journal was to counter the "liberal" views that prevailed in the American Bar Association and American law schools, and to rein in the "liberal" and "activist" judges who dominated the federal bench.[71] His own writing about the crèche case showed how he planned to do it.[72]

In the Pawtucket brief, McClellan found a weak rehearsal of the "confused and inconsistent" ideas of the Justices. He wrote, "Because the Solicitor General's brief did not question any of the Court's prior interpretations of the Establishment Clause, which emerged unscathed to haunt future generations, the Justices were not compelled to reexamine their holdings or defend their position."[73] That McClellan's comments could not be written off as crank became clear when another religion case came along, this time dealing with a prime item on the President's agenda.

As McClellan told the story of Wallace v. Jaffree, which addressed the constitutionality of an Alabama law permitting silent prayer in public schools and raised the question of spoken prayer, "Federal District Judge Brevard Hand, after meticulously examining the historical record, including countless new documents never before mentioned in any Supreme Court opinion, lifted his own earlier injunction against Alabama authorities and came to the startling yet compelling conclusion that the Supreme Court had been misinterpreting the Establishment Clause since 1947. Exposing in stark relief the constitutional flaws of the Supreme Court's wall of separation doctrine"—the doctrine about separation between church and state—"Hand also argued convincingly that the Federal courts do not even have jurisdiction over cases involving prayer in the public schools. Going one step further, Hand even challenged the Supreme Court's doctrine of incorporation, relying again on original sources to demonstrate the unassailable fact that the Framers and backers of the Fourteenth Amendment never intended to apply the Bill of Rights to the States or give Federal courts jurisdiction over disputes between States and their citizens where freedoms in the Bill of Rights were at issue."[74]

Approving Judge Hand's opinion, McClellan treated Hand's

series of "startling" conclusions as belated advances in legal reasoning rather than as judgments flying brazenly in the face of
thirty-five years of constitutional law. In his rendition, McClellan
failed to mention that it was his own research and thinking on
which Judge Hand had relied as authority for his assault on Supreme Court doctrine. (A footnote in the judge's opinion expressed "indebtedness" for McClellan's "vision"; and, according
to Forrest McDonald, a University of Alabama historian who
followed the case, McClellan also drafted Hand's opinion.) [75]
McClellan did comment about the background of one of the basic
ideas attacked by Hand.

In *A Lawyer Looks at the Constitution,* Rex Lee called the First
and the Fourteenth Amendments the two constitutional amendments most important to the country's fundamental law. [76] Many
hold this view. The latter was adopted in the aftermath of the Civil
War, and since 1925 the Supreme Court has understood it to mean
that a phrase called the Due Process Clause ("nor shall any State
deprive any person of life, liberty, or property, without due process of law") incorporates most of the guarantees of the Bill of
Rights and applies them to the states. To many historians, this step
of incorporation assured that all citizens would benefit from basic
protections: against unreasonable searches and seizures by police,
against government encroachments on private religious worship,
and the like. To McClellan, however, the Court had used the
doctrine "to acquire jurisdiction over civil rights disputes that
were originally intended to remain under the exclusive control of
the States." Giving his radical idea some mainstream polish by
tying it to an insistent theme of legal conservatives, McClellan
announced that incorporation was "the great seedbed of judicial
power in the modern Court." [77]

McClellan's ideas became more fashionable than Judge Hand
had made them when Bradford Reynolds decided to sponsor them
as well. Paul Bator recalled, [78] "The prayer story is the most con-
tinuous single story involving the tension between the legal and
the political, and the complexity that arises from the fact that the
SG's office has a relationship with both the Administration and the
Court. The first time I heard about the Alabama school-prayer case
was when memos started floating around as the case was going

from the district court to the Court of Appeals. Brevard Hand had issued an extraordinary opinion, saying that the Fourteenth Amendment didn't incorporate the First and therefore that the First Amendment does not prohibit a state from establishing a religion and therefore that Alabama is free to allow prayer in schools. A district judge was repudiating Supreme Court precedent! Brad Reynolds and other people in the Administration pressed us to file an amicus brief in the Court of Appeals arguing that Judge Hand had gotten the thing right. We were being urged to do this because the President had said the same in speeches and otherwise that it was his policy to restore prayer in the public schools. This came into the office very shortly after we had decided to go into the Pawtucket crèche case with my enthusiastic support. I was of the view that our office could be helpful and influential in that case. But when I heard about the prayer case, it made me very nervous. We couldn't do anything but insist on a reversal of Judge Hand. As a lower-court judge, he was bound by Supreme Court precedent. If not, what is the rule of law? The Justice Department cannot encourage lawlessness on the part of lower-court judges, and that's what we were being told to do. The question was a major one during the fifties, when desegregation cases came up and some federal judges refused to enforce the Justices' holding in Brown v. Board of Education. The principle that district-court judges must obey the Supreme Court is one that every lawyer ought to be clear on. In the Justice Department, the issue was up for grabs in the Jaffree case, but there was no doubt what the correct opinion should be."

Bator and Rex Lee agreed that the Solicitor General should not file an amicus brief supporting Judge Hand's opinion in the Court of Appeals,[79] and they persuaded Reynolds to back off. When the court overturned Hand, Reynolds again took up the fight. According to the *Wall Street Journal*, Reynolds had the support of the White House.[80] "As you know," he wrote to the Solicitor General, "at the time we discussed our participation in this case in the Court of Appeals, there was general discomfort with the Government filing a brief that would effectively ask the Eleventh Circuit to overrule" major precedents.[81] "The consensus was, as argued by both you and Paul, that such a position should be advanced only in the Supreme Court, and that the government would be acting irresponsibly were it to urge a lower federal court to disregard Supreme Court rulings. There was the added concern that the district court's rejection of the 'incorporation doctrine' opened a Pandora's box with which we were not prepared to deal. We are now in the Supreme Court," he pointed out, and he contended that the government should urge the Justices to overturn the precedents forbidding school prayer.

The primary issue of dispute between Reynolds and the Solicitor General was the appropriate extent of the government's call for reversal of the Court of Appeals. As Reynolds put it, referring to the Supreme Court's major precedents in this area of law, which prohibited spoken prayer in public schools, "It would be counterproductive for the Government to argue strenuously for a narrow exception to the Schempp and Engel doctrine . . . if, in so doing, we effectively endorsed the existing school prayer precedents." He wrote, "Our position in the Supreme Court must be crafted in such a way as to make abundantly clear that we view Schempp and Engel as wrong and unworthy of respect." [82]

When Rex Lee opposed the Reynolds line, Attorney General William French Smith asked, "What am I going to tell the White House?" [83] Paul Bator again took charge of the government's brief and provided the Attorney General with an acceptable explanation to give to the President's aides. He framed the choice differently than Reynolds. "The important question," Bator said, [84] "was whether we should ask the Court to uphold the part of the Alabama statute that would allow a teacher to recite a verbal prayer, which would have required the Solicitor General to tell the Court that Schempp and Engel were based on an erroneous principle. There's nothing wrong with the government doing that. The 'independent' judgment of the SG at this juncture—that is, our professional judgment—was that going to the Supreme Court on the spoken-prayer issue was a kamikaze mission, that we would not get a single vote on it, that we would receive a stinging rebuff, that it would be unprofessional in a more subtle sense. It would put to the Court an issue for which the intellectual preparation had not been done. You go to the Court when there are lower-court decisions and law-review articles and other expressions in the legal culture showing serious and thoughtful controversy about a matter. In the case of the prayer decisions, the intellectual preparation had not been done, and more work was still required to make that a question worth bringing to the Court. I had a strong feeling that we would jeopardize our other religion cases if we just said to the Court, 'Throw out your jurisprudence about the wall of separation between church and state.' We would have lost nine to zip. Instead, I believed the SG should go in on the silent-prayer issue, and everyone finally agreed. Our view was that it was perfectly legitimate for the government to say that the major precedents did not bar a moment of silent prayer. The theme I wanted to stress was that of tolerance, including tolerance for those who are under a claim of conscience to make religious observance a part of daily life. My thought was that intolerant secularism is as out of harmony with the religion clauses of the Constitution as an official religion would be."

A majority of the Supreme Court treated Bator's thought that a moment of silent prayer could be "an instrument of toleration and pluralism, not of coercion or indoctrination" as a generalization that didn't apply to the case. The state senator who sponsored the law permitting a moment of silence in Alabama had stated that he intended to give children the chance to share in the spiritual heritage of their state and country. His purpose was obviously religious, not secular. It was "to return voluntary prayer to our public schools," he said. The law was "a beginning and a step in the right direction." Writing for a majority of the Justices, John Paul Stevens reminded that this purpose conflicted with the "freedom of conscience protected by the First Amendment"—what he called "the right to select any religious faith or none at all." [85] Religious beliefs "worthy of respect," he pointed out, are "the product of free and voluntary choice by the faithful," and "the political interest in forestalling intolerance extends beyond intolerance among Christian sects—or even intolerance among 'religions'—to encompass intolerance of the disbeliever and the uncertain." There was no more poignant expression of intolerance than the ostracism by other students of a couple of second-graders and of a single child in kindergarten—in this case, the Jaffree children, whose father brought the lawsuit—when they refused to take part in various acts of religious worship led every day by their teachers.

Answering the argument favored by Reynolds, Justice Stevens also referred to Judge Hand's "remarkable conclusion that the Federal Constitution imposes no obstacle to Alabama's establishment of a state religion." [86] The Justice went on, "Until the Fourteenth Amendment was added to the Constitution, the First Amendment's restraints on the exercise of federal power simply did not apply to the States. But when the Constitution was amended to prohibit any State from depriving any person of liberty without due process of law, that Amendment imposed the same substantive limitations on the States' power to legislate that the First Amendment had always imposed on the Congress's power." The Justice declared, "This Court has confirmed and endorsed this elementary proposition of law time and time again."

The government's brief drew a compliment from a concurring opinion by Justice Sandra Day O'Connor, who agreed that "moment of silence laws in many States should pass Establishment Clause scrutiny because they do not favor the child who chooses to pray during a moment of silence over the child who chooses to meditate or reflect." [87] But this endorsement did not quiet the noise from the right. In *Benchmark*, James McClellan complained about the school-prayer case, "Here was an historic occasion for the Solicitor General to lay the foundation for a conservative constitutional revolution." [88] Instead, the SG filed a brief about a moment of silence—"a secondary issue of the case"—and bowed to precedent.

McClellan's writing appeared under the title "A Lawyer Looks at Rex Lee," a takeoff on the titles of Lee's books. It singled out the SG as he had never been before, but Lee did not benefit from this attention. The piece called for Rex Lee's "prompt removal" as Solicitor General, and it was a cutting and inaccurate polemic. McClellan twisted Lee's personal history to improve the sound of the case against him. Soon after Lee's Supreme Court clerkship in the early sixties, for example, he had been asked for legal advice by the American Civil Liberties Union. McClellan turned this into an insinuating pejorative, calling it Lee's "ACLU Connection." He criticized Lee for failing to follow what McClellan said was the tradition of Robert Jackson, SG from 1938 to 1940, claiming that Jackson had been blunt about pointing out the errors of the Supreme Court's ways during the Roosevelt era and that in one year he had been willing to lose two-thirds of his cases rather than follow mistaken doctrine.[89]

On both points, McClellan was telling half-truths. In political speeches outside the Court before and during his tenure as SG, Jackson did criticize some Court decisions; and in the 1935 Term, under Jackson's predecessor, Stanley Reed, the government did lose the lion's share of its cases. But by the time Jackson assumed the office, in March 1938, the Court had already swung in favor of the New Deal. In his own appearances before the Court, he proved to be both a respectful and a successful advocate. As annual reports of the Justice Department indicate, under Jackson the government's record in the Court was better than at any time in the previous decade.[90] Far from being at odds with the Court as SG, Jackson maintained cordial relations with most of the Justices and even called on the Chief Justice in his chambers to obtain special dispensation for the scheduling of an argument.[91]

In the categories of abortion, religion, states' rights, labor law, and the interpretation of statutes, McClellan faulted Lee's management of government litigation in the Supreme Court. This judgment rested on a redefinition of the SG's mandate rather than on twisting the facts, though McClellan did both. He complained that Lee had not urged the Court to overrule "a single prior decision," and that the SG had "opposed the idea that his primary responsibility as Solicitor General was to advocate the Administration's policies, insisting instead that he had an independent relationship with the Court based on trust between the Justices and the Solicitor General's office." McClellan accused Lee of "orthodox liberalism," and of "slavish submission" to prior rulings of the Supreme Court: "Lee ha[d] consistently addressed the Court as a dutiful and fawning serf might approach the Czar."[92]

McClellan seemed especially irked by the interview Lee had given to the Los Angeles *Times*. "In that same interview," McClellan went on, "Lee also remarked that such social issues as prayer in the public schools and abortion were 'an albatross around my neck,' and asserted that he would resist the 'enormous pressure' he was under to take stronger positions on those issues. Lee has, in fact, stoutly resisted not only the so-called social or children's issues, but also basic principles of limited constitutional government and many of the policies of the Administration he was appointed to serve. Upon a close examination of actions taken by Lee before the Supreme Court, we find that he has repeatedly taken positions that are directly at odds with the President's program, and has regularly advanced points of law that are calculated to preserve intact existing case law and the doctrines of the Supreme Court." [93]

To any Court-watchers but those on the Solicitor General's right flank, Lee's opposition to the President's program was news. In an unpublished essay called "Another Lawyer Looks at Rex E. Lee: A Reply to James McClellan," Richard Wilkins, who had worked as an assistant to Lee in the SG's office and was now an assistant professor of law at Brigham Young University, wrote that the SG understood "what some of his conservative critics do not; that is, that the law moves in careful modulations rather than great leaps. It has taken a number of years and some patience, but because of Rex Lee's careful persistence and craftsmanlike presentation of the government's position, the Administration's views on a number of important social issues are—for the first time—beginning to bear substantial fruit in the Supreme Court. And when that occurs, Rex Lee is not the only winner. President Reagan wins too." [94]

Lee was caught between the New Right's impatient call for change and his own sense of the limits required by the law's "careful modulations." It was not surprising that his performance drew irreconcilable reviews, as it did in a prominent case about abortion. Instead of being marked by "servile deference to recent judicial precedents," [95] as McClellan contended, Lee's role in 1982 in a pair of abortion cases out of Ohio and Missouri known as the Akron case led some observers to think he'd pushed the bounds of government advocacy farther than any SG before him. Under the heading "No Friend of the Court," *The New York Times* ran a lead editorial about his brief: "The Reagan Justice Department filed a curious document with the Supreme Court last week in connection with pending abortion cases. Though called a brief for the United States as a friend of the court, it is in fact a 20-page lecture. 'The time has come to call a halt,' it says, to the way the Court has been dealing with abortion disputes. The document goes out of its way to disparage the Court's famous 1973 abortion decision, Roe v. Wade. Then it goes on to urge the Court to uphold some of the nation's most restrictive abortion regulations.

"We trust that the Court, which needs no such lecture, will ignore this political tract, for it is of scant help in deciding the complex cases to be heard in the fall term. The brief is better suited to the partisan purposes of an Administration eager to appease its disgruntled right wing." The editorial went on, "With this brief, Solicitor General Rex Lee has vented his deep personal quarrel with most of the Court's abortion decisions while distorting the function of his respected office."[96]

When Lee argued the case before the Supreme Court, Justice Harry Blackmun, who had written the majority opinion nine years before in Roe v. Wade, said he could not understand the government's position. Was the Solicitor General asking the Court to overrule Roe? Distinguishing himself from McClellan, Lee replied, "I am not, Mr. Justice Blackmun."[97] Though the SG viewed the abortion case as one of the few in which he was willing to risk irritating the Court by promoting the President's policy when restraint told him not to ("There is the point of view that the election results give you the four-year right to drive the engine of government," Rex Lee said about the agenda cases, in the Los Angeles *Times*. "There's no sense in leaving the car in the garage."),[98] he stopped short of doing what he considered disrespectful.

Justice Lewis Powell, whose caution and pragmatism made hime the Court's leading promoter of traditional judicial restraint, wrote the opinion about the abortion case, and he suggested that Lee's amicus brief had still gone too far. Powell lectured about the legal doctrine of stare decisis—that is, abiding by precedent. According to the Justice, following a principle laid down in a previous case that is like the new one before the Court "is a doctrine that demands respect in a society governed by the rule of law."[99] Though no precedent is shielded from scrutiny about its continuing vitality in the law, the Justice found "especially compelling reasons for adhering to *stare decisis* in applying the principles of Roe v. Wade." The case had been "considered with special care"—it had been argued and then reargued before the Justices were ready to decide it. After the 1973 ruling, the Court "repeatedly and consistently" had "accepted and applied the basic principle that a woman has a fundamental right to make the highly personal choice whether or not to terminate her pregnancy." For a six-to-three majority, Powell reaffirmed a woman's right to abortion.

In June 1985, Rex Lee resigned after four years as Solicitor General. "My wife and I were shopping," he reported, "and she reached for some English muffins. They were the Thomas's brand, and I said to her, 'We can't afford those.' I don't want to dwell on this, but I can't afford to send three kids to college and support four others on a government salary. That's the immediate reason why I'm leaving." Lee added, "It seems that this is the right time to move on." [100]

Lee also, however, spoke to what most observers of the SG's office believed was the true reason for his departure. It was the constant hounding from the Reagan Right, from critics outside the Administration like James McClellan and from lobbyists inside like Bradford Reynolds, that drove him from the post he considered the best job for a lawyer in America. "Stare decisis is an important part of American law," Lee said. "I know that. Even though I might have some misgivings about certain precedents, where they are well established and it's obvious the Court isn't going to depart from them, it isn't smart to lecture the Justices about where they went wrong. It accomplishes nothing. I have no qualms about taking a position that might not be immediately persuasive, but which might bear fruit down the road. That's not what we're talking about. If I had done what was urged on me in a lot of cases, I would have lost those cases and the Justices wouldn't have taken me seriously in others. There has been this notion that my job is to press the Administration's policies at every turn and announce true conservative principles through the pages of my briefs. It is not. I'm the Solicitor General, not the Pamphleteer General." [101]

BY COINCIDENCE, the same week that Lee resigned the Senate Judiciary Committee opened hearings on the nomination of William Bradford Reynolds to serve as Associate Attorney

General. The hearings revealed much about the nature of the pressure Lee had faced as Solicitor General. The insights had to do with the question of Reynolds's attitude about the law. Events recounted to the senators showed him to be a lawyer whose dedication to the ends of the Reagan agenda made him headstrong and, often, insensitive about his choice of means. The Judiciary Committee documented the performance of a radical conservative whose impatience for results made him deaf to the appeals for craftsmanship made by lawyers in the Civil Rights Division and the SG's office. The senators also heard substantial testimony that went to the issue of character. From a considerable record—the report on the Reynolds hearings filled 1,037 pages—it appeared to some senators that Reynolds pressed to have his way as expeditiously as possible and that at times he overlooked or hid the truth to get it. [102]

A group called the Lawyers' Committee for Civil Rights Under Law submitted to the senators a detailed account of Reynolds's record. [103] The committee was organized in 1963 at the request of President Kennedy, who wanted private attorneys to help in the effort to assure civil rights for all Americans, and it had continued its work with the encouragement of every President until Ronald Reagan. It was composed of liberals and conservatives, and Democrats, independents, and Republicans, and for the first time in the committee's history, they felt compelled to oppose a Presidential nomination. The main author of the committee's report was Thomas Barr, [104] a senior partner in the prestigious New York law firm of Cravath, Swaine & Moore and as weighty a figure as the American legal establishment could offer to criticize Reynolds.

Barr wrote that Reynolds's performance on behalf of the Reagan Administration represented "a sharp break with the past." For twenty-four years, under every head of the Civil Rights Division since it was founded in 1957, the Justice Department had followed a steady, moderate course in enlarging and defending the rights of minorities. Under Reynolds, the Civil Rights Division had abruptly and dramatically "undercut" those rights. "As a result of those policies," Barr stated, "the Lawyers' Committee and lawyers affiliated with it now find themselves in a novel and regrettable position. In increasing numbers of civil rights cases throughout the country, where we represent the interests of minorities and women, we are encountering for the first time the fervent and vigorous opposition of the federal government." [105]

The Lawyers' Committee divided their conclusions into three sections: areas where Reynolds had violated the "obligation faithfully to execute the law," [106] by ignoring or overriding "clear and well-established law"; where he had tried to weaken the law in a way that would "impede the progress of minorities toward equality under law"; and where enforcement of the law had been "lax or virtually non-existent."

Barr summed up: "Our concern over the policies of the Civil Rights Division under Mr. Reynolds runs far deeper than any differences of opinion in a few isolated cases; it runs deeper than any simple dispute over Administration policy. The record of the present Administration in civil rights—Mr. Reynolds's record—reflects an abdication of responsibility for the enforcement of civil rights and, even more disturbing, a disregard for the rule of law as it governs those rights." [107]

To career attorneys at the Civil Rights Division, the report refuted what they called "the big lie." [108] The main form of the "lie" was that the Reagan Administration and especially Bradford Reynolds had vigorously enforced civil-rights laws. The report contradicted this claim. Reynolds's determination to prosecute whites who had violated federal laws that were passed to punish severe abusers of civil rights (for example, some police officers and members of the Ku Klux Klan) made it difficult to write him off as a racist, but, criminal cases aside, the Lawyers' Committee noted that he often advised the United States to support whites contesting blacks.

A second version of the "lie" was that the only major differences between the views of past administrations and the current one came in the areas of school busing and affirmative action, on grounds of policy and not law. Among those convinced this was true was Griffin Bell, the former Attorney General to President Carter. "Mr. William Bradford Reynolds has been under sharp attack recently because of the Department of Justice's policies on quotas and school busing," [109] Bell wrote to the members of the

Judiciary Committee in a letter endorsing Reynolds, as if that were the whole story. As the Lawyers' Committee reviewed the record, it was not.

Reynolds had led the Reagan Administration to make obvious changes in policy as well as law, in the areas of housing, voting rights, the rights of the handicapped, and all other areas for which the Civil Rights Division was responsible. To the Lawyers' Committee, the Reagan Justice Department went beyond reversing the practices of previous administrations. It went beyond favoring whites over minorities whom the civil-rights laws were passed to protect. With Reynolds as the leader of the Civil Rights Division, the department had turned its back on the judgments of Congress and the Supreme Court about the dictates of the law.

Some of the examples considered during the Senate hearings concerned Reynolds's dealings with the Solicitor General's office. After the Supreme Court ruled in favor of the government's position about layoffs in the Stotts case, for example, Reynolds treated the holding as the deep blow to affirmative action in hiring and promotions that he had wanted the Justices to strike. All the Courts of Appeals that interpreted the Court's opinion disagreed, and treated it only as a ruling on the narrow question about layoffs. Reynolds spurned this uniform reading, and sent what became known as "the Stotts letter" to fifty-one state and local governments across the country. Disregarding the government's "legal obligation"[110] to defend lower-court decrees previously worked out by elected officials and judges, and signed by the government, he pressed the local governments to effectively end their affirmative-action programs in hiring.

Arlen Specter, a Republican from Pennsylvania, asked Reynolds about "what appears to be a pattern of elevating your own legal judgments over the judgments of the courts—stated differently, in disregarding the established law."[111] Referring to Reynolds's refusal to read the Stotts decision as the federal courts had done, Specter said, "We are all obliged to follow the law as it is finally interpreted by the courts."

Specter also rebuked Reynolds for misleading him at a hearing in 1982. The topic had been certain election laws in Burke County, Georgia, which the Supreme Court eventually struck down on the grounds that they discriminated against blacks. The Assistant Attorney General had told the senator that he would not challenge the laws because he lacked the resources. A federal statute required the county government to justify the new election laws when challenged, and Reynolds had given Specter the impression he was sympathetic to the suit that had been brought against the laws. But two months earlier, in a memo to the Solicitor General, Reynolds had taken the opposite position. He had argued that if the government entered the case, it should go in against the blacks on the side of the all-white county government. Despite the specifications of the federal statute, Reynolds would have preferred to shift the burden of proof to the people challenging the changes. Specter learned about what he considered Reynolds's dissembling when the Justice Department complied with the Judiciary Committee's request for documents. He was upset by the news.

"Wasn't your response to me deceptive?" Specter asked. Reynolds said, "I apologize to you, Senator, for leaving that impression," and explained that he had not wanted to discuss an internal memo. "Well, Mr. Reynolds," Specter commented, "I find that hard to accept." [112]

Charles Mathias, a Republican from Maryland, also focused on Reynolds's part in a case involving the Solicitor General. Earlier in the hearings, Reynolds had been asked whether there had been any controversial cases where the result pleased civil-rights groups. (The question went "Name me a close call where those folks thought, 'Doggone that Bradford Reynolds, he got it right this time.' ") Reynolds had answered, "Havens Realty," a Supreme Court case where the question was who had the right to sue a landlord for discrimination. In the past, people known as testers had played a part in suits against housing discrimination. When a black was turned down by a person renting a place to live, a white tester with similar credentials would come along to look at the same house. If the white was told he could have it, there was strong proof of discrimination against the black to use in a lawsuit. Blacks sometimes lacked the resources to take on the landlord. Testers representing public-interest groups could sue in their stead and have the same impact. Havens Realty, Reynolds said, where "the Supreme Court accepted our argument is another one that I would say the civil rights groups ought to be extremely happy with." [113]

In fact, while Rex Lee had urged the Justices to uphold the right of testers to bring suits, Reynolds had opposed that position. "My preference is to stay on the sidelines and quietly watch," [114] he wrote Lee in a lengthy memo telling the SG why to leave the case alone. As Mathias put it, ". . . the result was the opposite of the way you started." [115] Although it had not come out at the original hearing, Reynolds took credit for a victory the government had a hand in only after it overruled his objection to entering the case.

Reynolds had begun his tenure as Assistant Attorney General by refusing to enforce laws with which he disagreed, and he had compounded this show of contempt by trying to alter the spirit of the law where the letter did not explicitly prevent him from doing it. When Dennis DeConcini, a Democrat from Arizona and a member of the Judiciary Committee, explained why he had decided to vote against Reynolds, he said that the Assistant Attorney General hadn't "told the truth here." Reynolds had a "tendency to uphold the laws and decisions he like[d] and ignoring or refusing to follow or enforce the ones he [didn't]"; and "he altered the truth to suit his own purposes." [116]

The Senate Judiciary Committee voted ten to eight against Reynolds's confirmation, with Republicans Specter and Mathias joining the unanimous Democratic minority. As of July 1987, Reynolds's was the only nomination for a presidential appointment in the Executive Branch voted down by the committee during the Reagan Administration. [117]

When Rex Lee left the Solicitorship, he suggested that the main difference of opinion between himself and his critics on the right appeared to be about a matter of degree: how hard should a Solicitor press the Administration's policies? [118] In light of the Reynolds hearings, Lee's idea seemed naive. As a result of Reynolds's attitude, which, for want of a better phrase, amounted to disrespect for the law, and his authority within the Reagan Administration, Reynolds had managed to reverse the traditional relationship between the Solicitor General and the other senior political officials in the Justice Department.

"If the independent legal advice of the Solicitor General is to be preserved," the memorandum by the Office of Legal Counsel about the role of the SG had concluded, "it should normally be the Solicitor General who decides when to seek the advice of the Attorney General or the President in a given case." [119]

Rarely, however, had Reynolds waited for Rex Lee to call on him for counsel. As point man for the White House at the Justice Department, Reynolds had pressured the SG's office as hard as he had campaigned for the Reagan agenda in other forums. When it appeared that career civil-rights lawyers, who worked down the hall from the SG's office, were undercutting Reynolds by kibitzing about cases with Rex Lee's aides, Reynolds forbade his staff to talk to the Solicitor General's assistants until they cleared it with the front office in the Civil Rights Division. When assistants to the SG resisted his arguments, he effectively blackballed them from working on civil-rights cases and made sure that only lawyers he considered acceptable were assigned to work on later cases. [120]

It was a steady, driving, effective performance. Dealing with the Reynolds whose radical practices were copiously recorded by the Judiciary Committee, and with other senior Justice Department officials for whom Reynolds established a precedent by lobbying the Solicitor General, [121] Rex Lee was handicapped by the standards of restraint he thought he should maintain. At the end of his tenure, Lee reported that Reynolds had never bested him in an argument about which side the government should take in a Supreme Court case. But Reynolds prevailed in other ways. [122] He kept the SG from entering cases he otherwise would have, he changed the terms on which the SG presented cases, and in general, he played a major part in altering the SG's role. Lee tried to fulfill what he called "my obligations to the Court and to my office," [123] but he was inevitably worn down.

In the spring of 1985, a memo that circulated at the Justice Department explained how the promotion of Reynolds to the third-highest post in the department was intended to have direct consequences for the SG's office. [124] Since the permanent establishment of this post in 1977, the Associate Attorney General had been in charge of either civil or criminal matters in the department. The chain of command had been revised again, so that for the first time since 1870, when the office of the Solicitor General was established, an official besides the Attorney General—in this case, Reynolds—was to be given authority to oversee the SG's business.

The memo confirmed what Reynolds had achieved in his regular sorties against Rex Lee in civil-rights cases and a widening circle of other matters. [125] By 1985, the SG's independence had been officially and markedly cut back. Even without becoming Associate Attorney General, William Bradford Reynolds was already a Shadow Solicitor.

VIII

Meese's Law

DESPITE THE POWER of Bradford Reynolds over the Solicitor General in the Reagan Administration, his influence was only derivative. From the outset, Reynolds's authority stemmed from the Administration's dominant legal figure, Edwin Meese.

Meese first caught Ronald Reagan's attention as a deputy district attorney in California, where, in the sixties, he prosecuted students protesting at Berkeley as part of the free-speech movement.[1] As a prosecutor, Meese showed little interest in balancing the state's desire for public safety with the rights of individuals, and his views squared with Reagan's. He was appointed legal-affairs secretary to Governor Reagan, and later, moving with Reagan to the White House, he became the President's most powerful adviser.[2] Meese repeatedly expressed his legal views in recommendations on public policy. He was instrumental in the Administration's decision to concentrate its law-enforcement efforts on prosecuting criminals rather than vigorously protecting civil rights and liberties. (In a speech to a convention of policemen in California, he called the American Civil Liberties Union "a criminals' lobby.") He persuaded President Reagan to back the Administration's decision favoring tax exemptions for segregated schools in the Bob Jones case, called for abolition of the Legal Services Corporation, and approved lax enforcement of environmental, antitrust, and occupational health and safety laws.[3] When lawyers at the Justice Department said they felt pressure from the White House to take a position in a case, they invariably meant from Meese.[4]

Edwin Meese's attitude about the law was revealed in detail in the report of an independent counsel issued in September 1984 after questions had arisen about Meese's personal business affairs. [5] The report dealt with allegations of wrongdoing that led the Senate to postpone for eleven months a vote on Meese's nomination to serve as Attorney General. President Reagan called the 385-page report a "vindication," Meese said he was "very happy" with it, and his lawyers claimed that the independent counsel exonerated their client when he found "no basis with respect to any of the 11 allegations for the bringing of a prosecution against Mr. Meese for the violation of a federal criminal statute." [6] (In fact, while the independent counsel found no basis for prosecuting Meese on most of the charges that had been leveled, in some instances he did find a basis for prosecution but chose not to bring charges.) [7] Yet among the events that the report chronicled, a handful had the impact of a hard slap.

Meese cashed a check made out to him by the Presidential Transition Trust for his "moving expenses" from California not long before he came East to join the Administration in 1981. [8] He learned from the Justice Department that it was illegal for the trust to pay moving expenses for people taking government jobs, and after he cashed the check for its intended purpose, he had the record changed so that the check would be passed off instead as payment of a "consulting fee." Then he told the Senate Judiciary Committee that he had paid all the expenses when he and his family moved from California to Washington.

Meese sat on the White House Senior Staff Personnel Committee that approved a job as an Assistant Secretary of Commerce for Thomas Barrack, a real-estate developer who had helped Meese sell his house in California. Barrack had used $70,000 of his own money to cover the down payment for a buyer of the house and another $13,000 for general expenses related to the sale. Meese did not tell his colleagues on the committee about this help. [9] He also sat on the committee that approved an appointment to the Postal Board of Governors for John McKean, who loaned Meese $60,000, and did not reveal to the committee that McKean loaned him the money. And Meese approved government jobs for three officers and a director of the Great American First Savings Bank in San Diego, from which he had borrowed $423,000 to buy the house that he eventually sold in California and, later, a house in Virginia.

As chairman of Common Cause, former Solicitor General Archibald Cox wrote what was echoed by dozens of editorial pages across the country: "The Attorney General must symbolize the highest standards of honor, integrity, and freedom from self-interest in the performance of public office."[10] In the dealings chronicled by the report of the independent counsel, Cox concluded, Meese showed himself either contemptuous of these standards or oblivious to them.[11]

A rumor circulated in Washington during the Meese inquiry that his fellow presidential aides, James Baker and Michael Deaver, were tired of his bumbling, disorganization, and rigid ideology, and saw William French Smith's decision to leave the Attorney General's office as a chance to move Meese out of the White House and into the Justice Department.[12] The right-wing press (*Human Events*, the Washington *Times*, and other publications) portrayed Meese as a pillar of principle who was a victim of leaks, slurs, and innuendoes from moderates trying to banish him from the President's inner circle.[13]

In any case, the month after the Senate Judiciary Committee voted against the Reynolds nomination in 1985, and six months after it confirmed Meese as Attorney General, Meese began a series of speeches that confirmed which side he took in the fight between traditionalists at the SG's office and their antagonists, like Bradford Reynolds and James McClellan. Written by *Benchmark* contributors,[14] the Attorney General's first major speeches were delivered in Washington and then in London to the annual convention of the American Bar Association. His subject was the role of judges in the American system of government, and the proper limits on their reading of the Constitution.

Dwelling on certain opinions of the previous Term (like Wallace v. Jaffree, in which the Justices had rejected the Administration's call for change and had relied on a traditional analysis of the First Amendment's religion clauses), the Attorney General accused the Court of overstepping its constitutional bounds. In his words, ". . . far too many of the court's opinions were, on the whole, more policy choices than articulations of constitutional principle." The Justices' "voting blocs, the arguments, all reveal a greater allegiance to what the court thinks constitutes sound public policy than a deference to what the Constitution—its text and intention—may demand."[15]

Meese proposed that courts use what he termed a Jurisprudence of Original Intention. The way to assure that Supreme Court Justices and other federal judges did not jeopardize the separation of powers distinguishing American democracy was to have them "resurrect the original meaning of constitutional provisions and statutes as the only reliable guide for judgment." As he put it, "To make certain the ideal of the rule of law is given practical effect, the law must be fixed and known." By Meese's lights, the widely shared view of the Constitution as a living testament that takes "meaning from the circumstances of each age" was mere "chronological snobbery."[16]

Although these remarks were general enough to be construed in different ways, and they appealed to students of the Constitution who believed that, in the past generation, the Supreme Court has not been sufficiently mindful of the limits on judicial power inherent in that document, what Meese said went far beyond the bounds of mainstream thinking. Over the years, liberal and conservative scholars have agreed that the Framers of the Constitution deliberately chose ambiguous language as a form of compromise on many important questions. "No Constitution is the same on Paper and in Life," wrote Gouverneur Morris, one of the authors of the text, and, along with other Framers, he began to debate its meaning almost as soon as it was adopted.[17] Liberal and conservative Justices alike have declared that the words of the Constitution are capable of well-tempered growth, and that the Supreme Court must continually reinterpret the document, with its ambiguities, compromises, and internal tensions, in the light of new conditions. (In one glaring respect, Justice Thurgood Marshall has pointed out, the imperfections of the Constitution could not be fixed by interpretation. Its sanctioning of slavery had to be expunged, and women's suffrage added, by major amendments before the fundamental American law guaranteed equality to all citizens.) The most honored declaration about the idea of a living charter—John Marshall's warning that "we must never forget that it is *a constitution* we are expounding"—has been taken as given since at least

1819. (The Constitution, Marshall explained, was "intended to endure for ages to come and, consequently, to be adapted to the various *crises* of human affairs.")[18] Meese interpreted Marshall to mean the opposite, and said that kind of thinking "suffers the defect of pouring new meaning into old words, thus creating new powers and new rights totally at odds with the logic of our Constitution and its commitment to the rule of law."[19]

It took awhile for the legal community to recognize the breadth and depth of Meese's attack on conventional notions about constitutional law; but by the late summer of 1985, Meese found himself the center of attention from students of the Constitution. He regularly took advantage of the spotlight to promote his views. Instead of speaking in the measured tones of authority, of a powerful figure who felt accountable for the actions of a government which had held sway for a number of years, Meese addressed his audiences with the vigor of a young Turk challenging the old order.

"The past several decades of American life have been influenced by an aggressively secular liberalism often driven by an expansive egalitarian impulse," he told a gathering at the American Enterprise Institute. "The result has been nothing less than an abandonment of many of the traditional political and social values the great majority of Americans embrace." Meese's anchor against this drift was the "restoration of fundamental Constitutional values"[20]—that is, his Jurisprudence of Original Intention.

This included removing from the federal courts jurisdiction over social issues like abortion and school prayer. It meant questioning whether the independent agencies that for years had been operating as a wing of the government, with commissioners appointed by the President and a mandate directly from Congress, were constitutional. It meant giving up the form of affirmative action used by every Administration since Lyndon Johnson's in the nineteen-sixties. "A new version of the Separate but Equal doctrine,"[21] Meese labeled affirmative action.

Finally, Meese redoubled his effort to cut back on the protections afforded by the Supreme Court to individuals suspected of crimes. "Miranda only helps guilty defendants,"[22] he said about Miranda v. Arizona, the Supreme Court's landmark decision requiring the police to advise suspects of their rights to remain silent, to know that anything they say can be used against them, and to request the presence of an attorney for whom the state will pay if the suspects could not afford one, before they are interrogated. He finished, "Most innocent people are glad to talk to the police." (After the Attorney General's comment drew criticism, he said he had made "a poor choice of words,"[23] but stood by the substance of his remarks.)

The attack on Miranda was particularly odd because it was aimed at a target whose allegedly pernicious effect had already been greatly reduced since it was created by the 1966 ruling.[24] The purpose of the holding was to protect suspects' rights against self-incrimination under the Fifth Amendment and to guarantee them their right to counsel under the Sixth. Until Miranda, as long as a defendant's statement to the police was "voluntary," it could be admitted into evidence in court. By then, however, a double standard about criminal rights (one in the privacy of a police station, where a confession may have been coerced; the other in the public forum of a court, where due process usually prevailed) meant that a statement may have been voluntary only in the sense that a defendant had offered it to protect himself from a beating. The police often acted as if they had a right to hear a confession, regardless of how they obtained it, and Miranda dispelled that misimpression.[25]

A study published by the *Yale Law Journal* in 1967, a year after the Miranda decision, when the police still considered the landmark a rebuke, found that "not much" actually changed because of it. As subsequent rulings made clear, the landmark decision had balanced the interests of the police in convicting criminals and of individuals in maintaining their dignity,[26] and that is how it was applied. While law-enforcement officials had feared that Miranda meant they couldn't ever question a suspect unless they gave him the full warnings, the Justices said that the warnings were only required when the police took someone into custody. The Justices also decided that while the police could not use an illegally ob-tained confession in court, they could do something almost as good: they could use the confession to impeach the testimony of a defendant who contradicted it on the stand.[27] The Miranda decision proved not to hamper the police, and increasingly law enforcement officials came to believe that it actually helped: only a small percentage of convictions had depended on confessions and, despite getting their warnings, the same percentage of suspects confessed after the Miranda decision as before. [28] The warnings also raised the number of valid confessions. They were easy to give, and they helped the police avoid claims by defendants that their constitutional rights had been violated. Many law-enforcement officials decided they were better off with Miranda than without it. [29]

Meese's ideas eventually provoked an extraordinary response. For the first time since the drama caused by Roosevelt's Court-packing scheme in the thirties, when Chief Justice Charles Evans Hughes informed the Senate that the Supreme Court had no need for the six new Justices proposed by the President, members of that bench entered into debate with a senior figure from the Executive Branch. The Attorney General's speeches drew scholarly rebuttals from Justices William Brennan and John Paul Stevens.

Brennan has served since President Eisenhower appointed him in 1956, when he was fifty, and he is the Supreme Court's leading liberal. The Justice spoke a couple of months after the Attorney General, and appeared to respond to him point by point.

At a Georgetown University symposium about interpreting texts as different as the Constitution and the Bible, the Justice opened his remarks with a confession. He said, "The encounter with the Constitutional text has been, in many senses, my life's work." [30] To Brennan, the discussion sparked by Meese was "really a debate about how to read the text, about constraints on what is legitimate interpretation."

"There are those who find legitimacy in fidelity to what they call 'the intentions of the Framers,' " Brennan said. "In its most doctrinaire incarnation, this view demands that Justices discern exactly what the Framers thought about the question under consideration and simply follow that intention in resolving the case before them. It is a view that feigns self-effacing deference to the specific judgments of those who forged our original social compact.

"But in truth," Brennan continued, "it is little more than arrogance cloaked as humility. It is arrogant to pretend that from our vantage we can gauge accurately the intent of the Framers on application of principle to specific, contemporary questions. All too often, sources of potential enlightenment such as records of the ratification debates provide sparse or ambiguous evidence of the original intention."[31]

He went on, "One cannot help but speculate that the chorus of lamentations calling for interpretation faithful to 'original intention'—and proposing nullification of interpretations that fail this quick litmus test—must inevitably come from persons who have no familiarity with the historical record."

Brennan concluded, "We current Justices read the Constitution in the only way that we can: as Twentieth Century Americans. We look to the history of the time of the framing and to the intervening history of interpretation. But the ultimate question must be, what do the words of the text mean in our time."[32]

In remarks to the Federal Bar Association in Chicago, Justice Stevens also responded to the Attorney General's promotion of his Jurisprudence of Original Intention. Stevens was appointed to the bench in 1975 by President Ford, and he is known for either his independence of mind or his quirky, unpredictable opinions, depending on who is commenting. Stevens takes a centrist's approach to the law, and in his speech he criticized Meese for failing to evaluate "subsequent developments in the law as well as the original intent of the Framers"[33] when he offered judgments about the Supreme Court.

While the Justices' words were fresh in the public mind, Meese answered no questions about the responses from the Court to his speeches. He said only that he thought it was "a very good thing"[34] they had joined the debate: the rejoinders from the members of the Court brought Meese's ideas to wide public attention. Even though the "jurisprudence" was eventually dismissed by many in the legal commuity—including Justice Byron White, who has otherwise endorsed some of the Administration's most controversial positions, but who called Meese's notion "simplistic"—the Attorney General and his aides were pleased by the clamor.[35]

A few months later, in the winter of 1986, Meese changed his tactics. In a journal called *Policy Review*, published by a New Right think tank called the Heritage Foundation, Meese replied with an article called "The Battle for the Constitution." "In the main," he wrote, "a jurisprudence that seeks to be faithful to our

Constitution—a jurisprudence of original intention, as I have called it—is not difficult to describe. Where the language of the Constitution is specific, it must be obeyed. Where there is a demonstrable consensus among the Framers and ratifiers as to a principle stated or implied by the Constitution, it should be followed. Where there is ambiguity as to the precise meaning or reach of a constitutional provision, it should be interpreted and applied in a manner so as to at least not contradict the text of the Constitution itself."[36] These guidelines presented a mainstream view of constitutional review, and marked a retreat from some of Meese's earlier comments. Though his new statement addressed none of the hard questions about interpreting constitutional ambiguities, it was uncontroversial.

Now, instead of quarreling with Brennan and company on grounds of theory, Meese attacked their application of the law. If not *ad hominem*, Meese's strikes were unmistakably barbed. "Sadly," Meese continued, "while almost everyone participating in the current constitutional debate would give assent to these propositions, the techniques and conclusions of some of the debaters do violence to them. What is the source of this violence? In large part, I believe that it is the misuse of history stemming from the neglect of the idea of a written constitution." Invoking the spirit rather than the letter of America's basic law, Meese argued in response to Brennan, the Supreme Court had done lasting harm to the nation. It "read blacks out of the Constitution" in the Dred Scott decision, by holding that slaves were not citizens, and brought on the Civil War.[37] It "contrived a theory" to "support the charade of 'separate but equal' discrimination" in Plessy v. Ferguson.[38]

Making his argument, Meese seemed to misuse history. The Dred Scott case stands mostly for the proposition that racial prejudice runs deep in American experience and that institutions like the Supreme Court, which are capable of great deeds, can also inflict grievous wounds on themselves and the country. As to Plessy, according to Alexander Bickel, the idea of "separate but equal" flourished when the Civil War amendments, including the Fourteenth Amendment, were adopted as part of the Constitution—it was Brown v. Board of Education that, to use Meese's word, "contrived" a theory of equal opportunity to overturn

Plessy and call for desegregation of public schools, in a unanimous opinion widely cited as the worthiest precedent for judicial activism. [39]

Meese went a calculated step further. Without an acknowledgment that he was yoking one of the Court's champions of equality to its most notorious decisions endorsing racism, he suggested that those cases fairly represented the contribution of Brennan-type judges. "It is amazing how so much of what passes for social and political justice is really the undoing of old judicial mistakes," [40] he observed—and warned that the only way to protect the law from future Dred Scotts and Plessys was to apply it as Meese did, and not Brennan.

DURING THE WEEK that the Attorney General began riding circuit to air his views in the summer of 1985, the government filed a Supreme Court brief marking the official start of the Meese era for the office of the Solicitor General. [41] The subject was a pair of cases from Illinois and Pennsylvania dealing with the constitutionality of state laws regulating abortion. "In America," Meese told his London audience, "we face the difficult question of abortion. It is a question made more difficult by the entry of the federal judiciary into an area once clearly reserved, under our Constitution, for the states themselves to decide. We know there are fervently held opposing views about abortion. It is our responsibility and practical task to dedicate ourselves to the principles and purposes of our Constitution, particularly in areas of great controversy. This week the United States filed as amicus in the Supreme Court a brief arguing that the Court should return the law to the condition in which it was before the 1973 case, Roe v. Wade, was decided." The Attorney General declared, "The responsibility of the Justice Department to urge that constitutionally-wrong decisions be overruled is no less strong today in this case than it was in 1954 in Brown v. Board of Education." [42]

For the dozen years since the Supreme Court had struck down anti-abortion laws in forty-six states and had ruled by a seven-to-two vote that women have a constitutional right to abortion, the decision had troubled even constitutional scholars who agreed with the result. [43] According to John Hart Ely, the former dean of Stanford Law School, who was regularly cited as a legal authority by the Reagan Administration, "Roe v. Wade was the clearest example of noninterpretivist 'reasoning' on the part of the Court in four decades." Interpretivists, Ely wrote, hold that "judges deciding constitutional issues should confine themselves to enforcing norms that are stated or clearly implicit in the written Constitution," while noninterpretivists contend that "courts should go beyond that set of references and enforce norms that cannot be discovered within the four corners of the document." [44]

Writing for the majority in Roe v. Wade, Justice Harry Blackmun grounded the right to abortion in the Due Process Clause of the Fourteenth Amendment and the right to privacy staked out by the Supreme Court in a series of cases beginning in the late nineteenth century, in which the Justices had affirmed the right of individuals to decide whether and when to marry, whether to conceive and bear children, how to raise and educate them, and how much to disclose of their personal lives. Blackmun's critics, interpretivists and noninterpretivists alike, understood the Justice's conclusion, but they did not agree with his legal reasoning. The Constitution didn't "clearly reserve" regulation of abortion to the states, as Edwin Meese claimed, but, as John Hart Ely put it, there was nothing in the Constitution that marked the freedom to have an abortion as a special value. "A neutral and durable principle may be a thing of beauty and a joy forever," Ely wrote. "But if it lacks connection with any value the Constitution marks as special, it is not a constitutional principle and the Court has no business imposing it." [45]

The 1985 abortion case that Meese was describing raised a legal dilemma. Should the Court perpetuate a widely heralded constitutional right whose source was in dispute? Or should it remove from the books a troublesome holding, and wipe the slate clean? To Meese, the proper solution to this problem lay in the dramatic step of simply revoking the constitutional right to abortion. In making his proposal, Meese disregarded the opinion written only two years before, by Justice Lewis Powell, in the Akron decision affirming Roe v. Wade. (Justice Powell had reminded that stare decisis—abiding by precedent—"is a doctrine that demands respect in a society governed by the rule of law.")[46] Meese also seemed to ignore the workings of the law itself. Picking up on a theme of Justice Stevens, John Hart Ely explained what Meese was overlooking when the Attorney General supported the Reagan Administration's call for the Court to reverse its landmark decision about abortion.

"It's been almost a decade and a half since Roe v. Wade was decided,"[47] Ely said in 1986, "and it isn't sitting out there all by itself. The Justices have built a number of decisions on it, and the holding is now part of an elaborate system of legal doctrine. It's part of the law. I haven't changed my mind about the merits of the original judgment, and if the whole subject could come up fresh, I'd still be against the Court ruling as it did. But in this case that's no longer possible. If I were on the Court, I'd feel bound to uphold the decision." (Both Congress and the state legislatures seemed to assent to this development of the law by making no serious move to reverse the abortion ruling with an amendment to the Constitution.) Just as Meese's initial proposal for a Jurisprudence of Original Intention was based on the idea that the meaning of the Constitution was frozen in time, Meese appeared to think that rulings like Roe v. Wade marked legal moments that could be judged right or wrong no matter how far in the future, as if nothing in the interim counted for the law.

The abortion case drew special notice from lawyers because it was the first in which the Solicitor General had asked the Supreme Court to decide that a right the Justices had previously found in the Constitution was no longer there.[48] Important as this was, it paled in significance next to another insight that the case revealed about the Reagan Administration's view of the law. The Attorney General's statement in London about the right to abortion was the first of several in which he indicated the most radical belief that he and other Reagan officials seemed to hold: that their judgments about the law were as authoritative as those of the other two branches of government, if not more so.

Once again, Meese suggested that his idea was grounded in "original intention," but now it was found in the Constitution's provisions about the structure of government. As Meese put it, "Some of the chief problems of government today stem from the fact that how the federal government works in practice doesn't always resemble how it is supposed to work according to the Constitution."[49] But, while the Framers were deeply concerned about the government's structure, they never directly addressed the question of which branch would have ultimate responsibility for interpreting the Constitution, and certainly did not resolve it the way Meese claimed they had. By voting down a proposal for a body called the Council of Revision, which would have given the President a role in judging the constitutionality of federal statutes, the Framers explicitly rejected the very principle that Meese was now proposing centuries later. The Attorney General, however, was not deterred by history. He invented a new axiom of constitutional law: if the Supreme Court handed down decisions with which the Executive Branch disagreed, then officials in that branch of government should treat their own views as authority for the true meaning of the law.

The Attorney General developed his argument with an illustration from Cooper v. Aaron—the only opinion in the history of the Court that was individually signed by all the Justices. The Court's statement of unanimity was prompted by a dramatic series of events: the school board in Little Rock, Arkansas, sought to desegregate the city's public schools in 1957, under a plan approved by a federal court; after declaring his commitment to defending the Southern way of life, Arkansas's Governor Orval Faubus claimed he was not "bound" by the Supreme Court's call for desegregation in Brown v. Board of Education, and he ordered the National Guard to place Little Rock's Central High School "off limits" to blacks; the case rose quickly to the Supreme Court, which built on one of its venerable themes and declared, according to "the basic principle that the federal judiciary is supreme in the exposition of the law of the Constitution,"[50] that Arkansas had to abide by the Brown decision.

Almost thirty years later, Meese disagreed and reopened the argument. He took Faubus's side in the debate. He insisted that while the decision in Cooper "was binding on the parties in the case,"[51] it was not binding on anyone else. The error of his position was easy to show, because if the Attorney General was right, Brown v. Board of Education would have pertained only to the public schools in Topeka, Kansas. To force schools to desegregate throughout the rest of the country, children and their parents would have had to bring lawsuits in every single district, which was not how the law had worked before, not what the Supreme Court intended, not how lower-court judges eventually responded, and not what most Americans understood the law of the land to be after Brown.

Although the Attorney General attacked the Supreme Court's judgment in Cooper v. Aaron, which reaffirmed the long-settled duty of the states to obey federal law, he seemed primarily interested in the Court's relationship to Congress and the President. He skirted the question at the core of this subject—which branch of government the Constitution empowers to resolve disputes between them when, for example, the Congress passes a law the Supreme Court finds unconstitutional, or the President and the Supreme Court disagree in a case about the meaning of the Constitution. He overlooked the enduring answer provided in Marbury v. Madison, or in McCulloch v. Maryland, when Marshall wrote, "On the Supreme Court of the United States has the Constitution of our country devolved this important duty"[52]—namely, of deciding the law of the land. Instead, the Attorney General invoked the Dred Scott case once more.

Dred Scott dealt with the legality of slavery in a territory not yet part of the United States. Abraham Lincoln feared that the ruling was a step toward what he called "the nationalization of slavery," because since the Court had already decided that neither Congress nor the legislature of a territory could constitutionally outlaw slavery, the Justices could as easily rule the same about the states. Lincoln recognized that he couldn't challenge the Dred Scott case as it applied to the parties whose controversy had been resolved by the Court ("We offer no resistance to it," he emphasized), but, as he put it, "All I am doing is refusing to obey it as a political rule. If I were in Congress, and a vote should come up on a question whether slavery should be prohibited in a new territory, in spite of that Dred Scott decision, I would vote that it should."[53]

Meese interpreted this to mean that Abraham Lincoln, like Orval Faubus, had refused to honor the Court's holding because he believed that the Justices were wrong about the law.[54] He thought that the Reagan Administration could make a laudable contribution to the law by doing the same. While the Administration's legal logic was not completely wrong—the Constitution is different from constitutional case law; the Supreme Court isn't irreproachable, and it has regularly demonstrated its commitment to the Constitution by correcting what it considers errant decisions—Meese and the Reagan team never acknowledged some crucial facts.

Dred Scott was unlike any other legal case in American history. It is an irrefutable example of why the Supreme Court cannot claim to be infallible. If it had been resolved otherwise, the debate about the Court's authority as the supreme source of American law would have been very different. Rather than observing the tension between the lessons of Dred Scott and Cooper noted perennially by constitutional scholars (the Court is fallible, and yet it has the authority to state the law of the land), and noting that the tension can be partially resolved by understanding how the facts in each case explain their current significance in the law (Abraham Lincoln interpreted Dred Scott narrowly because the decision favored slavery and held that blacks were not citizens; the Justices in Cooper warned Governor Faubus and his cohorts about the need to comply with the Court's desegregation order handed down in Brown), Meese lectured about the dangers of equating judges and lawgivers, and of submitting to government by judiciary.

The Attorney General belittled the principle of judicial review, which the Justices in Cooper v. Aaron called "permanent and indispensable,"[55] and which Chief Justice William Rehnquist defended in 1987 by calling the Supreme Court "the final arbiter of questions of constitutional law."[56] Using the word "interpret" in a very active sense, Meese approved the notion that "each of the three coordinate branches of government created and empowered by the Constitution—the executive and legislative no less than the judicial—has a duty to interpret the Constitution in the performance of its official functions," and announced that the Supreme Court's interpretations of the Constitution do "not establish a 'supreme Law of the Land.' "[57]

Whether he meant to or not, Meese thereby licensed an attitude about the law that, if taken seriously, leads to conflict, chaos, and lawlessness. That was the result in Little Rock after Governor Faubus refused to integrate Central High. In an effort to restore order, the federal district court granted a request from the school board that the desegregation plan be postponed for many months. The court explained that the "chaos, bedlam and turmoil" caused by Faubus were "intolerable."[58] President Eisenhower sent in troops to enforce the law, and Faubus backed down.

Examples abound of Meese's and the Reagan Administration's inclination to read the law according to their own lights and to reallocate power among the branches of the federal government—above all, to increase the authority of the Executive Branch. Meese castigated the Justices because, in his opinion, "far too many of the Court's opinions were, on the whole, more policy choices than articulations of constitutional principle."[59] Bradford Reynolds broadly interpreted a narrow Supreme Court ruling about layoffs and affirmative action, counter to every reading of the opinion by Courts of Appeals. Roger Clegg, a young lawyer who held a number of political jobs in the Justice Department before becoming an assistant to the Solicitor General, suggested how casually the Administration did this in a memo criticizing a widely respected, three-decade-old precedent applying the Constitution's Equal Protection Clause to the District of Columbia, just like any state. He doubted it should apply. "I know the Supreme Court thinks so," the lawyer wrote, "but that does not make it true."[60] Clegg did not mention the consequence of his judgment, which was as telling as his statement about the authority of the Court: if the Equal Protection Clause was not applied to the District as the Justices did in the decision the lawyer criticized, then because of the District's odd status in American law, there would be no apparent way to outlaw segregation in the District under the Constitution.[61]

When Archibald Cox was Solicitor General, he warned that "the very fabric of a free society is strained when criticism and efforts to change the law slip over into efforts to frustrate or revile the courts."[62] The Reagan team regularly strained that fabric, and went beyond lack of respect for court rulings. They often elevated legal judgments of the Executive Branch over those of Congress as well. At its most dramatic, this took the form of unlawful acts rationalized by patriotism: many students of the

Iran-Contra affair concluded that Ronald Reagan's aides violated the law to carry out a clandestine foreign policy. When Secretary of State George Shultz was asked by Congress about these operations, even he testified, "Some things took place that were illegal." [63] Once the President disclosed his knowledge and approval of some of the secret dealings, it became impossible not to ponder the degree of his complicity too. But in the present administration, these acts are distinguished mainly by their scale; they are not an aberration. Whether the subject was national security, the environment, on-the-job safety, labor, housing, or civil rights, the Administration regularly violated or failed to enforce statutes it disapproved of. [64] The attitude prevailing among many Reagan aides was described by an official who helped supervise the Administration's role in the Nicaraguan war: "Legality," he advised the Washington *Post*, "was viewed as an obstacle that had to be gotten around." [65]

The President's lawyers sought to alter the relationships between the branches of government in other ways as well, less publicized but just as revealing. The Meese Justice Department came up with a new technique for elevating the judgments of the Executive Branch to equal standing with those of Congress in cases raising statutory questions, where the Executive's were, by custom, essentially irrelevant. As if the President's understanding of the purpose of a statute were as important as the Legislature's in guiding interpretations of the law, the department decided to expand the statements made by the President at media events where he signed congressional bills into law. The department expressed a new view about separation of powers, and turned what had long been ceremonial speeches into Presidential proclamations about congressional intent.

Then the Attorney General arranged to have them published in the same volume as the official legislative histories of major statutes. [66] His reasons for doing so strayed far from standard legal thinking. The President's only choice about a bill forwarded to him for signature by Congress is to sign it or not, because the Chief Executive is to execute and enforce, not to make, the law: he has no constitutional role in stating the purpose of a law or the intent of its framers except when he proposes legislation. Even when he does, his comments are at best peripheral to understanding the history of a federal statute, since he is a secondary figure in the lawmaking process. The President does make a statement when he vetoes a bill, but the statement merely explains his decision to veto. It does not become the official history of the proposed law.

The Attorney General wrote to the president of West Publishing Company, a major publisher of official legal records, and insisted on "the importance of presidential signing statements as an aid to statutory interpretation."[67] Like many of Meese's statements, the letter appeared plausible on first reading, though it was in fact a distortion of the President's role in lawmaking. The publisher took his word for it. "We appreciate your suggestion," West's Dwight Opperman wrote back. "I am surprised nobody thought of it before."[68]

The Meese Justice Department adopted another policy that involved a deliberate encroachment by the Executive Branch on the authority of the Legislature. A statute called Public Law No. 96-132 requires that in any case where the Attorney General decides to refrain from enforcing a provision of a statute passed by Congress because he thinks the act is unconstitutional, he must report that decision to both Houses of Congress.[69] For many years, through the Carter Administration, the Attorney General closed his report to the Vice-President of the United States, in his role as President of the Senate, and to the Speaker of the House with a paragraph acknowledging the gravity of this judgment whenever he exercised it. "I should like to conclude by reiterating my belief that the Attorney General is obliged to defend the constitutionality of Acts of Congress in all but the most unusual circumstances,"[70] Attorneys General Griffin Bell and Benjamin Civiletti began their paragraph. In the Reagan Justice Department under William French Smith, the boilerplate was trimmed. "I believe that the action I am taking is consistent with my responsibility to support and defend the Constitution and at the same time will facilitate prompt judicial consideration of the constitutional issues,"[71] Smith wrote. And in the Justice Department under Edwin Meese, even though career attorneys in the Solicitor General's office continued to forward for his signature the old language about defending the Constitution,[72] the Attorney General cut it out altogether.[73]

In the Reagan Administration, then, the Executive Branch

decided it was empowered to judge the law as well as the Congress or the courts, and believed it had little obligation to show, through protocol or other means, deference to the other branches of government even as co-equals. To the Reagan team, separation of powers appeared to mean that the Executive Branch could decide which laws to enforce, that it owed no deference either to Congress or to the courts in determining how to interpret the law until the other branches of government recast it as the Reagan Administration wished them to.

One measure of the Administration's true interest in results instead of restraint—and of its cynicism about the process by which laws are made and interpreted—may lie in the clear willingness it has shown to go counter to its own professed views on the proper role of the judiciary, when this suits its purposes. Thus, after failing to persuade Congress to enact into law various elements of the Reagan agenda, the Administration turned to the courts as the main forum for the pursuit of its domestic objectives. Perhaps most important, it sought to pack the courts with judges who appeared willing to put aside conservative canons of judging in order to fulfill the Administration agenda. According to Sheldon Goldman, a political scientist at the University of Massachusetts, during the first six years of the Reagan Administration, it relied on ideology as a primary test of a candidate's fitness for the bench more than any government since Franklin D. Roosevelt's and perhaps more than any in American history.[74] Largely rich, male, white, and Republican; younger on average than the judges appointed by the five previous Presidents; and, according to the American Bar Association, diminishing in quality as the pool of acceptable ideological candidates appeared to be drained[75]—the judges chosen by Ronald Reagan made up forty percent of the federal bench by 1986.

The last administration to draw attention to the law as Ronald Reagan's has done was Richard Nixon's, during Watergate. But unlike the Nixon Administration, which became notorious for holding that it was *above* the law, the Reagan Administration in essence has regularly proposed that it *is* the law. In doing so, the Administration has encouraged a climate of lawlessness in its private dealings as well as in its public acts. Members of the Administration have compiled a record of misdeeds, impropriety, and unlawful behavior that defies comparison with that of any of its predecessors. To take one measure: By the count of the Washington *Post*, between January 1981 and April 1986, one hundred and ten senior Reagan officials were accused or found guilty of unethical or illegal conduct. This was months before word of the Iran-Contra affair leaked out, adding names to the list like Oliver North, and before the Wedtech scandal implicated yet another group of top officials, including Edwin Meese. The Reagan record of ignominy dwarfs that of any other administration, including Nixon's.

By contravening the standard reading of the Constitution, the Reagan Administration has flouted the will of Congress and chosen not to execute laws with which it disagrees. In theory and practice, it has sought to redefine the role of the judiciary, by claiming that judges lack the authority that scholars have long agreed the Constitution gives them and, at the same time, packing the courts and turning to them (after failing in Congress) as a key instrument of change in social policy. But the Administration's elevation of the Executive Branch's judgments about the law to equal or greater status than those of the other two branches explains why the Reagan team could overlook the logic of the 1977 memorandum from the Office of Legal Counsel about the traditional role of the Solicitor General. To Griffin Bell's Justice Department, the major safeguard against errors of an independent Solicitor General was the Supreme Court. If the SG made a mistake, the Court could correct him. If the Justices upheld him, "then all the better, for his legal judgment and not that of his superiors was correct."[76] But if, as Edwin Meese made clear in his speeches on constitutional law, the Reagan Administration did not grant the Supreme Court this authority, then the SG's dual responsibility to the Court and the Executive Branch lost its point. There was no need for the Solicitor to defer to the Court if the Court's rulings did not establish what the law was any more than did the judgments of the Executive Branch, and the SG might then just as well carry to the Justices the policies of the Administration even where they conflicted with the law as previously expounded by the Court. In the abortion case, Acting Solicitor General Charles Fried served notice that this was what he intended to do.

IX

The Abortion Brief

CHARLES FRIED'S VIEWS about the law were an uncanny match for the Reagan Administration's. Born Karel Fried (pronounced Freed) in Prague, Czechoslovakia, he and his family fled the Nazis in 1939 and settled in Manhattan when he was almost six.[1] He once wrote that he "loves his country as a lover would, not as a child loves the parents he never chose."[2] Tall and sharp-nosed, Fried has deep lines etched in his forehead and a pliant mouth that stretches from a tight line, when he is watchful, to a broad grin. Like Paul Bator, whom he replaced in the winter of 1985, Fried had been a professor at Harvard Law School before joining the Reagan Administration as the political deputy in the SG's office. (Fried was political deputy for four months.) In fact, before the Administration brought in Bator, two years earlier, officials in the Justice Department got in touch with Fried about the job. Instead, Fried recommended his old friend and colleague as an expert in constitutional law. As a scholar in the philosophy of law and a teacher of subjects like contracts and torts, where judge-made rules comprise the heart of the law and the Constitution is not central, he had no special knowledge about the work of the Solicitor General, he explained.[3] Though he also taught criminal law, where the Constitution can figure prominently, he had no background in litigation or federal courts. But, as a member of Scholars and Educators for Reagan in 1980, co-chairman of Law Professors for Reagan-Bush in 1984, and a consultant to Edwin Meese in 1984 and 1985, Fried was eager to find a place in the Administration, and he eventually accepted one in the SG's office. In pictures of him taken not long before he left Harvard for Washington, Fried's glasses had thick black frames and his hair jutted out from the sides of his head in a windswept, bohemian look. [4] By the time he became Acting SG, in June of 1985, his frames were silver and streamlined, and his wiry graying hair was close-cropped, giving him the aura of an investment banker.

Fried had earlier showed his sympathy with the Reagan agenda by writing occasional Op Ed and magazine pieces, [5] on topics like "Curbing the Judiciary," "Questioning Quotas," and "The Trouble with Lawyers." The hallmark of a Fried piece was an argument rocketing along on the strength of its own self-evident truth: though federal judges have usurped power from the other branches of government, this is a symptom as well as a cause of problems; the legal theory in which many judges have been schooled—"that law is policy, and nothing but policy"—has bred a "corrosive cynicism" that explains why "judges feel there is little inherent in their role as expositors of the law to constrain them"; [6] to relieve judges of this symptom, Fried proposed shrinking the power of courts over the daily business of government. Or: "The problem with lawyers, critics say, is the maldistribution of legal services," because only "big business and the very rich benefit from the legal system," but "this is nonsense," because the "rich and big corporations are more victims than beneficiaries of the legal system"; the law firms that serve the big corporations charge high fees, and the work done for a company by a firm can be handled more efficiently and just as well by in-house counsel. As for the middle class, wrote Fried, it "gets quite enough legal services," and "the poor need other things far more urgently than they need lawyers." [7] (In a commencement speech at Georgetown University Law Center, Justice Sandra Day O'Connor offered a different view about the need of the poor for legal services. "The gap between the need for legal assistance and the ability to pay for it seems to be widening," she said. "Costs of legal services have escalated beyond the means of many.") [8]

One of Fried's more memorable comments about law and society came at an unusual gathering about the curriculum at Harvard Law School, before he left the faculty to go to Washington. The school was intensely divided between the academic legal right and left, and the faculty was asked to attend an open meeting with the student body. One student complained that the school taught too much corporate law and too little poverty law. Fried lectured the student on the error of his views, and concluded that Harvard should teach more corporate law. An impulsive man who likes to cause a flap, Fried finished his remarks with an analogy. The Massachusetts Institute of Technology "teaches nuclear physics," he said, but it doesn't tell students "how to repair toasters." The room erupted in hisses and boos.[9]

Fried's 1976 law-review article, called "The Lawyer as Friend,"[10] argued that an attorney who defends a big corporation has as much claim to being morally correct as a poverty lawyer. The piece contended that as long as they provide faithful counsel, lawyers should be free to live as they wish, because each individual has the freedom to choose, as well as the responsibility for, his own destiny. There is no sense living as if we are preparing for the Day of Judgment, Fried maintained, because what happens if it never comes? The article was treated by Fried's academic allies as a casual effort, and was greeted by students and a number of law teachers with scorn. "Many conservatives who see a bad or obnoxious or ugly practice in society have a recognition of grim reality for what it is," Robert Gordon, who is a professor at Stanford Law School, told the *National Law Journal.* "Charles is perversely determined to defend some of the obnoxious social practices as not only being tragically unavoidable but as somehow morally compelled."[11]

Fried's writing grew out of his background in the philosophy of law, and the core of it was a series of books about legal principles (*An Anatomy of Values, Right and Wrong,* and *Contract as Promise*) amounting to a grand declaration (not an argument, the philosopher Alasdair MacIntyre said about the second book, for "if we do not already agree with Fried's premises, so much the worse for us")[12] that absolute commands of right and wrong should take precedence over the dictates of utilitarianism—that is, doing the greatest good for the greatest number of people. From his early law-journal articles ("I propose to examine the foundations of the right of privacy—the reason why men feel that invasions of that right injure them in their humanity")[13] to his more widely known book about right and wrong ("This is a book about how a moral man lives his life: how he approaches choices between his own interests and those of others, what he should do if helping one person means hurting another, how far he must take on himself the burdens of the world's suffering"), [14] Fried made a spirited case for the autonomy of the individual. He made no great mark in the worlds of law or philosophy, but his work was respectfully reviewed by major journals. The *Yale Law Journal* wrote, "Fried is haunted by the nightmare of our being saddled with excessive personal responsibility for the state of the world." [15]

Fried had begun to express his belief in individual autonomy as early as the year he graduated from Columbia Law School (he already held degrees from Princeton and Oxford), when he clerked for Justice John Harlan. During the 1960 Term, the Supreme Court decided Poe v. Ullman, a case where the majority had chosen not to rule on the merits of a challenge to a Connecticut statute on birth control. Harlan dissented, and Fried worked with the Justice on his opinion. Harlan wrote, "I believe that a statute making it a criminal offense for *married couples* to use contraceptives is an intolerable and unjustifiable invasion of privacy in the conduct of the most intimate concerns of an individual's personal life." [16] Relying on the Due Process Clause of the Fourteenth Amendment, as Justice Blackmun would a dozen years later in Roe v. Wade, Harlan went on, "Due process has not been reduced to any formula; its content cannot be determined by reference to any code. The best that can be said is that through the course of this Court's decisions it has represented the balance which our Nation, built upon postulates of respect for the liberty of the individual, has struck between that liberty and the demands of organized society."

The value of privacy that Fried favored, as a law clerk to Harlan and as a young scholar, was embraced by the Supreme Court in its landmark decision about abortion, Roe v. Wade. Among his Harvard colleagues, Fried applauded this ruling and defended it from attack by others then on the faculty, including his colleague John Hart Ely. [17] To Fried's fortune as a prospect for political appointment in the Reagan Administration, he did not emphasize his support for Roe v. Wade in print. One of his law-school colleagues said, "Right before he went to Washington, we were together and someone asked him flat out: 'Does the Administration know your position on abortion?' He smiled and said,

'Well, I've never written it down.' " When a reporter for the Washington *Post* asked him about this in 1986, Fried answered, "You never know when you're 50—you have said a lot of things. I don't remember what I thought about the case in 1973." [18]

Not long after Fried filed the abortion brief as Acting SG, he said, "My passion is philosophy. Everything else is an excursion." He commented about himself, "I think a person who has lived life as a practicing lawyer is somehow restricted in what he sees in the law—that someone who has a larger, subtler view, as I inevitably do from my training, sees more issues." [19] Fried's commitment to his brand of philosophy explained why his approach to the Solicitor Generalship fit the legal view of the Reagan Administration. A friend of his, Philip Heymann, who is a professor at Harvard Law School and was the head of the Criminal Division at the Justice Department during the Carter Administration, noted the connection. Heymann clerked for Justice Harlan the same year as Fried and served as an assistant to the Solicitor General during the Kennedy Administration. He reflected, "When you get to the Reagan Administration, you find that the Solicitor General is in a different position. It is basically the view of this Administration that courts have misbehaved, including the Supreme Court, making law where they shouldn't, and doing social justice instead of law. They regard it as an important responsibility of the Department of Justice to straighten out the courts, both through judicial appointments and through declarations in briefs that they should stop what they've been doing. Charles Fried believes this, and he thinks that he does not have an obligation to the courts as much as to the law. He substitutes for a concern about the law as shaped by the courts a broad philosophical view. The law, whether in the Constitution or in statutes, is there to be interpreted by the Solicitor General; the law is not necessarily what the Supreme Court says it is. In fact, in his view courts regularly ignore the law or make it into something it isn't. Charles would say he's as committed to holding the Administration to the law as any of his predecessors, but for him the law is something that any right-minded lawyer can see." [20]

Fried's usual response when he was asked about the Reagan Administration's abortion brief after it became a legal event was

"You won't get a whisper of my views on abortion in that document. It's about the law."[21] Roe v. Wade should be overturned, Fried contended in the cases called Thornburgh v. American College of Obstetricians and Gynecologists and Diamond v. Charles,[22] because the decisions of the lower courts in the cases at hand had failed to balance the interests recognized in Roe v. Wade ("the state's interest in maternal health and in unborn and future life" versus "a woman's unfettered right to an abortion"). The Court's previous judgment about abortion, in the Akron case, had "expressed considerable impatience" with attempts by state legislatures to strike the proper balance. "To the extent this is so," Fried argued, "these cases and Akron itself are not just wrong turns on a generally propitious journey but indications of an erroneous point of departure. Indeed, the textual, doctrinal and historical basis for Roe v. Wade is so far flawed and, as these cases illustrate, is a source of such instability in the law that this Court should reconsider that decision and on reconsideration abandon it."[23]

The strongest language of the Acting Solicitor General's brief was directed at the courts below. "The courts of appeals betrayed unabashed hostility to state regulation of abortion and ill-disguised suspicion of state legislators' motives,"[24] it read. Where the Court of Appeals for the Third Circuit, in Pennsylvania, found obstacles to abortion in the state legislature's regulations, the Acting Solicitor General found law that was constitutional. For example, the appeals court struck down requirements that: a pregnant minor be obliged to persuade a state judge she was mature enough to give her informed consent for an abortion; two doctors attend an abortion for a woman during the third trimester of her pregnancy, after the term of potential viability for a fetus; a woman's consent to an abortion be considered informed only if her doctor had told her in detail about the medical risks of the procedure; a doctor report to the state about each abortion he had performed, and why he determined "a child" was "not viable" from the pregnancy he ended. Charles Fried argued that these requirements were valid.

The last section of the government's brief made a general argument. The analysis in Roe v. Wade had "no moorings in the text of our Constitution or in familiar constitutional doctrine," the brief claimed, and it gave courts scant guidance for ruling on the lawfulness of statutes. "The result has been a set of judicially crafted rules that has become increasingly more intricate and complex, taking courts further away from what they do best and into the realm of what legislatures do best," it concluded. Roe v. Wade had divided pregnancy into trimesters, for example, and drawn an arbitrary line between them, on grounds that whenever the prospective childbirth posed a danger to the life of a pregnant woman, an abortion in the first trimester might be most defensible, and an abortion in the last, when an abortion might be more dangerous than childbirth, least defensible. But look at the confusion in the courts about the general meaning of the decision, Fried admonished: a state could require that information about abortions be given to a woman by a doctor and his assistant, but not by the doctor alone; a state could require that second-trimester abortions be performed in clinics, but not in hospitals. The Supreme Court's key standard for judging the lawfulness of an abortion was "viability" (the ability of the fetus to survive outside the womb), but in the words of the government's brief the notion of viability was "particularly unworkable" because the meaning of the term was changing with "advances in technology." [25]

More important than the practical problems caused by the Supreme Court's ruling, Fried observed, "There is no explicit textual warrant in the Constitution for a right to an abortion. It is true, of course, that words, and certainly the words of general constitutional provisions, do not interpret themselves. That being said, the further afield interpretation travels from its point of departure in the text, the greater the danger that constitutional adjudication will be like a picnic to which the framers bring the words and the judges the meaning." In Roe v. Wade, the Justices had brought along the conviction that "free access to abortion is a fundamental expression of individual freedom, and that such freedom is the first principle of a just society," but the conviction did "not constitute constitutional argument." [26]

On one level, Fried's brief presented an urbane version of a standard criticism of Roe v. Wade. Though he said that his brief presented "a fresh constitutional methodology," [27] it did little more than summarize the twelve-year-old view that the Constitution includes no explicit right to an abortion and that therefore the Supreme Court was wrong to find one in its provisions.

On another level, it was a bold misrepresentation of the facts

and law before the Supreme Court. "The courts of appeals betrayed unabashed hostility to state regulation of abortion and ill-
disguised suspicion of state legislators' motives,"[28] the brief
stated. But in the Pennsylvania case, it turned out, the Court of
Appeals had struck down parts of only six of twenty sections in
a twenty-four-page statute[29] which was described by State Representative Stephen Freind, its chief sponsor, as "the most comprehensive abortion control act in the United States, and the
most publicized bill in Pennsylvania history."[30] Fried's brief did
not say so, but most of the statute's provisions were left intact.
They were as significant to the law as were the sections struck
down. The lower court's ruling hardly amounted to "unabashed
hostility."

As for the court's "ill-disguised suspicion," the history of the
law indicated why the suspicion was justified. In 1981, the Pennsylvania legislature passed a bill designed to limit abortions that was
based on a model statute written by an anti-abortion group in
Chicago. Governor Dick Thornburgh vetoed the bill. In 1982, the
legislature revised the bill to satisfy the governor, and passed it
again. "Was my bill intended to discourage abortion?" Representative Freind asked rhetorically in an interview. "You use the
word you want. It certainly counsels extreme caution to women
and, by forcing them to understand what abortion is, tries to get
them to think twice before going ahead with an abortion. I won't
mince words: our goal is definitely to outlaw abortion."[31] Rather
than supporting the view that Roe v. Wade and its progeny had
been interpreted by state legislatures to require "free access to
abortion," as the Acting SG's brief contended, legislatures like
Pennsylvania's were testing to see how strongly their laws could
discourage women from having abortions and still pass muster
with the Supreme Court.

Instead of presenting a measured view about a vexing question
of fact and law, Charles Fried had submitted a piece of advocacy
that was marked by taunting phrases (like his comparison, already
noted, of constitutional adjudication to a "picnic") and irrelevant
asides (a comment on the meaning of the Establishment Clause, for
example)[32] that made most sense as tips of the hat to the Attorney
General and his ideological circle. In the estimate of many long-

time observers of the SG's office, Fried's brief was more strident than any ever submitted by a Solicitor General.[33]

In a speech to federal judges in Little Rock, Arkansas, the month after the government entered the Pennsylvania and Illinois cases as a friend of the Court, Justice Blackmun called Fried's submission "a very amazing brief."[34] (Blackmun did not yet know that the SG assistant who had helped Fried write the brief was Albert Lauber, an ex-Blackmun clerk who kept his name off it so as not to offend the Justice.)[35] Blackmun also suggested that the Supreme Court was not likely to overturn Roe v. Wade. "There are always four votes" to hear an abortion case, he said, referring to the Court's rule to hear a case presented for review through a petition for certiorari if four Justices agree to.[36] "And the other five of us heave a deep sigh and wish we didn't have to go through this traumatic experience again."

Among the many amicus briefs filed on the other side from the government in the Thornburgh and Diamond cases, the best publicized was by Senator Bob Packwood, a Republican from Oregon; Congressman Don Edwards, a Democrat from California; and eighty other Republicans and Democrats from both Houses of Congress. It was written by four professors at Harvard Law School: Susan Estrich, Martha Minow, and Kathleen Sullivan, with Laurence Tribe as lead counsel.[37] Tribe is the author of a widely used treatise on constitutional law. Through the 1986 Term, he had argued fourteen cases before the Supreme Court—a notable accomplishment for anyone but a lawyer in the SG's office.[38]

At a press conference sponsored by Planned Parenthood in September of 1985, the day his brief was filed, Tribe described what Blackmun might have found amazing about the SG's submission. "The basic proposition" of the Tribe brief was "that the government's plea that the Supreme Court overturn Roe v. Wade is unprincipled, is divisive, and is dangerous." It was unprincipled "because it offers no coherent reason, at all, for the Supreme Court suddenly to repudiate this basic liberty." As the Tribe brief declared, "For the first time in the history of the Solicitor General's office, in a case in which the United States is not even a party, and a case in which the issue was not presented by the parties, the Department of Justice has urged the repudiation of a liberty long since declared fundamental by this Court." The SG's brief was divisive because it would "toss" the rights of women and of the unborn into "50 different political arenas, there to be resolved by a majority vote in 50 separate state legislatures." And it was dangerous because it threatened "every woman in this country with turning over her reproductive freedom to the powers that be in government," and because it advocated "radical surgery on our form of government and the body politic." The government had claimed that it wanted "to turn back the constitutional clock to 1973." It really called for turning back the clock "at least another half century," and repudiating "a long line of decisions about personal and family privacy which cannot be distinguished, in principle, from Roe v. Wade."[39]

A footnote in Tribe's brief emphasized the anomalous character of the role Fried had chosen to play:[40]

> In argument before this Court in Akron, the Solicitor General expressly refrained from asking the Court to overrule Roe v. Wade:
> Question: Mr. Solicitor General, are you asking us to overrule Roe v. Wade?
> Mr. Lee: I am not, Mr. Justice Blackmun.
> Question: Why not?
> Mr. Lee: That is not one of the issues presented in this case, and as amicus appearing before the Court, that would not be a proper function for us.

In an interview on National Public Radio in 1985, Lee was asked the same question. "When you come to cases like that," he said, "it's simply a question of 'Do you want to blow the bugle?' or 'Do you want to win the war?'"[41] In a draft of a speech he planned to give once he was out of office, written before his successor filed the government's abortion brief, Rex Lee made the point one more time, in the plainest possible language.[42] Bringing together in an organized way ideas he had expressed in various interviews, he wrote, "Let me give you the practical reasons why I don't think the Solicitor General can or should take it upon himself to tell the Supreme Court what he may very well believe are its errors of constitutional doctrine.

"The Solicitor General, unlike his critics, cannot afford to lose sight of the fact that he is a lawyer, an *advocate*, whose first duty is to see that his client, the federal government, prevails in the case at hand. There is, I admit, a place for announcement of pure principle, and from time to time that place is in a Supreme Court brief. But a Solicitor General is a *Solicitor* General, not a 'Pamphleteer General,' and his role is to persuade the Court by legal arguments to decide cases in the way that best serves his client, the people of the United States. His audience is not one hundred million people; his audience is nine people, or more specifically, nine Justices, all of them sophisticated, capable lawyers who are not about to be influenced by lectures or slogans. You just don't win cases that way.

"The law, especially constitutional law, is made incrementally, on a case-by-case basis. No lawyer worth his salt would think of going before the Supreme Court, or any appellate tribunal, and telling its members point blank that they were wrong on some case they decided just several years before, even if the lawyer strongly believes they were. That approach would simply not be in his client's best interest, and the reason is obvious: the Court as an institution would find it offensive. In a close case—as so many of the cases are in the Supreme Court—the lawyer's impertinence might well cost the client the one or two votes needed to win. It would therefore be both a tactical mistake and a professional violation of the lawyer's ethical duty to advance his client's cause. But more than that, it would deeply injure the Solicitor General's personal credibility with the Court, without which the government would cease to enjoy its remarkable success both in getting the Court to review its cases and in winning on the merits.

"And so my practical argument against those who would have the Solicitor General rail against the perceived excesses and errors of the Supreme Court is simply that it would be bad lawyering, period. And I think most lawyers, and certainly most seasoned litigators, would agree. In his speeches, in his writings, or, in later life, in the classroom (if that's where he ends up), the Solicitor General has the right of every citizen and the duty of every lawyer to speak his mind on the issues, and to say where he thinks the law is going and where it should be going. He has no business doing so as an advocate, however, and I challenge any scholars or researchers to find an example of a Solicitor General, beginning with

Benjamin Bristow in 1870, who has ever let politics or personal beliefs interfere with his advocacy in the Supreme Court." [43]

After Fried filed his brief, in July 1985, Lee toned down the text of the speech which he eventually delivered at Franklin and Marshall College. [44] While uncompromising about the Solicitor's need to preserve his "unique standing" with the Supreme Court, Lee went on, "This is not to say that it is never advisable for a Solicitor General to take a position that he knows the Court will reject. There could be long-range objectives to be served by such a filing. All I am saying is that there are large costs, and it is rarely advisable. In my four years I never did it," Lee said, "though I always held open the possibility that in a sufficiently compelling case I might." Lee restricted his disagreement with Fried to the area of tactics. At a conference about constitutional law in Washington, Lee said, "The one thing you learn as Solicitor General is how to count to five." [45] When he joined the Akron case as amicus, he believed that the Administration couldn't win five of the Court's nine votes to overturn Roe v. Wade, so he didn't asked the Court to consider it—even though he was highly critical of the ruling. The makeup of the bench hadn't changed since Fried took over as SG, so it made little sense to ask the Justices to abandon Roe. The plea detracted from the SG's credibility, because it gave the Justices the impression he was using the Supreme Court as a political forum; and it gave the Court the opportunity to reaffirm the holding in Roe v. Wade, yielding "one more recent precedent to fight." Lee said his remarks were not meant as a criticism of his successor. "These are difficult judgments to make," he said, "and they can only be made by the current Solicitor General."

In time, both Fried and the Attorney General addressed Lee's points, but they responded differently. Terry Eastland, Meese's spokesman at the Justice Department, acknowledged that a majority of Justices were not likely to take the government's line in the case. "But a brief can stimulate public discourse on an issue," he said when he was asked about the abortion case. "Notice the commentary . . . that's already out there now. It wouldn't be there except for our brief." [46] Eastland corroborated Lee's belief that some in the Reagan Administration wanted the SG to serve as a Pamphleteer General, using submissions in the Supreme Court to address the larger audience of voters beyond the capital.

Fried tried to keep discussion on a higher plane than that of a pamphlet. "Some legal conclusions are compelled by logic," he said, "and candor requires us to present them squarely to the Court. That's the duty of the government, don't you think?"[47] In the circle of lawyers who once served in the SG's office, Fried's line recalled a story about one of his predecessors, William Mitchell.[48] The SG was out for a stroll in Washington, and he met Justice Holmes on the street. "Mr. Solicitor General," the Justice said, "I admire your candor before our Court." As Mitchell drew himself up proudly, Holmes quickly added, "I have always thought that candor is the best form of deception."

As far as the SG's tradition was concerned, however, Fried insisted that his brief was business as usual: the commotion about it said more about his critics than about his views. At a speech to the Chamber of Commerce in Washington, Fried said, "I haven't discussed our brief in the abortion cases, and I'm not going to, but you might actually be interested to read it, and see whether it has any bearing on what I've said. The press, which does not like to read things, but prefers to call people up on the telephone and provoke them into indiscretions, called me a lot when the brief was filed, and they said, 'Well, what was the reason for you to take the position you did?' And that gave me the chance to say, 'You don't understand. A brief is not like a symphony. It's not like a directive. It's not even like a proclamation. A brief is nothing but reasons. And to ask "What are the reasons for your position?" is to ask "May I read it?" ' "[49]

During his remarks, Fried presented a sketch of the outlook informing his judgments as SG. He referred to Herbert Wechsler, his former professor at Columbia Law School, and a giant in the field of American constitutional law, who is noted especially for his theory of neutral principles related to the traditional idea of judicial restraint. In an essay published in 1959, Wechsler argued that unless courts could find reasons that were general and neutral enough to apply beyond the immediate case, they had no grounds for overturning the judgments of the other branches of government.[50] "I'm a reverent student of Herbert Wechsler," Fried volunteered, and he indicated that his abortion brief was an expression of his belief in neutral principles.

One of the scholars who read Fried's brief was Wechsler. "On

balance," he said in February of 1986,[51] "my opinion is that the
Solicitor General made a mistake in the abortion case. The recency
of the reaffirmation of Roe v. Wade coupled with the fact that
there had been no change in the membership of the Court suggested to me that the government was posturing rather than practicing good law when it asked for a complete re-examination of the
issue. It's one of the oldest traditions of the Court, going way back
to Chief Justice Taney, that the Court stands ready to reconsider
its judgments if they are shown to be wrong. Over and over again,
this has been done and the notion persists. But I can't really believe
that Charlie Fried thought that this was an appropriate case for the
Administration to ask the Court to restate the law. You've got to
see the thing in long perspective. On the one hand, you've got the
tradition that the Court is prepared to reexamine its decisions.
And, on the other hand, that the Court considers that it speaks the
last word in cases about interpreting the Constitution. Where to
draw the line—between persistence and presumption—is more a
matter of common sense than abstract thinking, and I think the
Solicitor General was presumptuous in the abortion case."

Wechsler recalled, "I myself was in the SG's office during the
late thirties and early forties, and I briefed and argued cases. I got
the Court to overrule the Newberry case, in U.S. v. Classic.[52] That
was a case which was crucial in doing away with lily-white primaries in Southern states. There had been ballot-stuffing in a Louisiana
primary, and the Newberry case held that the election statute
outlawing that kind of shenanigan didn't apply to primaries, but
only to general elections. We got that overturned. Charles Evans
Hughes was then Chief Justice, and he had been the winning
counsel in Newberry. I had no reason to believe he would think
differently as a judge, and I was happily surprised. We were engaged then in asking the Court to overturn a precedent, but how
and when we did it marked the difference between persistence and
presumption.

"Charlie Fried was a student of mine in the fifties, and a very
brilliant fellow. I think his views as to what is right are close to
Meese's. But I was surprised he took the job as Solicitor General,
because he must have known he would confront the conflict between the office's and the Court's institutional values versus Administration policy. If Charlie Fried really believes that he has

things to say about Roe v. Wade that have not been said, and that he has a fresh objection to the case that the Court might consider determinative, then he has a right to say it. But he's obviously a damn fool if he thinks he has anything to say that hasn't already been said."

The review of the government's brief that Fried favored was an article by the politically moderate Edwin Yoder that appeared in the Philadelphia *Inquirer*. [53] "Needless to say, it strikes me as an accurate and balanced discussion," the Solicitor General said about the piece. [54] Yoder is a syndicated columnist who has won a Pulitzer Prize for editorial writing, and he opened his assessment with a disclosure. "I can, for once, shed some first-hand light on a relationship that threatens to generate an obscuring excess of steam," he began. "Charles Fried, an old friend, has come to Washington from a distinguished teaching career to serve as U.S. Solicitor General—chief legal advocate—for the Reagan Administration. Fried is a kind, jolly, and brainy man. He is, however, addicted to dialectics as others are to bourbon or baseball. Those unaccustomed to his manner tend to find him contentious." Yoder's thesis, however, was that the "misimpressions" about the SG's brief had more to do with the abortion issue itself than with Fried's personality. "To argue that the Court should return the power to regulate abortion to the states, as Fried does, is not to argue for an outright ban on abortion," Yoder wrote. "In fact, the judicial debate is only secondarily about abortion."

From the vantage of the SG's office, and several lawyers whom Fried had inherited as members of the staff, the problem with Yoder's column was that it missed an essential fact. When the columnist hazarded that "the brief undoubtedly represents Fried's best thought on the law of abortion, not a pose forced on him by Attorney General Ed Meese" and that "[i]nsinuations to the contrary drastically underestimate Fried's commitment to principled debate and the Constitution," Yoder wrote with the confidence of an old friend and not, apparently, with the conviction held by many people in the SG's office: if Fried wanted to be named Solicitor General, and shed his conditional status as Acting SG, he had no choice about what position to take in the abortion case. [55]

In the speech that Edwin Meese gave to the American Bar Association where he discussed the government's submission in the abortion case, the Attorney General tied it to his primary initiative at the Justice Department.[56] A lawyer in the SG's office, who became one of Fried's main supporters after he was named Solicitor General, explained that Meese's expectations inside the Justice Department matched his public comments, and that Fried acted accordingly. "The Attorney General made it absolutely clear how far the government was going to go. Charles couldn't afford to give a hint of ambivalence about the position or he would have dropped out as a candidate for the post."[57]

Fried had a different view about his freedom as SG to write what he wanted. With longtime colleagues at Harvard Law School, he was cavalier. "I have no trouble saying what the Attorney General and his crew want me to, because I'm much more conservative than they are," he said.[58] When former Solicitor General Erwin Griswold, who had hired Fried for the Harvard faculty a quarter of a century before, expressed the view that the Acting SG's abortion brief so clearly flouted the deference of his office to the Court that it "apparently was filed pursuant to instructions," Fried called the Dean's comment "a shameful thing for him to say."[59] Another time, he said, "Anyone who says I was forced to write what I did in the abortion brief doesn't know what the hell he's talking about."[60] His vehemence was prompted by, among other things, a story in the *Wall Street Journal* ("Justice Department sources say Mr. Fried wasn't immediately nominated in June so department officials could test his willingness to advocate administration positions")[61] stating the view that was common in the SG's office and elsewhere at the Justice Department: to Meese and company, the abortion case was Fried's loyalty test.

ON THE MID-OCTOBER morning in 1985 when Charles Fried appeared before the Senate Judiciary Committee for his confirmation hearing, committee members came and went, and there were never more than a half-dozen present at any one time.[62] Of the committee's eighteen members, only ten took part in the proceedings. Fried said afterward, "The fix was in."[63]

Fried's testimony was careful and well prepared, and he controlled the give-and-take. "Mr. Chairman,"[64] he said, in answer to a question from Strom Thurmond about his legal qualifications to be Solicitor General, "I think that of all the experience that I have had, that which qualifies me most, if I am qualified, is an experience I had twenty-five years ago, when it was my privilege to be law clerk to I think one of the finest Justices in the history of the Supreme Court, John Marshall Harlan, and I hope to carry his standards, and his values in my heart and mind, as I do this work." Like his invocation of Wechsler in speeches, Fried's reference to Harlan was shrewdly made, for Harlan was widely respected for his legal craftsmanship.

How did Fried plan to conduct himself if confirmed by the Senate?

"Nothing would be more important to me than to maintain that sense of confidence which I believe the Supreme Court has always had in the Office of the Solicitor General. That the Supreme Court can believe that the work that comes from the office represents the most objective, the most accurate, and the fairest presentation of the issues before it. To be sure, the Office of the Solicitor General is an advocate's office. Nevertheless, I think though we are the government's lawyer, we are also handmaidens to the Supreme Court, and the Supreme Court has always reposed a very special confidence in the quality of our work, in the accuracy of our work, and in the objectivity and restraint of our judgments, and I would hope very much to keep that up." [65]

What about the charges that "urging the abandonment of Roe versus Wade was an indication that the Office of the Solicitor General is being somewhat politicized?" Thurmond asked.

Fried answered, "Senator, I do not believe that our office has been politicized, and I would not wish to serve as Solicitor General in order to further a process of politicization. I suppose that the President has nominated me because he has some sense of what my philosophy is, and that philosophy enters my judgment of what the law is on a particular matter, and what arguments should be made. But certainly partisan political considerations have never entered into our judgments, never should enter into our judgments, and I would never allow them to enter into our judgments."

At one point, Joseph Biden, the senator from Delaware who was the committee's ranking Democrat, said, "I want to make sure you are rooted in Harlan and not in Meese. Do you understand my concern?"[66]

Fried replied deliberately, "I have been rooted in Harlan for a very long time."

A few days later, when told how comfortable he seemed answering questions from the committee, Fried scoffed, "These people don't have follow-up questions because they don't decide which questions to ask in the first place."[67] The quiet that greeted one of his remarks to the senators suggested the accuracy of his comment in this instance: either they knew little about the tradition of the Solicitor General, or were willing to accept Fried's recasting of it. "The office is, always has been, must remain independent," he said at the hearing. "I would like to explain what that means," Fried went on, "because the statutes and regulations which set up the Office of the Solicitor General plainly indicate that the Solicitor General is a subordinate official of the Attorney General. I think the original . . . 1870 statute speaks of the Solicitor General as a helper to the Attorney General, 'learned in the law.' Now, the way in which the Solicitor General serves the Attorney General, which he does, is by giving his own best independent judgment. That is how he renders that service. Now, the Attorney General does not have to accept that judgment, and he has got to make his own judgments, and that means that there will be occasions—there always have been and there will continue to be—in which the Attorney General, in rare cases, concludes that the judgment that his Solicitor General has given him is a judgment with which he does not concur, and in that event, he has the clear statutory authority to direct the Solicitor General to take a contrary position. There is no doubt about that."[68]

Until then, Fried's lesson had been unremarkable, a reading from a nuts-and-bolts chapter in a textbook. Then he turned the post of Solicitor General from a position of independence into the job of a good-natured mouthpiece.

When the Attorney General directs the Solicitor General to take a contrary position, Fried judged, "I think it would be *peevish* and *inappropriate* for the Solicitor General to be anything but *cheerful* in accepting that reversal."[69] His voice supplied the emphasis. He said that frequent reversals would give the SG "a right to wonder" whether the Attorney General had confidence in his judgment, and that the SG "should simply not" take a position "which he feels is influenced by improper factors, or, cannot conscientiously be urged to the Court," but the message he delivered most assertively was that he had already assumed a loyal position on the Reagan team.

Fried was also asked how the Justice Department determined its position in a case before the Supreme Court, and how he intended to resolve any differences of opinion within the Department. Again he gave a textbook answer. Some part of the government "will have won or lost a case in a court below, and will then request that our office take the matter to the Supreme Court." The request usually came on paper, and it was assigned to an assistant in the SG's office. "The assistants in the office are an extraordinary group of men and women," Fried said, "professional career lawyers of the highest degree of competence. That memorandum is then reviewed by one of the deputies who are even more remarkable than the assistants, and fewer in number, and that deputy and the assistants together make a recommendation to the Solicitor General, who then proceeds to make a final disposition whether the request of the agency or the department to bring a case to the Supreme Court will indeed go forward. If we determine it shall go forward, then we proceed to draft the papers, draft the brief, and argue the case."[70]

What Fried neglected to tell the committee—since he had never known the arrangement to be otherwise, he might not have thought there was any reason to mention it—was how differently from the textbook description the SG's office now worked. To anyone who knew about the change (none of the senators, apparently), Fried's answer sounded almost like part of a cover-up. He was frank about the deference he thought he owed the Attorney General (it would be "peevish" and "inappropriate" for the Solicitor to be anything but "cheerful" about taking orders from the AG), but he said nothing about how closely the Attorney General was keeping tabs on the SG's work. Nor did he refer to the agent selected for the task. The agent's name—William Bradford Reynolds—would have astounded at least the members of the Senate Judiciary Committee who had voted against his confirmation as Associate Attorney General four months before.

When Rex Lee was SG, Reynolds exercised influence far beyond his official status in deliberations about the government's position before the Supreme Court in civil rights cases, and many other cases where the President's agenda was at stake. Soon after Charles Fried replaced Lee, in June of 1985—and almost immediately after the Senate Judiciary Committee rejected Reynolds's promotion to Associate Attorney General—the civil-rights chief was rewarded for his past vigilance. The Attorney General announced he was giving Reynolds "important new duties" beyond his role as Assistant Attorney General and that he would be "part of our senior management team" with "a number of assignments."[71] Meese did not detail the new work, but he gave a large hint: Reynolds would operate on a par with the Deputy Attorney General and the Solicitor General, he said—above the rank of Assistant Attorney General and at the same level as Associate Attorney General. The arrangement had been set down in the memorandum describing what Reynolds's duties were supposed to be after he was confirmed as Associate AG. Reynolds could no longer use the Associate's post as a way station to becoming Solicitor General, as some of his allies in the Administration had planned he would and as many lawyers in the Justice Department and some senators on the Judiciary Committee expected him to do as well.[72] (Reynolds was asked, "Can you assure the Committee, that if you are appointed Solicitor General at a later date, you will come before the Committee for confirmation?")[73] But, instead of resigning, as some senators thought he should, Reynolds stayed on at the Justice Department. He was written up in a series of newspaper features in which the Attorney General praised Reynolds's "strength of character" and "tremendous statesmanship," and said how much he relied on his advice in a wide range of legal matters.[74] (In May 1987, Meese appointed Reynolds Counselor to the Attorney General, to supplement his title of Assistant Attorney General and finally make official the longtime close relationship between them.)

The week of the Fried hearing, and days before he was confirmed as SG, a lawyer in the SG's office reported matter-of-factly, "Reynolds now sits in on most meetings dealing with sensitive political cases."[75] One of Reynolds's assignments was to monitor Charles Fried's submissions as Solicitor General.

X

The Celestial
General

TO SOME CONNECTED with the SG's office, questions about their personal background seem beside the point. The details they like to talk about (where they went to law school, whom they clerked for, what cases they have argued before the Court) relate to the law. Louis Claiborne has a more spacious concept of autobiography. He has a handsome, weatherworn face, a dime-size scar on one cheek, and a charming, offhand manner, and he often wears casual clothes that give him the air of a man dressed for a summer evening on his porch. He is also a storyteller and his accent reveals his travels from New Orleans, where his family is from, to Europe, where he grew up, and from Washington, D.C., to London, between which he has shuttled half his life. In 1985, at fifty-eight, he was the oldest of five deputies. He had worked for six Solicitors and, within a tradition-minded institution, he was an institution himself.

"I theoretically come from Louisiana, but was in fact born in Europe and went to the University of Louvain, in Belgium—the Most Catholic University of Louvain—the head of which is usually called the Magnificent Rector, who is usually an Archbishop," Claiborne said in 1985.[1] "It was founded by Martin the Fifth, one of the Popes, or at least it was blessed by him, and mere attendance gives you something like a hundred days' indulgences in purgatory. As you can gather, I'm not a very good Catholic, but I was born Catholic and I went to the university not because it was Catholic but because it was meant to be the best university in Belgium. My father was an international banker representing a New York bank. He had been in Belgium before the war, which is why I was born there, in 1927, and he returned after the war, which is why I went to school there. I went there for a year, and did more social than academic things. Then went to the Science Politique in Paris, which was certainly more social than academic. That was three years. And then came back and went to Tulane Law School, which was the proper, traditional thing for me to do, being nominally from New Orleans, but not generally viewed anywhere outside Louisiana as a prime law school. I was blissfully unaware of that at the time.

"I practiced for a bit, and went into the local state district attorney's office, doing mostly appeals. Then there was a change in the local administration, and we in the reform group were removed for a more corrupt lot. I formed a little law firm and one of my cases took me to the Supreme Court of the United States in 1959, when I was thirty-one years old. It was called Louisiana Power & Light Company v. City of Thibodaux,[2] and it was an odd case. The city had expanded and annexed the territory next door. The city had a power authority of its own, but the new territory it was taking over was serviced by a private utility, the Louisiana Power & Light Company, and the city decided to appropriate the property of that company and integrate the system into its own. It invoked some relatively obscure Louisiana statute which seemed to cover the matter, but the Attorney General of Louisiana ruled that it didn't. Anyway, it was not clear-cut what was the right answer. The case was removed to the federal court where J. Skelly Wright was then a district judge. He did what was unexpected from him of all people—he was not noted for his deference to state courts, because those were the days when Southern courts were pretty backward when it came to people's rights—and he abstained, and said this is a question of local law that ought to be settled by the Louisiana courts, and therefore required the parties to go to the Louisiana courts and find out what the answer was. Well, that stunned both sides, neither one of which had argued anything related. So the case went to the U.S. Court of Appeals for the Fifth Circuit, and that's the point at which I was brought into the case on behalf of the Power & Light Company. I appeared before Judge Hutcheson, who was then a very senior judge in the Circuit, and he asked me how long I needed to argue the case. I said half an hour, or something like that, and he said, 'If I told you

Wright was wrong, how long would you need?' I said, 'Five minutes,' argued, and he told me he'd heard enough. The judges decided promptly to reverse Wright, and said Wright must proceed to trial. Very nice for me.

"The state of Louisiana filed a petition with the Supreme Court, which decided to review the case. Once more the case fell to me, and I came to Washington and argued my first case, as a relatively new lawyer, before the Supreme Court. I prepared like mad and I argued the case, and on one side of the bench there was Felix Frankfurter, who thought I was twelve years old and treated me like a law student and had fun by doing a very academic exercise, and at the other end there was Hugo Black, who said 'I don't know about the points of my brother Frankfurter, but doesn't it make sense to let the state courts figure this out? The Attorney General of the state couldn't make head nor tail of it, and Judge Wright couldn't—isn't it common sense to leave it to the state courts?' So I had common sense and academia against me, and my chances were very poor. In the end, I did get three votes—from Brennan, Douglas, and Warren.

"The performance apparently amused Frankfurter, and the next time he saw Skelly Wright, he said, 'Who's this young lawyer from New Orleans?' To which Skelly Wright said, 'Never heard of him.' Frankfurter told him he ought to do better and know the people in his jurisdiction who were up and coming and all that, and why didn't he try to persuade me to come and clerk for him. Wright wasn't interested in hiring me, and I wasn't interested in clerking, but we agreed, for the sake of Frankfurter, to try it out for six months. It lasted two years. We got along fine. In the meantime, the desegregation crisis had arisen and I was helpful to him. Thanks to Wright's strong stand on desegregation—he was famous for his fight against the powers of Louisiana to get them to comply with Brown v. Board of Education—the move to get him the hell out of New Orleans, where he was stirring too much trouble, and promote him to the Fifth Circuit, where his influence would be diluted, or, even better, to the District of Columbia Circuit, where he'd be out of harm's way, became very popular. Bobby Kennedy, who was by then Attorney General, and Jack Kennedy acquiesced in this latter idea, which was a promotion for the judge and meant getting somebody more tractable in the district court in Louisiana. The judge wanted me to remain his clerk in Washington, but I thought the time had come to move on.

"Louis Oberdorfer, who is now a trial judge in Washington and was head of the Tax Division at the Justice Department and a great friend of Bobby Kennedy's, came down to New Orleans just about then, and Skelly Wright persuaded me to invite him to dinner, which I did. Over dinner, Oberdorfer suggested I join the Solicitor General's office. I'd never heard of the Solicitor General, and I wasn't particularly interested in a government job, and I wasn't interested in Washington, but Oberdorfer kept on about it and Skelly Wright said what a glorious opportunity this was, so finally I found out that somebody called Archibald Cox was the Solicitor General and I wrote myself a letter to Cox saying that Louie Oberdorfer had suggested I might be interested in a position under him. I got a very swift note back from Archie Cox telling me that Mr. Oberdorfer was head of the Tax Division, and if I wanted to work for the Justice Department, perhaps I should apply to the Tax Division, and that he was *the Solicitor General*, and he didn't need Oberdorfer as a scout making offers for his office.

"There were a few vacancies, because a longtime staffer named Oscar Davis had just gone on the Court of Claims, and another named John Davis—not *the* John Davis—had just become Clerk of the Supreme Court. By now, we're in early spring of 1962. I was rather annoyed at Cox's rebuff, having decided that I did want the job, so I was as stubborn as Cox. I got John Minor Wisdom, who became a great Fifth Circuit Judge, and Skelly Wright, and others to write on my behalf, but it produced very little—a halfway polite correspondence. Ultimately, I was invited to come up for an interview, but I didn't get much more out of Cox than a suggestion that I go into training for a year with the Tax Division. At which point, Skelly Wright alerted Frankfurter to this impasse, and apparently Frankfurter picked up the phone and told Cox that he had no choice but to hire me. Frankfurter, being Harvard Incarnate, overcame the prime objection, which was that I wasn't from Harvard, or even Columbia, which is where many of the lawyers in the SG's office had come from until then. There's an unproved belief among staff lawyers that I was the first non–Ivy Leaguer ever hired by an SG. What is more, most of the people Cox took had been Supreme Court clerks, as opposed to a clerk for a district judge, and they had been a year or two training at Covington & Burling, or some such fancy place, and had started it all on the *Law Review.* I didn't fit any of these. When Frankfurter told Cox 'Never mind all that,' Cox swallowed hard and reluctantly agreed that he would take the enormous risk. We in fact got along fine.

"When Cox left, in the summer of '65, there was a farewell party, at which three people said very different things, but all of them appropriate for Cox. One of them was Hugo Black, one was Bobby Kennedy, and one was a fellow named Ralph Spritzer, who had been Cox's first deputy, even though we didn't have titles like that in those days because there were only nine lawyers in the office, including the Solicitor General. What Hugo Black said about Cox was what Hugo Black thought about this office. A slightly exaggerated view, but still. He said Cox had distinguished himself in this office because he had not been 'the attorney for the parochial interests of the federal government but the lawyer of the people of the United States.' Bobby Kennedy told the story of his brother calling him up to ask for a legal opinion. 'I'll get right on it,' Bobby said. 'No, Bobby,' the President explained. 'You don't understand. I want a *legal* opinion. *Ask Archie.* He's the Solicitor General.' It was all said very nicely. Ralph Spritzer, in a more serious vein, said, 'There is only one word that describes Archie Cox. That is *rectitude.*' A very old-fashioned word, but it was true. Cox's own comment to me at this gathering was that he had thought when he was so brave as to take me on that I might end up as Cox's Folly, but that it had turned out all right. That was as generous as you could get from Archibald Cox, who was the best Solicitor General I ever worked for."

Another lawyer at the SG's office said about Claiborne, "He's of the Skelly Wright school: You do what you think is right." Though Wright was an activist liberal judge, who believed that the role of law is to serve human ends, he tried to place decisions he reached in the line of legal principles on which he drew. In legal terms, he tried to make sure that "the doctrine lined up."[3] Claiborne came early in a long string of gifted lawyers who worked for the judge as a law clerk (from 1975 through 1985, Wright was the only lower-court judge in the country who sent all his aides—

thirty of them—on to clerk at the Supreme Court),[4] and he was schooled by the judge in this practice.

Claiborne made his mark as a young assistant to the Solicitor General arguing cases dealing with problems of race. An early case of his was reported by Tom Kelly, a columnist for the Washington *Daily News*. [5] "Mr. Claiborne," Kelly wrote, "stood in his braided frock coat, slim as a sword cane, his manner as aristocratically militant as General Pierre Gustave Toutant Beauregard, and his voice as Southern as Terrebonne Parish." In Claiborne's native Louisiana, blacks could register to vote in the southern parishes "as easily as they sign up to cut cane." But in the northern parishes they had been "discouraged from voting so well that in West Feliciana [no black had been] on the rolls for ten years." Between 1956 and 1958, the registrars in the northern parishes and some white groups known as "citizens councils" had purged about thirty thousand blacks from the voting rolls. No whites had been removed. To get back on, blacks had to pass a test that whites were not required to take. Claiborne told the Court, "Any test is harder than no test." He also quoted the late Governor Earl Long speaking to the state legislature: "There ain't ten people looking at me, including myself, who, if attacked, could qualify to vote."

On the list of parishes before the Supreme Court was Claiborne Parish. Justice Arthur Goldberg asked the attorney about it. "I regret to say Claiborne Parish is one of the worst," the *Daily News* quoted Claiborne as saying. "It is named after my great-great grandfather who was the first Governor of Louisiana." The paper had skipped a generation. "An upwardly mobile pol," Claiborne called his great-great-great grandfather. The story was that Aaron Burr and Thomas Jefferson received the same number of electoral votes to be President in 1800. Those were the days the candidate with the most votes became President and the runner-up Vice-President. Jefferson and Burr agreed to run as a team, with Burr expecting to serve as Jefferson's second. When the vote came in tied, Burr reneged, and the election was thrown into the House of Representatives. On the thirty-sixth ballot, Jefferson was elected President and Burr Vice-President, and, not long after, Congress proposed the Twelfth Amendment to the Constitution, which provided for separate balloting for the two offices.

One of the deciding votes for Jefferson was cast by Claiborne's forebear, William Charles Cole Claiborne, who was then twenty-five years old and had already served as a justice of the Supreme Court of Tennessee. His payoff was an appointment as Governor of Mississippi and, a few years later, when he was twenty-eight, he became the first non-French Governor of Louisiana.[6] Tom Kelly, who wrote the column about the parish voting case, kept up with Claiborne long after. "My wife is a sprig off the old aristocracy of New Orleans," Kelly said in 1985, "and she's always said that the Claibornes are the first family of Louisiana society."[7]

Claiborne's genealogy has exotic shoots as well as deep Louisiana roots. His brother Omer sells primitive art and antiques in Santa Fe.[8] His sister is Liz Claiborne, and in her world Louis is the one who needs an introduction. In 1976, Liz and her husband founded a women's clothing company named after her. On the strength of its elegant line, the company took less than a decade to climb into the Fortune 500 with over half-a-billion dollars of sales.[9]

In 1970, after eight years of arguing civil rights cases, Louis Claiborne left the SG's office for the first time. He said, "I left with a pull and a push."[10] The push was his sense after a year working for the Nixon Administration that his role in shaping arguments before the Supreme Court had been diminished. He was not the only valued lawyer to leave the SG's office during the Nixon years. The impression given by some senior Administration officials that they considered themselves above the law prompted rapid turnover in the SG's office. At one point, Erwin Griswold noticed that he was the only lawyer left who had graduated from Harvard Law School. At a dinner for his staff, the former Harvard dean went around the table introducing everyone by his credentials. When he came to Claiborne, he said, "And then there's Louie. Louie and I are the Alpha and Omega of the office. I won't say which is which."[11]

The pull was that Claiborne had an English wife who wanted to go home. The Ford Foundation had offered him a fellowship to write about the law, and he took it. "Three or four years later," Claiborne said, "I became a barrister and practiced for a few years with modest success."

In the mid-seventies, Claiborne began to come back to the SG's office during summers to make some extra money by filling in for lawyers on vacation. Once, he arrived before the close of Term and had the chance to argue a case in the Supreme Court. With a nudge from a colleague,[12] he proposed a departure from the SG's traditional garb. He had already set himself apart from other men in the office by buying his own formal outfit. (Most pass around five sets of hand-me-down gear, distinguished by size and wear and tear; they put on the one that fits best and, fastened in with safety pins, appear elegant only when they are viewed from a generous distance.)[13] With his own sense of folderol, Claiborne had another thought.

He explained: "I was a full-fledged barrister. The rules of the bar of England and Wales are that whenever you appear, whether in Great Britain or at a distant bar, you must always appear in the wig and gown. Using that as a pretext, I called Warren Burger's chambers at the Supreme Court and asked if I could have audience with him. His secretary was rather testy, so I told her it was to talk about a subject dear to the Chief Justice's heart: proper dress in the courtroom for lawyers. He called me back immediately, all ears. By way of asking him if I could appear in my wig and gown, I told him about the British rules. Then he said that he himself should be in a wig and gown, and had been cheated out of it by Thomas Jefferson. I didn't follow, so he told me about an exhibit in the Supreme Court lobby showing Chief Justice John Jay in a magnificent red robe, with a proper gentleman's wig. It followed that Burger should be so adorned, and would be, if Jefferson hadn't changed the rules. I wasn't sure whether he was being humorous or not, but I brought him back to my predicament, and asked him what I should do. He said he thought it was entirely appropriate for me to appear in my wig and gown, but warned that others might disagree. I went down to the Solicitor General's office—he was then Bob Bork—and told about this conversation. He said I had been a damn fool to ask permission, that I should have just done it. In any case, discretion got the better part of valor: I, not forbidden either by the Chief Justice or the Solicitor General, decided to go back to the standard getup of the SG, and so I did."[14]

In 1978, Claiborne returned full-time to the SG's office. He was put in charge of cases rising from the Environmental Protection Agency, the Department of the Interior, and the Lands Division at the Department of Justice, dealing with Indian affairs, environmental questions, and so on. "My cases dealt with the land and the sea and the air," he said. The subject appealed to his sense of grandeur, and it fit his arch prose. "With this decision," he wrote about a case dealing with a lagoon near Venice, California, over which the state had exercised authority he thought it didn't have,[15] "the California Supreme Court appears enthusiastically to have embraced a new legal Renaissance, in which modern 'humanists' rediscover old texts and invoke the distant past to liberate the spirit from the confining 'shackles' of a more conventional era. But we are not witnessing Petrarch, mildly unorthodox in reviving Cicero, or Boccaccio retelling irreverent stories borrowed from Ovid. Here, the half-forgotten ancient models are the codes of the Emperor Justinian and Alfonso the Wise of Castile, the Magna Carta wrested from King John and the treatise of Henry de Bracton. We may question whether such a revolution, not in literature or philosophy, but in the law of property, even on the claim of returning to an earlier wisdom, is equally to be applauded."

Claiborne also took responsibility for an area known as original jurisdiction. It was a classic SG assignment: becoming expert in a hidden area of the law that can have deep importance to the parties before the Court. (According to the *Stanford Law Review*,[16] the Justices decided 123 cases under original jurisdiction between 1789 and 1957, for an average of between one and two a Term, but even the Supreme Court does not know how many OJ cases have now been before the Justices.)[17] Though Claiborne was linked to Judge Skelly Wright as a liberal activist, and was sometimes accused by colleagues of taking liberties with the law to see justice done, original jurisdiction showed him to be as meticulous a craftsman as anyone in the SG's office. "Louie's one of those gemstones with a number of facets not all of which you'd expect on the same rock," a former assistant to the SG said.[18]

"In all cases affecting Ambassadors, other public Ministers and Consuls, and those in which a State shall be a party," the Constitution reads, "the Supreme Court shall have original jurisdiction." The idea was that cases about the structure of the federal government or controversies between the United States and foreign countries should be resolved by a tribunal worthy of the parties before it. Because diplomats have immunity from most lawsuits, only three cases involving Ambassadors have arisen,[19] but OJ cases have raised serious questions about the relationship between the states and the federal government.

In recent years, the big OJ cases have involved disputes about America's offshore boundaries, because the limits on the territorial lines of the United States determine where states can allow drilling for oil and gas, and huge sums of money (three billion dollars in some cases) are at stake. By coincidence, given Claiborne's native state and his expertise, a good number of conflicts involved Louisiana and its craggy, inverted coast. For many years, the Solicitor General has delegated OJ cases to one lawyer. The part calls for thinking and writing about arcane notions that change little over long spans of time, and the Supreme Court almost always takes the lawyer's advice. Out of the limelight, Louis Claiborne became the world's leading expert on original jurisdiction.[20]

The Solicitor General who asked Claiborne to pick up the OJ brief was Wade McCree, in the Carter Administration. Claiborne admired his commitment to the SG's office. "He was very conscious of the independence of the office. He never hesitated to make the decision that might well stir questions. He took the position that, as SG, you didn't need to seek permission for a judgment, you just made it. Nobody would have dared ask him to fudge his views."[21]

When the Reagan Administration came in, and Rex Lee became SG, Claiborne wondered what his impact on the office would be. "Frankly, I was apprehensive, not because it was Rex Lee, but because it was a new Administration. But I was pleasantly surprised to find Lee extraordinarily likable and pretty clear about maintaining the independence of the office. He even took the advice of the civil servants, for which he was hounded. One assumes that some of the grumbling voiced in the legal press represented the views of the political leaders: that he was too timid about forcing the President's agenda in the Supreme Court, that he preferred to tap on the door instead of kicking it down. Unlike any other Administration, with the possible exception of the Kennedy Administration, this one has a clear idea where it wants to go and thinks it sees how to get there. The law is one of the obvious tools, and the Supreme Court is an obvious forum, and it's quite unacceptable for the Solicitor General or anyone else to filter the message."

Soon after Lee arrived, he arranged a breakfast so that Attorney General William French Smith could meet the Deputy SGs. He asked each one to say something about his background and responsibilities. "When my turn came," Claiborne said, "I told him I was a holdover from the Thomas Jefferson Administration. French Smith apparently lacked my sense of humor: he looked as if I had just uttered an obscenity. An aide leaned over and said, 'He means Kennedy,' not knowing about my comings and goings during most of the Nixon era as well, and that was worse."

In the fall of 1981, Claiborne caused Lee what the SG later called his "first major crisis."[22] "Here was a case that shows the unpredictable twists that there are more of in the Reagan Administration than in any other,"[23] Claiborne recalled. In Nevada, a federal district judge had parceled out water rights to the Carson River. An irrigation project had diverted water from that and another river, "to increase irrigation for Sunday farmers who waste water at a scandalous rate," Claiborne said, and, because of the project, water had fallen in Pyramid Lake, "which is a great natural wonder." The drop had jeopardized the fishery of the Pyramid Lake Paiute Indian tribe.

In the Alpine case, as it was called, the government originally argued that the farmers were entitled to no more water for irrigation than certain long-term contracts provided. The trial judge ruled that the farmers could take as much water as they needed. "That was a preposterous notion that ought to have agitated the Department of the Interior," Claiborne recalled, "but it chose not to appeal the case." Senator Paul Laxalt, the Republican from Nevada, also urged the government not to appeal. Laxalt wrote a "Dear Bill" letter to William French Smith:

RE: ALPINE APPEAL

While it's fresh in my mind . . .

—This has immense political overtones out there. All those ranchers—who are our friends—feel they're finally going to get some relief from this Administration. To have to go through the legal expense and hassle of an appeal will be a real "downer" for them.

And:

> —If Rex's shop thinks the Indians can intervene, let them. Even have Justice assist in fulfillment of whatever fiduciary responsibility exists, if any. Then at least the monkey won't be on our political backs.
> —Lastly, this would be a badly needed signal—that in a proper case the Attorney General will overrule the careerists in Justice who have never been with us and will never be. [24]

Having the man known as President Reagan's best friend on Capitol Hill serve as a lobbyist for the farmers put extraordinary pressure on Lee. But the Solicitor General took the advice of Claiborne and another lawyer, and appealed. He lost.

In an internal memo recommending that the Solicitor General join the Indians in asking the Supreme Court to consider the case, Claiborne wrote, "It is, of course, arguable here—as in most cases—that 'enough is enough' and that we ought not to pursue a hopeless cause, however meritorious, to the bitter end when four judges below have rejected our arguments. But, needless to say, there can be no such inflexible rule." [25] Though the Department of the Interior had "never favored" the SG with "a complete report," there were "at least 350 *recent*" cases in which the trial judge's ruling in favor of the farmers would raise serious problems. If the judge's decision stood, the amount of water available for the Pyramid Lake fishery would be diminished. If the government pulled out of the case, the Indians would not be represented in the case, since the tribe had failed to gain permission to intervene. To Claiborne's mind, the U.S. government was "not as free as otherwise we might be to abandon ship, leaving the tribal interest to sink uncaptained." The memo was initialed in Claiborne's Declaration of Independence–worthy hand: a swooping "LC."

While Rex Lee believed that the Court of Appeals had been wrong to favor the farmers, he also thought that the holding had limited importance. He approved the request of the Indians to intervene as a formal party, but opposed their petition asking the Supreme Court to take the case. The Justices declined certiorari, and the case rested as the lower courts had decided. "In the Court of Appeals, Rex did the bold thing," Claiborne said, "and stayed with the case. But he learned the wrong lesson. Instead of realizing his independence, he figured he should be more politically sensitive. In those days, with James Watt running the Interior Department, they wanted to give away the store: to grant mineral leases that should not have been; to grant leases at lower royalties than was warranted; to let developers exploit land instead of preserving it in its natural state; to let oil companies drill on the outer continental shelf, on the theory that the United States should be independent of Arab oil. They wanted to favor the white farmer over Indian tribes regardless of legal rights. They cut corners in indefensible ways."[26]

Claiborne had never interpreted his responsibility as a lawyer in the SG's office to mean he should engage in no-holds-barred advocacy for either the Administration in power or the government. He sometimes gave what he called "my lecture on the self-destructive habits of the American legal establishment, both lawyers and 'jumped-up lawyers' sitting on the Bench, calculated to bring the law into disrepute by encouraging needless complexity, indulging in undue prolixity and tolerating endless procedural maneuvering," in the service of unjust results. He took the lecture to heart. A case about the decision to restart a nuclear power plant in Pennsylvania, after another one partially melted down in the 1979 accident known as Three Mile Island, particularly bothered him. Claiborne's judgment about the slowness of the nuclear regulatory process convinced him to support the government's position that the plant should go on line again. In an internal memo with his recommendation, he explained "that our system permits scandalously protracted and costly proceedings, even at the administrative level, and the consequence of acquiescing in the present decision would be to delay restart for much too long." But he also said, "Accordingly, I must agree that we should ask the Supreme Court to announce a rule that no non-lawyer will ever understand: that THE LAW does not care whether people living next door to a nuclear power plant, whose twin has recently gone bad, lose their peace of mind (or even their sanity), their family harmony, their community cohesion, or their property values. As it happens, the prospects of the High Court so ruling are very good.

And so," he concluded, "I cannot counsel against seizing the opportunity to win a predictable 'victory.' " The government won the Court's unanimous backing. [27]

As the Alpine case suggested, the problems created for the SG's office during the Reagan Administration were often of a different order. With William Bradford Reynolds setting the example, Claiborne's adversaries in the Environmental Protection Agency, the Lands Division of the Justice Department, and the Department of the Interior pressed the Solicitor General to approach the law as radically as they did. Claiborne said, "In the past, more often than not, when an assistant to the Solicitor General or a deputy disagreed with other parts of the government, he could persuade them to go along. He was that much better a lawyer, and they respected his judgment about the law. In the Reagan years, if there has been disagreement, the SG has been seen as a pushover. It's often been done nicely, but still, Lee didn't like to say no to the political appointees. Maybe he felt vulnerable because of all the carping from the New Right. He wanted to show himself as independent of the careerists. But everything became a controversy, and it made for a lot more work. The truth is that nine out of ten times this office got it right. That's our job. The telling point was the predictability with which the staff, when they wanted to hold the line, lost ground because of the Solicitor General. The old-time practice in the SG's office usually succeeded at keeping politics at bay. The Reagan style seemed to accent the politics, and sometimes made the law an afterthought. In the end, I think Lee was quite happy to call it a day and be free of the nagging from both sides. I doubt he had a single day of peace." [28]

In the fall of 1985, Claiborne announced he was retiring from the SG's office. The fun had gone out of the job for him, he said, and his wife was eager to move back to England. The last argument he made on behalf of the government came in December. The case was called U.S. v. Maine, No. 35, Original Jurisdiction, but Maine had long since dropped out of the case, so the cover of the SG's brief included a parenthesis identifying it as a Massachusetts boundary case. [29] The more accessible of the questions before the Court was whether the waters of Nantucket Sound qualified as inland waters, as Massachusetts insisted, or as "high seas," under a doctrine called "ancient title." The more remote of the questions dealt with the standard of evidence the Justices should impose.[30]

Before the argument, in his morning coat, a starched white shirt, and a striped silver tie, Claiborne admitted,[31] "It's of no practical importance, unless they find gold there, or buried treasure. The truth is that the case is still before the Court because of an ambiguity that arose through an accident of timing. When the last decision was shaped, one law clerk to a Justice wrote the first part but couldn't finish before his year ended. Another wrote the second, and therein lies the problem." The two clerks had adopted different theories of the case, according to Claiborne, and confused a special master appointed by the Justices to help resolve the case on a key point of law.

The government's brief was vintage Claiborne.[32] "In light of our acquiescence in the Special Master's recommendation that Vineyard Sound be declared part of the inland waters of Massachusetts, the only issue now before the Court is whether the waters of Nantucket Sound also qualify as inland (as the Commonwealth asserts), or, rather, constitute territorial sea and high seas (the Master's conclusion, which we support)." And: "That single question, alas, has spawned a dozen sub-issues and no lack of words, some apparently self-contradictory and many of them wide of the mark as it seems to us. Our endeavor will be to put the case back on track in as short a space as possible."

In his argument before the Justices, as well as his brief, Claiborne tried to do that and he eventually won the case.[33] His opposing counsel was Henry Herman, a lawyer for Massachusetts who also made a well-spoken presentation. After the argument, while Claiborne was catching his breath in the SG's office at the Supreme Court, Herman knocked on the door and asked Claiborne if he was free to meet later for a drink. They made a date, and the Massachusetts lawyer said, "The Great Claiborne. I've always wanted to argue a case against you, and now I have."[34]

Several weeks before, at the Officers' Club of Fort McNair in Washington, many current and former members of the SG's office had gathered for an event labeled "A Farewell Buffet upon his Departure to Reside in England," in Claiborne's honor.[35] A quartet of SGs (Erwin Griswold, Robert Bork, Rex Lee, and Charles

Fried) made generous remarks about Claiborne, and then Claiborne spoke. He offered a challenge for the future instead of nostalgia. He had written out his remarks in longhand on small sheets of buff-colored paper, in stanzas of blank verse, and, in bright yellow Magic Marker, had highlighted the words he wanted to stress. [36] "I fear that most of you are here under some *deception,*" he began, "that I am about to *fade* into the wilds of Essex, never to be seen again on this side of the Atlantic. Which perhaps augurs for a last look at this disappearing species, and certainly explains the extravagant remarks I have heard this evening: they were obviously spoken in the firm expectation that their truth would never be tested." He announced his intention to begin a transatlantic practice as a private counselor. ("Louis Fenner Claiborne, onetime public and private practitioner in Louisiana, sometime common lawyer at the bar of England and Wales, longtime Deputy Solicitor General of the United States, is now resuming the occasional private practice of law before the American appellate courts and international tribunals [standing, sitting or off-stage parts]," [37] read the formal announcement he soon mailed: it came with a Claiborne sonnet titled "Have Quill, Will Travel," which argued that it was not foolhardy to hire a lawyer based in England ["Why care about proximity today?/Concorde exists and so does Express Mail"] to argue in the United States Supreme Court, and ended: "If this be puffery, make the most of it./Or, better still, reward the joke of it.") Eventually, he shifted to a more serious tone.

"So far as my education in the law is concerned," he said, "I am proud to say that my principal post-graduate tutor was Judge Skelly Wright, who is here tonight." Judge Wright's health was poor, and though he had not yet notified the President, he had decided to take senior status as a judge. The Reagan Administration would be able to name a replacement who would give the President's appointees a conservative majority on the D.C. Circuit, which, two decades before, Wright had helped make the most liberal in the country. "For better or worse, he is responsible for my coming to the Solicitor General's office some twenty-three years ago," Claiborne continued. "With such a tutor, it follows that I was raised right, as they say in the South, and have, by and large, behaved accordingly. For me, it is too late in the day to cast off what we call the Old Humility in order to take up the New Arrogance that now prevails. And so I leave with no reluctance."

Claiborne asked a young member of the SG's staff to fetch a large, oddly shaped crate, made from cardboard boxes used by laundries to pack clean shirts, and went on, "So you will not forget me too quickly, I have something to leave behind, which I hope the new Solicitor General will put on display, perhaps in his office. The object inside the box is one of a very rare species called *Egretta Caelesis Generalis.* You will notice its pure white coat and its aloof stance. Originally, I painted him showing only his left profile, but, in deference to the times, I decorated the other side as well. He is therefore reversible, but he will not bend or stoop for anyone. I am encouraged to think that my creation bears a strong resemblance to the next Solicitor General. But, just in case, I leave him behind to watch over you all."

To understand Claiborne's gift, it was necessary to know a story from the SG's past. Robert Jackson was Solicitor General before becoming Attorney General and then a Justice on the Supreme Court. Justice Louis Brandeis thought that Jackson was so skilled an advocate he should be made SG for life.[38] During Jackson's tenure, a letter addressed simply to "The Celestial General, Washington, D.C.," found its way to him.[39] Until the Reagan Administration, the lofty title was an emblem of the Solicitor General among lawyers in the office.

Out of the box Charles Fried took a wooden cutout of an erect white egret, of the Celestial General species. The room filled with delighted clapping, and brows were raised in mild astonishment. Fried was momentarily speechless.

XI

Charles Fried

CHARLES FRIED'S DÉBUT as Solicitor General was a celebration of the Reagan Right. It took place at the Hyatt Regency Hotel at the foot of Capitol Hill one November night, and it was convened not in honor of Fried but as an event called "Saluting an American Hero: A Tribute to Wm. Bradford Reynolds."[1] The buffet for Louis Claiborne a few weeks before had been a quiet affair dedicated to memories and tradition. The Reynolds salute was a campaign rally, a great time, an exercise in forgetting. The pretext was the presentation to Reynolds of the Winston Churchill Award, but the hum of voices, the glee and rounds of applause, brought to mind a giddy political roast where all the speakers had been guaranteed they could say whatever they wanted about their absent nemeses with no ill consequences. The tables were set with lilies, the head table was draped in red so it would show up well on TV, and about six hundred people gathered in a large hall to let the world know, as the evening's host put it, "When anyone attacks Brad Reynolds, they're attacking us."[2]

The host was Burton Yale Pines. He is chairman of the National Center for Public Policy Research, the group that sponsored the dinner, and a vice-president of the Heritage Foundation, of which the Center for Public Policy Research is a neutrally named part, and he gave the welcome to the network of New Righters, Religious Righters, Cultural Conservatives, Pro-Lifers, and others who helped pay for the party: Joseph and Holly Coors, whose family controls Coors beer; the Liberty Institute; World Youth Crusade for Freedom; National Pro-Life PAC; National Right to Life Committee; and other organizations whose names filled a page in the evening's program. 3 In the audience, among others, were former civil rights lawyers who had become allies of Reynolds while working on cases with the Justice Department, and who paid fifty dollars each to show their admiration. Some realized they had crossed a line by attending the dinner. "Coming here was harder than it would have been to tell my mom I'd come out of the closet," one said, with an embarrassed laugh. "I'd just as soon people didn't know I was here." 4

The master of ceremonies was Representative Henry Hyde, a Republican from Illinois, whose amiable liberal-bashing set the evening's tone. "One of the senators that gave Brad rather an unpleasant time over in the Upper Chamber, as we laughingly call it—I don't want you to think he was liberal, but I once asked him what he thought of the Indianapolis 500, and he said, 'They're not guilty!' "

Congressman Hyde initiated the list of Reynolds's virtues, and others took the next several hours to fill it out: courage; integrity; brilliance; idealism; patriotism; morality; incandescence; faithfulness to public service; commitment to important and traditional values; conservatism; warmth; genuineness; honesty; painstaking concern; humanitarianism; humor; and, the evening's theme, heroism. 5 Hyde also read a telegram from Ronald Reagan, who declared that "Brad has fought the good fight with energy, enthusiasm, and an unflinching commitment to the principle of equality under the law." His "dedication to justice, to professional excellence, and to civil rights for all Americans is a shining example for public servants." The President told everyone that "Nancy joins me in sending best wishes for a memorable event," and signed his greeting, "God bless you."

On the dais sat a rainbow coalition of Reagan conservatives: Roy Innis, black chairman of the Congress of Racial Equality; Madeleine Will, Assistant Secretary of Education in charge of services for the handicapped; Clarence Pendleton, chairman of the U.S. Civil Rights Commission; Senator Orrin Hatch; and Attorney General Edwin Meese. Pendleton was the most prominent black in the Reagan Administration, and he summarized the Reagan-Meese-Reynolds line on civil rights. He took as his text a passage from Rousseau.

"People once accustomed to masters are no longer in condition to do without them," he read. "If they try to shake off the yoke, they still move farther away from freedom, because they confuse it with an unbridled license and their revolutions nearly always deliver them into the hands of seducers who only make their chains heavier than before." The specific "yokes and chains" he had in mind were goals and timetables in affirmative action. He ended, "Brad, I'm proud to be your colleague and your friend, and together we will make this country a place where, as Langston Hughes once said in a poem, 'Freedom,' where 'Freedom is just the frosting on someone else's cake, till we learn how to bake.' Let's turn the ovens on, Brad!"

Hatch made the keynote speech. He asserted that the Senate Judiciary Committee owed Reynolds a deep apology. He made no mention of the reasons that had led a majority of the members, including two Republicans, to doubt Reynolds's truthfulness and commitment to the law. Hatch joked that the Democrats had voted against Reynolds to keep him on the civil-rights watch. He also suggested that they had "tarred and feathered" Reynolds. The Assistant Attorney General's was the "toughest" confirmation hearing Hatch had ever taken part in, and during it "Brad sat stoic as a bust at Mount Rushmore." Hatch stated that Reynolds had done "more than anyone to shape civil-rights policies in the United States since Abraham Lincoln."

When Reynolds spoke, he sounded shy and almost wary. The day before, the Washington *Post* had run a story under the banner "REYNOLDS SAYS HE'S BEEN TO THE MOUNTAINTOP," in which he advised that he was extending the tradition of Martin Luther King, Jr., and other civil-rights leaders of the nineteen-sixties. "I was pretty much in lockstep with that whole effort," he said.[6] At the tribute, Reynolds did not mention Dr. King. He called the event "a great affair," and identified himself as a "foot soldier" in Reagan's army. His "battle scars acquired in our struggle to preserve for all Americans those fundamental ideals that distinguish this country from all others" were "badges of honor." Reynolds also invoked Lincoln. "Let every man remember that to violate the law," he read without irony from the President's words, "is to trample on the blood of his father, and to tear the character of his own, and of his children's liberty."

As part of the program before Reynolds spoke, his onetime aide and Assistant Attorney General–designate, Charles Cooper, offered ornate reflections on "the contemporary state of the 'public man.' "[7] The quote was from a 1760 speech by James Otis denouncing the British. Reynolds was cast as an American revolutionary. "The only principles of public conduct that are worthy of a gentleman," Cooper pronounced with Otis's help, "are to sacrifice estate, ease, health, applause, and even life, to the sacred calls of his country." In Cooper's eyes, Reynolds had met this standard. He was "an honorable man who has had his integrity called into question." He was "a sensitive and friendly man who was cruelly defamed, excoriated, and ridiculed." Skipping to the words of Edmund Burke, Cooper said that the "slander" was all right: "obloquy is a necessary ingredient in the composition of all true glory"; "calumny and abuse are essential parts of triumph. . . . He may live long, he may do much more; but here is the summit: he never can exceed what he does this day." Cooper paused to let his words sink in, and, in a hushed voice, finished, "Brad, dear friend, here is the summit."

Charles Fried introduced Cooper. To most of the lawyers in the Solicitor General's office, few of whom were invited to the dinner or later heard about Fried's appearance, it would have been an enlightening performance. Among staffers in the SG's office, Cooper was known for his hot temper and his habit of fighting to the limit on every issue.[8] Like Reynolds, his friend and compatriot from the Bob Jones team, Cooper seemed to see every case involving a disagreement between the Civil Rights Division and the SG's office under Rex Lee as a test of will. Fried noted only that Cooper was "famous in Alabama as one of the most brilliant graduates" of the University of Alabama Law School, where he was editor-in-chief of the *Alabama Law Review,* and "famous at the Supreme Court as one of the most brilliant law clerks to Justice Rehnquist."

Before Fried praised Cooper, he made general remarks that drew applause. For an academic without much experience at political rallies, it was a good outing. To the assembly of Reynolds and Reagan supporters, Fried's talk confirmed what they had figured from his briefs: he was a team player.

"By 1980," Fried lectured, "this country was in danger of becoming a quota society. By 1980, we were in danger of a situation with jobs—private and public sector—educational opportunities, housing, judgeships—all the good things were being handed out, not on merit, but by a racial and ethnic and religious and gender spoils system. The American people elected Ronald Reagan to restore the idea of equality of opportunity and the great ideal of the unity of all mankind. Today that danger is further from us than it was in 1980. And if Ronald Reagan has been able to keep his promise, it is largely because of the work of Brad Reynolds. It has been a great honor to have Brad as a collaborator in the Department of Justice. It has been a great honor to agree and disagree with Brad, to learn from him, to persuade him, and be persuaded by him. It has principally and overwhelmingly been an honor to have Brad as a friend. It is that friendship, after all, that we are all here to acknowledge and celebrate. Let me say that in the last few months we have all learned that Reagan people make the very best friends."

CHARLES FRIED is a vivid, angular man who makes expansive gestures. His admirers call him passionate and charming. When he arrived as the political deputy in early 1985, lawyers who worked in the SG's office described Fried as "strange." [9] In November, not long after the start of his tenure as SG and the week following the Reynolds dinner, this writer had an experience with him that led me to think that, at least sometimes, he floated in his own world. When I came into the Solicitor General's suite one morning to keep an appointment, [10] Fried was sitting in a chair pulled up to the middle of an oblong conference table, looking through a large window to a spectacular vista down Constitution Avenue toward the east. In the foreground was the classical headquarters of the National Archives (with a Corinthian portico, a huge pediment framing statues of "Heritage" and "Guardianship," and the largest bronze doors in the world); [11] in the middle distance was the marble palace of the National Gallery of Art; and, a mile away, against a background of sky, the United States Capitol. The Supreme Court peeked over trees to the left of the Capitol dome.

Compared to every office at the Justice Department except the Attorney General's, the SG's is a dominion. Soon after former

Solicitor General William Mitchell became Attorney General, in 1929, he took charge of the design for the Justice Department building, which opened in 1935. Since the SG was then the second-ranking officer in the department, and served as Acting AG when the AG was out of town, Mitchell thought that the SG's suite should match the Attorney General's. Right up to the private elevator, it does. [12] The ceilings are twenty feet high, the decoration is aluminum Art Deco, and the space extends into a nook which holds a standard lawyer's desk, to a back room with a TV, and up a flight of stairs to a hideaway equipped with a sofa bed. The day of the visit, the space over the mantelpiece was bare. "John W. Davis used to be there," Fried explained with a smile, either amused by what he was about to say or anticipating future pleasure from a higher form of art. "Even though he was one of my predecessors and said to be a very good lawyer, and had hung there a very long time, I thought I could do better." Fried strode to his desk to get a copy of a letter he had written to the Chief Curator of the National Gallery of Art, in which he compared his office to Charlie Chaplin's quarters in *The Great Dictator,* and asked for a fine painting to hang over the fireplace.

We talked for a while in the office, and then Fried suggested we continue over lunch nearby. The restaurant at the National Gallery where we planned to eat was crowded when we got there, so we decided to try someplace else. But on the way, Fried said, "Have you got time? I want to show you a picture that captures the feeling of my view down Constitution Avenue." We entered the Gallery's old West Building, threaded through a series of galleries, and stopped in front of a painting by Nicolas Poussin, done in 1648. [13] "There!" Fried said. "That's my view."

Called "Holy Family on the Steps," it was a portrait of the Virgin Mary and Jesus Christ, and Joseph, Elizabeth, and her son John the Baptist. I had expected a literal depiction of the view from Fried's window, and was faced with a historical painting by the dominant French artist of the seventeenth century. It required a leap of imagination to see the painting in relation to the view from the SG's office.

While the ground for the figures of the Holy Family included a brilliant sky and the classical temple before which they were pictured had a portico with Corinthian columns, the painting focused on the boy Jesus accepting an apple from the young John and other symbols of Christian tradition. It seemed to have far more to do with religion and humanity than with architectural vistas. As in his understanding of the law, Fried made a connection that was grand and idiosyncratic, and spurned the obvious.

"Don't you see?" Fried asked. "The temple is in the place of the National Archives, and there's the sky, just like mine." He paused, and beamed at the painting. "I'm in your hands," he said.

AT THE GREAT HALL in the Folger Shakespeare Library, a couple of blocks from the Supreme Court, one February evening in 1986, Charles Fried gave an address called "Framers' Intent: A Meditation on Sonnet 65 and the Constitution."[14] It was a cold, blowy night, and the audience was small: regular library patrons, graduate students, and a corps of Fried's friends, including writers like Henry Brandon, formerly with the *Times* of London; William Safire, of *The New York Times;* and columnist Edwin Yoder.

Fried describes himself as a polymath ("I've probably taught more subjects and practiced less law than anyone who's been SG," he said),[15] and, like many academics, he had noted similarities between debates about constitutional interpretation and debates about literary theory. He wanted to share his thoughts about them.[16] Fried asked, Does the meaning of a poem reside in the author's intent, or of the Constitution in the Framers'? Or does it spring from "the critical reader's free response to contemporary conditions, whether it be in the Constitution or a poem?" He began with the poem, Shakespeare's Sonnet 65:

> Since brass, nor stone, nor earth, nor boundless sea,
> But sad mortality o'ersways their power,
> How with this rage shall beauty hold a plea,
> Whose action is no stronger than a flower?
> O, how shall summer's honey breath hold out
> Against the wrackful siege of battering days,
> When rocks impregnable are not so stout,
> Nor gates of steel so strong, but time decays?

O fearful meditation! where, alack,
Shall Time's best jewel from Time's chest lie hid?
Or what strong hand can hold his swift foot back?
Or who his spoil of beauty can forbid?
   O, none, unless this miracle have might,
   That in black ink my love may still shine bright.

"Well," Fried said, "let's take a first and, I apologize, rather obvious cut at what the poem is about, and you will see in a moment why I burden you with these perhaps obvious observations." There was the contrast between the solid and the extremely transitory: brass, stones, rocks, and gates of steel versus beauty, the strength of a flower, honey breath, and love. As time was to brass and steel, so stone and steel were to beauty and love, which showed how transitory and weak the latter were. Fried said, "So what we have in the end is yet another poem about the potency of time, a poem about change and about decay. And, really, it's about the potency of time and its cunning, its kind of implacable potency, for if you try to hide from time, the way Jonah tried to hide from the Lord in the belly of the whale, you can't evade it. Time's chest is not a place for safekeeping, but an engulfing, kind of an active force, a voracious rage, which sucks up matter and puts it into nowhere."

The rage of impermanence seemed unstoppable, except by "black ink." A pot of ink dumped into the sea might disappear immediately, but that was Shakespeare's miracle. On paper, it could outwit time, and save what was flimsier than stones. "And for how long?" Fried queried. "Well, for about four hundred years." He observed offhandedly, "Now, this of course is the standard poet's theme. One might almost say that it is the perennial theme of poetry. The ravage of time, the impermanence of things, and the reason for that is worth pondering for a moment, because time is after all the greatest mystery of human experience, because it is the sense of time which animals do not have which allows us to plan, which allows us a sense of our own continuity, which gives us a sense of the future, and makes us human." Fried paused, and said, "Well, all of that is rather obvious, so let's change the subject."

Referring to Justice William Brennan in particular, whose work he presented in caricature, Fried went on, "There are those who say that to attempt to understand the words of the Constitution according to the intention of those who conceived it almost two hundred years ago is so obviously, so hopelessly unavailable, that the invocation of that is either foolish or a subterfuge, what has been called 'arrogance cloaked as humility.' The objection is that we cannot know the intention of those so distant from us in time's circumstance. I think the objection is not that it is inconvenient or even bad to ask about the original intention of the Framers, but that the 'wrackful siege of battering days' has made that very enterprise devoid of sense. Words simply cannot now mean what they did then, surrounded as they now are by new contexts. They may seem comprehensible and familiar, but a proper historical sense reveals that they are mere homonyms of their present counterparts. And so meaning too cannot hold out 'when rocks impregnable are not so stout, nor gates of steel so strong, but Time decays.' And that, of course, is a 'fearful meditation' indeed."

On the one hand, Fried conjectured, perhaps it was not so fearful after all. "Maybe in our impotence is potency, since freed of past meanings we are free, quite marvelously free, to make new ones, according to our present needs, visions, whims, what have you—so the idea that we cannot know the Framers' intent is perhaps a great liberation from the chains of the past." He asked, "Should we accept this line of argument? Is it true? Recall for a moment my exegesis of the obvious—the transparent meaning of Sonnet 65. Put aside for the moment the contents of that exegesis and recall just the act of it. You went along with it, or you didn't, and if you didn't, it was perhaps because you had a different, perhaps a better sense of what the poem meant. And in a way I tricked you, because in following along with me in my exegesis, whether you agreed with it or not, you agreed with my unstated, major premise—that the poem had meaning and that we could understand it, and that the intent to do so, rather than making up the meaning as we went along, was not arrogance cloaked as humility, but an ordinary act of human intelligence."

To Fried, the sonnet was not about the perennial theme of poetry at all, but about the nature of writing. "I think it's about words," he said. "The miracle that black ink can make the most fragile and evanescent of entities shine bright and that it can do so through time. But how do we know this? Why do we believe it? The poem is like one of those logician's tricks where the thing provides its own proof. The poem proves itself, for I contend that we all understand what the poem is claiming, and in understanding what the poem claims, we prove Shakespeare's contention that black ink can perform the miracle of causing meaning to shine bright across years. So it seems to me that the final meaning about the poem is about the power of poetry, and it proves its own thesis, just as the enterprise of discoursing about the Constitution and the possibility of understanding it, or not, proves that such discourse is possible. In addition, understanding the subject of the discourse, whether it's a poem or the Constitution, is also possible."

He went on, "Well, what about freedom?" As a straw man, Fried admitted, he had said that our inability to understand Shakespeare or the Constitution might be liberating. It might allow us to be creative and innovative. But, he continued, the ability to create something, like Shakespeare's poem, was an ability to stress thoughts and actions in words and transmit them over time. Fried declared, "It is the ability to transmit original intentions, if you like, Framer's intentions, across the void of time. Without that ability, we would be powerless to create and innovate."

Then Fried addressed the claim that "the Framers of the Constitution no more envisioned every application of their general terms than Shakespeare did the use I am making here of his sonnet. I think that's a dreadful red herring, which does indeed ignore the miracle of language and the miracle of general terms. For it's the very essence of language and the very essence of general terms to govern particular cases which were not envisaged by their authors. General terms are not mere compendia of the very specific instances which those who first employed them had in mind when they spoke them. If it were otherwise, we could never generate meanings." He continued, "What the miracle of language requires is that words, ideas, concepts reach new instances but that they do so definitely. Those who deny that language can reach new cases and those who claim that they can reach new cases but only indefinitely are really in the same camp. They are the enemies of meaning, and therefore the enemies of the very conditions of human creativity."

To Fried, a great deal was at stake here: "the integrity and meaning of human communication in general," and "the integrity of the tools of legal and political discourse." If he was correct about Shakespeare's meaning, then politics and law were not just a matter of power, but could be bound by words and reason as well. "And this is what law is," Fried stated. "It is a constraint, not of force but of reasons. The reasons that one man offers to another for his judgment and his action, the reasons that one age offers to another for its judgment and its action. So it means that the enterprise which the Framers embarked on in Philadelphia two hundred years ago was a possible enterprise, the establishment of a foundation of government, the structure for relations of power in a written Constitution—that is, in black ink." If we could understand Shakespeare's meaning in Sonnet 65, we could understand the Framers' meaning in the Constitution. "Not necessarily without difficulty," Fried admitted, "but that is not an objection in principal to making the effort. And the effort is what we owe to the texts of both."

Fried said, "The striking thing is that the courts are physically able, they can ignore the provisions of the Constitution, as can the President or a sheriff." The law was not a machine gun. It did not disable anyone from disagreeing. Whatever coercion the law exercised was guided by reason. "That's why the suggestion that we cannot understand the intentions of framers of laws, whether it's the Constitution or a law in its humbler manifestations, whether twenty years ago or two hundred years ago, is such a disturbing suggestion," Fried insisted. "It is that suggestion which I think Shakespeare refutes in Sonnet 65, and it is that miracle of meaning which we as free persons whose freedom is underwritten by the rule of law should celebrate."

Fried's lecture was intended as a contribution to the ongoing debate about the Jurisprudence of Original Intention between Attorney General Edwin Meese and Justice William Brennan, among others, and to throw in his lot with Meese. For many lawyers who heard about it in subsequent weeks, the most tactful thing to say was that, whatever the current vogue among scholars for using the techniques of literary criticism to explain the law, Fried had skipped over the obvious point that the Constitution is not a sonnet and that the meaning of a law is different from that of a poem. Like the Attorney General, Fried had also declined to answer the hard question of how you interpret America's fundamental law when the text is ambiguous about its meaning. As David Lauter, then of the *National Law Journal,* put it, the Solicitor General had displayed a gift for phrases that rose like perfect bubbles, and then burst, leaving nothing behind to help solve the problem they were meant to address. [17]

But cast in terms of constitutional metaphor rather than text, and in metaphor generally (with the word "intention" redefined to mean not the "mere compendia of the very specific instances which those who first employed them had in mind when they spoke them"—that is, Meese's understanding of the Framers' intent—but as the Framers' general "concepts" that could grow to cover "new instances"), the lecture sounded surprisingly like an affirmation of Brennan. The answer Fried gave to a question from William Safire strengthened this view.

" 'O fearful meditation,' " Safire said. "In Shakespeare's time, the word 'fearful' meant 'filled with fear,' not 'striking fear,' so 'O fearful meditation' might mean 'O meditation that strikes us with fear,' though, in his time, it meant 'the thought is filled with fear.' Now, the question, recognizing the ambiguity, is what do you think we ought to do about it? Do you think we ought to find out what the context was in 1660 to determine what he meant by that? Or do you think we ought to have that creative tension between that meaning and the one of today?" Fried replied, "If you were to persuade me that in 1660 it meant 'filled with fear' instead of 'striking fear,' and, in fact plainly so, but it reverberates with other meaning for you, so much the better."

Earlier, Fried had declared, "I think the nature of the legal debate is this: Are we people of the law, people of the book, if you like, or people who are governed by judges? I think that is very much the issue. Maybe the text isn't the last word, but it certainly ought to be the first." Yet when a "judge"—in this case, a reader and columnist and man who writes best-selling books about the meanings of words—posed a choice between a meaning from the time Shakespeare used it in a text and one from today, Fried told him to choose the contemporary meaning, if it "reverberated" for him, and "so much the better."

It was a confusing answer. As with other examples from Fried's scholarly and government record, the specific advice was ambiguous, and seemed to contradict his general pronouncement on the law. If not, the point was lost in nuances that the Solicitor General did not clarify.

XII

Friends
of the Court

CHARLES FRIED summed up the events that shaped his
outlook as a lawyer in March of 1985, at a seminar titled "Crisis
in the Courts," sponsored by the Manhattan Institute for Policy
Research. "I think by now there is a large measure of agreement
that many significant, yet misguided, policy trends developed in
the law during the mid-1960s,"[1] he said, and "a growing institutional paralysis—a kind of celebration of self-hatred for national
values and institutions—was fed by the emergence of what many
have called the 'new class,' a class in which lawyers and judges
played a large role." Fried reduced his ideas to a caustic phrase.
"Looking back at that time," Fried said about the sixties and
seventies, "I think it is clear that judges were among those who
'did it to us.' "

Judges "did it to us" by creating too many new rights, and by
"departing from common sense and moving in the direction of
elaborate rule systems," through landmark decisions like Miranda.
They did it by saying a psychiatrist could be sued for not warning
a woman that one of his patients had threatened to kill her. (The
doctor went to the police instead.) They did it by declaring that
every product on the market carried an implied warranty that
could never be disclaimed, or, after a business ran into trouble, by
undoing good contracts made by executives in moments of bad
judgment, to protect them from their folly.[2]

To Fried, these examples of "judicial activism" represented "an
attitude." He told the Chamber of Commerce at a speech in 1985,
"It's an attitude which says that everybody is constrained by law
except the judges. The judges do justice. The rest of us are con-

strained by law. Now, I think that is the philosophy which is so dangerous to us, and which, in a sense, represents"—here Fried digressed to another example before making his point—"lawlessness." As Solicitor General, the "most important function" he could serve was to fight this "attitude" and help "maintain the rule of law." He came to Washington "to do something about this terrible drift."[3]

In some ways, Fried's critique went wider than the Attorney General's. Meese directed his attack at the Supreme Court, and faulted the Justices for interpreting the Constitution more broadly than the Framers intended. Fried contended that judges in state courts whose responsibility was to make law in areas like torts and contract were just as blameworthy. "If somebody is hurt, you find a way to put money in their pocket,"[4] he said. "That's the crudity of the logic." As SG, Fried could do little about the drift in judge-made, or common, law except through lecturing. The Constitution was a different matter, and he recognized the choice he faced.

"If you are to respect other institutions, be less activist, and adhere to precedent," he observed at the Manhattan Institute, "you're going to be stuck with many of the ill-conceived legal decisions which occurred between 1960 and 1980. If you're less activist, you're going to be less creative about interpreting some really silly statutes which were passed during this period, which could do with a dose of negative activism." To return the law to its proper role in society, he believed that lawyers with his beliefs had to urge federal courts to undo doctrine left over from ill-founded decisions by liberal judges during the past generation. Putting the idea in the negative, he said, "Judicial restraint may require judges to be faithful to a lot of things which, in the abstract, don't deserve fidelity."[5]

The Solicitor General with whom Fried often compared himself in the first year of his tenure was Archibald Cox. He knew how well-regarded Cox was as SG, and Fried thought it would be instructive to show how his approach to the job closely followed Cox's.[6]

Both had come from Harvard Law to serve as Solicitor General in Administrations with well-defined notions of what they hoped to accomplish in the Supreme Court, he pointed out, and, as Cox had done a generation before, Fried believed that the role of the SG was to enter into a Socratic dialogue with the Justices—what he called "a conversation with the Court." Both men cut stern, impressive figures when they argued cases before the Justices, and the lawyers who worked for each described their bosses as pompous but dedicated, and eager to take an active hand in shaping the briefs submitted by the government under their names. Instead of writing briefs in longhand on yellow pads, as Cox did, Fried composed on his computer, but he was equally engaged in the business of his office. [7]

In the field of constitutional law, Cox made a study of the Warren Court that raised questions related to Fried's complaints about that Court's decisions. In a series of lectures delivered not long after his term as SG, Cox said that Earl Warren's appointment as Chief Justice "marked the opening of a new period in our constitutional development. In the next 15 years the Supreme Court rewrote, with profound social consequences, major constitutional doctrines governing race relations, the administration of criminal justice, and the operation of the political process." [8] To Cox, the Court's choice was whether to play a role equal to Congress's and the President's in shaping the nation's destiny, or leave new departures in social policy to the political branches. In theory, Cox found the predicament insoluble. The "extraordinary character" of the issues presented to the Warren Court meant that the Justices could not "ignore the political aspects" of their decisions, yet the best result for the country, according to social consensus, was often inconsistent with what was required by current law. In practice, in times like the fifties and sixties when the Justices felt obliged to act because the other branches of government hadn't, the Supreme Court could best uphold its constitutional duty through far-reaching decisions—and by searching for principles that gave the decisions the force of law. "I cannot prove these points," Cox granted, "but they are the faith to which we lawyers are dedicated." [9]

According to Fried, the costs of the Warren Court era were evident in the social tatters left by the explosion of law since the nineteen-sixties. The rate of crime was up, the amount of litigation had multiplied, the costs of insurance for doctors had driven some of them out of practice because of the rise in malpractice suits.[10] Too much law had stripped the law of its power, and, in Cox's term, led people to withhold their "consent" from judicial opinions when consent was essential to the authority of courts in society. Writing in the late sixties about constitutional law, Cox had wondered if this might come about as a result of the Warren Court's activism. The majority had sometimes been "notably unsuccessful in rationalizing new departures" and, "when cynically minded," Cox confessed, "one wonders whether it has made much effort. Occasionally decisions seem to turn on intuitive judgments of right and wrong rather than the impartial application of principle."[11] Without the power of reason to command consent, the Justices' opinions undermined the rule of law. They robbed the Justices of authority to solve problems when the Court became the institution of last resort.[12]

For all their agreement, Cox and Fried acted differently as SGs. As a former law clerk to Judge Learned Hand and a onetime junior lawyer in the SG's office, Solicitor General Cox believed it was his duty to restrain the recommendations for activism that rose through the rest of the Justice Department, and to exercise similar restraint on the arguments it made to the Supreme Court.

At the Kennedy Justice Department, according to Victor Navasky, in *Kennedy Justice,* Cox was known as the Solicitor "who couldn't see beyond the law."[13] He regularly challenged proposals of Attorney General Robert Kennedy and his aides by insisting that the law constrained them from doing what they wanted. In a series of suits known as the sit-in cases, the question appeared to be whether the government should file an amicus brief to support civil-rights protesters who had staged sit-ins at lunch counters, stores, and other Southern establishments that refused to serve blacks. To Cox, the question was not so elementary. The Fourteenth Amendment guaranteed equal protection of the laws against state action, but what was that? Cox equated state action with official action—the deeds of police, the rules governing city parks, admissions policies to state universities. The NAACP Legal Defense and Educational Fund, Inc. and other liberal groups equated state action with "public" action and distinguished it from private action, so that even if a restaurant or a hotel was privately owned, its services and legal character were public. If the owner of a segregated restaurant called in the police to throw out blacks who had staged a sit-in, the combination of the public nature of the restaurant and the official help of the police in getting rid of the protesters amounted to state action. The Civil Rights Act of 1964 removed the issue from the Supreme Court to Congress, which resolved the question as the civil-rights groups wanted.

Burke Marshall, who is now a professor at Yale Law School, was the head of the Civil Rights Division during Cox's tenure. Though he disagreed with Cox about the sit-in cases, he respected the SG's concern about the law. "He was determined to understand and be persuaded that these pro-civil-rights positions were the right positions to take because they were constitutionally and legally sound," Marshall said. "His concern was 'Don't mislead the Court into doing something that might look right now, but wrong a hundred years from now.' "[14] Cox fretted that advocates who thought the new definition of state action would benefit blacks had paid no attention to its potential costs. He thought that blacks as well as whites might lose the safeguard of private law if doctrines like trespass were eclipsed by expanding the notion of state action.[15]

Cox rarely made an argument as SG until he was convinced it was the logical solution to a legal problem, and when he could not make up his mind, he refused to choose a position just to have one. In one government case, he presented both sides to the Supreme Court. This was an antitrust suit against the St. Regis Paper Company, in which the Federal Trade Commission had subpoenaed records including the firm's confidential responses to questions from the U.S. Census Bureau. The FTC and the Justice Department's Antitrust Division said the reports could be subpoenaed. The Census Bureau and the Bureau of the Budget said they couldn't, because they contained privileged information. As Navasky told it, Cox "chose to go before the U.S. Supreme Court, and as the nine robed men sat there slightly awe-struck he commenced to argue both sides of the case as fully and honestly and persuasively as he knew how." With some pique, Justice Frankfurter asked, "How do you expect us to decide this matter if you can't even get an agreement inside the Justice Department?" Cox replied, "Oh, Mr. Justice. If the dispute were only inside the Justice Department, I'm sure I could settle it."[16]

The major clash between a favored social policy of the Kennedy Justice Department and Cox's judgment about the constraints of the law came in a series of cases dealing with reapportionment of state legislatures. The first case was Baker v. Carr,[17] in which the plaintiffs claimed that they had been denied the equal protection of the laws guaranteed by the Fourteenth Amendment. In Tennessee, where the case arose, legislative districts were apportioned according to a 1901 state law. Though major changes in the pattern of the population had occurred since then, the legislature had failed on many occasions to redraw district lines. As a result, the votes in some parts of Tennessee, where districts were sparsely settled, counted much more than votes in others.

The issue for Cox was not whether the district lines in Tennessee were fairly drawn. He recognized that in Tennessee, and in many other states as well, the votes of many citizens had been seriously diluted with the passage of time. In Tennessee, the population had quadrupled. The number of voters in a district ranged from 2,340 to 42,298.[18] He also believed that the case involved "one of the most basic rights in any democracy, the right to fair representation in one's own government."[19]

The legal constraint for Cox was that the Supreme Court, less than two decades before, had called reapportionment "a political question" best left to the legislature. Even though Cox's predecessor, Lee Rankin, had decided that the government should enter the case as an amicus on behalf of the plaintiffs, Cox was not sure he should argue the case. After overcoming his misgivings, he did, and, according to Navasky, the government's amicus brief was "crucial in persuading at least two members of the U.S. Supreme Court—Justices Potter Stewart and Tom Clark. Without their vote the decision below would have been reaffirmed and there probably wouldn't have been any reapportionment cases."[20] The Supreme Court ruled that the plaintiffs were entitled to a decision in federal court.

Philip Heymann served as an assistant to the Solicitor under Cox. In 1985, he said, "Archie took the biggest cases, and he liked to argue a lot. [Between 1942 and 1981, Cox argued eighty-seven times in the Supreme Court, sixty-seven as SG.][21] He was a very good advocate—exceptionally orderly, upright, clear. He was always a teacher. He would say, 'There are three issues here,' and what was happening was that, above all, he was imposing his structure on the question. He gave a very sharp sense of definition. The impression of the Justices was that he was telling the Supreme Court what the law was. He would tell the Court what was acceptable and persuasive, as a professor in the best sense. To some of them, it must have been very irritating, though Archie was very much in tune with the Warren Court. Baker v. Carr was one of his big cases. My impression in the courtroom was that a majority of the Court wanted to take jurisdiction in the case, but they were afraid of what they were getting into because of Frankfurter, who had objected to that position and who was a very powerful intellect. Archie unlocked the door for that majority, and Frankfurter ended up dissenting. Archie stood up and said, 'It is respectable and nothing terrible will happen if you take on reapportionment.' He wrestled with it—he spent a lot of time wrestling with questions because he sensed his influence on the Court. He wrestled with Baker v. Carr a long time, and it's one of those cases where the lawyer made all the difference."[22]

Cox's second struggle in the reapportionment cases was with the standard the Court should adopt as the measure of apportionment in a district. The question arose in Reynolds v. Sims,[23] which dealt with the constitutionality of the apportionment of legislatures in six states. Robert Kennedy and his aides believed that each person should have one vote, and that districts should have basically the same number of voters. According to Cox's estimate, that standard would lead to an extreme outcome, because the makeup of forty-six of the fifty state legislatures would be found unconstitutional,[24] requiring each of them immediately and at the same time to face the volatile task of reapportionment. The Solicitor General also thought the Attorney General's standard was simplistic. It would do nothing to avoid the problem of gerrymandering, because districts could be drawn so that they were equal in population but favored one party or the other. (In 1986, a generation later, the Supreme Court decided that federal courts could review gerry-

mandering by a state legislature.) [25] It ignored special circumstances presented by geography, because in some states mountains
divided areas that might be required to vote as a unified district if
the one person/one vote standard was adopted. The SG's hesita-
tions were supported by liberal and conservative scholars. [26] But
Bruce Terris, the assistant in the SG's office who was working
with Cox on the case, disagreed. "I think it is plain that it would
significantly benefit the country if our state legislatures were reap-
portioned on the basis of population," he wrote. "It would be a
tragedy if the great victory in Baker v. Carr were thrown away by
our persuading the Supreme Court to accept a weak substantive
standard." [27]

Terris anticipated by fourteen years what the Office of Legal
Counsel said the Solicitor General should do in a case like Reynolds v. Sims. (As noted earlier, in the 1977 document called "The
Role of the Solicitor General," the Office of Legal Counsel advised, "If the independent legal advice of the Solicitor General is
to be preserved, it should normally be the Solicitor General who
decides when to seek the advice of the Attorney General or the
President in a given case.") [28] In 1963, Terris wrote, "I recognize
that the choice between the various standards largely depends on
questions of policy. I have therefore gone on to suggest that the
population standard is, as a matter of policy, best for the country
because it is most consistent with contemporary concepts of democracy and with a strong federal system. However, despite my
views on the correct policy, I recognize that this vital issue is
largely outside my province. It seems to me to be a political decision properly made at the highest levels of government. Until that
decision is made, I do not believe that our legal position can be
formulated." [29]

Terris's memo was one of several documents sent to Cox to
persuade him to argue on behalf of the one person/one vote standard. Unwilling to order Cox to make an argument the SG did not
believe in, Robert Kennedy orchestrated a quiet campaign to
change the Solicitor's mind. Cox responded by drafting a memo
of his own, in which he argued that the one person/one vote
standard was sound social policy but questionable law. "In a state
constitutional convention my vote would go to apportion both

houses of a bicameral legislature in accordance with population," he wrote, "but I cannot agree that the Supreme Court should be advised to impose that rule upon all 50 states by judicial decree. In my opinion any such decree would be too revolutionary to be a proper exercise of the judicial function and too rigid to comport with the principle of federalism." In a meeting with the Attorney General and his advisers, Navasky reports, Cox lectured about his views until Kennedy interrupted, "Archie, isn't the real issue: 'Should some people's vote count more than other people's vote'?"[30]

That was as close as Cox and Kennedy ever came to a confrontation. The Attorney General never told Cox what to argue before the Court ("Archie, I know you can put this issue in a way that will convince the Supreme Court," he said), and when Cox faced the Justices, he stopped short of advocating one person/one vote. He said, ". . . my appraisal of sentiment within the legal profession—and probably outside—is that while the invalidation of the egregiously malapportioned legislatures would command a consensus of opinion, a 'one man, one vote' decision would precipitate a major constitutional crisis causing an enormous drop in public support for the Court."[31]

Cox says the meeting with Kennedy did not take place. "The one case that got sticky," he recalled in 1985, "and where my views of what good lawyering required and where the political views of others came into collision was here. I—I now think wrongly—I thought one really couldn't press a one person/one vote rule in a clear-cut form. I thought we couldn't ask the Court to require that legislatures draw district lines so that each person's vote counted the same. It wasn't that I didn't like the idea. I just doubted whether the Constitution required it. I had my heels dug in, and I wasn't going to budge. On the other hand, the President's aides were all gung ho that we push that standard. There was a meeting all set up in Bob Kennedy's office, and we were all going to thrash out the case. As I say, my heels were dug in. Well, that conference in Bob's office never happened. Burke Marshall and I happened to ride an elevator together one day. We were walking down the hall, and he said, 'We can't let this come to a head. You ought to recognize that Bob won't file a brief in the Supreme Court that you won't sign. You ought to recognize that he can't get into a position of filing a brief against the groups that have been pressing for one person/one vote.' I said, 'All right. I've got the germ of a solution, and I think I can work it out.' As I remember it, we filed a brief that didn't press that standard, but suggested a close alternative. Our brief provided the basis for much of the Court's decision, but the Justices took the final leap, which my intellect wouldn't allow me to. Poor prophet."[32]

Voting was a fundamental right, the Justices ruled, and any inequality of treatment for voters should be subjected to strict scrutiny. They ordered the states to establish districts with equal numbers of voters. Cox was not confident about the prospects for compliance with the Court's 1964 order, but far from causing a citizens' revolt, the Court initiated an orderly modernization of state government. Reapportionment in every state was virtually complete within two years.[33] Cox said, "I dug in my heels on one person/one vote, and I'm not especially proud of it. But my stubbornness was based on my sense of the law."[34]

A decade after the reapportionment cases, Cox's sense of the law was intensified by Watergate. He sees a close relationship between the secret of American constitutionalism and the resolution of that crisis. In a 1985 lecture, he asked, "Upon what does our constitutionalism ultimately rest? Why have the Constitution and the Supreme Court served so successfully for almost two centuries that the people, at least until now, have always rejected attacks upon the Court? The question confronted me with extraordinary personal intensity during the Watergate crisis." In the summer of 1973, the investigation he led as Watergate Special Prosecutor was stalled. Allegations that Richard Nixon and his White House aides had planned the Watergate break-in and then engaged in a conspiracy to obstruct justice through a cover-up hinged on the credibility of suspect witnesses like Nixon's onetime counsel John Dean. Then another aide disclosed that the President had installed a taping system in the Oval Office, which raised the possibility that hard evidence existed by which to judge the witnesses. When Cox subpoenaed the tapes, Nixon refused to cooperate, and continued to stonewall after federal trial Judge John Sirica and the U.S. Court of Appeals ordered him to turn them over. Cox said, "The habit of compliance—the notion that a powerful executive official has no choice but to comply with a judicial decree—is a fragile bond. Who could say in an age of Presidential aggrandizement that if one President succeeded in his defiance, others might not follow that example until ours was no longer a government of law?"[35]

On a Friday night, Nixon announced that he would not give up the tapes. He also ordered Cox "never again to resort to judicial process" to get White House evidence. Cox explained that he was obliged to pursue the inquiry as he had pledged he would to the Senate, and Nixon ordered Attorney General Elliot Richardson to fire Cox. After Richardson and William Ruckelshaus refused, on Saturday night, in Cox's words, the "third in command carried out the President's wish"—Solicitor General Robert Bork.

To Cox, what happened next is crucial: "Public support for the rule of law was then put to the test. A firestorm of public outrage overwhelmed the White House." By Tuesday, the President had promised to comply in all respects with the court order that he turn over the tapes. He did not in fact do so, but nine months later, when the Supreme Court itself ordered him to turn over the withheld tapes, he finally did. His resignation swiftly followed.

"The rule of law prevailed," Cox wrote, "because the people did rise up morally and politically. The response doubtless flowed from many sources; but I think there was present a deep and enduring realization, partly conscious and partly intuitive, that all our liberties depend upon compliance with law, because the principal bulwark of those liberties against executive or legislative oppression is respect for constitutionalism: the law and the courts."[36]

EVEN AS CHARLES FRIED compared himself with Cox, he sometimes tried to chip away at Cox's reputation for rectitude. "Why has Archie Cox been picked on by the right?" Fried asked. "He's been very partisan lately. At Common Cause"—for which Cox served as spokesman while criticizing Edwin Meese's fitness to be Attorney General—"he's Mr. Clean turned into a regular pol running a nickel-and-dime lobby."[37] Fried's apparent purpose was to show that Cox was no more a saint than Fried was a sinner: the similarities between their practices as SG outweighed any differences. The example Fried selected was their respective uses of amicus briefs in the Supreme Court.[38]

Part of the complaint that Fried had "politicized" the SG's office was the charge that he had submitted amicus briefs in agenda cases where the federal government's interest was "attenuated" rather than "direct."[39] Responding to this, Fried would ask, "What was the federal interest in the abortion case? Why, it was the same interest Archie Cox was required to articulate when he filed his brief in the reapportionment cases like Baker v. Carr and Reynolds v. Sims."[40] The answer was double-edged. It could mean that Cox had stated no federal interest in Baker v. Carr, so that Fried did not have to either, or, cutting the other way, that the interest Cox stated in Reynolds v. Sims was no less general than Fried had declared in some of his briefs. Fried's assertion raised a technical point. As a matter of Supreme Court procedure, Cox did not have to state a federal interest as part of a government brief. The rules under which Cox operated were issued in 1954.[41] When Cox was SG, from 1961 to 1965, no rule required him to state a federal interest, though he usually did. The Supreme Court rules were changed in 1970, and the new ones obliged Fried to declare the government's interest in every case.

Even when Fried discussed points less technical than the federal interest, he was concerned with a subject that draws the attention of only a small group of lawyers. But its significance has grown considerably in recent years. Since 1823, when the Justices let Henry Clay argue as an amicus, the Supreme Court has allowed lawyers to argue for clients as friends of the Court. The main requirement imposed on all friends of the Court (except the government) is that they present facts and law not well addressed by the parties. Amicus briefs answer a shortcoming of the adversary system: specific cases raise general questions that the parties do not always reckon with.[42]

During the presidency of Theodore Roosevelt, beginning in 1907, Attorney General Charles Bonaparte entered fifty-six cases before the Supreme Court in a little over two years, to press for an increase in the rights of blacks.[43] This was the first attempt by the government to spur social change as a friend of the Court. The Justices mentioned amicus briefs in the Court's rules of procedure for the first time in 1937, and by the forties, when cases arose dealing with desegregation, the Supreme Court began to ask the Solicitor General to give counsel through amicus briefs. [44]

Until the sixties, however, the subject of amicus filings was largely academic to the government. In 1956, for example, the government was an amicus in only two cases decided by the Justices. [45] From 1961 through 1966, the number of amicus filings by the government began to climb, and averaged seventeen a year. About one-fifth of the government's appearances in the Court during that period were as amicus curiae. The number in that era peaked in 1963, when the government filed twenty-eight amicus briefs, representing one-third of the cases in which it appeared before the Court in that Term.

In a speech before the Chicago Bar Association in 1962, when the subject of amicus briefs was as topical to lawyers as it became again during the Reagan Administration, Archibald Cox described the standards he followed as Solicitor General in deciding which cases to enter as a friend of the Court. [46] First, the question had to be important to constitutional law. Next, a large number of people should be affected. Then, the case had to have an impact on the government's "more direct interests"—this last standard being the hardest to define. (Though Cox did not cite them, Baker v. Carr and Reynolds v. Sims provided ready examples of cases meeting all three requirements. The government had a general interest in the suits because of the fundamental constitutional issues they raised, but that interest was also "direct" because the federal government would be directly affected by the outcome of the cases. What the Supreme Court decided about the apportionment of state legislatures would apply to Congress as well.) Finally, Cox asked, "Can we really help the Court?"

In 1985, Cox said about the government's use of amicus briefs during his tenure, "We had the feeling when we filed an amicus brief that we had an even stricter responsibility to the guardians of the law than we normally did. We couldn't just take a strong position on behalf of a state, for example. We had to be especially careful about what we said the law was or should be." Cox did not raise issues that were doomed to fail, because he thought it was the Solicitor General's duty not to waste the Court's time. He didn't raise issues not raised by the parties to the suit, or inject new issues not raised at trial. [47]

Though Cox felt constrained, the use of amicus briefs by private attorneys during his tenure was not constrained. In 1963, Samuel Krislov wrote in the *Yale Law Journal* that "the amicus is no longer a neutral amorphous embodiment of justice, but an active participant in the interest group struggle." [48] Between the late sixties and the early eighties, on average, amicus briefs were cited in almost one-fifth of the Supreme Court's opinions, and the average number of amicus briefs filed each Term was over sixty. [49] In that period, according to Karen O'Connor and Lee Epstein, who are professors of political science at Emory University, liberal groups like the American Civil Liberties Union and the NAACP Inc. Fund took part in over 40 percent of the Supreme Court's cases either as parties or as friends of the Court. Conservative groups played a role in almost 20 percent. In the dozen years from 1969 to 1981, while liberal participation stayed relatively steady, the percentage of appearances by conservative groups tripled. In civil-rights cases, defined to include abortion, affirmative action, and other topics on the Reagan agenda, conservatives played no role at the start of the period. They entered almost half by the end. Conservative groups became as accomplished in using amicus briefs to push their agenda as they had in mastering the use of political action committees, direct mail, and other new tools of politics. As O'Connor and Epstein put it, "Conservative as well as liberal groups now aspire to be 'private attorneys general.'" [50]

After the number of amicus filings by the government rose in the Cox era, it leveled off and did not jump to the next plateau until Robert Bork was Solicitor General. [51] The average number of cases in which there were amicus filings by the government between 1973 and 1977 rose to thirty-two, or 30 percent. The figures stayed about the same during the Carter Administration, and then they leaped again under Reagan, to an average of forty-three amicus filings, or 37 percent, through the 1984 Term. In short, between Cox's era and Bork's, amicus filings as a percentage of all of the government's briefs went from around 20 to 30 percent. Between

Cox's era and Rex Lee's, they doubled to almost 40 percent. And in the 1985 Term, the first full year Charles Fried was Solicitor General, the number of briefs climbed again to a rate of almost 50 percent of the government's filings in the Supreme Court for most of the Term, until the rate dropped off during the last few months to yield an annual figure of 41 percent. [52]

The increase in amicus filings in the seventies and eighties can be explained by several factors: the constitutionalization of the law; the growth in the number of federal statutes; and the tendency by government, private lawyers, and citizens alike to view the courts, and the Supreme Court in particular, as a proper forum for addressing social issues. But the Nixon, Ford, and Carter Administrations, in office when the number of filings began to increase, showed no special urgency about changing the law through amicus filings. [53] In many areas, lawyers in those Administrations believed the law was in equilibrium. Where the Solicitors General sought new doctrine, they were careful not to upset the general balance. The Reagan Administration, on the other hand, took a new tack, and used the amicus brief as a tool of change.

By Fried's time, according to a lawyer in the SG's office who was appointed by the Reagan Administration and who studied the filings of its predecessors, the type of amicus briefs filed by the Reagan team spelled a significant difference between how it viewed the office and how prior Administrations had. Fried defined the federal interest as broadly as possible—"threadbare," the lawyer called this definition—in order to enter any case where the Administration and the Solicitor General wanted to make a point. Instead of submitting briefs that were seen as attempts to help the Court, Fried filed position papers to put the Administration on record about questions of law it considered important for whatever reason. "I don't think you've been useful or not useful in terms of just wins or losses," he said. "It's a question of whether you've told the truth in a way that is persuasive and effective, and if in the end it's wrong, at least it's clearly wrong, not just a muddle." [54]

While the nature of practice before the Supreme Court had changed since Cox's day, the behavior of Reagan's second Solicitor General was not fully explained by this shift. Both Cox's staffers and Fried's agreed that the cardinal difference between the two Solicitors was that while both men declared beliefs in law as a constraint, Cox's record underscored that he felt bound by what the courts said was law, while Fried's showed that he did not.[55]

Cox often tells a story about his days as a law clerk to Learned Hand. "Sonny," Hand asked him, "to whom am I responsible? No one can fire me. No one can dock my pay. Even those nine bozos in Washington, who sometimes reverse me, can't make me decide as they want. Everyone should be responsible to someone. To whom am I responsible?" Then the judge pointed to the shelves of his law library. "To those books about us!" he answered. "That's to whom I'm responsible!"[56] Judges had a body of law to which they were accountable. They could change it, but they had to recognize their duty to the ideal of law or it would lose its force.[57] In the SG's post, Cox believed he stood halfway between the Supreme Court and the President, and he owed a duty to each. He kept the President and the Attorney General from ignoring what the Court said the law was, and from asking the Justices to reach judgments that, in his view, could harm the Court. He also argued the Kennedy Administration's position in terms he thought were consistent with the Court's reasoning about the law.

Philip Heymann can draw on as much experience as anyone in commenting about the difference between the Cox and Fried outlooks on the law. He has known both men well since the early sixties. It was Heymann who noted that, unlike Cox, Fried believes that "the law is not necessarily what the Supreme Court says it is," that "the law is something that any right-minded person can see."[58] As Fried put it, "Law is nothing but reasons."[59] The divergence between Cox's and Fried's views about the law and the Supreme Court led to a difference in their stewardships as Solicitors General that was summed up in their use of amicus briefs.

For Cox, representing the government required caution, patience, and steps of moderation. He tried to fulfill the SG's responsibility to the Supreme Court as well as the President, and by Republicans and Democrats, liberals and conservatives, he was hailed as a great SG. Serving an Administration that governed during the midst of a revolution in constitutional law, when he might have been expected to call for radical changes in the law,

Archibald Cox believed that, for the good of the Court and the SG's office, he should advocate restraint. [60]

Charles Fried, on the other hand, felt no such compunctions. "There are two reasons why you don't file an amicus brief in an important case," Fried said in 1986 when asked to explain the high number of filings he had made compared to his predecessors. "Either you are very deep and have too much to say to reduce it to a simple brief. Or you have nothing to say at all." [61] Except for his regular references to Archibald Cox, who said the "choice of words" in Fried's briefs ran ahead of "sober reasoning," was "too polemical" and "strident," and was "weakening the rule of law," [62] Fried declined to comment on the appraisals of him made by some of his predecessors. He did not answer the charge of Erwin Griswold that the Reagan Administration "intervenes too often, a) for the good of the law, and b) for its own good." (Fried described a piece on NBC News that reported Griswold's view—"Three former U.S. Solicitors General accuse the Reagan Administration of turning that historic post into little more than a political mouthpiece for the President"—as "a hatchet job.") [63] He did not respond to the comment of President Carter's Solicitor, Wade McCree, that the SG's briefs appeared to be less "dispassionate" and "objective" than they had been "traditionally." Fried, however, contended that his briefs made arguments compelled by logic, and not by overt pressure from the Attorney General and his circle, or by the instinct to placate his masters, [64] as Louis Claiborne called it, that might overtake a Solicitor General trying to get along in an expressly ideological Administration.

"TAKE OUR BRIEF in the Wygant case," Fried said about an amicus filing he made in Wygant v. Jackson. [65] "The reaction of some of our critics to that brief shows you how bad the polarization has become. Compared to the bland stuff that Archie Cox submitted, the Wygant brief was wonderfully well written. And that was my main problem. If that's the problem, I plead guilty." The Wygant case dealt with affirmative action. In 1972, the Board of Education and the teachers association in Jackson, Michigan, agreed on a plan: ". . . at no time will there be a greater percentage

of minority personnel laid off than the current percentage of minority personnel employed at the time of the layoff." [66] The goal
of the plan was to have at least the same percentage of minority
teachers on the staff of each Jackson school as there were minority
students throughout the Jackson public schools.

Though the SG's brief did not say so, until 1954 no black
teacher taught in the Jackson schools. By 1969, minority teachers
accounted for less than 4 percent of the school system's faculty,
and the Michigan Civil Rights Commission found that the school
board had discriminated in hiring. The board worked to improve
its record, and two years later the share of minority teachers had
doubled to almost 9 percent. But Jackson had to lay off some
teachers, and because the minority teachers were the most recently
hired, according to the superintendent of schools, the layoffs "lit-
erally wiped out all the gain." [67] In 1972, racial tension in the
Jackson schools tripped over into violence, and the school board
decided to integrate students and faculty. When teachers were
asked to consider abandoning the "last hired, first fired" layoff
scheme, all but a small fraction voted to retain it. The board and
the teachers' union negotiated, and they came up with the Jackson
plan.

In 1974, some white teachers in Jackson were laid off under the
agreement. They sued in federal court, and a judge ruled against
them. He found "a sound basis" to conclude that "minority under-
representation is substantial and chronic," that the "handicap of
past discrimination is impeding access of minorities," and that the
affirmative-action plan met standards laid down by the Supreme
Court. The U.S. Court of Appeals for the Sixth Circuit upheld the
trial court's ruling.

The core of the Solicitor General's argument asking the Supreme Court to overturn the lower courts was familiar. The white
teachers in the Wygant case had been laid off solely because of
their race, and because the school board had bound itself "to an
absolute layoff preference for 'employees who are Black, American, Indian, Oriental, or of Spanish descendancy.' " Neither the
school board, the lower courts, nor anyone else had found that
members of these groups had been victims of discrimination by the
school board, the city of Jackson, or the state of Michigan. "All

there is by way of justification for the racially based misfortune visited upon petitioners are references by the district court and the court of appeals to a history of 'societal discrimination' . . . 'under-representation' of minority teachers . . . and the need to supply 'role-models' for minority students."[68]

The conclusions of the SG's brief went as follows: "So casual a waving aside of the fundamental Fourteenth Amendment principle of equal treatment for all persons regardless of race and of our republic's basic moral vision of the unity of all mankind cannot be countenanced."[69] What Fried meant by the phrase "the unity of all mankind" was not explained. In any case, he went on, the courts below had "drawn a wholly unwarranted connection between the general history of racial discrimination in this country, and the statistical underrepresentation of minority group members in the teaching corps relative to the student body—without even the semblance of an attempt to relate that disparity to some pattern or practice of conduct by the school board." Then the courts used this "suppositious discrimination to justify a remedy which further undoes the connection between wrongdoer and victim," and let a person, "say of Asian descent whose ancestors suffered discrimination in the early history of California," gain an advantage over the white petitioners. "The third and final step in the shambling logic of this enterprise would justify the explicitly racially based layoff of petitioners on the ground that this is necessary to provide 'role-models' for minority group students. Stripped of its veneer of unsupported psychological and sociological conjecture, this justification can only mean one of two things. It may mean that black, Hispanic, or Asian students learn better if they are taught by black, Hispanic, or Asian teachers. Or it may mean that such students, conscious of the injustices done to the groups of which they are members, will draw encouragement and a practical moral lesson from seeing members of their own (or some other) minority group in positions of authority and respect."

To Fried's mind, the claim about role models missed the point that the "most powerful role models are those who have succeeded without a hint of favoritism." It also begged the question at issue in the case. "For one must assume that these students will be aware of the very system of racial preference which delivers role models in supposedly sufficient numbers. But what is the moral lesson that such a system teaches? Surely not that ours is a society in which each person can succeed as a result of his or her own work and talent. On the contrary, one may likelier suppose that such a system (its actual working laid bare) will teach a different and more sinister lesson: that one hundred and twenty years after the end of slavery government may still advance some and suppress others not as individuals but because of the color of their skin."[70]

Much of the SG's brief came off as a lesson about morals and role models rather than as a statement about law. But the brief reached a legal conclusion: "Equality before the law, so magnificent in principle, is often a difficult and uncomfortable concept in practice. There have always been and perhaps will always be voices seeking to carve out special exceptions to this principle based on history, prevailing social conditions, temporary need, or expediency. After the era of Reconstruction, such voices prevailed, and the true meaning of the Equal Protection Clause was long suppressed. In 1896, this Court approved the concept of 'separate but equal' facilities for blacks and whites and thus upheld the arrest of Homer A. Plessy for occupying a railroad coach reserved for whites. . . . In one of the most famous and prescient dissents in the history of this Court, the first Justice Harlan wrote . . . : 'Our Constitution is color-blind, and neither knows nor tolerates classes among citizens. In respect of civil rights, all citizens are equal before the law. The humblest is the peer of the most powerful. The law regards man as man, and takes no account of his surroundings or of his color when his civil rights as guaranteed by the supreme law of the land are involved.' This vision became the creed of the Civil Rights Movement, and eventually the nation."[71]

To brighten its argument, the SG's brief also included an attention-grabbing example: "Henry Aaron would not be regarded as the all-time home run king, and he would not be a model for youth, if the fences had been moved in whenever he came to the plate."[72] In a brief about the kind of affirmative action used by the school board in Jackson, Michigan, the example was wholly misleading. It implied that affirmative action in the case of a Henry Aaron would mean moving in the fences, as if minority teachers in the schools were permitted to impart less knowledge to their students than other teachers. For the analogy to work, however, it had to describe how a black athlete like Aaron might realistically benefit from affirmative action—how he might get a special chance to prove his talents as a ballplayer and earn a job as a major leaguer. A minority teacher hired through affirmative action in Jackson was expected to perform in the classroom at the same level as his colleagues. Similarly, once an athlete whose entrée to the majors had been helped by affirmative action stepped up to the plate, he would face the same pitcher and have to hit a home run over the same fence as anyone else.

At the Justice Department, the Wygant brief stirred a lot of talk. Some lawyers agreed with Fried's judgment that it was "wonderfully well written." Others did not. Lawrence Wallace commented on Fried's style, "His writing is of a more disputatious nature, written with an admixture of styles you might find in the *New Republic* or the *National Review.*"[73] And one senior lawyer in the department remarked, "It doesn't read like SG stuff. It reads like a combination of what you'd see in a neo-con editorial and a snarky Harvard book review."[74]

The strongest criticism of the Wygant brief faulted it on the grounds described by Charles Fried and Philip Heymann as the basis for the Solicitor General's legal arguments—that is, legal philosophy. In a 1964 lecture called "Civil Rights and the Limits of Law," Paul Freund addressed the question "Is not the Constitution color-blind? Can a preferential treatment of Negroes be squared with the requirement of equal protection of the laws? Is it not an unconstitutional discrimination in reverse?" Freund instructed, "The first thing to note about Justice Harlan's phrase is that it is not a constitutional text, it is a constitutional metaphor." No reference to the "color-blindness"of the law appears anywhere in the Constitution. The phrase had been taken by the Justice from a brief written by Albion Tourgée, a lawyer and novelist. (Tourgée's collaborator in the case, though not on the brief, was Samuel Phillips, an admired former SG whose thirteen-year tenure toward the end of the nineteenth century was almost twice as long as that of any other Solicitor either before or since.) Harlan's reading of the Constitution (for example, in a case where he judged that the right of an employer to hire and fire at will could not be tampered with by a statute protecting an employee's right to join a labor union) was not so pure that a lawyer should take the Justice's metaphorical teachings over the lessons of the text itself. As for the text, Freud said, "the most obvious fact" about the Fourteenth Amendment was that "it grew out of the Civil War in an effort to raise Negroes from the level of legal inferiority." In two cases, at least, there could be little doubt about the lawfulness of preferential treatment: where public facilities were unequal and de facto segregation shunted blacks to inferior ones; and where de facto segregation was "a product in part, a remnant, of the governmental discrimination in the past." Freund also said, " . . . if pushed to a drily logical extreme," the phrase "the Constitution is color-blind" can become "the reverse of liberal." He noted what Charles Fried did not: ". . . the moral, and it may be the legal, difference between a preference in favor of a minority and one against it."[75] The Supreme Court had acknowledged the distinction and, by authorizing affirmative action, turned it into law.

Laurence Tribe, the professor who filed a brief against Fried in the abortion case, who holds the only chair in constitutional law at Harvard Law School, and who is seen by some lawyers as the private lawyer's equivalent of an SG, was quoted by NBC News as saying, "The Solicitor General now is hardly a friend of the Court. He is a friend of the Administration and of Ed Meese."[76] When he was asked to comment about the Wygant brief, he said, "What's striking about the Wygant brief is not that it explores the underlying philosophies of equality that might give rise to either a condemnation or an acceptance of affirmative action on constitutional grounds. What's striking is its pamphlet-like quality: the offhand discussion of Hank Aaron as a role model, the cavalier assertion that life would have been different for Plessy if only he had lived in another state besides Louisiana, because he was just one-eighth black. Those are things I would have expected to find in a public speech by an Attorney General, or by a President, and not in a Solicitor General's brief. Not because it is wrong or unhelpful for a brief to have a colorful flourish here or there, but because, at least in my conception of a powerful brief, more work must be done to connect the flourishes to substantial and careful examination of law, and to the underlying philosophical issues in the case. What is striking in the Wygant brief is that those observations float free of any anchor in the law itself. There is a casual examination of three or four arguments made by various people chosen almost at random who are in favor of affirmative action, and then a rather sweeping non sequitur defending the principle that the Constitution should be color-blind." [77]

Tribe also commented, "It seems to me that the problem isn't that the SG's briefs are philosophical, it's that their rhetoric is not carefully connected with a legal theory that is made coherent and brought to bear on cases themselves. In Wygant, for example, the fact which is clear from the record that prior to 1954 there were no minority teachers at all in Jackson is surely not irrelevant. The case is about whether an agreement entered into by the local government which is designed to assure a more integrated society is lawful. And yet from the SG's brief you wouldn't even know that that was an aspect of the case. The use of a case pending in the Supreme Court as an occasion for a grand pronouncement about a subject in ways not connected to the case, or to the history of legal development on the matter, unbolstered by a careful, comprehensive, and rounded statement of the relevant philosophy is less than one is entitled to expect from the Solicitor General's office operating at its best."

When the Supreme Court decided the Wygant case, in the spring of 1986, the Justices handed down the kind of mix of opinions that normally appeals to the Court-watchers in the SG's office. There were five opinions, and none was joined by more than three Justices. A majority of five struck down the Jackson scheme, on the ground that the school district had never proved how its affirmative-action plan was justified by discrimination against minority teachers in the schools. Writing a separate opinion to explain her part in the Court's majority, Justice Sandra Day O'Connor was clear about the evidence that would have accomplished that end. For her, proof that the share of minorities in the Jackson work force was much greater than the percentage of those hired as teachers could have settled the case of "deliberate discrimination." [78] Three Justices who formed the core of the majority were represented by Justice Lewis Powell, and he addressed another defect of the Jackson plan. While hiring goals diffused the burden of affirmative action throughout society, he said, making a large concession to those who favor affirmative action, goals in layoffs requiring whites to give up their jobs to blacks imposed "the entire burden of achieving racial equality on particular individuals, often resulting in serious disruption of their lives." Powell wrote, "That burden is too intrusive." In sum, the Jackson scheme was not "sufficiently narrowly tailored."[79]

The Court's opinions otherwise amounted to a rejection of the Reagan Administration's views about affirmative action. Attorney General Meese had boiled the Administration's position down to one line: "The idea that you can use discrimination in the form of racially preferential quotas, goals and set-asides to remedy the lingering social effects of past discrimination" was "nothing short of a legal, moral and constitutional tragedy."[80] Even the Powell opinion in the Wygant case refuted him. "In order to remedy the effects of prior discrimination," the Justice wrote, "it may be necessary to take race into account. As part of this nation's dedication to eradicating racial discrimination, innocent persons may be called upon to bear some of the burden of the remedy."[81] For the first time, eight of the Court's nine Justices (only Justice White signed no opinion commenting on the subject) appeared to endorse the voluntary use of hiring goals by government employers, like public schools, to correct their past discrimination against minorities.

Justice O'Connor explained, "[T]he Court has forged a degree of unanimity: it is agreed that a plan need not be limited to the remedying of specific instances of identified discrimination for it to be deemed sufficiently 'narrowly tailored,' or 'substantially related,' to the correction of prior discrimination by the state."[82] Though the Court's holding was no ringing endorsement of affirmative action, and it favored the side supported by the SG's brief, the O'Connor opinion explained why the case was a defeat for the Administration. The Solicitor General had taken a position that none of the Justices endorsed.

To Charles Fried, the style and substance of the Wygant brief was a fair sample of the amicus briefs that he filed in the 1985 Term.[83] He told the *Congressional Quarterly*, "There are cases where what is at stake is not some particular government program but an important and pervasive view of the law or the Constitution." While Fried suggested that his goal was to win cases instead of grandstanding ("The really important part of the story," he said, before the Court gave him his report card in the Wygant case, "is whether we got it right"), Steven Puro, a political scientist who studies amicus briefs, said it was notable that people often read about the substance of the government's filings in the newspapers, as if they were speeches or position papers, before the briefs ever made it to the Supreme Court.[84]

Burt Neuborne, a professor at the New York University School of Law who was then legal director for the American Civil Liberties Union, offered another judgment. He said that Fried had "demoted the Solicitor General's office to our level, the level of an ideological interest group, a salesman for a partisan line just like the ACLU is."[85]

XIII

The SG's Lawyers

LAWYERS IN THE SG's office describe themselves as nerds, wonks, and idiot savants,[1] who wear dull gray suits and thick-soled wing-tips, and sometimes relieve the intensity of analyzing cases with a quick game of darts.[2] They have an aversion to simplicity, one said, but in 1985 and 1986 some were anxious about what the SG's office was becoming and they spoke about it plainly.

In discussing their reasons for finding the traditions of the office to be under assault, the assistants meant to be careful. They balanced the list of wrongs against the office with an acknowledgment that the laws and cases in dispute could usually be interpreted in several ways. But they seemed to be a wounded, bewildered lot. They were contemptuous of what they considered, crude legal notions emanating from the AG's office and often supported by Charles Fried as SG, yet fully aware that Meese and Fried had the power and they did not. These were smart, highly trained, articulate people who had a passion for the law. Though some expected to go into private practice or to teach, many hoped to spend their careers right where they were. They took the challenge to the way of doing things in the SG's office as an affront to a great institution and, because of the SG's role, an attack on the integrity of the law.

Edwin Kneedler, then a six-year veteran, explained the value that the SG's office had long attached to process.[3] He sketched how the SG's office traditionally worked and added a new dimension to the standard description. Ordinarily, an agency like the Department of Health and Human Services would recommend to a division of the Justice Department, say the Civil Division, that the government appeal a case. The Civil Division would then make its recommendation to the SG about what should be done. The case would be assigned to an assistant to the SG, like Kneedler, who would write a memo assessing the pros and cons of the recommendation. Making a proposal of his own, he sent the memo to a deputy, who added his thoughts in a brief note that was sometimes handwritten on a modest slip of yellow paper. The memo and note went to the SG, who made a decision. If there was any disagreement about what to do, lawyers from the agency and division involved might be invited to a meeting with the assistant to the SG, the deputy, and, perhaps, the Solicitor General, to resolve the case. In rare instances, the Attorney General was asked to help decide.

These steps represented a form of due process. The assistant to the SG would seek out the views of officials from all parts of the government with a stake in the case, to make sure his recommendation was informed by their experience. He had the freedom to write his own thoughts, but he was forced to put down on paper his assessment of the position the government should seek, making it clearer and easier to grasp than it would have been if he had made only an oral report, and harder to ignore if it ran counter to a claim with support elsewhere in the bureaucracy. The deputy was forced to articulate his ideas on paper, as well, if they clashed with the assistant's. Each point of view had a chance to be aired, and when there was a reckoning, it was with ideas rather than some form of posturing. The Solicitor General could rely on both the balanced approach of his aides and the clarity of the record as a foundation for his judgment. Being independent, as the Solicitor General usually prided himself in being, did not require riding roughshod over the rest of the government. The SG's office sat at the top of a very large pyramid—with lawyers in the ninety-four U.S. Attorneys' offices at the base, the Justice Department's trial divisions in the middle, and its appellate sections just below the apex—and a skillful SG used the government to help make a reasoned decision about the law.

"If you think about it," Kneedler reflected, "there are few occasions when one branch of government speaks directly to the other: the State of the Union address; proposals for new laws; vetoes of legislation. There is a great deal of diplomacy about them. Our filings in the Supreme Court are on this short list, and our faith in the separation of powers requires us to be respectful as well. For justice to be done, it must be seen to be done, too, and that's what this process is about."

Harriet Shapiro also talked about what had been. Her commitment to the SG's office was as serious as Kneedler's. Shapiro was editor in chief of the *Columbia Law Review* in 1955, when less than 10 percent of Columbia's law-school classes were women, and in 1972 she became the first woman hired as a regular attorney by the SG's office. (The highest number who have served at one time is four, and by 1986 there had been nine in all.) On her own hiring, she explained, "The young Turks in the office persuaded the SG it was time to hire a woman. They said he had never hired a woman before because nobody qualified had ever applied." [4]

The aspects of the SG's work that animated Shapiro, like Kneedler, dealt largely with the lawyer's craft. "In some sense," she said, "authorizing appeals in the lower federal courts may be the most important thing we do. Once a case gets to the Supreme Court, we have an information-gathering function, because the government as a whole is a repository of specialized information about all kinds of law: the Social Security Act, the Freedom of Information Act, and so on. One role we play is to translate this information for the Supreme Court, to tell the Justices about the impact of a possible decision on the workings of the government. On the other hand, the Justices sure as heck can read cases. They've got a terrific staff of law clerks who can help them with the reading, and in many cases they can get along without us. But when we're deciding about an appeal in the lower courts, we've got to decide whether the government should swallow a defeat or, if not, why we should take a crack at a case in an appeal. We serve a kind of judicial function, and it's ours alone."

In Shapiro's view, the SG's office served as a well-placed information booth, advising judges about the law (in the Courts of Appeals and the Supreme Court), answering questions from law reviews about legal developments worth noting, fielding questions from major newspapers about how to improve their coverage of Supreme Court cases. [5] What set it apart was its judicial function, and its attention to process. "The office makes decisions on paper," she said, "because it couldn't function otherwise. It's important to have a written record, because the government tries to take consistent positions—or, if it takes an inconsistent one, to know why." And: "Anyone who wants to talk to the SG's office about a case he has a part in, especially from the government, is welcome. The door is always open." Like many assistants, Shapiro took pride in her ultimate accountability for the office's work. "After a brief comes back from the printer in final form," Shapiro said, "it comes back to the assistant who worked on it. He's responsible for final checking—of proofreading, substantive stuff, everything. When he's done, he marks it 'O.K. for Filing,' and initials it. For me, that's a very special moment in the process. I look at the paper and say, 'This is the best I can do.' I believe in the process. When I put my initials on some paper, that's my stamp of approval."

David Strauss spoke shortly before he left the SG's office in 1985 to teach at the University of Chicago Law School. "I wanted to say what the office meant to me," [6] he said soon after a farewell lunch in his honor. "It's been a huge experience working for the Solicitor General. More important than law school at Harvard, working on the *Harvard Law Review,* or clerking for Judge Irving Goldberg on the Fifth Circuit, whom I greatly admire. I believe, when I look back on my career, this will have been the formative experience. So there was something I wanted to say: the office believes in the sovereignty of reason. It's very much the ethos, and Ken Geller and Andy Frey, who are deputies, represent it best, since almost 70 percent of the work goes through them. In the SG's office, what you know is that you don't say anything or write it on paper unless you can defend it. If you do, and you can't, you'll be attacked and torn to shreds. But if you can defend it, you say it and, more importantly, you write it, so it's down in black-and-white. No one can misrepresent or mess with it. And even if your colleagues aren't predisposed to agree with you, even if they disagree with your larger judgments about policy, if you're right on the law and you convince them, they'll listen and back you."

Kenneth Geller came to the SG's office in 1975, after serving as a member of the Watergate Special Prosecutor's force. [7] By 1985, he was in charge of civil cases, and he was known at the Justice Department for his intense dedication.

"Reviewing cases from the Civil Division," one assistant said, "is very hard. It deals with a lot of really boring, technical things that are difficult to grasp, and Geller had a remarkable ability to see ill-founded notions the division wanted to push that no one else caught. A case came up from the Second Circuit on the question whether a resident alien"—someone without American citizenship living in this country—"could get Social Security benefits. A district court said yes. The Second Circuit said yes. To anybody but the political folks at the Civil Division, the answer seemed to be yes. The division wanted to appeal, and Geller wanted to avoid a big fight. No one else could figure out how to avoid it. So he asked about the alien, and what was likely if the Supreme Court ruled the way the division wanted. The alien turned out to be seventy-two years old and very sick, and she had been in the United States for twelve years. She qualified for benefits on a number of grounds, and it wasn't likely she would be deported, even if Geller took the division's side and won the case. So what was the point of the suit? If she wouldn't be deported, it was a lousy suit to push. It was such a simple point, yet nobody had thought of it."[8]

In his dealings with the Civil Division, Geller was often acerbic. "As usual," he sometimes began notes about the division's papers to the SG, "the Civil Division has missed the point."[9] Lawyers who received this sort of note hoped that they were not supposed to take it personally. Ridicule and sarcasm sharpened Geller's principal tool—reason—and if work from these lawyers gave him grounds to exercise it, they were willing to be corrected. One government lawyer, whom Geller described as "dumber than a stone" after they met about a case, called Geller the rudest person she had ever talked to. She said he was arrogant, and told him so, and he was not surprised. But generally his professional reputation (monklike devotion to the law, firm commitment to the government's interests, competence to match) was excellent. Some of his colleagues held him to be the best lawyer they had ever worked with.

Geller created a series of notebooks that played a characteristic part in the due process of the SG's office.[10] In a special binder he kept statistics about his caseload, the names of pending cases, and the outcomes in cases already resolved. Then came pages from a loose-leaf publication called *U.S. Law Week,* showing a table of Supreme Court opinions from 1978 to the present, so Geller could quickly locate a citation in the Supreme Court's *United States Reports* for each, and memos written at his request by assistants to the SG about various topics of legal analysis that were frequently of use.

The heart of the book was a collection of aphorisms. They were quotations taken from Supreme Court opinions and copied by Geller into his book during the course of the previous few years. "These are the sorts of things you could never find by standard legal research," Geller said. "Opinions aren't indexed by aphorism," he pointed out, but he wanted to have them at hand. His entries included one in particular that appealed to him: " 'Unless we wish anarchy to prevail within the federal judicial system, a precedent of this Court must be followed by the lower federal courts no matter how misguided the judges of those courts may think it to be.' Hutto v. Davis." It summarized a traditional view now under attack by Edwin Meese and his supporters.

Geller also recorded in his book statistics that were available nowhere else in the government. Among other things, they revealed that for the judicial year beginning on June 30, 1984, and ending June 28, 1985, of 2,089 appeals handled by the Office of the Solicitor General, Geller had been in charge of 782, or 117 more than any other deputy in the office.[11] He had overseen about 37 percent of the office's work, and with Andrew Frey 69 percent. Of 110 briefs on the merits filed by the government in the Supreme Court, he handled 27, or almost a quarter of the government's primary statements about the law.

On file carts parked by the side of his desk, Geller kept rows of black binders storing all the memos he had reviewed as Deputy Solicitor, and all the memos dealing with civil matters going back more than a decade. Though they lacked the force of law, because they were internal documents used only to decide what position to take in a federal court, the papers made up a bank on which Geller and other lawyers in the SG's office could draw to ensure that the government took consistent positions before the courts (or, if not, could say why it had departed from previous submissions). The binders were part of the record of the SG's due process. They were a piece of the SG's memory, to which Geller served as the index, and they helped the office play its role in the law.

Andrew Frey was the office den leader: almost every day around twelve-thirty, he would knock on doors along the SG's corridor, and in an announcer's voice—"Lunch!"—round up a half-dozen lawyers for a session about the law over sandwiches in the Justice Department cafeteria. He was in charge of criminal appeals, and in that area was known as a persistent, sometimes obstinate, conservative. When Wade McCree became SG, he was told by people in the Carter Administration to "watch out for Andy Frey," McCree said, "because he just wasn't a liberal." (Frey became a favorite of McCree's.) Frey's job was to argue for rules that "promote efficient law enforcement," Frey said. "Everybody agrees that these aren't the only goals of the law, but I generally tried to move the law in the direction of helping the police do their job and prosecutors get accurate verdicts."[12]

Like Edwin Meese, Frey was preoccupied by problems caused by the Miranda decision. In an article for the *University of Pittsburgh Law Review* in 1978, he contended that, instead of trying to identify and punish those who commit crimes, the "first principle" of the law about confessions had become "solicitude for the interests of the arrested suspect." In the best of circumstances, confessions were difficult to obtain, Frey judged, and the "central inquiry" for lawyers should be how to balance the interest of police in obtaining "honest" confessions against the interest of a suspect in not being coerced to confess. Unlike the Attorney General, Frey acknowledged that the concerns prompting Miranda were "real and valid." But he also advised that the law should be changed to take a more "realistic view of society's needs"—that is, the needs of the police as opposed to suspects. The police should not be restricted to taking "statements only from those suspects who are unequivocally willing to give them."[13] Frey used SG briefs to guide the Court toward this view of Miranda, and if the Justices had not intended to strike the balance that Frey counseled when they handed down the landmark, as some legal scholars believe,[14] they did in cases he argued a decade later. By 1985, with a traditional, evolutionary approach, Frey had already helped accomplish without fanfare what the Attorney General contended was still left to do.

The most compact example of Frey's ability to persuade the Justices to take a position on the side of the government and against criminal defendants came in the area of double jeopardy. The principle of double jeopardy is reputedly the oldest of the procedural guarantees included in the Bill of Rights ("The laws forbid the same man to be tried twice on the same issue," Demosthenes wrote in the fourth century B.C.),[15] but, as a field of constitutional law, it was only sketchily developed before Frey joined the SG's office. Until then, most American lawyers with reason to think about the subject assumed that the Double Jeopardy Clause of the Fifth Amendment ("nor shall any person be subject for the same offense to be twice put in jeopardy of life or limb") meant that a criminal defendant had almost complete protection from further proceedings after any ruling in his favor by a federal court.

Frey's concern about double jeopardy was spurred by events that prompted the Supreme Court to re-evaluate this area of law as well. In 1969, the Court ruled that the clause applied to the states, where the vast majority of crimes are prosecuted.[16] In 1971, an omnibus crime law sponsored by the Nixon Administration included a provision explicitly allowing the federal government to challenge rulings by judges that raised questions about double jeopardy.[17]

The Double Jeopardy Clause protects a defendant against a second prosecution for the same offense after he has been acquitted; against a retrial for the same offense after he has been convicted and the conviction has been overturned; and against more than one punishment for the same offense. But the meaning of terms like "acquittal" and "conviction" is not always simple, and the Supreme Court has struggled to define them in this context.[18] Frey persuaded the Justices to read the clause as he did in most cases and limit the reach of this safeguard. His theme was that unless there was the threat of an entirely different trial, there was no second jeopardy, because the Double Jeopardy Clause does not bar the continuation of proceedings that could be carried on without making a defendant go through a new trial. Balancing the defendant's interest in receiving a final judgment and the state's interest in effective law enforcement, the Court accepted Frey's proposal that the latter be given more weight.

According to Peter Westen, a professor at the University of Michigan Law School and an expert on double jeopardy,[19] "The truth about Frey's work is that it was just highly intelligent advocacy. It didn't raise any red flags, because his were the same arguments that someone could make who was not pro-government, so few scholars in the law, let alone anyone else, picked up on it. He just tested old myths about doctrine, and came up with ideas based on good legal reasoning. It was a careful, methodical, incremental process."

To Westen's mind, the process that Frey used at the SG's office to craft his arguments was reflected in the Supreme Court's development of the law. Retired Supreme Court Justice Potter Stewart concurred with this judgment. "While a seat on the Supreme Court may be the best job in American law,"[20] Stewart said, "the Solicitor General's office provides the best lawyers' jobs. It's a small office, and it's independent. The Solicitor General has his own staff, and they argue fully half the cases before the Court. They participate in the development of the law. Andy Frey is a good example how they do it."

IN MARCH OF 1986, it had been nine months since Charles Fried took over as Acting Solicitor General and five since he was confirmed as SG. In that period, over one-quarter of the lawyers in the office had left and been replaced. On a Wednesday during the first week of March, Andrew Frey, Kenneth Geller, and an experienced assistant named Kathryn Oberly, three of the most respected lawyers in the office, announced to Fried that they, too, had decided to leave. A lawyer in the office recounted,[21] "At three-thirty the next afternoon, a couple of secretaries wandered down the hall and told us we were wanted in Mr. Frey and Mr. Geller's offices immediately. People knew something was afoot. There was an inkling. But we weren't sure what. We all crammed into the suite where Andy and Ken worked next door to each other in adjoining offices, and Charles said there were some announcements. Andy started, and told us that he and Ken and Kay were going to be leaving to join Mayer, Brown & Platt"—the Washington, D.C., branch of that Chicago law firm. It also employs former Acting Solicitor General Robert Stern and former Deputy SG Stephen Shapiro, who are two of the three co-authors of Stern, Gressman, and Shapiro on *Supreme Court Practice;* former (political) Deputy SG Paul Bator, who now teaches at the University of Chicago Law School and who is of counsel to the firm; and former assistant to the SG Mark Levy.

"Andy said it was a bittersweet moment for all of them, because the SG's office meant a lot to them. But the law firm had offered a wonderful opportunity. Then Charles piped up, and that's when the offensiveness began. He said, 'We're sorry to see Andy and the others go, but I have some really good news.' Then he told us about their replacements. He went on for a long time, and finally Larry Wallace, who hadn't planned to speak, felt compelled to deliver a kind of apology for Charles. There was a lot to apologize for. The combination of Charles's remarks and his press release about the new appointments, which didn't mention Andy or Ken or Kay, made it seem as though he had asked them to leave. Neither he nor anyone else said the unspoken, but it was definitely there. Of course, that was the farthest thing from the truth and it was a terrible thing for him to do. It was as if somebody had given a eulogy and he had said, 'The deaths of this trio are too bad, but life goes on and besides there are three less mouths to feed. And let me tell you about my three *new* friends.' He must know that it's bad for the office to lose three first-rate, experienced professionals in one blow, but he had no idea of the depth of feeling that people have about all this. It is going to mean the end of an era, and I blame Charles."

The press release the lawyer had in mind was dated Thursday, March 6, 1986. It began, "Solicitor General Charles Fried today announced the appointment of three new deputy solicitors general—a United States attorney from California, the former chief appellate lawyer for the Justice Department's Criminal Division, and a partner in a prestigious Washington law firm. All three have clerked for justices of the United States Supreme Court." [22] On the face of it, the release justified Fried's enthusiasm about the new appointments. The three lawyers were very well qualified and showed every promise of meeting the standards set by the deputies they were going to replace. But, according to an official of long tenure in the Justice Department, [23] the release departed from Justice Department tradition by failing to mention the three lawyers leaving the SG's office to join Mayer, Brown & Platt. It was also misleading. The release suggested that the new deputies were each directly replacing the three who were departing. In the case of William Bryson, a Special Counsel to the Organized Crime and Racketeering Section of the Criminal Division, and a onetime assistant to the SG, who was taking the place of Andrew Frey as deputy in charge of criminal matters, it was true. In the others it was not. Donald Ayer, the U.S. Attorney in Sacramento for the Eastern District of California, was filling the job of political deputy held by Carolyn Kuhl. Louis Cohen, a partner in the law firm of Wilmer, Cutler & Pickering, and, like Fried, a former law clerk to Justice Harlan, was assuming the post vacated by Louis Claiborne five months before. Oberly and Geller were not being "replaced."

A few days later, *The New York Times* ran a small article about the new appointments. [24] It mentioned the outgoing trio, but it reversed the order of the departures and arrivals, and implied that the former lawyers had been dismissed. ("Two top deputies in the Solicitor General's Office have said that they are leaving for a private law firm after the Solicitor General, Charles Fried, announced their replacements," it began.) A lawyer outside the Justice Department who deals regularly with the SG's office commented about this gloss on the departures of Frey and Geller, "It really irritates me that a lot of lawyers are asking whether they were forced to leave, or whether they resigned. They were the top lawyers in the government, and people should know they weren't fired." [25]

From Fried's vantage point, Geller and Frey had brought the problem on themselves. While the SG had known for months that Oberly and Geller were thinking of leaving (Geller was a candidate for a judgeship that he was not offered), Fried said that neither they nor Frey had given him adequate notice. (When the lawyers told Fried they were leaving, they said they would stay as long as he wanted.) Fried also said that Frey's decision was a complete surprise. [26]

To others, Frey had seemed the most likely to leave. In 1984, he had been nominated for a judgeship on the local, as opposed to the federal, Court of Appeals in Washington. According to an official familiar with the District bench, as a former editor of the *Columbia Law Review* who had won Columbia's award for its outstanding graduate and then risen to become Deputy Solicitor General, Frey had the "best legal credentials" of anyone ever nominated to that court.[27] But after the Washington *Post* reported that Frey was a member of the National Abortion Rights Action League, the National Coalition to Ban Handguns, Planned Parenthood, and the Legal Aid Society of D.C., conservatives opposed him and the Reagan Administration asked the Senate Governmental Affairs Committee to cancel the hearing it had scheduled to confirm Frey.[28]

He had done more than any advocate since the mid-seventies to persuade the Supreme Court to take conservative positions in criminal law,[29] and his views about criminal law were relevant to his possible duties as a judge: half the docket in the D.C. court is made up of criminal cases while less than one-sixth of the cases deal with criminal law in the average federal appeals court.[30] Frey's thoughts on social issues like abortion and birth control were close to irrelevant, because few of the cases before the local court were likely to involve them. But the nomination lapsed at the end of the Congressional session in 1984, and after President Reagan was reelected, he chose not to follow the local bar's recommendation and name Frey again for the judgeship. The experience embittered Frey (about the press, about the New Right senators who attacked him, about the members of the Reagan Administration who sympathized with them and made his life difficult at the SG's office). Almost everyone who worked with him in the SG's office expected he would eventually leave.

The *American Bar Association Journal* wrote up the departures under the banner "SOLICITOR GENERAL: HAS OFFICE BEEN POLITICIZED?"[31] The piece was neither trenchant nor harsh, but after it was published, the SG followed his habit of correcting the reporters of pieces he did not like ("You hit all the sour notes," he complained to the reporter from a newspaper about a story on the departures) and wrote the *ABA Journal* to protest the opinion of its feature. A lawyer from Alaska, who had once worked with

Kathryn Oberly on a Supreme Court brief, also read the account of the departures, and wrote her a letter.[32] He had just finished reading the *ABA Journal*, he began, "and by luck opened to page 20 and saw your picture at the bottom of the page so I read the article. The article disturbed me greatly—I would hate to see the 'most prestigious little law firm' in the United States lose that great institutional credibility it has both with the court and with members of the practicing bar. So much for the myth that conservatives protect our institutions, values, and traditions!"

With the departures of Claiborne, Frey, and Geller, the SG's office had lost three of its four nonpolitical deputies in five months. They had a combined total of over forty years of experience as government lawyers, and in the history of the SG's office there had never been a wave of departures like the one under Fried.[33] Oberly had four years of experience in the SG's office, and she had thought about making a career in the government.[34] After she and her colleagues left, three-fourths of the lawyers in the office had been there less than two years.[35] Counting all the lawyers who had left on Fried's watch, the rate of turnover in the office was 50 percent in his first year, or double the normal rate.[36]

Lawyers in the SG's office recognized that Frey, Geller, and Oberly had each left for different reasons, but they also believed that the trio had been increasingly disturbed by Charles Fried's advocacy and had finally lost patience with him. No matter how lawyers who were left behind rationalized the departures ("Andy is a splendidly capable lawyer, but he's a very hard grader," said one, "and the only SG he's ever worked for who measured up to his standard was Bob Bork"), the lawyers took them as a judgment on Fried that spoke for itself.[37]

During the week after the changing of the guard, lawyers in the SG's office said: "Charles is hiring very good people, but there's a sort of affirmative-action program for right-wingers. He gives them a big preference. He's on a hot seat. He wants to maintain professional standards and not everything he does is indefensible or plainly wrong, but something always grates." "Geller didn't know the difference between himself and the United States. He was about as loyal and dogged a civil servant as you can find in the government. His slot won't be easy to fill. It can't be done by a mere mortal. You've got to have real penetration and quickness to do the job. I'd heard he was looking, but this is a sure sign that he was disgusted." "The people and the traditions in the SG's office can be dispensed with. There's nothing that makes it so special that can't be changed overnight."[38]

Not long afterward, the pitch of emotion fell and leveled off. Many of the SG's assistants were exhausted from months of pressure generated by work and worry, and some wondered if they should remain to uphold traditions that newcomers might not know about, or if they should take a hint from Fried's decision to hire all but one of his deputies from outside the staff. ("Why am I here at 2 a.m. if I'm not appreciated?" one assistant asked.) Others were struck by a newfound grace in Fried. On the last day that Frey, Geller, and Oberly spent in the SG's office, the Solicitor held a small ceremony to honor them and told his full staff that the trio was irreplaceable. "It was something that needed to be said," an assistant commented. To fill the assistant's slot for a tax specialist that recently belonged to Albert Lauber, Fried chose a career lawyer from his permanent staff. (Lauber had planned to return to private practice, but he decided to stay when the SG asked him to replace Geller as a deputy.) The SG used the hire to soothe the feelings of the civil servants who worked for him. Fried also let the new tax lawyer know he was not the first who had been offered the job, and turned a bright note flat.[39]

IN AN ARTICLE ABOUT the SG's office, Robert Stern once wrote, "The Office, experience proves, molds the Solicitor General, who usually comes from an entirely different background from that of his staff, but almost invariably prides himself on conforming to the standards of the Office. The consequence is that the Office operates pretty much the same way no matter who is Solicitor General."[40] Through the end of the Carter Administration, longtime lawyers in the office later said, Stern was essentially correct. The SG's office held the image of a talented, hard-working, compulsive band who put great store in legal reasoning and who were accustomed to almost total deference from the rest of the government. In reality, the assistants and deputies knew, they got their way more often in dry technical cases about tax law than they did in front-page tests of the Constitution, and they thought this was appropriate. Some admitted they were occasionally less punctilious than tradition suggested, and counseled the government to override the interests of other litigants in court. They could also be high-handed about basic details. If they did not like the draft of a brief written by a lawyer elsewhere in the Justice Department, they often discarded it and wrote one they liked instead. But the lawyers admitted their lapses because they were confident about the general value of their prudent ways. [41]

Under Rex Lee, Bradford Reynolds's frequent clashes with lawyers in the SG's office led to his "running to the AG" on an almost regular basis, and the SG's office became the subject of increasingly common front-office arbitrations. When Charles Fried became SG, Reynolds didn't have to go to the AG, because Edwin Meese had designated him the SG's overseer. "It used to be that the SG's slip"—the piece of paper on which the Solicitor General announces his judgment in a case—"represented the last word," an assistant said. In Lee's time, if Reynolds disagreed with the SG, it was grounds for a new debate. By Fried's day, lawyers in the SG's office expected that in almost any controversial case the SG would have made the SG's slip an afterthought: by the time a case reached him for decision during his first year as SG, according to some of his assistants, Fried had figured out what was expected of him in the front office by speaking with his "kitchen cabinet." This was composed of lawyers from the Bob Jones team—Reynolds; Carolyn Kuhl, whom Fried promoted from Deputy Assistant Attorney General for the Civil Division to take his place as political deputy; and Charles Cooper, who was promoted from his post as Reynolds's deputy to be Assistant Attorney General for Legal Counsel. (Fried saw the same facts differently. He often turned to Reynolds for advice because he respected the lawyer's judgment, he said—Reynolds was one of the few top officials as old and experienced as Fried at the Justice Department. The others were talented lawyers whose ideas he valued.) [42]

Lawyers in the SG's office especially resented what one called the "shadow process"—Fried's freewheeling method of taking part in the office's development of positions. It came about slowly. Soon after Fried arrived as political deputy, he asked an assistant to rewrite a memo because he did not like its tone. ("There is a standard set of tropes to characterize the arguments of an adversary which I don't like," he said later. "I can't stand 'multiply flawed.' I can't stand any suggestion that an argument is made in bad faith. In my book, that charge is inadmissible.") The assistant reminded him of the office tradition that every lawyer was responsible for his own arguments, and said that if Fried didn't like what he'd read, he was welcome to set his own thoughts on paper and append them to the memo bound for the SG, according to the practice of the office. Fried asked the lawyer once again, emphasizing it was the tone and not the outcome of the argument that he disagreed with. What happened next suggested otherwise. After the lawyer submitted a milder statement of the case, Fried made it appear toothless by flatly disagreeing with it on substance. [43]

Once Fried was confirmed as SG, the shadow process was stepped up. In some cases, according to lawyers in the SG's office, he picked up the phone and called the general counsel of the agency with a grievance in a sensitive case, so they could work out a deal. The lawyers in the agency, the division with responsibility for the case at the Justice Department and especially at the SG's office, who had laid the groundwork for the judgment of the Solicitor General, were left in the dark about the arrangement he had made. In the agenda cases, lawyers in the SG's office were certain, the problem of ad hoc negotiation was worse. Fried held secret meetings with his kitchen cabinet and others to set a position for the government, or excluded lawyers in the SG's office from meetings that were not secret. He did not consult assistants who had written the basic memos for cases, and used their papers to legitimize the agreements he struck on his own. He also undermined the status of his assistants with the rest of the Justice Department. Where they had been accustomed to dealing as equals with older and more senior officials (an admiral would come in from the Coast Guard to ask a young assistant to forward his service's appeal in a case about the placement of a navigation buoy; [44] an Assistant Attorney General would realize he had to persuade an assistant about the merits of his case if he wanted the Solicitor General to

rule his way), [45] the assistants became prey to phone calls from the
Attorney General's special assistants, fresh off clerkships, who
took their cues from other front-office lawyers checking up on the
Solicitor General. [46]

"Part of our being upset over this is the arrogance of the people
in the SG's office," one lawyer admitted. "We think we're good
lawyers. But there's also a value to putting arguments on paper,
so everyone knows what the choices are and other lawyers are
forced to deal with the merits or get the chance to offer a counter-
view. We're also the only lawyers in the government who take a
relatively neutral view. The agencies have axes to grind, because
their programs are at stake in litigation. This Administration's
senior executives are so political their legal views are colored as
well. That leaves the SG's office, and one of the things that people
in the office like least is that Fried gets advice from the agency
involved, the responsible part of the Justice Department, his
kitchen cabinet, and us, as if they were all on the same footing. He
treats us like any other part of the government. That is what
people in the office find most difficult to take." [47]

Through most of 1985, some assistants and deputies to the SG
did not want to believe that the office was changing. They re-
criminated about the pressures that drove Rex Lee out of office but
insisted that the SG's office would regain its form if only the
Administration would appoint someone, like Charles Fried, whose
legal credentials assured that his mandate was to serve the law and
not politics. [48] Then they detailed the pressures on Fried to submit
briefs that carried the Administration's message beyond the Supreme Court to American voters, and said Fried would declare his
independence once he was elevated from Acting Solicitor General
to SG. After Fried was sworn in, they contended that the agenda
briefs he filed were distinguished from the great majority of government papers, and that the Supreme Court would separate the
former from the latter as long as the SG's filings on traditional
subjects met the government's longtime standards. When the com-
pass of the Administration's agenda expanded so it appeared to
include almost any topic that caught the attention of a member of
the Reagan team, the lawyers in the SG's office came up with new
reasons why what many other observers of the office thought was

happening there was not as bad as it looked. The lawyers in the SG's office believed so strongly in the tradition of the place that they were sure Fried would come around. "Optimism springs eternal," explained one assistant to the SG after he was reminded about this series of rationalizations. [49]

Despite Fried's obvious intellectual quickness and his eagerness to engage in the work of the office, he did not make this brand of loyalty easy for his staff. In February of 1986, the Justice Department advertised the opening for an assistant to the Solicitor to handle tax cases. [50] The notice carried six requirements for candidates who wanted to fill the job. The next week, the government sent out an amended notice, which the Solicitor General had written. Fried had added a seventh requirement ("On occasion will be expected to work on special assignments of particular difficulty or delicacy outside the field of tax") that announced to lawyers they should be ready to work without qualms on agenda cases. Assistants still retained their optimism. They often spoke in melodramatic terms ("Not long ago, I thought Charles was going to succeed in destroying the traditions of the office") tempered with hope ("but I think things have finally turned the corner"). A Supreme Court law clerk harshly criticized Fried one day in an interview. "I resent the fact that there is any suggestion that Fried is an honorable man," he said. "He is an opportunistic, scheming, manipulative, mean-spirited man, and he's led a great institution into disgrace." One of the lawyers in the SG's office was asked how he thought Fried could continue to serve the government's interests if anyone with even modest influence in the law held such a black view. "Things are turning around," the lawyer said. [51]

Lawyers in the office volunteered a range of explanations for Fried's behavior: When he became Acting SG, in June of 1985, he still knew relatively little about how the government worked or about litigation; the first case he had ever argued was in the Supreme Court the winter before, as Rex Lee's deputy; he didn't know enough to see the fault in the political arguments pushed on him. [52] Or: He wanted to win the favor of the Meese team so they would appoint him SG, and "he went to absurd lengths to accommodate them." Or: Once he became SG, he meant no harm to the SG's office, but he was insensitive and didn't realize that the manner he used to ingratiate himself with members of the Bob Jones team "insulted lawyers who weren't targets of his charm." He also, at least at work, seemed unconcerned and neglectful of social skills or small courtesies—hello's, goodbye's, please's, thank-you's. He was an impetuous, enthusiastic official who had never managed an office before, and he appeared to overlook the value of basic pleasantries.[53] Or: He had little appreciation for good lawyering and cared less about a tight analysis than a bold, memorable declaration.[54] "He's very smart, he's very conceptual, he likes to put things in a general framework, which is always a help," Paul Bator said about his friend; "he's stronger on the conceptual side than on the detail side."[55]

On the other hand, Lyle Denniston, a legal correspondent for the Baltimore *Sun,* and now the dean of Supreme Court reporters, described Fried as an upbeat, naïve, refreshing intellectual, who believed deeply in the principles he espoused and was oblivious to pressure from political officials who wanted him to push ideas he had already come to on his own.[56]

The most sympathetic appraisal of Fried from career lawyers in the SG's office, which was shared by some who followed it from outside the government, was an explanation about circumstances: in the Meese Justice Department, Fried had little room to maneuver between the Attorney General's inner circle and the traditionalists in the SG's office—social revolutionaries with no regard for the law, on the one hand, and intransigent holdovers, on the other, as they saw each other. It was a clash of forces, and Fried was caught in the middle. He was the right man at the right time, in this appraisal, because his cleverness, good nature, and intelligence equipped him as well as anyone to satisfy both sides. ("You don't survive by appearing disloyal to the Meese team," observed a lawyer in the SG's office who was in Fried's corner. "You've just got to fool them.") Fried might join a group within the Attorney General's inner circle known as the Committee on Religious Liberty for regular meetings to discuss how to promote their extreme version of that concept before the Supreme Court. But he also recognized, on advice from his deputies, the value of hiring lawyers who met the standards of the SG's office. Aligning Fried with Meese missed the complexity of his role, his appreciation for the tradition of the SG's office, and the moderation of his lawyering, even though the Attorney General went beyond valuing the Solicitor General's "intellectual breadth" and considered Fried a reliable member of his inner circle. [57] While Fried always insisted that he was frank when he spoke about his judgments as SG, one of his allies advised that the SG's need to satisfy Meese often prevented Fried from saying what he truly believed about his advocacy for the Administration. [58]

One of Fried's critics was asked to comment on the theory of his supporters. The lawyer said, "Charles sees himself as a consensus-builder. He thinks he hammers out deals that make everyone happy. The problem is they leave no one happy." The defiant edge of this remark seemed to bear out Fried's explanation for the bad feeling expressed about him at the SG's office: it was grousing from a bunch of prima donnas who were angry they had lost their sway. Fried said that making the SG's office more accountable to a democratically elected President was bound to cause resentment. Several former aides to the Solicitor, including one who shared and one who criticized Fried's ideas, supported this view. One former deputy, who is now a federal judge, said that the Solicitor General was inevitably engaged in judgments about policy; the surprise about the office was that it did not get more guidance from the White House. Surely Charles Fried was correct, though deputies like Andrew Frey and Kenneth Geller disagreed, that the job of the Solicitor General was not to extend the power of the government virtually every time it went to court. That was not the meaning of "doing justice." It was to represent the policies of the current government as well as he could, and still perform his other duties as SG. [59]

To some observers of the office, the deputies and assistants were finally getting their comeuppance. They invariably judged someone by how smart he was (when lawyers in the office heard a comment they considered worthy, they said, "That's a thought," [60] as if awarding a star), and sometimes forgot that the clever answer was not always the right one. The real tradition of the office was a clubby sense of self-importance—what one ex-assistant called "a collective smugness." [61] Some of the SG's aides from Columbia, Harvard, and other élite law schools looked down their noses at political officials like Bradford Reynolds, Charles Cooper, and Carolyn Kuhl, as if where the three studied law (Vanderbilt, Alabama, and Duke) were enough to explain why they failed to defer to the wisdom of the office's career lawyers. ("They don't know any better because they didn't go to the right schools," one of the SG's lawyers explained seriously.) A bunch of well-credentialed white men (no matter how calmly the women in the office took their poor representation among the regular attorneys, it was conspicuous—and, since 1870, the office had employed only five blacks, including two SGs) had used a vague tradition as a cover for insisting on arguing whatever made sense to them in the law. "Their sort of know-it-all stuff is O.K. for a law clerk who is drunk from his first proximity to power," one legal reporter said about the SG's lawyers, "but at some point you've just got to grow up." [62]

However compelling some of the criticism about the career lawyers in the SG's office, Fried consistently brought the focus back to himself. "I'm feeling very upbeat about the office," [63] he said one day in April of 1986. "The Term is coming to a wonderful end." Not long after, he talked about the changes he had weathered. He said, "When Andy and Ken and Kay walked in and said they were leaving, my heart fell into my shoes. I thought, This is a potential disaster. The buzzing about the office would have just what it wanted: a sign of vulnerability. I was very upset, and I was hurt because they'd given me no warning. If the word got out, the vultures, very much in the press—they like to see an event, a trend that corresponds to a cartoon-like quality—if the word got out, the event would prove itself. Those were five of the worst days of my life, but today I think we are in very good shape. After the assistants got over the shock, they were entirely with me." Confident that the office was finally under his control, he downplayed continuing rumblings as the harmless mutterings of a temperamental staff. Repeating a phrase some assistants used to describe their efforts to persuade Fried not to send one of his flightier notions to the Court, [64] the SG gamely made fun of himself. "Of course I appreciate it when the assistants 'scrape me off the ceiling,'" he said, as if it were the job of the young lawyers, a few years out of law school, to protect the Solicitor from his foibles, and not the other way around.

He went on, "I have a sense that when this Justice Department got started five years ago, the SG's office pictured itself as a bulwark against the barbarians. An embattled station. That seems to me just an untenable way to talk about your work. It's poisonous. If that's the way you feel, you shouldn't have the job. When I took it, I thought I should develop collegial relations with the rest of the department. I thought the rest of the people in it were serious and impressive, and I was sympathetic to their agenda. They got into government for the same reason I did. I don't push the views I do because I'm their Solicitor General, but they probably picked me to be SG because I have these views. I also thought there was a difference between saying that the SG's office contained the vestal virgins of the law, and that it could maintain its own special standards while representing the President's interests. Don't you think we've done that?"

The image Fried wanted to convey was of a Solicitor General who served both the Reagan Administration and the tradition of the SG's office. He blamed the lawyers in the office for the problems they had encountered in dealing with political officials at the Justice Department before he took over. An observer of Fried at the office was asked why he thought the SG did this. He explained that Fried said things like this for public consumption, to keep Attorney General Meese and the "idiots" around him happy, but that he actually relied increasingly on the lawyers in the office, especially the ones he had chosen. [65] "To get along in this Justice Department," the lawyer recounted, "you've got to be a hypocrite. You try to keep Meese and everybody happy, you try to operate by the traditions of this office, and you sometimes say things to grease the wheels that you'd rather not have to. Charles understands this."

Fried did not acknowledge that he faced anything like the dilemma described by his observer in the office. The observer was asked whether, in private, the Solicitor General ever spoke about either the unusual circumstances under which he served, or the different faces he presented to the front office at the Justice Department and to the office he led, in order to survive and carry on as SG. "I've never heard him mention a word about this," the lawyer replied. "You just have to intuit it from his behavior." The lawyer was told that Fried had defended the Attorney General and the

Meese team as energetically as he had criticized the SG's office
under Rex Lee. The lawyer did not say anything for a moment
and then answered, "Sometimes Charles goes beyond the call of
duty." [66]

Fried emphasized the warmth and collegiality in the SG's
office, as if the days of the Vestal Virgins v. the Barbarians ended
when the disgruntled former deputies left, and a new era of harmony began. He made a point of going through the roster of
lawyers in the office, and saying how well he got along with each
one. Some of the lawyers he mentioned had different views.

"He's a bizarre fellow," one said. "To a lot of the assistants,
Fried's actually gotten to the point where he can do no right. They
are still upset over Geller and Frey leaving, and they blame Fried
for that. They remain loyal to a couple of lawyers who were
extremely able deputies. Fried is not seen as an ally of theirs. Even
when he does something right—the new deputies he brought in
are fine—he gets no credit. The case for him is that he has tried
to maintain the quality of the office, but when there are get-
togethers among lawyers who used to be in the office and lawyers
who still are, you can see a closeness between Rex Lee and the staff
that you don't see between them and Fried. You feel that you work
for him, not with him. He has private meetings about cases. The
collegiality Fried talks about is between him and the rest of the
political appointees, not between him and the office. In the Department of Justice, there is a group that is in—in every section of the
department—and there is everyone else, and Fried concentrates on
the people who count. Most of them are not in the SG's office." [67]

"It's definitely the end of an era," another lawyer said, "in the
sense that the SG no longer has the final say on what the law is.
At least through the late sixties there were few challenges to the
SG's authority, and there was little pressure on assistants and the
deputies to change their minds about a legal problem. As recently
as the tenure of Wade McCree, during the Carter Administration,
you felt you could say what the law was, and be protected by the
Attorney General. That was still true of Rex. You got the feeling
that even if Lee felt pressure to take a different position, once he
acted, one way or the other, the chance of reversal wasn't high.
These days, it's pretty clear that Fried doesn't have free rein. Now

there's a constant need to find a middle ground and accommodate the political folks. The SG is not making decisions that are the best for the government to take, in the best of all possible worlds. Sometimes the accommodations work fine. You also hear there are secret meetings that people in the office don't get invited to on political cases. From the Administration's point of view, that makes sense, because they came in with a prejudice against career people and thought the SG's office was trying to subvert the President's program. But it's still a big change.

"As for a sense of cohesiveness and spirit, it's hard to have that when only four of the seventeen assistants have been here for more than two years. It's hard to imbue the new people with the traditions of the place, even if they like tradition. Charles has come to appreciate the value of the organization more than he did when he came in as a loner, and he puts stock in collegiality. I don't see him as a captain on a bridge far removed from the deck. But he sees a different way of doing things. Even if the office isn't going down the tubes, the underlying question is: What is the role of the office? What is his job? How much independence should the SG have? Under Fried, you get the sense that he has less to say about how these questions are answered than do people outside the office. Even if he's not told what to do, there's a way of exerting pressure. An Assistant AG comes to see him over and over, and after a while Fried must get the idea he'd better do what the guy wants, or else. He has less authority to turn people down than the SG did in the past. If you're not willing to go along, you're obstructing the President's program. And Fried doesn't have trouble going along. He's not constrained by the government as a client, by precedent, or by standard legal reasoning. He takes a longer view, of who might be on the Court and what the law might become. If you're on the receiving end, that is, if you're up at the Court, it must be hard to distinguish between the abortion-type briefs and traditional ones. They get lumped together. That's the cost to the office, the cost of not having credibility."[68]

"It's difficult to draw any firm conclusions," said a third lawyer, "but my assessment isn't so rosy. In the first place, there is a low level of experience in the office. People just don't have the knowledge to draw on about how the government works, which makes it more difficult to resist badgering since they also don't know about what it means for the SG to be independent. In the second place, regardless of what Fried says about his support from the Attorney General and his independence, and I can't think of a recent case where he was overruled, there's a reason why we no longer have disagreements with the rest of the department as we did under Lee. Fried is completely in tune with Meese and company, who have a radical vision of the law. He has a very good sense of how far to go in pushing their agenda, so this office has become a tool of the Administration rather than the legal conscience of the government. In the third place, Fried loves talking about being in a dialogue with the Court. The idea of engaging in a dialogue with a judge is a peculiar view of the lawyer's role, but Fried doesn't take a traditional lawyer's view. He sees himself as being as much an originator of law as the Justices, and says he refuses to pander to the Court by telling them what they want to hear. But traditional lawyers don't see interpreting precedent that way. They see it as respecting the law." [69]

XIV

October Term,
1985

FROM THE DAY that Charles Fried filed the government's brief in the abortion case during the summer of 1985, the most often asked question about the SG's office was how the Solicitor General's aggressive advocacy would affect the office's standing with the Court. Whether the SG is seen as serving only the interests of the President who appointed him, as maintaining loyalty to both the Executive Branch and the Judiciary, or as serving all three branches of government through his duty to the law, the Solicitor General's credibility with the Justices is indispensable to him: he can be effective only as long as the Justices have confidence in his competence, integrity, and legal judgments.

Not long after the start of the 1985 Term, Charles Fried made a short argument before the Justices that some people at the Court cited as a good point of departure for a discussion about the SG's standing. [1]

One of the main tools of a courtroom advocate is his voice, and to observers at the Supreme Court, Fried's is his most distinctive physical feature. Fried speaks in the accent that some American Anglophiles pick up when they go to England for graduate school. Though he is married to an Englishwoman, it has been almost five decades since he lived briefly in England as a baby and refugee from Czechoslovakia en route to the United States, and almost three decades since he studied at Oxford. He grew up in Manhattan. Fried's accent strikes some as an affectation and it is singled out, even by people who like him, as a peculiar mannerism. When Fried-watchers at the Supreme Court recounted his performance in this case, they often imitated his voice. [2]

The case was Bender v. Williamsport, and it dealt with the right of a group of high-school students to meet during a free period at school and pray in a private club called Petros.[3] Bender drew attention because it was part of a series of divisive religion cases that had topped the Court's docket the previous Term. Attorney General Edwin Meese had discussed them at length in his speeches on constitutional law at the end of that Term, and his interest had influenced the government's position in Bender. When Fried took the podium to speak for five minutes as a friend of the Court, Justice Stevens immediately began to quiz him about problems of jurisdiction—the question of the Supreme Court's authority to consider the case. Fried's first answer was confusing. "I am not sure of what your answer is," the Justice told the SG. Fried tried again, and when Stevens began to correct him, Fried cut him off. "On the jurisdictional point," he said, "we do discuss that on page five of our brief. It is fairly intricate." The SG lingered on the last word, and then began his argument about accommodation of religion. Stevens heard him out, but at the end of Fried's speech he came back to the point that bothered him.

Stevens could not understand whether the case presented a true legal controversy for the Court to resolve. It was not clear to the Justice that John C. Youngman, Jr., who had pursued the appeal as a member of the school board and as a parent of a student, had shown how he or his son was harmed by the prayer meetings. To use Fried's word, the question was intricate, and it seemed that Fried was nervous or that he was not confident he knew the answer or that, from the vantage point of an amicus concerned with a lofty issue of constitutional law, he thought the Justice's preoccupation with this technicality was trivial—that the answer must exist somewhere in the case file.

"But at the time the appeal was taken," Stevens asked, "what was the controversy? Who was fighting with whom? Was there any allegation that any non-Petros child was offended by these meetings?" Fried replied, "Mr. Youngman, I believe, at that time was claiming on his behalf as a parent." Stevens persisted, "Where in the record do you find that?" Fried paused, and said, "I cannot point you to the section of the record."

During this second exchange, Stevens took off his glasses,

leaned over the bench to glower at Fried, and spoke in an increasingly agitated voice. Stevens does not have a naturally imposing presence, and he often seems grateful that lawyers before the Court are willing to help him and the other Justices solve the hard legal problems they consider. He normally addresses counsel in a respectful, easygoing manner. Now, however, he showed signs of anger at the SG's unsupported assertion and his attempts to dodge the question.

During the summer before the case was argued, Stevens had joined three of his colleagues in an extraordinary dissent from the Court's decision to let the SG argue in the Bender case as a friend of the Court. The senior deputy in the Court Clerk's office couldn't remember a similar dissent from any previous Term. [4] Stevens eventually wrote the Court's opinion dismissing the case, on the same procedural grounds that Fried had been unprepared or unwilling to discuss in response to the Justice's questions. [5] "A lot of people up here thought Fried's performance in the Bender case was shocking," said one law clerk. "He came in with a little speech about freedom of religion, and wouldn't answer Stevens's questions. He gave the impression that either he was a windbag or he was not telling the truth." [6]

Fried's performance in Bender was selected by career lawyers in the SG's office from the Supreme Court arguments, odd events, and amicus briefs submitted by the office in October of 1985 as what they called the "Embarrassment of the Month." [7] It was the first of a string of incidents that earned this sobriquet during the 1985 Term. The details of these encounters seemed to indicate that even if the career lawyers were not blameless in their disagreements with Fried and his allies, they understood better than anyone the long-term costs to the SG's office of his and the Administration's tenure. Under Fried, according to some of his aides, the SG's advocacy for the Administration often seemed to vanquish craftsmanship in the law.

Part of the new SG's problem was the insensitivity that he projected to the Court. During November, Fried argued for the government in a case called Davidson v. Cannon. [8] He later won it, and was proud of the victory. But at the oral argument, the SG began with what he judged a worthy piece of legal history, and what Justices and law clerks at the Court heard as tasteless commentary.[9]

The case concerned whether the negligence of a prison warden should make the government liable to a suit by an inmate. A prisoner had helped break up a fight between two other inmates, and one of them threatened to retaliate. The prisoner sent a note to the warden telling him about this threat; the warden read it, and passed it to one of his sergeants. The sergeant heard that the note was on its way and what it was about, but he did not bother to read it. Over the weekend, he forgot about it. Two days later, the inmate who had threatened the prisoner attacked him and beat him up badly, and the prisoner sued for damages. The Court eventually ruled that the warden's lack of care did not approach "the sort of abusive government conduct" that the Fourteenth Amendment's Due Process Clause was designed to prevent.[10]

Rather than going directly to the question of the government's liability, Fried opened his remarks with a comment about the prisoner who had been beaten up. "If I may," he began, "before I enter the details of what we consider to be the defects in petitioner's claim, may I suggest a more distant perspective on this case? A hundred years ago, Oliver Wendell Holmes began *The Common Law* by insisting on a distinction which he said was so basic that it is part even of our animal nature, the distinction, in his words, 'between being stumbled over and being kicked.' In this case, respondent"—that is, the warden—"can at most be said to have stumbled. If anyone kicked petitioner, it was his fellow prisoner, McMillan, against whom, of course, Davidson retains a cause of action."[11]

Fried saw his paraphrase of Holmes as a tribute to the scholarly tradition of the SG's office, but, as the opening comment on a case about the beating of a prisoner, the reference was jarring and crude. A number of Supreme Court law clerks mentioned it as an example of a Fried "snapper"—one of the showy fillips of language or law that he regularly employed. The Solicitor had the taste to sanitize Holmes's remark, by referring to "our animal nature" instead of quoting the Justice directly and saying it was "a dog" who knew the difference between "being stumbled over and being kicked." But, if not as a dog, was the Court supposed to think of the prisoner as another kind of animal? Did being a prisoner mean a man had to suffer incompetence from a warden, as an animal had to accept being stumbled over in the outside world? Although the SG's brief on the case was cited by some longtime lawyers in the SG's office as sound, Fried's oral argument in the case joined his performance in the Petros case as evidence of an odd insensitivity to his impact on the Court.[12]

In December, Fried's performance in two cases vied for honors as "Embarrassment of the Month," according to staffers in the SG's office.[13] The more poignant was called Batson v. Kentucky,[14] and it was argued by Lawrence Wallace. When Wallace became a target for the anger of Reagan conservatives after the Bob Jones debacle, they tried to link the source of his obstinacy to his political views, overlooking his loyalty to the SG's office. Wallace's sense of commitment was matched by his eagerness to get on with his work, and after an early period of uneasiness with Fried, he and the Solicitor formed a mutual-admiration society. Their legal experiences (Columbia Law School; Supreme Court clerkships; years as professors) were sufficiently alike to explain the alliance. Fried's quest for support among career lawyers in the SG's office also helped create this bond with Wallace, and each man praised the abilities of the other.

In the Batson case, the Supreme Court was being asked to revise a precedent set in the mid-sixties. During the heyday of the civil-rights movement, the Warren Court had held that prosecutors who systematically excluded blacks from juries solely because of their race, and "for reasons wholly unrelated to the outcome of the particular case on trial,"[15] violated the Constitution. But the Justices also held that it was lawful for prosecutors to strike blacks from juries by using peremptory challenges (a set number of challenges to potential jurors that prosecutors can exercise without any explanation) even if they excluded from the final panel all the blacks in a pool of potential jurors.

At Fried's request, Wallace argued in Batson. He had made his reputation as a civil-rights lawyer for the government, and, according to lawyers in the SG's office,[16] Fried believed that the Justices would think Batson was not an agenda case if Wallace represented the government. Wallace dutifully squared off against the

NAACP Legal Defense and Educational Fund, the American Civil Liberties Union, the Lawyers Committee for Civil Rights Under Law, and other groups, and made the prosecutors' case— that peremptory challenges should be available even to exclude from a jury every black in the jury pool for no reason other than race. The Justices rejected his arguments. [17] In a seven-to-two ruling, the Court overturned a twenty-one-year-old decision and made it easier for black criminal defendants to keep prosecutors from excluding blacks from juries. Justice Lewis Powell wrote the Court's majority opinion, which united Justices from across the Court's spectrum. Although Wallace was embarrassed as the government's spokesman, the blame lay at Fried's door. He eventually accepted it. "I think the Supreme Court, on reflection, was right," he said. "I think they taught us something about adhering to our own principles more rigorously than we had thought to do." [18]

In another December case, Thornburg v. Gingles, Fried argued for the government. [19] In 1982, Congress amended the Voting Rights Act of 1965, which had let voters sue state governments for unfair districting, unfair registration, and other discriminatory election practices. With the help of the 1965 law, the percentage of blacks registered to vote in the South had almost doubled (from 29 to 57 percent between 1965 and 1980), and the number of blacks holding office increased from fewer than three hundred to over twenty-four hundred. [20] The Supreme Court had held that in order to win suits under the original law, voters had to prove that legislators who set district lines intended to discriminate against them when they diluted the voting power of minorities. The voters could not rely simply on a showing that the effect of the change was to dilute minority votes. In the wake of this ruling, Congress decided to amend the law. The Reagan Administration fought to have it retain the "intent" standard, on grounds that any form of an effects test would require "proportional representation" and lead to "a quota system for electoral politics." In 1982, both the House and the Senate rejected the President's view and voted overwhelmingly (389–24 in the House, and 85–8 in the Senate) to amend the law so that it allowed voters to use an effects test when seeking fairer elections. Under the 1982 amendment, voters had to prove that the "results" of redistricting denied them an equal opportunity to take part in elections and to choose the representatives they wanted.

The Gingles case arose in North Carolina, where several blacks challenged the state's redistricting plan for the North Carolina General Assembly, and a federal trial court found that the plan violated the new standard. The case was the first to test the 1982 amendment before the Justices, and it raised elementary legal questions. How should the Court interpret the new standard? What kind of evidence should it tell lower courts to rely on in making the judgment?[21] The state of North Carolina argued that the "results" that a voter had to show to get relief were the outcomes of elections in suspect districts. On that theory, if any blacks had been elected, the black voters could not have been victims of discrimination. The NAACP Legal Defense and Educational Fund, Inc., on the other hand, attempted to give substance to the new law's "totality of the circumstances"[22] test: even if some blacks had been elected, the lawyers contended, there were other factors to consider in assessing the "results" of an election.[23] In North Carolina, black districts had been submerged in white districts where voters elected several representatives, and blacks were only occasionally elected. The share of white voters who chose blacks on their ballots was extremely low. Even when whites voted for blacks, they ranked the blacks last or next to last. Blacks who won the highest number of votes from blacks regularly carried the smallest number from whites. After a century of official hostility to their voting in North Carolina, blacks still registered to vote less often than whites, and according to the Inc. Fund, black candidates sometimes lacked the money and know-how to compete against whites. As the lower court acknowledged, blacks occasionally won in the elections under scrutiny only because they picked up votes from whites who hoped to prove to the Court that the new districts treated blacks fairly. The Inc. Fund pointed out that North Carolina had long had the smallest percentage of blacks in its state legislature of any state with a sizable black population (blacks made up 22.4 percent of the state's residents, but had never been more than 4 percent of either house of the state legislature), and the first black had not been elected to the state House of Representatives until 1968.

In the Supreme Court, Fried articulated views primarily associated with Edwin Meese and Bradford Reynolds, and argued that North Carolina blacks should get elected "the old-fashioned way—through politics." [24] He agreed with the state of North Carolina that "results" meant "election outcomes." [25] Since blacks had been elected to office, he said, the new districting scheme could not have impeded the rights of blacks to play a role in politics. Fried's was a skillful presentation, and on the surface it was difficult to fault. But to lawyers interested in the case—and to civil-rights attorneys, because it dealt with the right to vote, Gingles was as important as any case on the Court's docket—the SG gave no help on the central question. As longtime lawyers in the Civil Rights Division at the Justice Department put it, it was impossible to tell from the SG's brief or from his argument how he thought the Supreme Court should interpret the amendment's new standard, except to rule that the districts in North Carolina were legal. [26] On the lawyer's issue, which a Solicitor General could be expected to see as the most significant in the case and the one on which the Justices might most value his counsel, Fried was silent.

The SG saved his voice for chiding the Republican Party of North Carolina; the then Senate Majority Leader, Robert Dole, Republican from Kansas; Senator Charles Grassley, Republican from Iowa; and eight other co-sponsors of the 1982 amendment, who together had filed an amicus brief siding with the NAACP Inc. Fund against the government. In their brief, the co-sponsors stated that the lower court had interpreted the new law as Congress intended.

On the steps of the Supreme Court after the argument, Julius LeVonne Chambers, the director-counsel of the NAACP Legal Defense and Educational Fund, Inc., who argued against the Solicitor General, observed that Gingles was the first case in his long career as a civil-rights lawyer in which he had faced the Solicitor General as "the enemy." [27]

The morning the Justices announced their decision in the voting-rights case, at the end of the 1985 Term, Charles Fried happened to be at the Court sponsoring a group of lawyers for membership in the Supreme Court bar. When he heard the Chief

Justice say that Justice William Brennan would announce the holding in the voting-rights case, Fried's back stiffened and involuntarily, it seemed, he sucked in his breath. [28] Brennan was a liberal and, if one of the Court's two liberals had written the majority opinion, Fried knew that it was not likely to favor the Administration's views. Brennan's first sentence confirmed this fear. Brennan handed down the Court's opinion on behalf of all his colleagues (though some filed separate opinions concurring or dissenting about peripheral questions), essentially rejecting the SG's interpretation of the law. [29] At forty-seven pages, the opinion was long. At least half of it was devoted to rebutting the Solicitor General's arguments, point by point.

The Court's opinion took care to identify and criticize the SG's departures from standard methods of legal reasoning. When the voting-rights case was briefed for the Supreme Court, the NAACP Inc. Fund complained that the Solicitor had offered "an account of legislative history" that was "substantially inaccurate." According to the Inc. Fund, in 1982 the entire Senate Judiciary Committee had favored amending the Voting Rights Act as it was ultimately amended, and two-thirds of the full Senate stood ready to support the bill in case any of the remaining senators should consider holding the bill in committee until it was changed to suit them. But the SG's brief focused on the views of a few senators who were overwhelmingly outvoted; it called the result of their stubborn bit of maneuvering a "deadlock" [30] instead of acknowledging the general harmony of the decision. After the amendment was passed, the Senate followed its usual procedure and wrote up the history of the new voting-rights legislation in an official Senate Committee Report. In his brief, the SG urged the Supreme Court to pay slight attention to this official Senate Report.

For the full Court, the Brennan opinion indicated that the disagreement about whose version of legislative history was accurate touched a deeper issue of law. "The Solicitor General urges this Court to give little weight to the Senate Report," the Justice wrote, "arguing that it represents a compromise among conflicting 'factions,' and thus is somehow less authoritative than most Committee Reports." The Court expressly rejected the SG's contention. "We have repeatedly recognized that the authoritative source

for legislative intent lies in the committee reports on the bill."
Later in the opinion, the Court again repudiated an argument
presented by the SG, not because of any larger disagreement about
philosophy but because of its faulty legal reasoning. "The United
States," Justice Brennan complained about the SG's stated interpretation of the district court's original opinion in the case, "iso-
lates a single line in the court's opinion and identifies it as the
court's complete test."[31]

In January, February, and March 1986, the roster of agenda
cases on the Supreme Court's docket expanded from school
prayer, abortion, affirmative action, and other familiar topics, to
include medical treatment of handicapped infants, land-use regulation, the conflict between federal labor law and local regulation,
school discipline, and the legality of an established doctrine called
associational standing, which makes it possible for an organization
like the United Auto Workers or the Chamber of Commerce to
sue on behalf of its members.[32] The agenda now seemed to include
almost anything of interest to a member of the Reagan (and, really,
the Meese) team. Though the cases raised eyebrows for different
reasons, they were all notorious among regular observers of the
Supreme Court. They continued to strengthen the concern that
serious harm was being done to the SG's office.

In March, the talk was about the SG's brief in the case brought
by the United Auto Workers against the Secretary of Labor. The
government's filing prompted a united response by the improbable
coalition of the Chamber of Commerce, the AFL-CIO, the American Medical Association, the NAACP, the Alliance for Justice, the
Chemical Manufacturers Association, and the Sierra Club. At issue
was a federal supplement to state unemployment insurance for
auto workers who had lost their jobs because of foreign competition. In a highly unorthodox move, the SG's office waited until
presenting its brief in the Supreme Court to raise the question of
whether the United Auto Workers had standing to sue on behalf
of its members. (According to the key precedent, an association
like a union could sue on behalf of its members if members would
have had standing to sue on their own, the suit brought by the
association was related to the group's overall purpose, and the
nature of the suit did not make it necessary for individual members

to take part.)[33] The SG's approach was particularly odd, because when the government had earlier opposed the union's petition for certiorari, the SG had acknowledged that the Court of Appeals correctly applied the law of associational standing when it let the UAW represent its members and supporters in court, and appeared to endorse this doctrine, which it called "well-settled."[34]

Some of the associations that responded to the SG's brief had not planned to. They saw no reason to burden the Supreme Court "with a brief arguing that the Court should adhere to 'well-settled' principles that neither party had questioned in the Court of Appeals or at the certiorari stage."[35] Because of the surprise about-face by the SG, the associations suddenly saw a need to participate. Written by a trio of attorneys in the law firm of Sidley & Austin, which Rex Lee joined after he left the government, the amici's brief criticized the SG's office in unusually blunt terms for a paper filed at the Supreme Court. One of the brief's authors was the former assistant to the Solicitor, Carter Phillips ("that quota lover!"), who had tangled with Bradford Reynolds.

"Without any previous hint of doubt about the petitioner union's basic right as an association to have standing to represent its members' interests," the brief observed, "the federal government has asked this Court to hold as a matter of 'policy' that the petitioner union should be denied standing to assert the rights of its members in federal court. It is particularly inappropriate for the federal government to raise an issue as fundamental and important as the validity of associational standing without submitting the issue to the adversarial process at any time prior to the Court's grant of certiorari. Because the government's litigating tactics on an issue of such national importance are not proper, the Court should simply refuse to entertain the Solicitor General's suggestion, in this case."[36] (The Court did.)

In April, the case on the docket that captured the most attention at the SG's office was called City of Los Angeles v. Preferred Communications.[37] It was about the L.A. decision not to let that company provide cable TV service to city homes. The company's challenge to the city's judgment was based on the belief that Los Angeles had abridged the First Amendment's guarantee of free speech by insisting that the city had the authority to award a cable

franchise to one company only, which was not Preferred. Bradford Reynolds and the circle of young lawyers around the Attorney General became interested in the case and, operating outside
the sphere of civil rights once more, Reynolds urged Charles Fried
to take a vigorous line in favor of competition and against regulation of the company's access to the city's cables.[38] He argued that
the city's telephone poles, on which the winning cable company
had hung its lines, had room for another set of cables as well, and
that deregulation of cable and competition between companies
would improve the choice of fare for viewers.

To lawyers involved with the case, the Reynolds argument had
a number of problems. To begin with, it appeared to run counter
to the Supreme Court's reading of the Constitution.[39] It also prevented the Solicitor General from defending a 1984 statute called
the Cable Communications Policy Act. As a report by the Congress about the law announced, the act "expressly affirmed the
authority of local governments to issue franchises for cable television service" and it reinforced their power "to determine the
number of cable television service" and it reinforced their power
"to determine the number of cable operators."[40] Reynolds wanted
the SG to ask the Supreme Court to overturn the Court of Appeals' opinion upholding the city's cable regulations, and to overlook the new federal law about cable TV.

Charles Fried thought he should not push the Justices that far.
He filed a brief advising the Supreme Court to do what it eventually did: to send the case back to the trial court to gather more facts
as a basis for judgment about the First Amendment issue at the
heart of the case. In contrast to the wave of cases in which he had
appeared to capitulate to pressure within the Administration to
promote the President's social agenda, Fried's decision in Preferred was hailed by lawyers in the SG's office as a sign of back-
bone.[41]

Nonetheless, the substance of Fried's brief had all but contradicted its conclusion. "What respondent seeks to do is to com-
municate messages—some of its own choosing, some of its own
devising—on a wide variety of topics and in a wide variety of
formats," the brief stated. "Surely this enterprise is every bit as
much the enterprise of speech, of the communication of ideas, as

are the traditional enterprises of newspaper and book publishers, of public speakers, and of pamphleteers." The brief extolled the virtues of competition in the marketplace of ideas, and left to a footnote any discussion of the statute regulating cable TV that was central to the case. If not a pamphlet, the Solicitor's brief lacked the qualities of a traditional brief. The assistant to the SG assigned to the brief was unhappy enough about its contents to ask that his name be removed when it was filed with the Supreme Court. [42]

By late April, however, the Solicitor General was pleased with his performance on the job. His new team was in place and he was happily immersed in the details of the case that commanded attention outside the Justice Department. It dealt with the constitutionality of the Balanced Budget and Emergency Deficit Control Act of 1985, widely known as the Gramm-Rudman Act. [43] A panel of lower-court judges, in an opinion written by Antonin Scalia, had ruled that the feature of the act calling for automatic budget cuts made the act unconstitutional. [44] The judges found that the provision violated the Constitution's requirement for separation of powers between the branches of government by giving authority of the Executive Branch to the Comptroller General, who works for Congress.

The Comptroller General's task under the Gramm-Rudman law was to tell the Executive Branch how much it had to cut the federal budget to stay on schedule for eliminating the government's deficit. As head of the General Accounting Office, which is a nonpartisan agency of Congress founded in 1921 to monitor the Executive Branch's enforcement of the laws, the Comptroller General is appointed by the President for a fixed term of fifteen years. To assure his independence, the law setting up the agency says he can only be removed from office by impeachment or by a joint resolution of Congress. [45] Through the tenures of six Comptrollers, none had come close to being removed.

This fact made the appeals court's ruling appear speculative and largely abstract, and the lower-court judges knew it. "It may seem odd," Scalia commented, "that this current curtailment of such an important and hard-fought legislative program should hinge upon the relative technicality" of who had the power to remove the Comptroller General. "But the balance of separated powers established by the Constitution consists precisely of a series of technical provisions that are more important to liberty than superficially appears, and whose observance cannot be approved or rejected by the courts as the times seem to require." In their opinion, it was illegal for the Executive Branch to delegate power to the Comptroller General, because, no matter how farfetched it sounded, he could be fired only by the Legislature and thus was not an Executive official.

In Fried's argument in the Gramm-Rudman case, which was his last of the Term, he showed polish and admirable control. He supported the lower court's reasoning that the Act was unconstitutional, which eventually prevailed. [46] But he still drew the Justices into unusual exchanges. Early in his presentation, the SG tried to divorce himself from the contention he appeared to make in his brief that all independent agencies (not just the provision affecting the Comptroller General in the case) might be unconstitutional. The Attorney General had pursued the subject in speeches, and it was widely understood to be an agenda item. Fried began: "I would like to say at the outset that this second argument does not in our view in any way cast any doubt on the validity of agencies such as the Federal Reserve Board, the Federal Trade Commission, or any such agencies, and that the notion that the second argument in some sense endangers those agencies or would embark this Court on some constitutional adventure is simply a scare which we don't intend to throw into the Court and I don't think need be thrown there." To Justice O'Connor, the idea expressed in the SG's brief was "a novel doctrine" without precedent "in any of this Court's previous decisions." Drawing a nervous murmur from the courtroom gallery, she observed, "Well, Mr. Fried, I'll confess you scared me with it." (When the Court decided the case, it did not endorse the doctrine suggested by the brief.) [47]

Fried's "novel" approach came up again when the Supreme Court ruled on the Pennsylvania abortion case. By five to four, the Justices upheld the right to abortion. The Court's majority opinion was written by Harry Blackmun. He recalled that three years before, in the Akron case, the Justices had reviewed state and local laws regulating abortion. "In Akron, the Court specifically reaffirmed Roe v. Wade," Blackmun emphasized. "Again today, we reaffirm the general principles laid down in Roe and in Akron." The Justice attempted to clarify why a majority of the Court thought that the Constitution protects the right to abortion. "Our cases long have recognized that the Constitution embodies a promise that a certain private sphere of individual liberty will be kept largely beyond the reach of government," Blackmun stated. "That promise extends to women as well as to men. Few decisions are more personal and intimate, more properly private, or more basic to individual dignity and autonomy, than a woman's decision—with the guidance of her physician and within the limits specified in Roe—whether to end her pregnancy. A woman's right to make that choice freely is fundamental. Any other result, in our view, would protect inadequately a central part of the sphere of liberty that our law guarantees equally to all." [48]

When the abortion case came down, Fried held the first major press conference ever given by a Solicitor General. He admitted that the case "was a defeat in the sense that the position we urged was not adopted by a majority of the Court." Now that the Court had spoken, Fried said, he wouldn't make a "pest" of himself by looking for another case that would allow him to press a similar claim. But he also hazarded that the government had done "a useful thing and a responsible thing in provoking a very restrained and a very probing constitutional inquiry which I believe is far from over." [49]

The inquiry he had in mind was a dissent by Justice Byron White—"one of the most remarkable and profound statements of constitutional principle which I have read for a long time," [50] Fried called it. Joined by William Rehnquist, White contended that decisions reading values and principles into the Constitution that are not explicitly stated usurp the power of the people, "for such decisions represent choices that the people have never made and that they cannot disavow through corrective legislation." The majority's was a "warped point of view," White concluded. "In my view, the time has come to recognize that Roe v. Wade," like other previously overturned Court decisions, " 'departs from a proper understanding' of the Constitution and to overrule it." [51]

The Solicitor General did not answer questions about the substance of another opinion criticizing White's. Justice John Paul

Stevens dissected what he considered errors in White's logic. As Stevens indicated, in 1965 Justice White had written for the Court when it struck down a statute outlawing birth control. In White's words, the law then in question deprived people of liberty without due process because of its "telling effect on the freedom of married persons." In the latest abortion case, White recognized that a woman's ability to decide whether to have an abortion was a "liberty" protected by the Constitution, but he announced that it was less fundamental than the rights associated with marriage. Stevens failed "to see how a decision on child-bearing becomes *less* important the day after conception than the day before. Indeed, if one decision is more 'fundamental' to the individual's freedom than the other, surely it is the post-conception decision that is the more serious." Stevens concluded, "In the final analysis, the holding in Roe v. Wade presumes that it is far better to permit some individuals to make incorrect decisions than to deny all individuals the right to make decisions that have a profound effect upon their destiny."[52]

The exchange between Blackmun, White, and Stevens about how the Court should interpret the Constitution carried wide significance, and it distracted attention from the Court's more focused response to the Solicitor General. Fried had asserted that the lower courts showed "unabashed hostility" to attempts by states to regulate abortion. For a majority of the Court, Blackmun found that the hostility came from the states. "In the years since this Court's decision in Roe," the Justice observed, "States and municipalities have adopted a number of measures seemingly designed to prevent a woman, with the advice of her physician, from exercising her freedom of choice." He added, "The States are not free, under the guise of protecting maternal health or potential life, to intimidate women into continuing pregnancies."

Like the Court's comments in the voting-rights case, Blackmun's statement transcended the question before the Court. A majority of the Justices seemed sufficiently concerned about the way the Solicitor General had argued for the Administration that they went out of their way to correct his presentation.

The Court's comments about the SG's arguments were prickly and virtually unprecedented, and they were restricted neither to cases the SG lost nor to agenda cases. [53] In a case where the Justices ruled in favor of the government, they corrected the SG on a technical doctrine known as equitable estoppel. [54] Explaining his understanding of a legal point endorsed by the Court, Justice Stevens instructed: "The [SG] has argued . . . that the remedy ordered by the District Court was improper because it rested on an equitable estoppel theory. The Court today correctly—and unanimously—rejects this argument, thus answering the central question of law that prompted it to grant certiorari in a way that completely repudiates the submission of the Solicitor General." [55]

To some lawyers in the SG's office, the opinions indicated that it was time for a statement of contrition from Fried and other senior Administration officials. The Solicitor General did not make one. When he commented on his record after the 1985 Term closed, he noted that he had won "a respectable 71 percent" and predicted that "the clarity of our arguments" would help shape the law in the future even though the arguments had not won the Court's "triumphant embrace." [56] Though the government's winning percentage had declined (in the 1984 Term, the government had won 77 percent of its cases, which was the average winning percentage during Rex Lee's four years as Solicitor General), [57] favorable holdings in uncontroversial cases about the details of government assured Fried a large enough share of victories that he seemed to feel comfortable reading the Court's high-profile opinions to find what he wanted.

After the voting-rights opinion was handed down, Fried declared that he was "very pleased" the Court had not endorsed the principle of "proportionate representation" [58]—which was never at issue in the case because, as briefs for all parties and the Court's opinion itself made clear, it was specifically excluded by Congress from the statute in question. In the wake of the affirmative-action cases, the Solicitor General explained the Court's holdings like this: "I think what they said is that while we feel using discrimination to get rid of discrimination is something you must never do, they said, 'No, not never, but hardly ever.' " [59] The Court had said nothing like Fried's interpretation. "To summarize our holding today," Justice Brennan wrote in Local 28 of the Sheet Metal Workers' International Association v. the Equal Employment Opportunity Commission, "six Members of the Court agree that a district court may, in appropriate circumstances, order preferential relief benefiting individuals who are not the actual victims of discrimination as a remedy for violations of Title VII" of the 1964 Civil Rights Act.[60] The Justice offered explicit directions on how to read the holding so no government official would do what Bradford Reynolds had done two years before, when he took a narrow decision and read it broadly as the basis for an attack by the Administration on affirmative action,[61] but Fried did not heed the Justice. The complexity of the Court's opinions about affirmative action gave Fried ample grounds for asserting that the Justices had been cautious in their judgments, but, instead, he pulled from the decision a strict limitation that simply was not there.[62]

It was not as far as Fried went to put his advocacy in the best light. He regularly emphasized that in Bowers v. Hardwick,[63] upholding a Georgia law that made oral and anal sex between consenting adults a criminal offense, the Supreme Court had used the same reasoning offered by the SG in the Term's major abortion case. Fried said the argument the Justices had adopted was that the Court should not "invent rights," and called this "the most dramatic example" of his salutary influence on the Court.[64] This claim astonished former and current lawyers in the SG's office. In the first place, Bowers was a case in which the government had not participated. (To former colleagues at Harvard Law School, Fried confided that the Attorney General and his aides didn't dare suggest that the SG file an amicus brief in the case, because they knew his reservations about the state law.)[65] In the second place, a reading of the opinions gave no reason to believe that any of the Justices, whether in the majority or in dissent, had actually relied on the Solicitor General's abortion-brief reasoning that rights should not be "invented."

Finally, to the extent that the SG's argument in the abortion case had any similarity to the holding of the majority in the sodomy case, it was like an argument that several Justices on the Court had been making for many years, and certainly did not reflect any novel contribution by the SG.[66] In fact, as one of Fried's deputies reminded him, the Justices in the majority in the sodomy case had done precisely what the SG had advised against in other cases when they read into the state law a distinction between homosexuals and heterosexuals that the law itself did not make, to uphold the law's application to homosexuals. The SG had no basis for taking credit for the Court's reasoning either way, and even one of his unshakable defenders in the SG's office admitted that Fried had engaged in "puffery" by doing so. (Another lawyer in the office explained, "We got a run of bad decisions, so that was a pretty bleak period for us. Charles meant to cheer the place up.") [67] Attorney General Meese embellished the Solicitor General's line and called the Court's decision to uphold the anti-sodomy law the Administration's biggest victory of the Term. Meese and Fried used identical language to present the Administration's public position. They said, "We don't have to be in a case to get our view across." [68]

Fried's habit of representing Court opinions to be as he wanted them understood, and not as they were written, was related to the theme of the Court's sharp criticism of him as Solicitor General—serious concern about his repeated departures from settled practices of legal reasoning, in order to press for results favored by the Administration. The pretense that the law is a system of scientifically applied rules was abandoned in the nineteen-thirties, [69] but lawyers still agree on certain principles for reading cases and statutes. One of the most basic, as Fried regularly stated, was to begin with the text of a decision or a law itself to understand its meaning. Fried seemed not to do this when it did not suit his purpose. Not long after decisions were issued in two cases on the Reagan agenda (not because they were obviously part of the President's social program, but because someone in the Justice Department had added them to the list), Fried was asked what he thought of the rulings. In each instance, a Justice representing the Court's right or left flank had rejected a theory supported by the Solicitor General.

"I'm gratified that Justice Rehnquist recognized the middle ground we carved out," Fried said about the first case, which concerned sexual harassment. [70] The main question before the Court had been: When should a company be liable to one of its employees for harassment by another employee? The Solicitor General argued that unless someone let the employer know about an incident of sexual harassment (for example, by filing official charges), the company could protect itself from liability simply by declaring its opposition to harassment and setting up a grievance procedure. [71] Rehnquist had declined to rule on the question of liability. (The factual record in the case wasn't clear enough.) But, in his opinion for the Court, the Justice "reject[ed] petitioner's view"—and the SG's—"that the mere existence of a grievance procedure and a policy against discrimination, coupled with respondent's failure to invoke that procedure, must insulate petitioner from liability." [72] When Fried was asked about this apparent rejection, he replied, "Isn't it nice we can go to the written record, and let the words decide for us?" [73] While the Court may have "recognized the middle ground," its rejection of that position was as plain as words could make it.

Fried's second mischaracterization dealt with the Court's dismissal of the Solicitor General's request that the Justices overrule the precedent giving groups like the United Auto Workers the authority to represent their members in court under the doctrine of associational standing. "Well," Fried said, "I couldn't have been happier with the treatment the Court gave us. Read the Marshall opinion. He said, 'We are not prepared to dismiss the government's argument out of hand.' That was a very respectful thing to say.' " [74]

While some, with Fried, may have found respect in that single phrase of Marshall's, which Fried paraphrased, no one could find that quality in Marshall's complete statement. It closed, "[t]he Secretary" (by proxy, the Solicitor General) "has given us absolutely no reason to doubt the ability of the UAW to proceed here on behalf of its aggrieved members, and his presentation has fallen far short of meeting the heavy burden of persuading us to abandon settled principles of associational standing." [75]

By the end of the Term, the record showed that the Solicitor General's victories were less grand than he claimed, that his losses were more emphatic and severe, and that, in general, the Court had rejected the arguments of the Solicitor General more often than ever before in history. Coming from a moderately conservative Court, these judgments were all the more indelible.

XV

The View from
the Court

TOWARD THE END of the 1985 Term, a young lawyer who
had recently clerked for a Justice remarked that the question about
Charles Fried was not whether his advocacy had diminished the
standing of the SG's office before the Court, but how much he had
aggravated a problem that had started before his arrival. "Every
year,"[1] the former clerk said, "the law clerks from each chamber
have lunch with each of the Justices. Invariably, during the past
few years, the subject of the SG's office has come up. The impression the clerks get is that the Justices feel they can no longer trust
the SG's office as they once did. While the briefs dealing with the
merits of cases on the Reagan agenda are one thing, the skepticism
has spilled over to other sorts of filings. In some cases, clerks found
that the SG's statements carried the stamp of a sharp-edged advocate more than a dispassionate scholar. There were definitely papers that were less honest about the facts and case citations than
they should have been. In order to dissuade the Court from taking
a case, for example, a petition opposing certiorari would downplay
conflicts in the Circuit Courts and claim support for its argument
which existed only weakly in the cases the SG's office cited. On
the whole, the office continued to file good briefs and to make
more polished and confident arguments than other lawyers. But
from the Court's point of view the politicization of the SG's office
marked an important change. In the past, the Justices had counted
on the SG as a kind of partner, an officer of the Court whose
inclusion in the list of officials at the front of every volume of the
United States Reports symbolized his special duty and loyalty. By
filing amicus briefs in cases where the federal interest was attenu-

ated and asking the Court to overturn recently reaffirmed precedent, or by attacking landmark holdings, the SG turned himself into a partisan before the Court and a kind of adversary of the Court itself. This was a major topic of conversation at the Court. It was significant because it determined how the clerks and the Justices first looked at material from the SG's office, and it was clear that the Court didn't trust the SG's office the way it used to."

It would not have been surprising if observers' opinions about Fried conformed to their views about the desirability of the results he sought: liberal law clerks would be his biggest critics, conservative clerks his boosters, and moderates somewhere in between. Since liberal Justices do not necessarily hire liberal clerks, or conservative Justices conservative clerks, there was no foolproof way to test this theory. But when, at the end of the 1985 Term, law clerks from each of the nine chambers agreed to be interviewed, as long as they were not identified by name, the results *were* surprising.

Except for one clerk, known by others for his devotion to the Federalist Society (a meeting ground for rising and established Reagan conservatives),[2] who chose not to speak, with the comment that "most of the clerks up here are very liberal and aren't likely to give the Solicitor General a fair shake,"[3] every clerk interviewed said that Charles Fried had pushed the Administration's political agenda more aggressively than any SG they had heard of from the Justices and prior law clerks. Two clerks praised the SG's office and said that, for all Fried's excesses ("He is definitely a maniac," said one, with obvious overstatement. "Even staunch Republicans tell lawyers thinking about government service not to go near the Justice Department or the SG's office, because they are now bastions of extremism"), the Court paid little attention to the Administration's rhetoric and found little reason to fault the craftsmanship of most of the SG's work. Discounting the notion of a special role for the Solicitor, as if anyone familiar with the law realized that the days of dispassionate advocacy were long past, one clerk said that the SG's work met the highest standard for lawyers urging a hard line on the Justices.[4]

But the majority of the clerks, who described themselves variously as moderate conservatives, moderates, or liberals, gave

many reasons to conclude that the reputation of the Solicitor
General at the Court had slipped dramatically during the 1985
Term. From all nine chambers, and very different political visions, they accused him, or the office under his command, of bad
lawyering, intemperance, deceit, arrogance, extreme partisan-
ship, and disgracing a long, great tradition. The language they
used often seemed exaggerated, but a clerk who described himself as a moderate conservative commented, "A guy gets up there
and he flaps his arms like a duck and he quacks like a duck, what
do you think of his work? He claims, 'This contravenes all notions of legal history,' or says, 'This contradicts known principles of law.' The Justices aren't idiots, and neither are the clerks.
They know what he claims is often hyperbole. It just rolls off his
tongue, and sounds like a lot of rot. He's the one who uses
strong language without cause." One of his fellow clerks said
more succinctly about Fried's advocacy, "My government lies to
me. My government *lies* to me!"[5]

The clerks also offered wide agreement about a concrete measure of the erosion in the SG's influence at the Court. A principal
chore of the Solicitor's office is to help the Supreme Court set its
docket by screening petitions for writs of certiorari. In the 1985
Term, parties from around the country filed 3,876 cert. petitions;
the Court granted only 146 of them.[6] As in previous Terms, the
task of winnowing out about 96 percent of the petitions was
tedious but important. No party came close to matching the Solicitor General's record of success with cert. petitions. The government derailed some cases on their way to the Court by opposing
petitions from other parties; it boosted the chances of other petitions by joining at the request of the parties submitting them; and,
where only a tiny fraction of petitions from any other party succeeded, the SG's office persuaded the Court to take an extraordinary share—83 percent—of its own petitions.

The rate of success in the 1985 Term was slightly higher than
during Rex Lee's last Term as Solicitor, when the Court granted
80 percent of the government's petitions. But while the government filed about the same number of amicus briefs to support
petitions from other parties, the Court granted only 57 percent of
these petitions, as opposed to the 80 percent it had accepted on

average during the previous four Terms.[7] This fact suggested that while the SG continued to affect the Supreme Court docket through its cert. petitions, Charles Fried had pressed the Administration's agenda at the cert. stage more aggressively than Rex Lee, and certainly more than previous SGs, who rarely entered cases at the cert. stage as an amicus.

Fried appeared to pay a price for it. In most chambers, reading and thinking about cert. petitions is a job that the Justices share with their clerks. The chambers of Justices Brennan, Marshall, and Stevens handle petitions independently,[8] but during the 1985 Term and before, the other six Justices decided which petitions to grant by forming a pool of all their law clerks, assigning one clerk to write a "pool memo" about each position, and basing their individual votes largely on information provided by the pool memo. The clerks had legitimate firsthand views about the petitions, since they had a significant hand in helping the Justices rule on them.

A law clerk: "The SG's cert. petitions cause law clerks a lot of consternation. When the Court sees 'The United States' at the top of a petition, it tends to be especially interested. The Court respects the government. When you're up here, you assume that the United States knows when not to bring a case to the Court. That's one of the main purposes of the SG's office, to determine which cases to bring to the Court's attention. The problem is that a lot of the petitions the Court now gets from the SG aren't what the Justices expect. As a law clerk, you go over them with a fine-tooth comb, because the petitions don't cite cases and they make huge assertions that don't always stand up. A whole lot of cert. memos begin with phrases like 'It's puzzling why the SG is bringing this petition.' You see that language quite often. The Supreme Court grants cert. if four Justices vote in favor of hearing a case, and on the 1985 Court there were three Justices—Burger, Rehnquist, and White—who used to give the SG the benefit of the doubt and were usually inclined to vote for his petitions. But now clerks often suggest: 'We know you want to hear cases the government says to, but not this one.' When the year started out, sometimes there wasn't a fourth vote. Now, though there are no official statistics kept about this, sometimes the SG gets none at all."[9]

Another clerk: "The clerks resent Fried, in part, because he makes our job harder. We don't trust the SG's submissions the way previous law clerks told us they did. That's no big deal, really. We're supposed to be here to do legal research. But the people who do the work for the highest Court in the Judicial Branch of government can use the SG's help. Nine Justices, thirty-three law clerks, sixteen secretaries, the people in the Clerk's office, the messengers, the library staff—it's not very many. It matters that the SG is less trustworthy, because the Court tends to get a less balanced picture of the law and the facts than it expects. The SG used to play a valuable role of processing information about the impact on the law of a possible holding, but that's been changed. Now he omits key cases, which, in the law, is a form of dishonesty, or he sneaks around precedents. This is not just a bureaucratic squabble. It's a break with a long tradition." [10]

A third clerk: "As a little kid, I actually wanted to be a lawyer. The first time I saw a picture of the Solicitor General on the steps of the Supreme Court, I thought, That's great, I aspire to that kind of integrity. When I got a little older, I read about the office and it measured up. I wanted to go there. Now it's over. This isn't something I want to be part of. It's tainted. The office doesn't seem to be a place where integrity reigns. It might change, but not for a long while." [11]

When Fried was asked about the government's cert. submissions during his tenure, he said, "You make an assertion in a cert. petition, and not an argument, so you want to be especially sure you're confident about what you say in them. I will never stretch a point about a conflict between the circuits. I will never say something is important to the government if it's not. I don't think our record this year is any different from in the past. On the whole, I think we do a fine job. On that, I would be very distressed if I learned otherwise, because with cert. petitions I am trying to be the faithful servant of the Court." [12]

During the Term, the Justices made a number of other minor decisions that signaled a decline in the SG's status before the Court. In two major cases—the Wygant affirmative-action case and the Akron abortion case—the Justices denied the Solicitor General's request for time to present an oral argument as a friend of the Court. According to Richard Revesz, an assistant professor at New York University School of Law, the denials fit a larger pattern. From the 1953 Term through the 1985 Term, he discovered, the Supreme Court refused to let the Solicitor General argue as an amicus curiae only eighteen times. The Justices turned down the SGs' requests on twelve occasions in the first five Terms of the Reagan era, when the Reagan SGs had asked the Justices for permission to argue as a friend of the Court as many times as their predecessors had in the previous twenty-seven Terms. In a third major case during the 1985 Term—about a school's authority, consistent with the First Amendment, to punish a student for making lewd remarks in assembly—the Justices denied Fried argument time even after the school had agreed to his request for ten minutes to present his views in favor of civility in schools. According to the Clerk's office, it was the only time in the history of the Supreme Court that this had happened. [13]

The denials were the only public sign that a majority of the Court sometimes disagreed with Charles Fried's insistence that he had the prerogative of stating the government's position as a friend of the Court in cases where there was no federal interest. But inside the Court the topic was a regular source of tension among the Justices. One Justice explained, "In those instances where the SG had requested time to argue and had shown that one of the parties was willing to give him ten minutes, the Chief Justice invariably approved. When another amicus asked for the same thing, on the same grounds, he invariably said no. That created some flak among the Justices. It was an irritant. All the rest of us didn't always agree with the Chief, and there was at least one case where we decided the government should not be given time to argue, because there was no federal interest." In the cases where no party had given the SG time to argue, even the Chief sometimes agreed with his colleagues. When the SG asked for time in the abortion case, Warren Burger issued an unusual internal memo in which he said the government should not be allowed to argue before the Court because there was clearly no federal interest in the case. [14]

Behind the scenes, there were other events, too, that reflected on the SG's increasingly shaky standing with the Justices. The Solicitor General asked the Clerk of the Court for a second extension of time to file a brief in a minor case called DiNapoli v. Northeast Regional Parole Commission.[15] The Criminal Division of the Justice Department had handed in its draft brief to the SG's office behind schedule, so the SG thought he needed more time.[16] To Charles Haydon, the lawyer from New York City opposing the government on behalf of DiNapoli, the second request for an extension of the deadline appeared to have serious consequences. His client was in jail. If DiNapoli was to win his appeal, every day of delay before a decision meant more unwarranted time behind bars. Haydon wrote a letter of protest to the Clerk's office. "I strongly object to a further extension and request that the Court act on the petition for the reason that it is inconceivable that three months are required for the response," the lawyer declared.[17] "If Petitioner's position is correct, he is being held illegally while the government takes its time in reviewing a response."

The letter went to Thurgood Marshall, the Justice who oversees the business of the U.S. Court of Appeals for the Second Circuit. Marshall dismissed the lawyer's protest,[18] but the incident reminded the Justice how unhappy he was about the state of affairs at the SG's office. As a former SG himself ("It's the best job I've ever had," he once said, "bar none!"),[19] Marshall has unusually high expectations of the office. During the 1985 Term, he complained to other Justices that the office had grown noticeably sloppy under Fried, and had taken advantage of its special relation to the Court. Some Justices also knew that Marshall believed in playing by the rules. ("I never got any special favors when I was representing the NAACP," he would say.) He raised the DiNapoli question at the private weekly conference of the Justices, and then asked a deputy clerk to come see him about their decision. The clerk let the SG know that the Justices would no longer tolerate repeated requests by him for extra time to file.[20]

As the Term drew to a close, the opinions of the Court rejecting the government's positions in agenda cases provided detailed evidence about the SG's loss of standing with the Justices. But the SG's defeats in the agenda cases were accompanied by a series of rejections in other matters as well. It was one thing for the Solicitor General to be chastised by William Brennan in cases where the sides could be easily identified as liberal and conservative. Charles

Fried suggested as much when he dismissed as "nonsense" charges that his advocacy had hurt the standing of his office with the Court. That sort of talk came from people who were so opposed to the Administration's views that they could not "bear" to have them stated, he said. (Fried also attributed the talk to vindictive lawyers who had left the SG's office and were out to settle a score;[21] to "smart-aleck insiders" who showed "disrespect for the Court" by suggesting that the SG's tactics as an advocate had backfired, irritating some of the Justices enough to cost the Administration victories it might have had if the SG had softened his approach in the agenda cases;[22] and to a flock of unnamed critics—"You know, there is a certain desire on some people's part to get the SG," he said on TV at the end of the 1985 Term.)[23]

But other rejections occurred in cases not obviously on the President's social agenda. The opinions were written by Justices ranging from liberals (like Brennan and Marshall), to centrists (Blackmun and Stevens), moderate conservatives (Powell and O'Connor), and even the Court's strongest conservative (Rehnquist). "The worst possible result of the aggressive Reagan policy would be for the Justices to take out their frustrations with the Administration's filings in agenda cases on regular government cases,"[24] concluded one assistant to the SG. This is just what appeared to have happened by the close of the 1985 Term.

In an opinion about the government's "secretive" policy to deny mentally disabled people Social Security benefits, Justice Powell wrote for a unanimous Court. Although the government argued that it had properly handled the appeals at issue, Powell sternly disagreed. He insisted that the people were entitled by law to a "fair and neutral"[25] procedure, and that the government had not given it to them. "While 'hard' cases may arise," Powell concluded in his opinion, "this is not one of them." Clerks and Justices at the Supreme Court spoke about the Social Security case as if it were another one of Fried's forays on behalf of the Administration's agenda. In a sense, this proved how thoroughly the SG's credibility had eroded. For his part, Fried wrote off the case. "That was a standard government case," he said. "We got a client, the client's got a problem, and you do the best you can for your client. That struck me as a down-the-line case. I didn't even handle it. I let the career lawyers worry about the case."[26] Fried might not have worried about it, but the Justices held him responsible for the government's position.

In a criminal case, the Court criticized the Solicitor General for making an argument the Justices had "expressly rejected"[27] when the government had first tried it a few years back. In a case dealing with attorneys' fees—an area of law where the Supreme Court had recently adopted the government's position in almost every instance—four Justices ridiculed the SG. They noted that the formula he had recommended for awarding fees in a civil-rights case would have inevitably, and unacceptably, yielded a paltry amount to lawyers who had worked for years to vindicate the rights of the Chicano plaintiffs. The Justices declared, "We reject the Solicitor General's suggestion that the prospect of working nearly 2,000 hours at a rate of $5.65 an hour, to be paid more than ten years after the work began, is 'likely to attract a substantial number of attorneys.' "[28]

Fried stated publicly that his advocacy had not damaged the reputation of the SG's office at the Court, but behind the scenes at the SG's office, lawyers said, Fried was profoundly disturbed by the Supreme Court's criticism of his advocacy. Inside the Justice Department, the SG spoke as if he believed he had been sold a bill of goods by Reynolds and other political officials who, on behalf of Attorney General Meese, convinced him to make the arguments he did in some controversial cases.[29] He declared his intention of finding a middle path between what he called "being obdurate and being abject before the Court."[30]

Fried was encouraged to seek this prudent course by Donald Ayer, the new political deputy who arrived with a sterling reputation from his post as U.S. Attorney in the Eastern District of California. Despite Ayer's partisan charter and his description of himself as a Reagan Republican, when he came to the Justice Department, in the spring of 1986, he was unprepared for the intensity of interest from political appointees outside the SG's office who expected to play a large role in shaping the SG's briefs. Lawyers in the SG's office said that Ayer was "shocked" by the pressure from Reynolds. After Ayer got caught in a shouting match with Reynolds about the government's briefs in a trio of

agenda cases, the usually reserved Deputy SG described Reynolds
to some of his colleagues as "a jerk," "a horse's ass," and worse,
and said that if Reynolds had been calling the shots throughout the
Reagan years, he finally understood why the President had such
a dismal reputation on civil rights. Ayer was loyal to the Solicitor
General, and the contribution of the new conservative political
deputy, ironically, was to remind Fried of his legal responsibilities,
and to press him to give up pamphleteering. "I'm especially concerned with the integrity of papers the government files saying
what the law is," Ayer said. "I think a lot of attention has to be
paid to conservative standards in the legal sense."[31]

ALTHOUGH MANY LAWYERS deduced a tie between the
changes in the SG's office and the Court's apparently negative
response, few could show a direct link. Members of the Court
themselves offered the evidence.

By the end of the 1985 Term, the Justices had each observed an
average of five SGs, and had more experience together as a panel
than any set of Justices in history, so they could provide well-
informed views. Although one Justice decided the topic was "a
sensitive one, too sensitive"[32] for him to discuss, and one did not
break his policy of not granting interviews to talk about Court
business, a majority of the Justices were willing to address the
subject of the SG. One Justice observed that the SG's standing as
an advocate was still relatively high, especially among members of
the Court's right flank. ("His writing always has influence," the
Justice said. "Chief Justice Burger, Justice O'Connor, Justice
Rehnquist—they've always been interested in what the present
SG says, and gain support from his briefs for positions they want
to espouse.") Another Justice treated the changes in the SG's office
as a faint bureaucratic rumbling in the Justice Department, barely
audible on Capitol Hill where the Supreme Court sits. Focusing
on the institution instead of the man, the Justice said that the
Court's high respect for the SG continued as usual.[33]

But others acknowledged a decline in the standing of the Solicitor General, and spoke in detail about their own views and those
of their colleagues on the topic. According to these Justices, the
expressions of concern and disapproval in the Court's opinions

were only a hint of the sadness and distress felt by at least a majority of the Justices (Brennan, Marshall, Blackmun, Powell, and Stevens, four of whom were appointed by Republicans) about the changes in the role of the Solicitor General. Interviews with Justices, law clerks, and other close observers of the Court also indicated that each of the four other Justices was sometimes put off by the SG's advocacy, because he had been too aggressive (O'Connor), too supercilious (White), or too willing to be spokesman for the "reactionary" Reagan Administration (Burger).[34]

While William Rehnquist was the only Justice who suggested that he was skeptical of the notion of the SG's dual responsibility, to the Executive Branch and to the Court[35] (to him, the SG is above all an advocate for the Executive rather than the Tenth Justice), apparently he, too, was somewhat critical of the role Fried was playing. When the Justice was asked whether he agreed with Rex Lee's statement that the SG should not be a Pamphleteer General, Rehnquist replied, "That's exactly right."[36]

"Charles Fried is a different type of Solicitor General," said one Justice. "I'm a little biased, I suppose. I think that Archibald Cox and Erwin Griswold got it right. They thought they had a basic responsibility to the Court as well as to the Administration, and they were not the political voice of the Executive Branch. They thought they had to say 'No' on occasion, and the Court was confident in them. Generally, until recent years, I've always welcomed any filing by the Solicitor General. Now the clerks tell me consistently that you can't trust the SG about the facts or the law the way you'd like, and I rely on their judgment. So we pause a bit longer in granting cert. just because the government says to, and we may grant a few less. I had always tended to apply the word 'integrity' to the SG's office. There was always an honest presentation made. When they took a position, even in the big policy cases, they were always straight on the law. I sense that there's less of that now. I've felt that I've had to watch for political overtones as I didn't from Wade McCree or other recent SGs. Of course, the current SG has taken a beating for it, more than in any Term I can remember. We're saying to him: 'Don't do this. You're going too far.' But if a couple of us old goats fall over, we'll be replaced—and who knows what will happen."[37]

Another Justice had been willing to speak the year before as well, and the turn in his opinions was conspicuous. At the close of the 1984 Term, he offered what he felt was a realistic view. "I don't criticize the SG for changing his views about policy matters from Administration to Administration," he had declared. "The Solicitor General is the government's attorney. I regret the shift that the SG's office was forced to make in the Bob Jones case, but it was not out of the question. There have to be some responsibilities on political grounds. Either the SG represents the Administration, or he quits."[38]

A year later, the Justice's tone had changed markedly. He was angry. He said, "I'm quite surprised that Charles Fried has departed so far from the standard that Rex Lee strived for, which is the standard that has governed the SGs since I've been here. While they were all very loyal to the Administration, they drew some lines. No one has ever gone as far as Fried.

"I get the impression that on abortion, affirmative action, and a whole range of other subjects, he's gone way out of his way to support the point of view of the Administration. On a lot of them, he has to know he faces an uphill climb to persuade us that the Administration is right. In a number of cases, we've already said rather definitely how we feel about them. In abortion, Justice Powell said what the Court thinks only a few years ago in the Akron case. But Fried came at us with the recommendation that we reverse ourselves as if it were old hat to do that. And in affirmative action he's persisted in reading into the Court's opinions ideas that our writings won't bear. It's hardly the mark of a reasoned approach to the law. It's ideology, pure and simple. It's an assault on settled practices. That's the thing that has distressed me most about it.

"I look at things from the SG's office a lot more closely than I felt I had to in the days of anyone else. I scrutinize the cert. petitions more so than I used to. Not that I don't think the government makes a case that we should grant its cert. petitions more often than we do for any other petitioner, but I don't give them the same benefit of the doubt I used to and I have to spend more time combing through their work. Now I don't have the feeling that every case is presented squarely. I'm not even sure that the facts are accurate, in some cases. In the past, I didn't have that uneasy feeling about the SG, but today I do.

"There's no question we've taken this SG to task in our opinions more than any of his recent predecessors. What we're saying to him and the other people in the Justice Department is simple: 'Listen, you guys, you're just dead wrong. This is an abdication of your responsibility.' The notion that the SG has no obligation to help the Court is an outrage. You might as well let the rest of the government argue its own cases. What good is the SG?

"The thing of it is, Fried hasn't learned a thing. He's really been boasting that he has an obligation to press on the Court the Administration's view. In the context of the traditional role of the SG's office, this is revolutionary. And he has persistently misstated what the Court has held in various opinions this Term. His suggestion that we had accepted the basic premise of the Administration except for a couple of wrinkles in the affirmative-action cases is irresponsible."

The Justice concluded: "Fried clerked for Justice Harlan, you know. Harlan had enormous respect for the SG's office, and if he were alive to see this, he'd be just as disappointed as some of the rest of us." [39]

XVI

The Rule of Law

NOT LONG BEFORE the close of the 1985 Term, Warren Burger unexpectedly announced his resignation as Chief Justice of the United States and Ronald Reagan selected William Rehnquist to succeed him. The President chose Antonin Scalia to take Rehnquist's place as Associate Justice. Though the appointments did not change the number of Justices who were likely to support the Administration's arguments before the Court (as does seem likely to happen with the replacement of Lewis Powell in 1987), they supplied an exclamation point to the Term. The end of the Burger Court prompted its students to compile some fascinating statistics about the era.

From 1801 to 1900, the average number of Supreme Court cases decided by a bare majority each Term was one.[1] During Warren Burger's tenure as Chief Justice, from the 1969 Term through the 1985 Term, the Court decided more cases by a plurality (a group whose opinion presents the Court's decision without commanding a majority of five) than ever before in its history, and in the 1985 Term one-quarter of the Court's cases were decided by a bare majority of five to four.[2] In the history of the Court, it had overruled its own precedents 184 times. Since 1950, it had overturned precedents 98 times, or more than half of the total. The Warren Court is generally thought of as reaching a high-water mark for judicial activism, but, according to the Library of Congress, the Burger Court overturned precedents more often (50 to 46), struck down more acts of Congress (31 to 21), overturned more state laws (288 to 150), and otherwise appeared to exercise its power to review the actions of government more actively than had the Warren

Court and, therefore, than any Court ever. Since the Burger Court decided about 15 percent more cases than the Warren Court, the absolute figures are less conclusive than they appear, but they are still significant as signs of evolution.[3]

As the Supreme Court's work shifted from resolving common-law questions of torts, property, and contracts (in the nineteenth century), to interpreting statutes and ruling on the meaning of the Constitution (during the twentieth), these numbers suggest that the Justices became increasingly divided about the substance of the law. During the past generation, when the number of cases dealing with important social policies like school desegregation and affirmative action rose considerably, the Court gradually exchanged a bold liberal outlook for a cautious, conservative one, and as the quest for neutral principles by which to decide these disputes foundered, the Justices settled for what Vincent Blasi, a professor at Columbia Law School, called "a rootless activism."[4] In cases about abortion, school prayer, and the rights of criminal suspects— principal items on the Reagan social agenda—Court decisions seen from afar as broad legal pronouncements appeared from close up to reveal an intense struggle among the nine Justices to agree on doctrine that expressed the most subjective human judgments.

The instability resulting from this struggle was underscored in 1986 by the Court's ruling in Bowers v. Hardwick, upholding the Georgia law that made a crime of oral and anal sex between consenting adults.[5] Justice Blackmun argued in dissent that the Constitution's concept of liberty includes a right of privacy requiring protection of intimacy among homosexuals as well as heterosexuals, and that the law should be struck down. For a five-to-four majority, Justice White dismissed that view ("We do not agree," he declared), and described one of the claims for the protection of privacy made by counsel as, "at best, facetious."[6] Soon afterward, Justice Lewis Powell confirmed a report by the Washington *Post*[7] that he had planned to vote with Blackmun, but because he thought the case wasn't the best on which to base a judgment about such a deep question of constitutional law, he had switched sides to join White.[8] As a result of this shift, instead of extending to homosexuals the full protection of the Constitution, the Court appeared to assent to an effort to push them to the margins of

society. "This was the most exhausting Term of any since I've
been on the Court,"⁹ Blackmun said at the end of his sixteenth
Term on the Supreme Court, and he attributed the exhaustion to
bickering and arm-twisting about cases like this.

The Court's rightward drift occurred in a period of bitter and
widespread political controversy about the law in general. While
most of the disagreement focused on the federal courts, Americans
expressed their conflicts about social issues by making the elections
for judgeships in the forty states that held them increasingly
contested affairs.¹⁰ Rose Bird, Chief Justice of the California Supreme Court, was re-elected with only 52 percent of the votes in
1978, and in 1986 was removed by a two-to-one margin through the
vigorous efforts of conservative critics and others. While her unqualified opposition to the death penalty marked her as a liberal,
she said, "It doesn't make any difference if the court is liberal,
conservative or somewhere in between. What [voters] want is
somebody who will do exactly what they want on particular issues,
so that when they push a button, you salivate on signal."¹¹ A
majority of the American people appeared to want the same, according to a 1986 NBC News poll. A representative sample decided that the Chief Justice of the United States should be elected,
too,¹² and overlooked the value of having the nation's highest
judge be above politics.

There are many reasons for these developments, but one of the
most dominant in the Reagan years has been the encouragement
by the President himself of a partisan and divisive view of the law.
His regular commentary about abortion provides a good example.
When members of the right-to-life movement send roses to members of Congress and of the Supreme Court each year to protest
the Roe v. Wade decision on its anniversary, and then gather on
the Ellipse behind the White House for a rally, the President offers
words of solidarity. When members of the movement gathered for
the funeral of sixteen thousand aborted fetuses one year, he sent
his condolences. Reagan's comment about abortion was "I don't
feel that I'm trying to do something that is taking a privilege away
from womanhood, because I don't think that womanhood should
be considering murder a privilege." Through the eighties, as the
number of bombings at abortion clinics rose, he did little to dis-

courage such tactics, and continued to pledge his support to the pro-life and anti-abortion movement. [13]

In 1986, a pro-life clergyman publicly urged a prayer for the death of Justice William Brennan as part of the answer to the country's abortion problem. He reasoned that Brennan's passing would allow the President to appoint a pro-life Justice, and shift the balance of the Court to achieve a majority ruling against the right to abortion. [14] Brennan became a renewed focus of pro-life criticism after Edwin Meese singled him out (though it was Justice Blackmun who wrote the majority opinion in Roe v. Wade). It was hard not to see a chain linking the President's encouragement of the movement, Meese's criticism of Brennan as the symbol of the kind of judicial activism that led to that landmark decision, and the "prayer" of the clergyman.

The President's confusion of the law with his own moral and social agenda was often repeated by the Justice Department under Meese. Again and again, in situations where the Administration's desired social policy required it to make a choice between conflicting values, whether the subject was pornography, AIDS, the rights of criminal suspects or some other item on the President's expanding agenda, the Reagan Administration chose not to follow established legal practices while presenting its position. It read cases, construed statutes, and represented both trial records and legislative history in radically unorthodox ways, and the Solicitor General sometimes did so for the President.

Was it inevitable that the Solicitor General would become a partisan advocate for the administration in power if the law is increasingly seen as no more than an instrument of politics and so much of the Supreme court's docket now deals with the legal aspects of social policy? Shouldn't an Administration's election to office entitle it to have arguments carried directly to the Court, without being filtered by an obscure office of civil servants, in these circumstances? How can the SG expect to fulfill a dual responsibility to the Court and the Executive Branch when neither can claim to apply neutral legal principles?

One of the hallmarks of legal scholarship in the Reagan era, as well as in the judicial and political arenas, is political polarization. [15] It has become difficult for a young law professor to avoid choosing between one of the movements in the law that correspond to the political far left or right. Even by choosing to do old-fashioned doctrinal analysis, by scrutinizing cases for new and insightful principles that transcend politics, a gifted legal scholar risks being considered trivial or anachronistic. In 1986, an able lawyer in the SG's office was interviewed at first-rank law schools for a teaching job that almost certainly would have been his a decade ago, when the skills of analyzing and writing about legal doctrine that he cultivated in the government would have been highly valued. He was turned down by all the schools, in part, they indicated, because he did not bring to teaching the special insights that came from looking at the law from the vantage point of a movement.[16]

As a balance to the right's Law and Economics, a school favored by the Reagan Administration, a movement called Critical Legal Studies sprang up on the left. A basic premise of CLS, as it is known, is that the law is ultimately defined less by abstract principles than by the political and moral views of the judges and lawyers who apply them, and that in the endless process of interpretation that it requires, the law becomes a forum for resolving larger social conflicts rooted in passion, reason, and, most of all, power.[17] Since the volumes of legal cases and statutes are full of contradictory doctrine, CLS holds, it is possible to make a respectable legal argument leading to any desired result.

Ironically, the aggressive advocacy of Charles Fried during the 1985 Term seemed to prove the wisdom of CLS scholars: choosing to question, rather than to reason from, the premises of earlier Supreme Court rulings, the more controversial briefs that he endorsed as Solicitor General appeared nonetheless to make presentable legal arguments. By this theory, the filings of the SG's office should have provoked no more distress than much current American legal scholarship—Fried had merely aggravated the problem by attracting attention.

But the judgments of the Justices about Fried's advocacy during the 1985 Term suggested other conclusions. For half a century, American lawyers have lived with the tension between the need, on the one hand, for legal ideals that command respect because judges make them appear to come from some higher authority and the knowledge, on the other, that the law is the imperfect creation of imperfect human beings.[18] They have recognized that the law is an art, not a science. Though there may be few "right" legal answers dictated by formula, legal reasoning can be done well or badly. When done well and honestly, it has a greater chance of illuminating either the purpose of the statute under scrutiny or the principle at the heart of the most relevant precedents in case law. In turn, it can fulfill its role of helping give order to society by contributing stability, predictability, and determinability to the law. If there were no overarching "neutral principles" guiding lawyers who worked on the most controversial problems before the courts in the mid-eighties, there were standard practices of legal reasoning that assured the law some integrity and helped define it as law.

The Justices of the Supreme Court indicated repeatedly in opinions at the end of the 1985 Term that the Solicitor General's office had failed to honor these practices as faithfully as they expected it to. The law was unsettled in some cases where the quality of the SG's advocacy fell down, and this was why the Justices seemed especially upset: the process by which the law is shaped is particularly important when the outcome of a case may be subject to controversy. Members of the Court knew little about the changes within the office that led to the decline in its work, but the Justices willing to speak about the topic did not think this deterioration had been inevitable. Unlike Archibald Cox, who, they concurred, demonstrated high legal scruples as Solicitor General during a similarly divisive period a generation ago, President Reagan's second SG bent reason and spurned restraint in order to try for results. By misusing accepted principles of legal reasoning in major cases, he made the government's rationales suspect in run-of-the-mill matters, and he threatened the law's stability when the legal system was unusually vulnerable. Instead of envisioning the law as a means for building consensus, as Cox did, Charles Fried advanced the President's positions without regard to the divisions they deepened in American society.[19]

The 1985 Term would have been an extraordinary one for the Supreme Court even if the Reagan Administration had not tried to press its agenda so aggressively, because the Justices resolved an unusually high number of cases presenting distinct choices about major issues in the law. The 1986 Term promised to be quieter and, at its opening, Charles Fried made a comment about the results of his advocacy before the Court during the previous Term: "We spoke last year," he told the Washington *Post,* [20] "they answered, we heard, and we go from there," which was as close as he'd come to conceding in public any errors of judgment as Solicitor General.

Out of optimism or an accurate sense of change, lawyers in the SG's office who spoke about Charles Fried's approach to cases for the new Term—before he had filed enough briefs for anyone outside the government to judge how they compared to submissions of the previous one—picked up on this comment. The lawyers were struck by the SG's new resolve to use his talents in the tradition he had previously compromised, and, adopting the coloration of his surroundings, to give up his ornate, frenetic style in favor of the less flashy manner of a reliable government lawyer. He had picked first-rank deputies who reinforced each other's devotion to craftsmanship, the lawyers said, and though he still overruled the deputies in favor of advice from Bradford Reynolds and representatives of Attorney General Meese, and had to be canny about warding off incursions from political appointees when he did not agree with them ("One whiff of treason, and they boot you out," a lawyer in the office said), Fried usually heeded the advice of his new deputies. He was committed to guarding the SG's office as well as he could, they said. [21]

Fried's eventual record in a number of the 1986 Term's major cases about affirmative action and other agenda items, in which the Justices again seemed to go out of their way to correct the government's reasoning while firmly ruling against it, suggested that the change noted in the SG by his staff had to do with tone more than substance—with his apparent attitude toward the Court rather than with what he actually argued, since he rejected the logic of its opinions and the importance of those statements as guiding judgments about American law. [22] His testimony before Congress in March 1987 that public criticisms of his approach as Solicitor were merely "subjective judgments" and that, during the previous eighteen months, he hoped that "the style and the content of the advocacy, the quality of advocacy, the thoroughness of the argumentation" by the SG's office under his leadership was "as good as it has ever been,"[23] raised questions as to how deeply his attitude had changed.

Still, for whatever it was worth, the change in tone, at least, was clear. At the end of the 1985 Term, according to the Philadelphia *Inquirer,* Fried had criticized one decision of the Justices by saying, "Who knows what these clowns mean?"[24] The words conveyed the disdain for the Court with which the SG was then increasingly associated. A year later, toward the close of the 1986 Term, the Attorney General's spokesman, Terry Eastland, commented that "a new appointment or two" to the Supreme Court would be the best way to reverse the Court's outlook on affirmative action. Fried called the remark "deeply troubling," and, drawing attention on the front page of *The New York Times,* the SG stated: "The way I should do my job is by crafting conscientious, scrupulous arguments in the light of the law. Personally, I wish every one of the Justices well." The Fried-Eastland exchange was only one of a series of minor incidents in which the Solicitor General and his right-wing allies within or outside the Justice Department not only acknowledged but magnified and seemed to relish a new distance between them. "I'm a very different man today than I was a year ago," Fried said after the Term ended.[25]

Lawyers in the SG's office also recognized a more general truth: the advocacy of Charles Fried, perhaps more than that of any other Solicitor General, could fairly be judged only by considering the Administration he served. Although he maintained that he had no grounds for complaint, the legal views pressed by Edwin Meese and the practices of Meese and Reynolds—which flabbergasted longtime observers of the Justice Department and exhausted the supply of synonyms for extremism in the law—severely limited Fried's independence.

Several weeks before the start of the 1986 Term, Reynolds gave a speech at the University of Missouri purporting to offer a serious comment about principles to apply in interpreting the Constitution.[26] Instead, Reynolds's remarks amounted to an attempt to blame one Justice for the discord between the Administration and the Supreme Court. In what a press spokesman at the Justice

Department later called the strongest personal attack on a member of the Court by any top member of the Administration, and what lawyers in the department described as the venting of an obsession, Reynolds denounced Justice Brennan for not reading the Constitution as Meese, Reynolds, and others thought it should be read. He declared Brennan's "radical egalitarianism" to be "perhaps the major threat to individual liberty" in the United States today.

The speech promoted the Attorney General's Jurisprudence of Original Intention more forcefully than Meese himself had done since its initial presentation, when critics on both left and right had given the theory low marks. After peppering his text with quotations from Brennan's major speech on the Constitution, Reynolds then accused the Justice of regarding the document as "a 'dead letter,' " placing quotation marks around this phrase so as to convey the false impression that it too was quoted from Brennan. In actuality, the Justice had argued the direct opposite. [27] Reynolds's speech was a reminder that the most powerful officials in the Reagan Justice Department sometimes skirted a practice without which the rule of law collapses—telling the truth.

A question about Meese, Reynolds, and their allies during the Reagan Administration that has often cropped up is this: Why did they do it? What moved them to defy the constraints of mainstream legal thinking, and sometimes the law itself, in their pursuit of the Reagan agenda? Neither the Attorney General nor his right-hand man would answer the question, in part because they did not grant its premise. They spoke about their reign in government as if they were meeting the highest standards of public service. [28] Because they were close allies of a President who was extraordinarily popular for almost six years and, perhaps, because many people who vilified them paradoxically wrote the pair off as unworthy of serious consideration, both men remained strong and untouchable long after the record warranted a harsher judgment.

In this period of free-for-all in the law, when a vocal group of scholars and advocates on the left joined Meese and Reynolds on the right in believing that, without cost, they could make almost any legal claim with a straight face, it was no wonder that the Solicitor General appeared to believe that, on behalf of the Administration, he could, too.

However much changes in the legal culture explain the transformation of the SG's office during the Reagan years, the story carries a lesson of its own. To understand how the Reagan Administration views the law, it is only necessary to know what it did to the office of the Solicitor General. If there is a thing called law, with a reassuring sense of continuity despite its contradictions, a measure of stability that contributes to social order, and an integrity provided by, among other things, the careful practice of legal reasoning, then one of the great misdeeds of the Reagan Administration was to diminish the institution that, to lawyers at the highest reaches of the profession, once stood for the nation's commitment to the rule of law.

A Note on Sources

Like many significant documents in American law, whether opinions of the Supreme Court or statutes passed by Congress, the briefs and other writings that express the legal views of Solicitors General were available to me, as they are to the public, at the Supreme Court and the Department of Justice libraries. These and other relevant books and papers are available at libraries around the country, and for this book I also used materials at the library of American University's Washington College of Law, the Boston Athenaeum, the Columbia University Oral History Project, the Georgetown University Library, the Harvard Law School Library, the Library of Congress, and the Montgomery County Public Libraries in Maryland. I used papers in the collections at the National Archives and the National Gallery of Art as well. I also relied on reports in newspapers, magazines, academic journals, and law reviews (in particular, on stories by David Lauter in the *National Law Journal;* Linda Greenhouse, Robert Pear, Philip Shenon, and Stuart Taylor, Jr. in *The New York Times;* Fred Barbash, Al Kamen, Howard Kurtz, and Loretta Tofani in the Washington *Post;* and James Stewart and Stephen Wermiel in the *Wall Street Journal*), and on radio and television reports (especially by Carl Stern for NBC News and Nina Totenberg for National Public Radio). Some papers on which I relied are not generally available to the public, and I'm grateful to the people who trusted me with these confidential documents.

Despite the value of this written record, much of the history of the Solicitor General's office has not been pieced together until now. To gather stories about past Solicitors and others who served in the office, during most of 1985, 1986, and part of 1987, I spoke with every living SG (nine in all), from Walter Cummings, appointed in the Truman Administration, to Rex Lee and Charles Fried, of the Reagan Administration; with Paul Freund, who ran the SG's office when he served there in the forties, and Robert Stern, who took charge during the early fifties; with scores of other lawyers who once worked in the office or do now; and with many other people who had facts and opinions about the Solicitor General to share. When I began this project, I expected to tell the unhurried and virtually unknown history of a tiny, great institution in the Justice Department. Not long after I started my reporting, it became clear that events at the SG's office were transforming the institution. The story took on an intense quality, and I began to concentrate as well on learning about the nature and significance of the changes.

Many in the SG's office or with special knowledge about it felt comfortable talking about general office lore, but believed they put themselves at risk by speaking with me about current events. In some cases, they cited their duty to honor the confidentiality of dealings between an attorney and his client (in this case, the government); sometimes they said they didn't want to be quoted criticizing lawyers they might deal with again in the future; sometimes they treated the questions I raised as if answering them required a breach of national security—which it never did, since none of the issues that interested me involved national security in the sense in which the phrase is ordinarily used.

In brief, some of the many people I spoke with did so on the record about subjects that they considered uncontroversial, but otherwise insisted on terms that would allow them to tell their stories without incurring the distrust of their colleagues or jeopardizing at least their ability to perform their jobs, if not the jobs themselves, through unwanted publicity. These are terms to which reporters regularly agree in Washington in order to get closer to the truth than official, on-the-record statements allow. They would talk about certain topics only if I promised not to name them as the source of their remarks.

In the past, some of the SG's former and current lawyers explained, they had cooperated with reporters for *The New York*

Times, the Washington *Post,* and other major news organizations to make sure the press accurately represented the meaning of Supreme Court opinions in cases in which the government had taken part. They thought that stories would be improved if the reporters knew how legal positions had developed inside the government. The lawyers protected themselves by providing this information on background only (i.e., not for direct attribution). A larger percentage of the lawyers in the SG's office told me that before they agreed to speak with me, they had never talked about their work with a reporter. They said that they had agreed to talk with me for one of two main reasons: they cared enough about the SG's office and how it was being changed to want to share their views about current events (even though some believed they would be fired if political officials in the Reagan Administration knew they had helped me piece together the story of the transformation); or they believed the story was more complicated than it seemed as it was passed along the grapevine of lawyers, judges, and journalists who follow the SG's office and the Supreme Court, and they wanted to counter the misimpressions they assumed I was gathering from other people.

Every reporter I know prefers to identify sources for readers so the readers can judge for themselves the sources' motives, biases, and reliability. Some reporters won't report the facts attested to by a source unless he is willing to be identified. In this case, I believe readers are better served by my reliance on some unnamed sources than they would have been had I ignored this material. I think the sense of the Solicitor General's office they gain is closer to the truth than it would otherwise be.

In every instance (and I asked permission to do this), I have tried to indicate a source's position, to let readers better judge the credibility of his observation ("a lawyer in the SG's office said"; "a Supreme Court law clerk commented"; "a Justice observed"). Although this may in given instances invite speculation about a source's identity, it seems a reasonable way of balancing the two concerns of protecting privacy and properly informing the reader.

Because this book focuses on the SG's office, I talked regularly with lawyers in that office during my reporting. In the heart of it, I spoke at length with more than half the current office staff and dozens of other lawyers who had served there and still kept up with the office. I tried to speak with at least three lawyers whenever my reporting centered on a controversial subject, to ensure that I heard several points of view. The lawyers from the SG's office identified in the notes are only some of those with whom I spoke during my reporting. I did not necessarily discuss other subjects with a lawyer who agreed to be quoted only about a certain topic.

I am grateful to the hundreds of people who told me about the history and lore of the Solicitor General's office, and what they thought has happened there during the Reagan years.

Notes

The notes in this book conform to the following rules of citation: Brown v.
Board of Education, 347 *U.S.* 483, 484 (1954), means that the Supreme Court
decided the case in 1954, that the opinions begin at page 483 of volume 347 of
the *United States Reports,* and that the passage quoted or mentioned begins
at page 484. I occasionally cite old cases by the name of the official reporter
of the case, which was the custom at the Supreme Court until 1875. Marbury
v. Madison, 1 *Cranch* (5 *U.S.*) 137 (1803) means that the case was reported in
the first volume compiled by William Cranch and the fifth volume of the
United States Reports. The other reporters whose volumes I cite are Henry
Wheaton and Benjamin Howard. Because there is a delay between the Supreme Court's decisions about cases and the publication of opinions in the
official reports, I sometimes refer to one of two other publications of Supreme
Court cases. 104 *S. Ct.* 2520 (1984) means that the case is reported at page 2520
in volume 104 of the *Supreme Court Reporter,* a service of West Publishing
Company that includes a quickly available softcover edition. 54 *U.S. Law
Week* 4095 means that the case is reported at page 4095 in volume 54 of *U.S.
Law Week,* a loose-leaf publication of the Bureau of National Affairs. I also
refer to some cases only by name and case number, without citing the volumes
in which they are reproduced, because when I collected these cases, the sole
version available was that printed by the Supreme Court. Finally, I sometimes
refer to other volumes reporting lower-court opinions: *F. Supp.* refers to the
Federal Supplement and *F. 2d* to the second edition of *Federal Reports.* Since
1932, district-court decisions have been reported in *F. Supp.,* and appeals-court
decisions in *F. 2d.*

Books are cited by author, title, publisher, year of publication, number of
pages, and pages of reference. Articles in law reviews and other journals are
cited by author, title, volume, and name of the review, page, and date. In most
instances, articles in newspapers are cited by paper, page, and date.

Some notes are labeled "Confidential interview." (These are marked "CI"
after the first, or "CIs" for more than one.) I explain my reliance on these
interviews in A Note on Sources, on page 280.

CHAPTER I

THE TENTH JUSTICE

1. In this note, "Government Litigation in the Supreme Court: The Roles of the Solicitor General," 78 *Yale Law Journal* 1442, 1442 (1969) means that the unsigned article appeared in 1969, in volume 78 of the *Yale Law Journal*, at page 1442, and the quotation appears on page 1442. Footnote 1 of the article quotes the original Act of Congress, passed June 22, 1870.

2. Interview with the late Justice Potter Stewart on June 5, 1985; confidential personal interviews with four Justices in 1985 and 1986; confidential phone interviews with two other Justices in 1985 and 1986; and a letter from Justice Lewis Powell to the author, July 2, 1986, quoted with his permission.

3. Letter from Justice Powell to the author, July 2, 1986.

4. Interviews with Paul Freund on April 12, 1985, and October 10, 1985; Erwin Griswold on April 5, 1985; and other long-time students of the Supreme Court and the SG's office, and with lawyers currently employed in the SG's office. In 1984, an opinion by Judge Patrick Higginbotham referred to "the historically unique and functionally important relationship between the office of Solicitor General and the Supreme Court." (Cotner v. U.S. Parole Commission, No. 83–1757.)

5. Statistics from October Term, 1983, available in the Docket Management Section of the SG's office and in "Annual Report of the Attorney General of the United States" for 1984 (U.S. Government Printing Office). "October Term, 1983" refers to the Supreme Court Term beginning then and continuing until the summer of 1984: each year the Court's Term is identified by when it opens—now the first Monday in October—and the calendar year. Cases argued after the turn of the year thus belong to the Term begun the previous October, and so a February 1984 case was heard in October Term, 1983.

6. In 1955, the Justice Department began using its current system for keeping Supreme Court statistics, and it applied the method retroactively to October Term, 1943. In the forty years prior to the 1983 Term, the Solicitor General won an average of 69 percent of the cases that he argued or presented on the merits to the Court. "Annual Report of the Attorney General of the United States," 1955 through 1984.

7. Homer Cummings and Carl McFarland, *Federal Justice: Chapters in the History of Justice and the Federal Executive* (Macmillan, 1937, 576 pp.); and Thomas Thacher, "Genesis and Present Duties of Office of Solicitor General," 17 *American Bar Association Journal* 519 (1931); Charles Fahy, "The Office of the Solicitor General," 28 *American Bar Association Journal* 20 (1942); Simon Sobeloff, "Attorney for the Government: The Work of the Solicitor General's Office," 41 *American Bar Association Journal* 229 (1955); Erwin Griswold, "The Office of the Solicitor General—Representing the Interests of the United States before the Supreme Court," 34 *Missouri Law Review* 528 (1969).

8. Op. cit., "Roles of the Solicitor General," *Yale Law Journal* 1442.

9. Cong. Globe, 41st Congress, 2nd Session, 3035, by Representative Jenckes, cited in Griswold, 34 *Missouri Law Review* 527, 530 (1969).

10. Benjamin Helm Bristow, *Dictionary of American Biography* (Scribner, 20 v. 1928–1936), Vol. III, 55–56.

11. Mark Sheehan, Assistant Director of the Office of Public Affairs at the Justice Department, letter to the author, March 6, 1986.

12. Interviews with Rex Lee on June 11, 1985, and Virginia Bolling, of the Docket Management Section of the SG's office, on August 11, 1986.

13. Op. cit., Soboloff, "Attorney for the Government," 230.

14. U.S. v. Mendoza, 104 *S. Ct.* 568, 573 (1984).

15. Interviews with Louis Claiborne on June 12, 1985; Andrew Frey on June 29, 1985; Kenneth Geller on June 20, 1985; and Lawrence Wallace on May 24, 1985.

16. Erwin Griswold, "Constitutional Cases in the Supreme Court," 24 *Oklahoma Law Review* 353, 354 (1971).

17. Op. cit., Stewart interview.

18. Op. cit., Soboloff, 232.

19. According to Virginia Bolling, of the SG's office, during the 1984 and 1985 Terms the SG was invited to enter as a friend of the Court in thirty-seven and thirty-one cases, respectively.

20. This is a phrase used by Justices in personal interviews during 1985 and 1986, and by law clerks at the Court who repeated the words of the Justices.

21. Interviews with Kenneth Geller, op. cit.; Edwin Kneedler on November 25, 1985; Joshua Schwartz on March 20, 1985; David Strauss on July 30, 1985; and Harriet Shapiro on December 3, 1985.

CHAPTER II

LORE

1. Interviews with Archibald Cox on April 11, 1985; John Davis (a onetime lawyer in the SG's office who became Clerk of the Supreme Court—no relation to Solicitor General John W. Davis) on June 9, 1985; Oscar Davis on June 21, 1985; Philip Elman on October 19, 1986; Daniel Friedman on June 22, 1985; Paul Freund, op. cit.; Warner Gardner on May 22, 1986; Erwin Griswold, op. cit.; Ralph Spritzer on February 26, 1986; Robert Stern on May 20, 1986; and Charles Wyzanski on April 12, 1985, among others.

2. William H. Harbaugh, *Lawyer's Lawyer: The Life of John W. Davis* (Oxford University Press, 1973, 648 pp.), 92.

3. Ibid., 92, 107.

4. Interviews with John Davis, op. cit.; Oscar Davis, op. cit.; and Paul Freund, op. cit.

5. Archibald Cox, "The Government in the Supreme Court," 44 *Chicago Bar Record* 221, 225 (1963).

6. Interview with Robert Bork on May 22, 1985.

7. DeMarco v. U.S., 415 *U.S.* 449, 451 (1974).

8. Op. cit., Cox, 225.

9. Young v. U.S., 315 *U.S.* 257, 258 (1942).

10. The facts about the Peters case, unless otherwise noted, are from the "Memorandum for the Attorney General from the Solicitor General Re: Peters v. Hobby," January 14, 1955.

11. Joseph Rauh, "Nonconfrontation in Security Cases: The Greene Decision," 45 *Virginia Law Review* 1175, 1178 (1959).

12. Confidential interview (hereafter CI).

13. Op. cit., "Memorandum for the Attorney General," 1.

14. Ibid., 13, 22.

15. CI.

16. Interviews with John Davis, op. cit.; and Oscar Davis, op. cit.

17. In the *Dictionary of American Biography*, op. cit., Vol. II, 508, the Bowers entry states, "It is well known that only his death prevented his nomination by President Taft to the Supreme Court of the United States." According to Charles Wyzanski, op. cit., another former SG, William Mitchell, might also have gone to the Supreme Court, but he turned down Herbert Hoover's offer of a seat because he believed Benjamin Cardozo should be appointed instead, as he was.

18. Including Sobeloff, the number of SGs who either left the bench to take the job or who later became judges is at least thirteen, or over one-third of the total of thirty-eight. (The SG's office has no records about past Solicitors and the *Dictionary of American Biography* does not have entries for every SG.) Of those who have served since 1930, the fraction is over half—ten of eighteen. In 1986, there were ten federal judges on active duty who once worked as lawyers in the SG's office.

19. CI.

20. Op. cit., interview with Paul Freund.

21. Op. cit., interview with Charles Wyzanski.

22. CI.

23. Interviews with Paul Freund, op. cit.; Erwin Griswold, op. cit.; and Charles Wyzanski, op. cit.

24. Frankfurter memo, March 15, 1933, Harvard Law School Library Manuscript Collection.

25. Leonard Baker, *Brandeis and Frankfurter: A Dual Biography* (Harper & Row, 1984, 567 pp.), 282.

26. CI.

27. Op. cit., Leonard Baker, 283.

28. CI.

29. According to Paul Freund, op. cit., the Democratic Party in Rhode Island, which McGrath had represented in the Senate, was badly divided. The Democrats' plan was for McGrath to gain some prestige in the Justice Department and return home to unify the party.

30. Francis Lorson, Chief Deputy Clerk of the Supreme Court, arranged access to Court files. The Court's records are not complete (the Court notes the titles of cases that lawyers have argued on their certificates of membership, but the Court only began using these certificates in 1925 and the records concerning lawyers who argued at the Court before then are spotty) and the current notation system is not foolproof (the Clerk's office follows no uniform system for crediting lawyers with arguments and sometimes fails to note that an advocate has made an argument), but, according to Court records, this is McGrath's score.

31. Richard Rovere, *The American Establishment and Other Reports, Opinions, and Speculations* (Harcourt, Brace, & World, 1962, 308 pp.), 85.

32. Interview with Walter Cummings on October 22, 1986.

33. Interviews with John Davis, op. cit.; Oscar Davis, op. cit.; and Robert Stern, op. cit.

34. Francis Biddle, *In Brief Authority* (Doubleday, 1962, 494 pp.) 98.

35. Interview with Sandy Nelson, of the Court Clerk's office, on January 27, 1987.

36. Interviews with Daniel Friedman, op. cit.; Paul Freund, op. cit.; Warner Gardner, op. cit.; and Charles Wyzanski, op. cit.

37. Op. cit., interview with Paul Freund.

38. Paul Freund, "Felix Frankfurter: Reminiscences and Reflections," Harvard Law School, 5, 6 (1982).

39. Robert Jackson, *The Struggle for Judicial Supremacy: A Study of a Crisis in American Power Politics* (Knopf, 1941, 361 pp.), xix.

40. Edward J. Bander, *Justice Holmes Ex Cathedra* (Michie Co., 1966, 381 pp.), No. 425, 207. Also, op. cit., interview with Paul Freund.

41. Thomas Reed Powell, "Constitutional Metaphors," *New Republic*, 314 (February 11, 1985).

42. Robert Stern, Eugene Gressman, and Stephen M. Shapiro, *Supreme Court Practice* (Bureau of National Affairs, 1986, 1,030 pp.), vii.

43. Op. cit., interview with Robert Stern.

44. Op. cit., interview with David Strauss.

45. Interview with Mark Sheehan, Office of Public Affairs, Justice Department, on October 22, 1986.

46. Op. cit., Biddle, 97.

47. Peter Irons, *Justice at War: The Story of the Japanese American Internment Cases* (Oxford University Press, 1983, 407 pp.), 278–310.

48. CIs with Justices, and interviews with Robert Bork, op. cit.; Archibald Cox, op. cit.; Paul Freund, op. cit.; Erwin Griswold, op. cit.; Rex Lee, op. cit.; Alan Morrison on March 20, 1986; Burt Neuborne on June 24, 1986; Laurence Tribe on November 15, 1985; and other lawyers.

CHAPTER III

THE SG AND THE SUPREME COURT

1. According to Erwin Griswold, op. cit., this occurred when he first joined the office in 1929. Paul Freund, op. cit., said that when he joined the office in the thirties, the practice continued and lawyers there talked about it as if it had happened before. The practice ended after Griswold's tenure as SG. "No one told me about it," said his successor, Robert Bork, op. cit.

2. Op. cit., interview with Paul Freund.

3. CI.

4. Op. cit., interview with Andrew Frey.

5. Interviews with Daniel Friedman, op. cit.; and Philip Elman, op. cit., the Frankfurter clerk and longtime assistant to the SG.

6. Op. cit., interview with Lawrence Wallace.

7. "Memorandum to the Solicitor General: Thoughts on Advocacy," May 14, 1980. Interviews with Andrew Frey, op. cit.; Kenneth Geller, op. cit.; and Harriet Shapiro, op. cit.

8. This occurred in the fall of 1986, for example, when the late Justice Potter Stewart was honored.

9. Interviews with Kenneth Geller, op. cit.; and Lawrence Wallace, op. cit.

10. Interviews on May 15, 1986, with Francis Lorson and the staff of the Supreme Court Clerk's office who handle membership in the Court bar.

11. Robert Jackson, "The Law Catches Up with the Times," broadcast on NBC Radio on November 21, 1938, on the National Radio Forum, sponsored by the Washington *Star*.

12. Op. cit., Stern, Gressman, and Shapiro, [*Supreme Court Practice*,] 898, Rule 36.4.

13. Op. cit., interview with Francis Lorson.

14. William H. Allen and Alex Kozinski, "Rules of the Supreme Court of the United States," 94 *Harvard Law Review* 312, 316 (1980). Also, op. cit., Stern, Gressman, and Shapiro, [*Supreme Court Practice*,] 895, Rule 33.2b.

15. Op. cit., interview with Francis Lorson.

16. Interviews with Francis Lorson, op. cit.; and Lawrence Wallace, op. cit.

17. Op. cit., interview with Francis Lorson.

18. Interview with Carter Phillips on June 19, 1985.

19. Op. cit., interview with Kenneth Geller.

20. Interviews with Robert Bork, op. cit.; Raymond Randolph on June 27, 1985; and Stuart Smith on September 17, 1986. Gregg v. Georgia, 428 *U.S.* 153 (1976).

21. Op. cit., interview with Raymond Randolph.

22. Charles Goetz, *Law and Economics: Cases and Materials* (West Publishing Co., 1984, 544 pp.), 491, 492.

23. Interview with David Kendall on July 1, 1985.

24. White had relied on the SG's office to report in his opinion for the Court that converting codeine into morphine is routine and "produces an

extremely noxious and penetrating odor which would make concealment of such conversion operations virtually impossible." Turner v. U.S., 396 *U.S.* 489, 497 (1970).

25. The SG had stated that it was "advised that the reductions involved did not exceed $6 per month for a four-member household if the household remained eligible for benefits," Stevens observed. "It does not indicate where in the record this information is located; nor does it indicate the source of the 'advice.' " Atkins v. Parker, 105 *S. Ct.* 2520, 2524, note 8 (1985).

26. CI.

27. Philip Elman, Columbia University's Oral History Project, December 3, 1983, used with permission of Elman and Columbia University. Also, "The Solicitor General's Office, Justice Frankfurter, and Civil Rights Litigation, 1946–1960: An Oral History," 100 *Harvard Law Review* 817 (1987).

28. Plessy v. Ferguson, 163 *U.S.* 537 (1896).

29. Bernard Schwartz, *Super Chief: Earl Warren and His Supreme Court* (New York University Press, 1983, 853 pp.), 1–3.

30. Richard Kluger, *Simple Justice: The History of Brown v. Board of Education and Black America's Struggle for Equality* (Knopf, 1976, 823 pp.), 672.

31. Ibid. Also, op. cit., interview with John Davis.

32. *The New York Times*, A-30, March 24, 1987. See also Randall Kennedy, "A Reply to Philip Elman," 100 *Harvard Law Review* (1987): "Offered as a behind-the-scenes report on his activities as an attorney in the Solicitor General's Office, Elman's memoir is instead a classic example of the treachery of nostalgia. In the end, its combination of factual errors and poor judgment makes it unreliable legal history and bad reminiscence."

33. Roe v. Wade, 410 *U.S.* 113 (1973).

34. Brown v. Board of Education, 347 *U.S.* 483 (1954).

35. Philip Elman quoted the Eisenhower addendum in his oral history, Wade McCree supplied a copy of the draft on which Eisenhower had handwritten his comments, and the Justice Department library confirmed that the copy from McCree matched the official copy on file there. The Eisenhower comments edited by Elman match the final printed version of the government brief on file at the Justice Department as well.

CHAPTER IV

"INDEPENDENCE"

1. Interviews with Archibald Cox, op. cit.; Thurgood Marshall on September 20, 1985; Erwin Griswold, op. cit.; Robert Bork, op. cit.; Wade McCree on July 11, 1985; Rex Lee, op. cit.; and Charles Fried on November 11, 1985, and June 28, 1986.

2. Op. cit., interview with Archibald Cox. Also, see proclamation of the American Bar Association to Erwin Griswold when the group awarded him its gold medal in 1978.

3. CI.

4. Interviews with Louis Claiborne, op. cit.; and Nathan Lewin on March 15, 1985. Also, Richard Harris, *Justice: The Crisis of Law, Order, and Freedom in America* (E. P. Dutton, 1970, 268 pp.), 193, 194.

5. Interviews with Louis Claiborne, op. cit.; and Lawrence Wallace, op. cit.; and CIs.

6. CIs.

7. Op. cit., interview with Erwin Griswold.

8. Sanford Ungar, *The Papers and the Papers: An Account of the Legal and Political Battle over the Pentagon Papers* (E. P. Dutton, 1972, 319 pp.), 224.

9. *The New York Times*, B-16, December 11, 1986.

10. New York Times Co. v. U.S., 403 *U.S.* 713 (1971).

11. Op. cit., interview with Erwin Griswold; and National Public Radio report by Nina Totenberg on June 8, 1975. Gutknecht v. U.S., 396 *U.S.* 295 (1970); and U.S. v. U.S. District Court, 407 *U.S.* 297 (1972).

12. "Statement of Information," Hearings about Watergate before the House Judiciary Committee, Book II, H 521–39, May–June 1974.

13. Op. cit., "Statement of Information," Book II, 1–9, memorandum by Erwin Griswold dated February 26, 1971.

14. Op. cit., "Statement of Information," Book II, 312 et seq., transcript of April 19, 1971, meeting in Oval Office of Richard Nixon, John Ehrlichman, and George Shultz.

15. Jack Anderson, Washington *Post*, D-15, March 3, 1972. "I'm so sorry that we got that call from the White House," an ITT lobbyist named Dita Beard wrote to her boss. "I thought you and I agreed very thoroughly that under no circumstances would anyone in this office discuss with anyone our participation in the Convention." She continued: "I was afraid the discussion about the three hundred/four hundred thousand committment [sic] would come up soon"; and "Certainly the President has told [Attorney General John] Mitchell to see that things are worked out fairly." She closed with a request that was ignored: "Please destroy this, huh?" Op. cit., "Statement of Information," Book II, 447, Beard memorandum, June 25, 1971.

16. Op. cit. "Statement of Information," Book II, 853, Richard Kleindienst statement. Also, op. cit., interview with Erwin Griswold.

17. Op. cit., interview with Erwin Griswold.

18. Op. cit., "Statement of Information," Book II, 853, Richard Kleindienst statement.

19. Op. cit., interview with Erwin Griswold.

20. Op. cit., interview with Robert Bork. He summed up these ideas in "Neutral Principles and Some First Amendment Problems," 47 *Indiana Law Review* 1 (1971).

21. Op. cit., interview with Robert Bork. At Yale, Taft and Bork were Chancellor Kent Professors of Law.

22. Symposium, "The Fire of Truth," 26 *Journal of Law and Economics* 163 (1983). Also, interviews with Guido Calabresi, Henry Manne, Richard Posner, and George Priest in February, March, and April 1984. Also, see Lincoln

Caplan, "Is the Supreme Court Ready for This Kind of Free-Market Justice?," Washington *Post*, D-1, September 30, 1984.

23. Op. cit., "The Fire of Truth," *Journal of Law and Economics* 183.

24. Robert Bork, *The Antitrust Paradox: A Policy at War with Itself* (Basic Books, 1978, 462 pp.).

25. Gerald Gunther, *Constitutional Law: Cases and Materials* (Foundation Press, 1975, 1,653 pp.), 731.

26. Op. cit., interview with Robert Bork.

27. Confirmation of Federal Judges, Hearings before the Senate Judiciary Committee, Senate document J-97-52, 8, 9 (1982).

28. J. Anthony Lukas, *Nightmare: The Underside of the Nixon Years* (Viking Press, 1976, 626 pp.), 439, and generally, 437–46. Also, Richard Ben-Veniste and George Frampton, Jr., *Stonewall: The Real Story of the Watergate Prosecution* (Simon & Schuster, 1977, 410 pp.), 123–57, 150, 156. Op. cit., interview with Robert Bork, Washington *Post*, A-8, July 27, 1987.

29. Interviews with Robert Bork, op. cit.; Raymond Randolph, op. cit.; and Stuart Smith, op. cit. Also, op. cit., Gregg v. Georgia.

30. CI.

31. Op. cit, Bork hearing, 11 et seq.

32. Interviews with Robert Bork, op. cit.; Daniel Friedman, op. cit.; and Lawrence Wallace, op. cit.

33. Interviews with Robert Bork, op. cit.; Andrew Frey, op. cit.; Raymond Randolph, op. cit.; and Lawrence Wallace, op. cit.

34. Op. cit., interviews with Stuart Smith and Robert Bork.

35. Interviews with Robert Bork, op. cit.; Daniel Friedman, op. cit.; and Lawrence Wallace, op. cit. Also, see "The President, the Attorney General, and the Department of Justice," the report on a conference at the University of Virginia, January 4–5, 1980. On page 86, Edward Levi said that President Ford was involved in the busing decision and that the Department of Justice made its own decision because "the president wanted it that way."

36. Morgan v. Kerrigan, 509 *F 2d.* 580 (1st Cir. 1974), cert. denied, 421 *U.S.* 963 (1975).

37. Op. cit., interview with Robert Bork.

38. Op. cit., Bork; NPR report by Nina Totenberg.

39. Regents of the University of California v. Bakke, 438 *U.S.* 265 (1978).

40. Interviews with Paul Bator on April 11, 1985; Bruce Fein on April 17, 1986; Charles Fried, on November 11, 1985; and William Bradford Reynolds on January 9, 1986. Also, see Stuart Eizenstat, "White House and Justice Department After Watergate," 68 *American Bar Association Journal* 175, 176 (1982).

41. Timothy O'Neill, *Bakke and the Politics of Equality: Friends and Foes in the Classroom of Litigation* (Wesleyan University Press, 1985, 325 pp.), 22.

42. Ibid., 42, 45.

43. Justice Department Memorandum from Drew Days to file, February 28, 1977.

44. Frank Easterbrook, Memorandum to the Solicitor General, June 9, 1977.

45. Ibid., 29, 36.

46. Interviews with Wade McCree, op. cit.; and Drew Days on July 1, 1985.

47. Press conference No. 12 of President Jimmy Carter, July 28, 1977.

48. Interviews with Drew Days, op. cit.; Stuart Eizenstat on July 3, 1985; Ben Heineman on July 24, 1985; Wade McCree, op. cit.; Lawrence Wallace, op. cit.; and others.

49. Interviews with Drew Days, op. cit.; Brian Landsberg on June 12, 1986; and others at the Civil Rights Division.

50. Joseph A. Califano, Jr., *Governing America: An Insider's Report from the White House and the Cabinet* (Simon and Schuster, 1981, 474 pp.), 237.

51. Ibid.

52. Griffin B. Bell, with Ronald J. Ostrow, *Taking Care of the Law* (William Morrow & Co., 1982, 254 pp.), 29.

53. Interviews with Drew Days, op. cit.; Frank Easterbrook on June 21, 1986; and Lawrence Wallace, op. cit. Also, see Easterbrook memorandum.

54. Stuart Eizenstat and Robert Lipshutz, "Memorandum for the President," September 6, 1977.

55. *The New York Times*, A-1, September 12, 1977.

56. Op. cit., Califano, 241.

57. Eizenstat notes of the meeting. He let the author copy his notes at his law office in Washington, D.C., and gave permission to quote from them.

58. Op. cit., Califano, 241; interview with Stuart Eizenstat; and Eizenstat notes.

59. Op. cit., Califano, 241.

60. Op. cit., Bell, 28–32. Also, interview with Terrence Adamson on July 10, 1985.

61. Letter from Chief Justice William Rehnquist to the author, October 2, 1986, used with permission of the Chief Justice.

62. Op. cit., Bell, 31.

63. TVA v. Hill, 437 *U.S.* 153 (1978).

64. Op. cit., interview with Wade McCree.

65. Ibid.

66. Op. cit., interviews with Terrence Adamson and Wade McCree.

67. Brief for the United States as amicus curiae, Regents of the University of California v. Bakke, No. 76-811, October Term, 1977.

68. Op. cit., O'Neill, 57.

69. Op. cit., Califano, p. 243.

70. "Memorandum for the Attorney General Re: The Role of the Solicitor General," September 29, 1977. Published as "77-56 Memorandum Opinion for the Attorney General: Role of the Solicitor General," in "Opinions of the Office of Legal Counsel," Vol. 1, 228 (1977).

71. Interviews with Miles Foy on July 23, 1985; Larry Hammond on June 28, 1985; and John Harmon on July 23, 1985.

72. Op. cit., Office of Legal Counsel, memorandum. The quotations cited in the rest of this chapter are on pages 1–11 of the memorandum.

73. Letter from Erwin Griswold to Attorney General Griffin Bell, May 13, 1977, used with permission of Erwin Griswold.

CHAPTER V

THE BOB JONES CASE

1. Brief for the United States, Goldsboro Christian Schools, Inc. v. U.S. and Bob Jones University v. U.S., No. 81-1 and 81-3, October Term, 1981, 1.

2. Interviews with Rex Lee. op. cit.; and Lawrence Wallace. op. cit.

3. Interviews with Andrew Frey, op. cit.; Kenneth Geller, op. cit.; Albert Lauber on July 30, 1985 and February 20, 1986; and Lawrence Wallace, op. cit.

4. Interviews with Francis Lorson, op. cit.; Supreme Court reporters; and Lawrence Wallace, op. cit.; and author's observations.

5. Interviews with Francis Lorson, op. cit.; and Lawrence Wallace, op. cit.

6. Louis Claiborne had about fifty in 1981, and was second to Wallace. As of 1987, Wallace had 97. Griswold used the figure of 127 cases, because he counted as two different cases some that were consolidated and argued at the same time. Other records, including the Supreme Court's, said 117. Also, op. cit., William H. Harbaugh, *Lawyer's Lawyer*, 531.

7. Kennedy School of Government, Harvard University, Center for Press, Politics, and Public Policy, "Ronald Reagan and Tax Exemptions for Racist Schools," 14 (1984).

8. Joint appendix in Bob Jones University (Nos. 81-3), A2–A3, A40–A41.

9. Washington *Post,* D-2, March 30, 1986.

10. Harvard Law School, Program on the Legal Profession, "Segregated Schools: Government Lawyers and Politics," 4 (1983).

11. Op. cit., Bob Jones joint appendix, 84.

12. Bob Jones University v. U.S., 468 *F. Supp.* 890, 894 (1978).

13. Op. cit., Kennedy School study, 25, quoting transcript of January 30, 1980, speech at Bob Jones University.

14. Op. cit., Kennedy School study, 14.

15. Op. cit., Harvard Law School study, 4.

16. CIs.

17. Op. cit., Kennedy School study, 9.

18. Ibid., 17.

19. CIs.

20. Bob Jones University v. U.S., 461 *U.S.* 574, 595 (1983).

21. Op. cit., Harvard Law School study, 8; quoting letter from Trent Lott to Rex Lee, October 30, 1981.

22. Op. cit., Harvard Law School study, 41.

23. Ibid., 10, 11.

24. Ibid., 23, 12.

25. CIs.

26. Op. cit., Harvard Law School study, 18, 54.

27. CIs. Also, see op. cit., Harvard Law School study, 26.

28. Op. cit., Bob Jones University v. U.S., 595. Also, Coit v. Green, 404 U.S. 997 (1971).

29. Hearings on the nomination of William Bradford Reynolds to be Associate Attorney General, Senate Judiciary Committee, No. J-99-29, 32, June 4, 5, and 18, 1985.

30. Interviews with Bruce Fein, op. cit.; and William Bradford Reynolds, op. cit. Also, see op. cit., Harvard Law School and Kennedy School studies.

31. CIs with Justices.

32. Op. cit., Kennedy School study, 49, 50.

33. Op. cit., Kennedy School study, 67.

34. Ronnie Dugger, *On Reagan: The Man and His Presidency* (McGraw-Hill, 1983, 616 pp.), 214.

35. Op. cit., Harvard Law School study, 48.

36. Op. cit., Dugger, 213–14.

37. Op. cit., Kennedy School study, 76.

38. Ibid., 107.

39. St. Louis *Post-Dispatch*, 1A, January 12, 1982.

40. CI.

41. Op. cit., interview with Lawrence Wallace.

42. Letter from Marvin Frankel to Lawrence Wallace, February 5, 1982, used with permission of Frankel and Wallace.

43. Op. cit., Bob Jones University v. U.S., 595, 598.

44. Op. cit., Kennedy School study, 111, 113.

45. Ibid., 115.

46. Interviews with Albert Lauber, op. cit.; and Lawrence Wallace, op. cit.

47. Interview with Brian Landsberg, op. cit. Also, see his remarks at Civil Rights Division farewell reception in his honor, June 20, 1986.

48. CIs.

49. *Wall Street Journal*, 16, September 6, 1984, quoting James McClellan.

50. Interviews with Paul Bator, op. cit.; Bruce Fein, op. cit.; Bradford Reynolds, op. cit.; and others.

51. CI.

52. CI.

53. Interviews with Paul Bator, op. cit.; Bruce Fein, op. cit.; William Bradford Reynolds, op. cit.; and others.

54. Op. cit., interview with Paul Bator. Also, see résumé of Paul Bator, March 1985.

55. Remarks by Paul Bator at the swearing-in of Kenneth Starr as a judge of the U.S. Court of Appeals for the D.C. Circuit, 2, 3–5.

56. Op. cit., interview with Paul Bator.

57. Interviews with Paul Bator, op. cit.; Charles Fried, op. cit.; and William Bradford Reynolds, op. cit.

58. Interview on January 27, 1987, with Jewel Lafontant.
59. Interviews with Andrew Frey, op. cit.; Kenneth Geller, op. cit.; and Lawrence Wallace, op. cit.
60. Op. cit., interview with Paul Bator.

CHAPTER VI
JUDICIAL RESTRAINT

1. Op. cit., interview with Robert Bork.
2. Interviews with Archibald Cox, op. cit.; Paul Freund, op. cit.; and others.
3. Council on the Role of Courts, *The Role of Courts in American Society* (1984).
4. Ibid., 1, 3.
5. Ibid., 4, 101.
6. Ibid., 6, 118–20.
7. See Joel Klein, "The Lawyers' Plot," *New Republic* 29 (February 4, 1985).
8. Remarks of the Attorney General before the Federal Legal Council, Reston, Virginia, October 29, 1981, 1.
9. Ibid., 14, 15, 17–18.
10. Ibid., 12.
11. Hearings on Justice Department confirmations, hearing on the nomination of Rex Lee to be Solicitor General, Senate Judiciary Committee, No. J-97-7-Part 2, June 19, 24, and July 17, 1981, 2.
12. Rex Lee, *A Lawyer Looks at the Equal Rights Amendment* (Brigham Young University Press, 1980, 141 pp.) and *A Lawyer Looks at the Constitution* (Brigham Young University Press, 1981, 229 pp.).
13. CIs.
14. Op. cit., Rex Lee, *A Lawyer Looks at the Constitution,* 9.
15. Op. cit., Lee hearings, 43.
16. Ibid., 45, 47.
17. CI.
18. Op. cit., interview with Rex Lee.
19. Op. cit., "Annual Report of the Attorney General," 1955 through 1985. The average percentage from the 1943 through 1983 Terms was 69. Except for the 1983 Term, the winning percentage was over 79 only twice: in the 1953 Term the percentage was 81; and in the 1981 Term the percentage was 82. Also, op. cit., interview with Virginia Bolling. She reports that some former lawyers in the SG's office claim the office did as well in the early years of this century.
20. Gerald F. Uelmen, "The Influence of the Solicitor General Upon Supreme Court Disposition of Federal Circuit Court Decisions: A Closer

Look at the Ninth Circuit Record," 69 *Judicature* 361 (No. 6, April–May 1986).

21. CIs.

22. "Judging the Judges," 1 *Benchmark* 1 (Nos. 4 and 5, July–October 1984).

23. Washington *Post*, A-2, March 8, 1982.

24. Los Angeles *Times*, A-1, July 25, 1983.

25. Ibid.

26. Learned Hand, *The Bill of Rights* (Harvard University Press, 1958, 82 pp.), 15, 29.

27. Hamilton wrote that limitations on the federal government contained in the Constitution "can be preserved in practice no other way than through the medium of courts of justice, whose duty it must be to declare all acts contrary to the manifest tenor of the constitution void." Charles A. Beard, ed., *The Enduring Federalist* (Frederick Ungar, 1959, 396 pp.), 333. Also, Marbury v. Madison, 1 *Cranch* (5 *U.S.*) 137, 177 (1803).

28. Charles Black and Eugene Rostow at the Yale Law School were key articulators of this view in the nineteen-fifties and -sixties.

29. Robert Jackson, *The Supreme Court in the American System of Government* (Harvard University Press, 1955, 92 pp.), 53.

30. Alexander Bickel, *The Least Dangerous Branch: The Supreme Court at the Bar of Politics* (Bobbs-Merrill, 1962, 303 pp.), 19.

31. James Bradley Thayer, "The Origin and Scope of the American Doctrine of Constitutional Law, 7 *Harvard Law Review* 129 (1893).

32. Reynolds v. Sims, 377 *U.S.* 533, 589 (1964).

33. Op. cit., Hand, 73.

34. Baker v. Carr, 369 *U.S.* 186, 270 (1962).

35. Op. cit., Bickel.

36. William Leuchtenburg, "Franklin D. Roosevelt's Supreme Court 'Packing Plan,' " in *Essays on the New Deal,* compiled by Harold M. Hollingsworth (University of Texas Press, 1969, 115 pp.), 76.

37. Interviews with Daniel Friedman, op. cit.; and Erwin Griswold, op. cit.

38. Op. cit., Leuchtenburg, 80.

39. Op. cit., Leuchtenburg, 75: "The question was debated at town meetings in New England, at crossroads country stores in North Carolina, at a large rally at the Tulsa court house, by the Chatterbox Club of Rochester, New York, the Thursday Study Club of La Crosse, Wisconsin, the Veteran Fire Fighters' Association of New Orleans, and the Baptist Young People's Union of Lime Rock, Rhode Island."

40. Richard B. Morris, *Encyclopedia of American History* (Harper & Row, 1970, 850 pp.), 356.

41. Interviews with Norman Dorsen on June 10, 1986; and Albert Sacks on June 9, 1986.

42. Karl Llewellyn, *The Common Law Tradition: Deciding Appeals* (Little, Brown, 1960, 565 pp.), 4.

43. Interview with Rex Lee, op. cit.; and CIs.

44. Speech by Rex Lee at Franklin and Marshall College, October 24, 1985, 23.
45. Op. cit., Los Angeles *Times*.
46. "Crisis in the Courts," *Manhattan Report*, 1985, p. 6.
47. Richard Posner, *The Federal Courts: Crisis and Reform* (Harvard University Press, 1985, 365 pp.), 210.
48. Résumé of Richard Posner, January 30, 1984.
49. Op. cit., Caplan, "Free-Market Justice."
50. George L. Priest, "The Rise of Law and Economics," a paper for a Conference on the Place of Economics in Legal Education, October 28–30, 1982, 49.
51. Richard Posner and Elisabeth Landes, "The Economics of the Baby Shortage," 7 *Journal of Legal Studies* 323 (1978).
52. Op. cit., interview with Richard Posner.
53. Los Angeles *Times* interview, released by the White House press office on June 23, 1986.
54. Knights of Columbus speech, August 5, 1986, released by White House press office.
55. Bruce Fein, "Why Ed Meese Is Right About the Supreme Court," Los Angeles *Herald-Examiner*, F-1, November 17, 1985.
56. Op. cit., *Benchmark*, 1. Also, see Bruce Fein, "Selecting a Supreme Court Justice Devoted to Judicial Restraint," 1 *Benchmark* 1 (No. 6, November–December 1984).
57. Op. cit., Los Angeles *Times*.
58. CI.
59. Op. cit., *Wall Street Journal*, 16, September 6, 1984.
60. Thomas Ferguson and Joel Rogers, "The Myth of America's Turn to the Right," *Atlantic Monthly*, 45–46 (May 1986).

CHAPTER VII

THE SHADOW SOLICITOR

1. Hearings on nomination of William Bradford Reynolds to be Associate Attorney General, Senate Judiciary Committee, No. J–99–29, 3, June 4, 5, and 18, 1985.
2. Op. cit., interview with William Bradford Reynolds.
3. CIs. Also, see *Legal Times*, 1, August 18, 1986, on Griffin Bell's testimony during the Rehnquist Chief Justiceship hearings.
4. Op. cit., interview with William Bradford Reynolds. Also, see op. cit., Reynolds hearings, 3.
5. Op. cit., interview with William Bradford Reynolds.
6. Interview with John Wilson, Office of Public Affairs, Justice Department, on January 9, 1986.

7. CIs.

8. Washington v. Seattle School District No. 1, 458 *U.S.* 457 (1982).

9. Interview with Gordon Foster on May 12, 1986. Also, see Fact Sheet About Busing, School of Education and Allied Professions, University of Miami, and "Covering School Desegregation," Educational Equity Project, Vanderbilt University.

10. Charlotte *Observer*, 1A, October 9, 1984.

11. "President's Busing Remarks Anger Schools Superintendent," Charlotte *Observer*, 1A, October 9, 1984.

12. "You Were Wrong, Mr. President," Charlotte *Observer*, 10A, October 9, 1984.

13. Carl Stern, "Nofziger memo," NBC News, October 16, 1981.

14. CI.

15. Robert J. D'Agostino, memorandum to William Bradford Reynolds about U.S. v. Yonkers, July 21, 1981.

16. Petition to William French Smith and William Bradford Reynolds about D'Agostino's July 21 memo.

17. CIs. Also, see letter from William Bradford Reynolds to the Civil Rights Division staff on September 17, 1981, using the same term.

18. CIs.

19. CIs.

20. Op. cit., Bakke, 407.

21. Glenn Loury, "The Color Line Today," *Public Interest*, Summer, 1985.

22. "The State of Black America 1986," National Urban League, i.

23. In 1986, Justice Thurgood Marshall took the occasion of a speech to the judges of the U.S. Court of Appeals for the Second Circuit, where he once sat, to explain why affirmative action was a required step toward the ultimate goal of a color-blind society. "We still have a very long way to go" before the United States finally closes the gap between whites and blacks that was brought about by slavery, he observed, and the "vestiges of racial bias in America are so pernicious and so difficult to remove that we must take advantage of all the remedial measures at our disposal." Remarks by Justice Thurgood Marshall, September 4, 1986, 3.

24. Op. cit., Interview with William Bradford Reynolds. Also, see remarks of William Bradford Reynolds before the Seventh Annual Convention, National Association of Police Organizations, August 1, 1985; before the Wilmington Rotary Club, October 31, 1985; and before the University of Chicago's Chapter of the Federalist Society, January 10, 1986.

25. Op. cit., interview with William Bradford Reynolds. Also, see file of news clips about Reynolds at the Leadership Conference for Civil Rights.

26. Interviews with Paul Bator, op. cit.; and William Bradford Reynolds, op. cit.

27. CIs.

28. Boston Firefighters Union, Local 712 v. Boston Chapter, NAACP et al., 461 *U.S.* 477 (1983).

29. Op. cit., interview with Carter Phillips.
30. CI.
31. CI.
32. Interviews with Rex Lee, op. cit.; and William Bradford Reynolds, op. cit.; and CIs.
33. CIs.
34. Op. cit., 461 *U.S.* 477 (1983).
35. "Assault on Affirmative Action," a production of WGBH broadcast in June 1986 by WETA in Washington, D.C.
36. Firefighters Local Union No. 1784 v. Stotts, 104 *S. Ct.* 2576 (1984).
37. Op. cit., WGBH.
38. CI.
39. Op. cit., Stotts.
40. CIs.
41. Op. cit., interview with William Bradford Reynolds.
42. 103 *S. Ct.* 3221 (1983).
43. CIs.
44. CIs.
45. CI.
46. Vasquez v. Hillery, 54 *U.S. Law Week* 4068 (decided January 14, 1986).
47. CIs.
48. Joshua Schwartz, Memorandum to the Solicitor General About Vasquez v. Hillery, No. 84-836, April 26, 1985.
49. Author's observation at oral argument on October 15, 1985.
50. Hillery v. Pulley, 563 *F. Supp.* 1228, 1234 (1983).
51. Op. cit., Vasquez v. Hillery, 4070, note 3.
52. Walter Barnett, Cover Memorandum About Vasquez v. Hillery to Charles Cooper, March 28, 1985, 1.
53. CIs.
54. William Bradford Reynolds, Memorandum for the Solicitor General Re: Vasquez v. Hillery, April 11, 1985, 2. All quotations in this paragraph are from this page.
55. CI.
56. Op. cit., Schwartz, 8, 9.
57. Strauder v. West Virginia, 100 *U.S.* 303, 308 (1880).
58. Rex Lee, Memorandum to the Attorney General, May 7, 1985.
59. Op. cit., Vasquez v. Hillery, 4070, 4072.
60. Op. cit., *Wall Street Journal*, 1, September 6, 1984.
61. Lynch v. Donnelly, 104 *S. Ct.* 1355 (1984).
62. Interviews with Paul Bator, op. cit.; Rex Lee, op. cit.; and Michael McConnell on May 28, 1985.
63. Lemon v. Kurtzman, 403 *U.S.* 602 (1971).
64. 525 *F. Supp.* 1150 (D.R.I. 1981) and 691 *F. 2d* 1029 (1st Cir. 1982).
65. Brief for the United States as amicus curiae supporting reversal, Lynch v. Donnelly, No. 82-1256, October Term, 1982, 23–24, 24–25, 1.

66. Norman Dorsen and Charles Sims, "The Nativity Scene Case: An Error of Judgment," *University of Illinois Law Review*, No. 4, 837 (1985).

67. CIs.

68. William Lee Miller of the University of Virginia argues that the religion clauses reflect a commitment to a liberty encompassing much more than religion. The religion clauses were intended to help guarantee the freedom of thought that is the foundation of free government. William Lee Miller, *The First Liberty: Religion and the American Republic* (Knopf, 1986, 373 pp.)

69. Op. cit., *Benchmark*.

70. Daniel Popeo, a contributing editor to *Benchmark* and a founder of the Washington Legal Foundation, one of the New Right centers that began during the Reagan years, said, "The Justice Department calls me up to go on the MacNeil/Lehrer Show, and I go." Interview with Daniel Popeo on November 14, 1985.

71. *Washington Post*, A-6, August 9, 1985.

72. Editor's brief, "A Lawyer Looks at Rex Lee," 1 *Benchmark* (No. 2, March–April 1984), 1 et seq.

73. Ibid., 5.

74. Ibid.

75. Jaffree v. Board of School Commissioners of Mobile County, 554 *F. Supp.* 1104, 1113, note 5 (1983). Also, interview with Forrest McDonald on March 17, 1987.

76. Op. cit., Lee, *A Lawyer Looks at the Constitution*, 31.

77. Op. cit., Editor's brief, 1–2.

78. Op. cit., interview with Paul Bator.

79. Interviews with Paul Bator, op. cit.; and Rex Lee, op. cit.

80. Op. cit., *Wall Street Journal*, 16.

81. William Bradford Reynolds, Memorandum to Rex Lee about Jaffree v. Wallace, June 29, 1983.

82. William Bradford Reynolds, Memorandum to Rex Lee about Jaffree v. Wallace, October 3, 1983.

83. Op. cit., *Wall Street Journal*, 16.

84. Op. cit., interview with Paul Bator.

85. Wallace v. Jaffree, No. 83-812, decided June 4, 1985; 4, note 22, 14.

86. Ibid., 10.

87. Ibid., O'Connor opinion, 11.

88. Op. cit., Editor's brief, 5.

89. Ibid., 16, 12, 15.

90. Op. cit., "Annual Report of the Attorney General" for 1938: "It is evident, therefore, that on the basis of reversals the percentage of success obtained by the Government at the last Term was better than at any time" since 1927. "It far exceeds that secured by its opponents as well as that obtaining in all cases, Government and non-Government. . . . Taking all cases decided on the merits at the last term in which the Government was a party, . . . the Government won, in actual numbers 91 cases and lost 23, a

percentage of 80," 37. In October Term, 1938, the government won 64 percent; in October Term, 1939, 84 percent. Robert Jackson's overall record as SG was 76 percent.

91. Eugene Gerhart, *America's Advocate: Robert Jackson* (Bobbs-Merrill, 1958, 545 pp.), 145.

92. Op. cit., Editor's brief, 2; 4–5, 14.

93. Ibid.

94. Richard G. Wilkins, "Another Lawyer Looks at Rex E. Lee: A Reply to James McClellan," 15.

95. Op. cit., Editor's brief [McClellan], 3.

96. "No Friend of the Court," *The New York Times*, A-22, August 4, 1982.

97. Brief Amicus Curiae of Senator Bob Packwood (R-Ore.), Representative Don Edwards (D-Calif.), and Certain Other Members of the Congress of the United States in Support of Appellees, Thornburgh v. American College of Obstetricians and Gynecologists, No. 84-495, October Term, 1985, 8.

98. Op. cit., Los Angeles *Times*, July 25, 1983.

99. City of Akron v. Akron Center for Reproductive Health, 103 *S. Ct.* 2481 (1983).

100. Op. cit., interview with Rex Lee.

101. Ibid.

102. Op. cit., Reynolds hearings.

103. Statement submitted, with testimony of Thomas D. Barr, by Lawyers' Committee for Civil Rights Under Law, June 4, 1985.

104. Interview with Thomas Barr on November 14, 1985.

105. Op. cit., Lawyers' Committee, 3–4.

106. Ibid., 6.

107. Ibid., 4.

108. CIs.

109. Op. cit., Reynolds hearings, 17.

110. Op. cit., Lawyers' Committee, 30.

111. Op. cit., Reynolds hearings, 887.

112. Ibid., 888, 889.

113. Ibid., 996.

114. Ibid., 997.

115. On page 208 of the hearing transcript, a Mathias sentence begins, "Now, they may be happy with the result, but the result really was the opposite of the way you started, and that is my concern." In the printed hearing record at page 997, the sentence reads, "Now, they may be happy with the result, but my concern is that the result really was what you originally wanted." The printed version is a misleading correction of the sentence the author heard Mathias speak, which the transcript records. It should read, "the result was *not* what you originally wanted."

116. News release from Dennis DeConcini, June 19, 1985.

117. Staff office, Senate Judiciary Committee.

118. Op. cit., interview with Rex Lee. Also, Rex Lee interview with Nina Totenberg on National Public Radio, May 28, 1985.

119. Op. cit., Office of Legal Counsel memorandum.

120. CIs.

121. A second good example is the Lands Division, but the Antitrust, Civil, and Criminal Divisions also did the same.

122. Op. cit., interview with Rex Lee.

123. Rex Lee, Memorandum to William Bradford Reynolds About *Irving Independent School District v. Tatro,* No. 83-558, February 3, 1984, 1.

124. "Inside: The Justice Department," Washington *Post,* A-23, May 3, 1985.

125. In the federal-court year that ended June 28, 1985, only six of the 110 briefs on the merits filed by the SG's office concerned civil rights. The low number was misleading as an index of Reynolds's dealings with the SG.

CHAPTER VIII

MEESE'S LAW

1. Hearings on Confirmation of Edwin Meese III to be Attorney General, Senate Judiciary Committee, No. J-99-1, January 29, 30, and 31, 1985, 723–725.

2. Ibid., 713. Also, *The New York Times,* A-1, July 23, 1985, quoting William Clark, who was National Security Adviser and then Secretary of the Interior in the Reagan Administration, and an old friend of the President. He observed about Caspar Weinberger and Meese that neither expressed purely personal views: "The thing to emphasize is that Cap and Ed Meese, for the past 18 years, have been the great articulators of the Reagan view of life, whether it be national security or domestic issues. They mirror the President on all the key issues. No one else can even come close."

3. Ibid., 713–763.

4. CIs.

5. Report of Independent Counsel Concerning Edwin Meese III, submitted to the U.S. Court of Appeals for the District of Columbia, Division for the Purpose of Appointing Independent Counsels, Ethics in Government Act of 1978, No. 84-1, September Term, 1984.

6. Common Cause, "The Case Against Edwin Meese for Attorney General," December 1984, 2.

7. Op. cit., Independent Counsel report, 8–12. Also CIs.

8. Ibid., 339–351.

9. Ibid., 151–225.

10. Op. cit., Common Cause, 4–5.

11. See Lincoln Caplan, "The Meese Affairs," Baltimore *Sun,* January 29 and 30, 1985.

12. CIs.

13. Op. cit., Meese hearings, 713–763.

14. "Theorists on Right Find Fertile Ground," Washington *Post*, A-1, August 9, 1985.

15. Address of Edwin Meese before the American Bar Association, July 9, 1985, 14–15.

16. Ibid., 15, 17, 12, 10.

17. H. Jefferson Powell, "How Does the Constitution Structure Government?: The Founders' Views," *A Workable Constitution* (forthcoming), 7.

18. McCulloch v. Maryland, 4 *Wheat.* (17 *U.S.*) 316, 407 (1819), 415.

19. Op. cit., Meese address, July 9, 18.

20. Address of Edwin Meese to the American Enterprise Institute, September 6, 1985, 1.

21. Address of Edwin Meese to Dickinson College, September 17, 1985, 10.

22. *U.S. News & World Report*, 67, October 14, 1985.

23. Office of Public Affairs, Justice Department.

24. Sidney Zion, "A Decade of Constitutional Revision," *The New York Times Magazine*, November 11, 1979, 27–28.

25. Interview with Yale Kamisar, professor of criminal law, Michigan Law School, on January 23, 1987.

26. "Interrogations in New Haven: The Impact of Miranda," 76 *Yale Law Journal* 1519, 1613 (1967). Also, op. cit., Zion, 28.

27. A few months before Meese's attack on Miranda, Justice William Brennan dissented from a decision in which the Supreme Court ruled that in some cases the police could ask questions first and later warn the accused of his rights. This limitation on Miranda prompted Brennan to write that the Supreme Court was "increasingly irrelevant in the protection of individual rights." Washington *Post*, A-17, April 4, 1985.

28. Op. cit., "Impact of Miranda," 1613.

29. Op. cit., interview with Yale Kamisar.

30. William J. Brennan, Jr., "The Constitution of the United States: Contemporary Ratification," October 12, 1985, 1.

31. Ibid., 4.

32. Ibid., 7.

33. Address of John Paul Stevens to the Federal Bar Association, October 23, 1985, 9.

34. NBC News, October 25, 1985.

35. Thornburgh v. American College of Obstetricians and Gynecologists, No. 84-495, decided June 11, 1986, White opinion, 4. Also, interviews with Terry Eastland on November 13, 1985; and Bruce Fein, op. cit.

36. Edwin Meese, *Policy Review*, 34, Winter, 1986.

37. Ibid.

38. Op. cit., Meese, *Policy Review*, 34.

39. Op. cit., Bickel, *Least Dangerous Branch*.

40. Op. cit., Meese, *Policy Review*, 34.

41. Brief for the United States as Amicus Curiae in Support of Appellants, Thornburgh v. American College of Obstetricians and Gynecologists, Dia-

mond v. Charles, Nos. 84–495 and 84–1379, October Term, 1985, filed July 15, 1985.

42. Address of Edwin Meese to the American Bar Association, July 17, 1985, 11.

43. Op. cit., Roe v. Wade, 410 *U.S.* 113 (1973).

44. John Hart Ely, *Democracy and Distrust: A Theory of Judicial Review* (Harvard University Press, 1980, 268 pp.), 1–2.

45. John Hart Ely, "The Wages of Crying Wolf," 82 *Yale Law Journal* 920, 949 (1973).

46. Akron v. Akron Center for Reproductive Health, Inc., 462 *U.S.* 416 (1983).

47. Interview with John Hart Ely on April 24, 1986.

48. Op. cit., Packwood-Edwards abortion brief, 3.

49. Address of Edwin Meese to the Federal Bar Association, September 13, 1985, 4.

50. Cooper v. Aaron, 358 *U.S.* 1, 18 (1958).

51. Lecture by Edwin Meese on "The Law of the Constitution," Tulane University, October 21, 1986, 12.

52. Op. cit., McCulloch v. Maryland, 401.

53. Saul Sigelschiffer, *The American Conscience: The Drama of the Lincoln-Douglas Debates* (Horizon Press, 1973, 488 pp.), 226, 133, 188.

54. Op. cit., Meese lecture, 9.

55. Op. cit., Cooper v. Aaron, 18.

56. Washington *Post*, A-3, February 16, 1987.

57. Op. cit., Meese lecture, 6–7, 11.

58. Op. cit., Gerald Gunther, *Constitutional Law*, 32.

59. Op. cit., Meese address, July 9, 14.

60. Roger Clegg, Memorandum to Charles Fried About U.S. v. District of Columbia, September 26, 1985.

61. CIs.

62. Op. cit., Cox, *Chicago Bar Record*, 229.

63. *The New York Times*, A-13. December 9, 1986.

64. See reports in the Washington *Post* about lax enforcement of environmental, occupational health and safety, civil rights, antitrust, and other laws, from 1981 through 1987.

65. Washington *Post*, D-2, December 7, 1986.

66. Letter from Edwin Meese to Dwight D. Opperman, December 13, 1985, supplied by the Office of Public Affairs, Justice Department.

67. Ibid., 2.

68. Letter from Dwight Opperman to Edwin Meese, December 26, 1985, supplied by the Office of Public Affairs, Justice Department.

69. Letters from Benjamin Civiletti to Walter Mondale on January 13, 1981, and from William French Smith to George Bush on November 21, 1984, supplied as public documents by Michael Davidson, Counsel in Office of Senate Legal Counsel, March 27, 1986.

70. Op. cit., Civiletti letter.
71. Op. cit., Smith letter.
72. CIs.
73. Letter from Edwin Meese to Thomas P. O'Neill, Jr., May 1, 1985.
74. Sheldon Goldman, "Reagan's Second Term Judicial Appointments: The Battle at Midway." 70 *Judicature,* April–May 1987.
75. Speech by Paul Simon, "Judging Judges: The Senate's Role in Judicial Appointments," National Press Club, March 10, 1986, 2.
76. Op. cit., Office of Legal Counsel memorandum, 11.

CHAPTER IX

THE ABORTION BRIEF

1. Interview with Charles Fried on January 22, 1987.
2. *Harvard Law School Bulletin,* 12, Winter, 1986.
3. Interviews with Paul Bator, op. cit.; and Charles Fried, op. cit., on November 11, 1985.
4. Charles Fried, curriculum vitae, 2; and op. cit., *Bulletin.*
5. Op. cit., vitae, 5–7.
6. Charles Fried, "Curbing the Judiciary," *The New York Times,* A-23, November 10, 1981.
7. Charles Fried, "The Trouble with Lawyers," *The New York Times Magazine,* D-56, February 12, 1984.
8. UPI, May 26, 1985.
9. David Lauter, "A Champion of the Reagan Agenda," *National Law Journal,* 1, 30, January 27, 1986. Also, CIs with Harvard Law School students and professors.
10. Charles Fried, "The Lawyer as Friend: The Moral Foundation of the Lawyer-Client Relation," 85 *Yale Law Journal* 1060 (July 1976).
11. CIs; op. cit., Lauter, 31.
12. Alasdair MacIntyre, review of *Right and Wrong, New Republic,* 29, May 6, 1978.
13. Charles Fried, "Privacy," 77 *Yale Law Journal* 475 (1968).
14. Charles Fried, *Right and Wrong* (Harvard University Press, 1978, 226 pp.), 1.
15. 88 *Yale Law Journal* 647 (1979).
16. Interviews with Charles Fried, op. cit., on November 11, 1985, and Philip Heymann on April 12, 1985. Also, Poe v. Ullman, 367 *U.S.* 497, 539, 542 (1961).
17. CI.
18. Washington *Post,* A-8, January 7, 1986.
19. Op. cit., interview with Charles Fried.
20. Interview with Philip Heymann on February 14, 1986.
21. Op. cit., interview with Charles Fried; and news accounts.

22. The Supreme Court dismissed Diamond v. Charles on jurisdictional grounds, and decided only Thornburgh v. American College of Obstetricians and Gynecologists.

23. Op. cit., SG's Thornburgh brief, 2.

24. Ibid., 3.

25. Ibid., 20, 21, 23.

26. Ibid., 24, 29.

27. Op. cit., interview with Charles Fried; and news accounts.

28. Op. cit., SG's Thornburgh brief, 3.

29. No. 1982–138, Chapter 32, Abortion, to amend Title 18, act of November 25, 1970 (Pennsylvania Law 707, No. 230).

30. Interview with Stephen Freind on June 12, 1986.

31. Ibid.

32. Op. cit., SG's Thornburgh brief, 26.

33. Interviews with Archibald Cox, op. cit.; John Davis, op. cit.; Erwin Griswold, op. cit.; Wade McCree, op. cit.; and others.

34. Washington *Post*, A-25, September 20, 1985.

35. CIs.

36. John Paul Stevens, "Deciding What to Decide: The Docket and the Rule of Four," *Views from the Bench: The Judiciary and Constitutional Politics*, edited by Mark W. Cannon and David M. O'Brien (Chatham House, 1985, 330 pp.), 81.

37. Op. cit., Packwood-Edwards abortion brief.

38. Interview with Laurence Tribe, op. cit., and summary of briefs and arguments from Tribe.

39. Planned Parenthood conference, September 3, 1985, 3, 17.

40. Ibid., 8.

41. Op. cit., Lee NPR interview with Nina Totenberg, May 28, 1985.

42. Rex Lee, draft of "History of the Office of the Solicitor General," 32.

43. Ibid., 32–34.

44. Op. cit., speech by Rex Lee at Franklin and Marshall College.

45. Notes of author from Bureau of National Affairs conference September 13 and 14, 1985.

46. *New Republic*, 11, October 7, 1985.

47. Op. cit., interview with Charles Fried; and CIs.

48. A letter from Paul Freund to the author, May 8, 1985, tells this story. Also, op. cit., Bander, *Justice Holmes Ex Cathedra*, No. 402, 195. After Fried's submission in the abortion case, and his comments about it, other lawyers who once served in the SG's office and who knew the Mitchell story told it in this context.

49. Audiotape of remarks by Charles Fried to the Chamber of Commerce on November 19, 1985, provided by Winston Leavell, Manager, News Department, Public Liaison, Chamber of Commerce, and transcribed by the author.

50. Herbert Wechsler, "Toward Neutral Principles of Constitutional Law," 73 *Harvard Law Review* 1, 19 (1959).

51. Interview with Herbert Wechsler on February 26, 1986.
52. 313 *U.S.* 299 (1941).
53. Philadelphia *Inquirer*, 15-A, January 17, 1986.
54. Letter from Charles Fried to author, January 21, 1986.
55. CIs.
56. Op. cit., Meese address, July 17, 17.
57. CI.
58. CIs with several of Fried's former colleagues at Harvard Law School.
59. Stuart Taylor, Jr., *The New York Times*, A-8, July 18, 1986.
60. Op. cit., interview with Charles Fried.
61. *Wall Street Journal*, 1, September 26, 1985.
62. Author's observation.
63. Comment by Charles Fried to author at party for Louis Claiborne on October 21, 1985.
64. Transcript of hearing on the confirmation of Charles Fried to be Solicitor General, Senate Judiciary Committee, October 17, 1985, 71.
65. Ibid., 72.
66. Ibid., 76, 88.
67. Comment of Charles Fried to author at party for Louis Claiborne on October 21, 1985.
68. Op. cit., Fried hearing, 94.
69. Ibid., 95.
70. Ibid., 73, 74.
71. Washington *Post*, A-7, August 9, 1985; A-1, August 25, 1985.
72. Op. cit., *Wall Street Journal*, September 6, 1984.
73. Op. cit., Reynolds hearings, 135.
74. Washington *Post*, A-7, August 9, 1985. Also, *The New York Times*, B-3, October 3, 1985.
75. CI.

CHAPTER X

THE CELESTIAL GENERAL

1. Op. cit., interview with Louis Claiborne on June 12, 1985.
2. Louisiana Power & Light Co. v. City of Thibodaux 359 *U.S.* 25 (1960).
3. CI.
4. Information supplied by Judge Wright's chambers.
5. Tom Kelly, Washington *Daily News*, April, 1965.
6. Joseph T. Hatfield, *William Claiborne: Jeffersonian Centurion in the American Southwest* (University of Southwestern Louisiana Press, 1976, 393 pp.).
7. Interview with Tom Kelly on December 12, 1985.
8. Claiborne Gallery, Santa Fe, New Mexico.
9. *The New York Times*, Business Section, 1, May 4, 1986.

10. Interview with Louis Claiborne on June 18, 1985.

11. CI.

12. Interviews with Louis Claiborne, op. cit.; and Raymond Randolph, op. cit.

13. Interviews with Edwin Kneedler, op. cit.; Joshua Schwartz, op. cit., and Lawrence Wallace, op. cit.

14. Op. cit., interview with Louis Claiborne.

15. Brief for the United States as amicus curiae urging reversal, Summa Corporation v. State of California, No. 82-708, October Term, 1982, 4.

16. "The Original Jurisdiction of the United States Supreme Court," 11 *Stanford Law Review* 665 (1959).

17. Interviews with Francis Lorson, op. cit.; and with Clare Bailey on February 18, 1986.

18. Interviews with Charles Fried, op. cit.; Edwin Kneedler, op. cit.; Rex Lee, op. cit.; and Joshua Schwartz, op. cit.; also, CIs.

19. Op. cit., "Original Jurisdiction," 665, 667, note 24.

20. Interviews with Louis Claiborne, op. cit.; and Michael Reed on June 5, 1986; and CIs with Supreme Court Justices.

21. Op. cit., interview with Louis Claiborne.

22. Rex Lee remarks at party for Louis Claiborne on October 21, 1985, and interview with Rex Lee on October 23, 1985.

23. Op. cit., interview with Louis Claiborne.

24. Letter from Paul Laxalt to William French Smith, October 7, 1981, reproduced in the appendix to the reply brief of the Pyramid Lake Paiute Tribe of Indians, in Pyramid Lake Paiute Tribe of Indians v. Truckee-Carson Irrigation District, No. 82-1723, October Term, 1983.

25. Louis Claiborne, Memorandum to the Solicitor General about U.S. v. Alpine Land & Reservoir Co., April 14, 1983.

26. Op. cit., interview with Louis Claiborne.

27. Louis Claiborne, Memorandum for the Solicitor General Re: Pane v. NRC, August 16, 1982, about that case, which was eventually decided by the Supreme Court and reported at 460 *U.S.* 766 (1983).

28. Op. cit., interview with Louis Claiborne.

29. Reply brief for the United States, U.S. v. Maine, No. 35, Original, October Term, 1985.

30. As the Washington *Post* summed up in the box labeled "Supreme Court Calendar," which it runs on days that arguments are scheduled, "No. 35 Original. U.S. v. Maine. Boundary dispute. Must state establish claim to coastline jurisdiction by 'clear beyond doubt' evidence?"

31. Comment by Louis Claiborne to author before oral argument on December 12, 1985.

32. Op. cit., reply brief, 1.

33. U.S. v. Maine, 54 *U.S. Law Week*, 4173, decided February 25, 1986.

34. Author's observation.

35. October 21, 1985.

36. From handwritten remarks of Louis Claiborne, which he gave to the author.

37. From announcement that Louis Claiborne mailed to associates and friends, and to the author.

38. Op. cit., interview with Paul Freund, a onetime Brandeis law clerk. Also, op. cit., Eugene Gerhart, *America's Advocate: Robert Jackson,* 199.

39. Op. cit., Gerhart, 143.

CHAPTER XI

CHARLES FRIED

1. November 6, 1985, sponsored by the National Center for Public Policy Research.

2. Videotape of the dinner provided by Amy Moritz, Executive Director of the National Center for Public Policy Research. All quotations from speakers at the dinner are taken from the videotape. Comments to the author are from the author's notes.

3. Program, Reynolds dinner, 3.

4. Comment to the author.

5. These are taken from the author's notes, and checked against the videotape.

6. Washington *Post,* A-3, November 5, 1985.

7. Remarks of Charles Cooper at Tribute to William Bradford Reynolds, November 6, 1985.

8. CIs.

9. CIs.

10. November 11, 1985.

11. Public Information Office of the National Archives.

12. Op. cit., Griswold letter to Griffin Bell.

13. Background on the history and contents of the painting provided by the National Gallery of Art. Also, see Colin Eisler, *Paintings from the Samuel H. Kress Collection: European Schools Excluding Italian* (Phaidon Press for the Samuel H. Kress Foundation, 1977, 639 pp.), 274–280.

14. February 10, 1986.

15. Op. cit., interview with Charles Fried on November 11, 1985.

16. The author taped and transcribed Fried's lecture; all quotations in this section are taken from the tape and transcription, and checked against notes provided to the author by Charles Fried.

17. Comment by David Lauter to the author on January 22, 1986, used with Lauter's permission.

CHAPTER XII

FRIENDS OF THE COURT

1. Op. cit., "Crisis in the Courts," *Manhattan Report.*
2. Fried Chamber of Commerce speech, op. cit.; and interview with Charles Fried, op. cit., on November 11, 1985.
3. Op. cit., Fried Chamber of Commerce speech. Also, Fried speech to the Academy of State and Local Government, February 13, 1986, reported by staff members and others who attended.
4. Op. cit., Fried Chamber speech.
5. Op. cit., *Manhattan Report.*
6. Interviews with Philip Heymann, op. cit.; Abram Chayes on October 9, 1985; and other members of the Harvard Law School faculty. Also, interviews with Charles Fried, op. cit., on November 11, 1985; and CIs.
7. Interview with Charles Fried, op. cit.; interview with Potter Stewart, op. cit.; author's observation of Fried and comments of Potter Stewart and other Justices about Cox; interviews with Philip Heymann, op. cit.; Nathan Lewin, op. cit.; Carolyn Kuhl, op. cit.; and Albert Lauber, op. cit.
8. Archibald Cox, *The Warren Court: Constitutional Decision as an Instrument of Reform* (Harvard University Press, 1968, 144 pp.), 1.
9. Ibid., 22.
10. Op. cit., interview with Charles Fried on November 11, 1985.
11. Op. cit., Cox, *The Warren Court,* 22–23.
12. To some scholars, Cox's criticism of the Warren Court played into the hands of its detractors by oversimplifying the role of the Supreme Court in American democracy. "Contemporary constitutional debate is dominated by a false dichotomy," John Hart Ely argued in the preface to *Democracy and Distrust:* "Either, it runs, we must stick close to the thoughts of those who wrote our Constitution's critical phrases and outlaw only those practices they thought they were outlawing, or there is simply no way for courts to review legislation other than by second-guessing the legislature's value choices." To Ely's mind, it missed the point to write off the cardinal decisions of the Warren Court as exercises in social policy. The accomplishment of the Supreme Court between 1954 and 1969 (the dedication of Ely's book to Earl Warren—"You don't need many heroes if you choose carefully"— emphasized that he considered it an accomplishment) was to fill in gaps left by other branches of the federal government and by state governments. The Court returned fairness to the political process, guaranteed that blacks and other minorities could vote, and otherwise safeguarded the workings of democracy.
13. Victor S. Navasky, *Kennedy Justice* (Atheneum, 1977, 482 pp.), 280.
14. Ibid., 291; and interview with Burke Marshall on May 20, 1985.
15. Op. cit., interview with Archibald Cox.
16. Op. cit., Navasky, 286, 296.

17. Op. cit., Baker v. Carr.

18. Op. cit., Navasky, 301.

19. The SG's brief, Reynolds v. Sims brief, 17.

20. Op. cit., Navasky, 299.

21. Supreme Court records.

22. Op. cit., interview with Philip Heymann.

23. Op. cit., Reynolds v. Sims, 533.

24. Op. cit., Navasky, 298.

25. Davis v. Bandemer, No. 84–1244, decided June 30, 1986.

26. Alexander Bickel, Paul Freund, Philip Kurland, and others.

27. Op. cit., Navasky, 308.

28. Op. cit., Office of Legal Counsel memorandum, 11.

29. Op. cit., Navasky, 309.

30. Ibid., 311, 314.

31. Ibid., 315, 313.

32. Op. cit., interview with Archibald Cox.

33. Herbert Wechsler, "Report of the Advisory Commission on Intergovernmental Relations," January 1967, footnote 25.

34. Op. cit., interview with Archibald Cox.

35. Archibald Cox lecture at Hunter College, "Storm over the Supreme Court," 1985, 18, 19.

36. Ibid., 20.

37. Op. cit., interview with Charles Fried on June 28, 1986.

38. Op. cit., interviews with Charles Fried. Also, according to lawyers in the SG's office and several of Fried's former Harvard Law School colleagues, he made the same point to them.

39. These are standard lawyer's terms, used by people in the SG's office and outside.

40. Op. cit., Fried speech to the Academy of State and Local Government, as reported by members of the Academy staff and by others at the event. Also, op. cit., interview with Charles Fried on November 11, 1985.

41. Interview with Steven Shapiro on March 27, 1986. According to Rule 42 of the 1954 Supreme Court rules contained in *Supreme Court Practice*, 2nd Edition, 1954, anyone who wanted to file an amicus brief in a case before the Court either had to obtain consent of the parties to the case, or to file a motion for permission to file a brief, which had to include a statement of interest. As one of the SG's prerogatives, on the other hand, the SG did not have to obtain permission to file an amicus brief, so he was never obliged to state a federal interest in a case. The rules changed in 1970. The Justices moved the location of the statement of interest. Instead of requiring that it be included in the motion for permission to file a brief, they directed that the statement of interest be included in the brief itself. The SG was still free to enter any case he chose without permission of the parties—he is one of the few advocates who enjoy that privilege—but he had to declare the government's interest just like any other advocate. The upshot was that when Cox was SG, no rule

required him to state a federal interest. By Fried's time, the rules had changed, and they obliged the SG to declare the government's interest.

42. Samuel Krislov, "The Role of the Attorney General as Amicus Curiae," in Luther A. Huston, ed., *Roles of the Attorney General of the United States* (American Enterprise Institute, 1968, 153 pp.), 89.

43. Ibid., 80.

44. Ibid., 85.

45. "Annual Reports of the Attorney General," 1920 through 1985.

46. Op. cit., Cox, *Chicago Bar Record,* 226.

47. Interview with Archibald Cox on August 5, 1985.

48. Samuel Krislov, "The Amicus Brief: From Friendship to Advocacy," 72 *Yale Law Journal* 694, 703 (1963).

49. Karen O'Connor and Lee Epstein, "Court Rules and Workload: A Case Study of Rules Governing Amicus Curiae Participation," 8 *Justice System Journal* No. 1 (1983), Table 2.

50. Karen O'Connor and Lee Epstein, "The Rise of Conservative Interest Group Litigation," 45 *Journal of Politics* 479, 481 (1983). The facts cited in the rest of this paragraph are on pages 482–487.

51. Op. cit., "Annual Reports of the Attorney General."

52. Clerk's office of the Supreme Court and Docket Management Section of the SG's office.

53. Interviews with Paul Bator, op. cit.; Andrew Frey, op. cit.; Charles Fried, op. cit.; Stephen Shapiro, op. cit.; and others.

54. CI; op. cit., interviews with Charles Fried; op. cit., David Lauter, *National Law Journal,* 24.

55. Interviews with Philip Heymann, op. cit.; and Nathan Lewin, op. cit.; and CIs.

56. Op. cit., Cox lecture, "Storm over the Supreme Court," 17; and interview with Archibald Cox, op. cit.

57. Op. cit., interview with Archibald Cox.

58. Interview with Philip Heymann on February 14, 1986.

59. In his Chamber of Commerce speech, Fried said, "A brief is nothing but reasons," and in an interview with the author, Fried said, "The law is nothing but reasons."

60. Op. cit., interview with Potter Stewart; and CIs with other Justices. Also, CIs with former lawyers in the SG's office. Op. cit., interview with Archibald Cox.

61. Op. cit., interview with Charles Fried on June 28, 1986.

62. Carl Stern, NBC News, October 21, 1985, transcript, 4.

63. Op. cit., interview with Charles Fried on November 11, 1985.

64. Comment of Louis Claiborne at the party in his honor on October 21, 1985.

65. Op. cit., interview with Charles Fried on November 11, 1985; brief for the United States as Amicus Curiae Supporting Petitioners, Wygant v. Jackson, No. 84–1340, October Term, 1985, and slip opinion, Wygant v. Jackson, decided May 19, 1986.

66. Op. cit., Wygant brief, 2.
67. Op. cit., Wygant decision, Marshall opinion, 4.
68. Op. cit., Wygant brief, 4.
69. Ibid., 5.
70. Ibid, 5, 6.
71. Ibid., 7, 8.
72. Ibid., 23.
73. Op. cit., interview with Lawrence Wallace.
74. CI.
75. Paul Freund, *On Law and Justice* (Harvard University Press, 1968, 251 pp.), 33, 44, 45, 46, 47. Also, Robert D. Miller, "Samuel Field Phillips: The Odyssey of a Southern Dissenter," vol. LVIII, No. 3, *North Carolina Historical Review*, 263, 273–79 (July 1981).
76. Op. cit., Carl Stern, NBC News, 2.
77. Interview with Laurence Tribe on November 18, 1985.
78. Op. cit., Wygant decision, O'Connor opinion, 3.
79. *The New York Times*, A–21, May 20, 1985.
80. Op. cit., Meese address to Dickinson College, 10.
81. *The New York Times*, A–28, May 21, 1986.
82. Op. cit., Wygant decision, O'Connor opinion, 3.
83. Op. cit., interviews with Charles Fried.
84. Elder Witt, "Reagan Crusade Before Court Unprecedented in Intensity," *Congressional Quarterly*, March 15, 1986, 616, 617.
85. Washington *Post*, A–7, July 7, 1986.

CHAPTER XIII

THE SG'S LAWYERS

1. Interviews with Kenneth Geller, op. cit.; Edwin Kneedler, op. cit.; Albert Lauber, op. cit.; Andrew Pincus on May 25, 1986; Joshua Schwartz, op. cit.; and David Strauss, op. cit.
2. During the seventies, for several years, five lawyers in the SG's office (Frank Easterbrook, Andrew Frey, Kenneth Geller, John Rupp, and Stephen Urbancyzk) held a regular dart game at 5:30 p.m.
3. Op. cit., interview with Edwin Kneedler.
4. Op. cit., interview with Harriet Shapiro.
5. According to Boisfeuillet Jones, general counsel of the Washington *Post*, he and Al Kamen, who covers the Supreme Court for the paper, had lunch with Kenneth Geller and Andrew Frey to discuss how the paper could improve its coverage of the Court.
6. Op. cit., interview with David Strauss.
7. Op. cit., interview with Kenneth Geller.
8. CI.
9. The facts in this paragraph are from CIs.
10. Op. cit., interview with Kenneth Geller and author's observation.

11. Deputy in charge of review:

of review:	Bator	Claiborne	Frey	Fried	Geller	Wallace
Number of appeals (Total: 2089)	38	142	665	49	782	413
Number of briefs on the merits (Total: 110)	8	23	23	7	27	22

12. Op. cit., interviews with Carter Phillips, Wade McCree, and Andrew Frey.

13. Andrew Frey, "Modern Police Interrogation Law: The Wrong Road Taken," 42 *University of Pittsburgh Law Review* 731, 732, 733 (1978), 736.

14. Op. cit., interview with Yale Kamisar.

15. Peter Westen and Richard Drubel, "Toward a General Theory of Double Jeopardy," *Supreme Court Review* 81 (1978), 81.

16. Peter Westen, "The Three Faces of Double Jeopardy: Reflections on Government Appeals of Criminal Sentences," 78 *Michigan Law Review* 1001, 1005, and 1006 at note 18, for description of Benton v. Maryland, 395 *U.S.* 784 (1969).

17. In 1971, Congress passed 18 U.S.C. 3731, Title III of the Omnibus Crime Control Act of 1970, explained at page S—146 of the Library of Congress "Constitution of the United States, 1978 Supplement," edited by Johnny Killian.

18. During a double-jeopardy argument, the then Associate Justice William Rehnquist asked, "Mr. Frey, you are not suggesting that all of the authoritative answers, as you refer to them, that have been given by this Court to these questions are consistent with one another, are you?" Transcript of U.S. v. Scott, No. 76–1382, October Term, 1977, 5, 6.

19. Interview with Peter Westen on July 11, 1985.

20. Op. cit., interview with Potter Stewart.

21. CI.

22. Press release, March 6, 1986, Department of Justice.

23. In a confidential interview, the official said the release "cavalierly disposed of" the three longtime SG lawyers.

24. "U.S. Solicitor General Announces Top Aides," *The New York Times,* March 7, 1986.

25. CI.

26. The facts in this paragraph are from an interview with Charles Fried on June 28, 1986, and from CIs.

27. CI.

28. Op. cit., interview with Andrew Frey; Ed Bruske, Washington *Post,* A-15, July 26, 1984; letters to Senate Majority Leader Howard Baker from Senators Jeremiah Denton, John East, Charles Grassley, and Orrin Hatch on August 9, 1984; to Andrew Frey from Senator Jeremiah Denton on September 7, 1984; and, eventually, to President Ronald Reagan from Senators Steve

Symms and Jeremiah Denton on March 6, 1985; CIs and Memorandum to the Full Committee Staff from John Duncan, the staff director of the Senate Governmental Affairs Committee, announcing the committee's plan to consider the Frey nomination, September 6, 1984, until the White House asked the committee to cancel the hearing.

29. Op. cit., interview with Potter Stewart.

30. Statistics in letter to the author from Alan Herman, Clerk of the Court, D.C. Court of Appeals, and from the Statistics Office of the Administrative Office of the U.S. Courts.

31. Nancy Blodgett, "Solicitor General," 72 *American Bar Association Journal* 20 (May, 1986).

32. CI; Charles Fried, Letter, 72 *American Bar Association Journal* 12 (July, 1986); letter from LeRoy E. DeVeaux to Kathryn Oberly, May 7, 1986, used with permission of DeVeaux and Oberly.

33. Interviews with John Davis, op. cit.; Oscar Davis, op. cit.; Philip Elman, op. cit.; Daniel Friedman, op. cit.; Paul Freund, op. cit.; and Erwin Griswold, op. cit.

34. Interview with Kathryn Oberly on March 13, 1986.

35. CI.

36. Until this change, most Deputy Solicitors General had served for many years. The SG's office generally hired three new assistants a year. From June 1, 1985, through April 1, 1986, excluding Solicitor General Rex Lee, eleven out of twenty-two lawyers left the office, for a 50 percent turnover. Though normal turnover before this wave was more like 15 percent a year—that is, three of twenty-three—the author assumed that an office of seventeen assistants who have an average tenure of three years, and whose arrivals and departures are spread evenly over the years, may have to replace four members in some years, which is 23 percent. Taking the figure of 50 percent and the figure of 23 percent as a basis for comparison, the author concluded that the rate of turnover jumped from about a quarter to half.

37. The facts in this paragraph are from CIs.

38. CIs.

39. The quotations and facts in this paragraph are from an interview with Charles Fried and CIs.

40. Robert Stern, "The Solicitor General's Office and Administrative Agency Litigation," 46 *American Bar Association Journal* 154 (1960).

41. The facts in this paragraph are from CIs.

42. The quotations and facts in this paragraph are from an interview with Charles Fried and from CIs.

43. The quotations and facts in this paragraph are from an interview with Charles Fried and CIs.

44. Interview with Bruce Kuhlik on November 1, 1985.

45. Op. cit., interview with Philip Heymann.

46. Unless otherwise indicated, the quotations and facts in this paragraph are from an interview with Charles Fried and from CIs.

47. CI.

48. Interviews with Andrew Frey, op. cit.; Kenneth Geller, op. cit.; and Lawrence Wallace, op. cit.

49. Unless otherwise indicated, the quotations and facts in this paragraph are from CIs.

50. Announcement of Career Opportunities, Justice Department, February 21, 1986.

51. Unless otherwise indicated, the quotations and facts in this paragraph are from CIs.

52. Author's observation and CIs.

53. Unless otherwise indicated, the quotations and facts in this paragraph are from CIs.

54. A lawyer, who claimed to be Fried's ally and whom the SG said he relied on, observed, "Charles has no patience for the intricacies of legal argument."

55. Interview by David Lauter with Paul Bator, used with permission of David Lauter.

56. Interview with Lyle Denniston on April 14, 1986.

57. Interview with Terry Eastland on June 26, 1986.

58. Unless otherwise indicated, the quotations and facts in this paragraph are from CIs.

59. Unless otherwise indicated, the quotations and facts in this paragraph are from CIs.

60. Interviews with Andrew Frey, op. cit.; and Kenneth Geller, op. cit.

61. Interview with Harlan Dalton on June 27, 1985.

62. Unless otherwise indicated, the quotations and facts in this paragraph are from CIs.

63. Interview with Charles Fried on April 28, 1986.

64. CIs.

65. CI.

66. CI.

67. CI.

68. CI.

69. CI.

CHAPTER XIV
OCTOBER TERM, 1985

1. CIs.

2. The facts in this paragraph are from interviews with Charles Fried and from CIs.

3. Bender v. Williamsport, No. 84–773, decided March 25, 1986.

4. Op. cit., interview with Francis Lorson.

5. Washington *Post,* A–8, March 26, 1986.

6. CI.

7. CI.

8. Davidson v. Cannon, 54 *U.S. Law Week* 4095, decided January 21, 1986.

9. Op. cit., interview with Charles Fried on June 28, 1986; CIs.

10. Op. cit., Davidson v. Cannon.

11. Op. cit., Davidson, transcript, 26.

12. Op. cit., interview with Charles Fried on June 28, 1986; CIs; interviews with Andrew Frey, op. cit.; Kenneth Geller, op. cit.; and Edwin Kneedler, op. cit.

13. CIs.

14. Batson v. Kentucky, 54 *U.S. Law Week* 4425, decided April 30, 1986.

15. Swain v. Alabama, 380 *U.S.* 202, 209–222 (1965).

16. CIs.

17. *The New York Times,* A–1, May 1, 1986.

18. Transcript of MacNeil/Lehrer News Hour, 6, July 2, 1986, provided by WETA.

19. Slip opinion, Thornburg v. Gingles, No. 83–1968, decided June 30, 1986.

20. Op. cit., Ronnie Dugger, *On Reagan,* 212.

21. CI.

22. Section 2(b), as amended, provides that Section 2(a) of the Voting Rights Act of 1965 is violated where the "totality of the circumstances" reveals that "the political processes leading to nomination or election . . . are not equally open to participation by members of a [protected class] . . . in that its members have less opportunity than other members of the electorate to participate in the political process and to elect representatives of their choice." Op. cit., slip opinion summary.

23. Brief for Appellees, Thornburg v. Gingles. Also, see press packet from the NAACP Inc. Fund.

24. Author's observation and transcript of argument.

25. Washington *Post,* A–4, December 5, 1985.

26. CIs.

27. Author's observation.

28. Ibid.

29. Op. cit., interview with Charles Fried on June 28, 1986; op. cit., Thornburg decision.

30. Op. cit., NAACP Inc. Fund brief, 32, referring to SG's brief, 8, note 12.

31. Op. cit., Thornburg decision, Brennan opinion, 10, 22.

32. Heckler v. American Hospital Association, No. 84-1529, October Term, 1985; MacDonald v. Yolo, No. 84-2015, October Term, 1985; Golden State Transit v. Los Angeles, No. 84-1644, October Term, 1985; Bethel v. Fraser, No. 84-1667, October Term, 1985; United Auto Workers v. Brock, No. 84-1777, October Term, 1985.

33. Hunt v. Washington, 432 *U.S.* 333 (1977).

34. Motion for leave to file on behalf of the Chamber of Commerce et al., UAW v. Brock, by Sidley & Austin, 3.
35. Ibid., 2.
36. Ibid., 5.
37. City of Los Angeles v. Preferred Communications, No. 85–390, decided June 2, 1986.
38. CI.
39. In the Red Lion case, 395 *U.S.* 367 (1969), the Justices ruled that the government could regulate media like radio and TV where there was a scarcity of broadcast frequencies. Instead of undermining the First Amendment, they judged, the government's commitment to assigning frequencies could enhance the freedoms of speech and press by assuring access for individuals and groups who might otherwise not get on the air. The Red Lion decision also approved government regulation of the content of broadcasts, which was a more difficult question for the Justices than the matter of awarding licenses.

The lower-court opinion in the Preferred case found an analogy between Los Angeles's rules for awarding its cable franchise and the federal government's policy about granting radio and TV licenses. The Supreme Court's prior judgment that the government could limit the number of licenses to avoid a cacophony of voices seemed to settle the case. If the government could control radio and TV licenses, a city could regulate cable. Experts also said that regulation of cable improved the content of programs. If the rules enforced by Los Angeles were upheld, they said, the city's cable company would have to maintain time for community programs. If the bid for competition prevailed, the need to win customers with commercial fare might squeeze public-service programs off the air.

40. Brief for United States and the FCC as Amicus Curiae Supporting Affirmance, No. 85–390, 12. One of the reasons for the federal law was to help companies like Preferred. Before the law was passed, cities had extracted from companies bidding for cable franchises pledges to build production studios, to train citizens how to produce cable programs, and to provide other benefits, as part of deals awarding the franchises. It was a form of "holdup," according to a lawyer in the SG's office familiar with the practice. The federal law was designed to settle the process for awarding cable franchises across the country.

41. CIs.
42. Op. cit., SG's Preferred brief, 9, 11; CI.
43. Interview with Laura Kopelman, of the General Accounting Office, on June 19, 1986.
44. Synar v. U.S., 626 *F. Supp.* 1374 (D.C. 1986).
45. Impeachment requires a majority vote in the House of Representatives and a two-thirds vote in the Senate. A joint resolution requires a majority vote of both houses, unless the President vetoes it, in which case Congress can override the President by a two-thirds vote.
46. Washington *Post*, A–1, February 8, 1986.

47. Bowsher v. Synar, No. 85–1377, transcript, 51, decided July 7, 1986.

48. Op. cit., Thornburgh v. American College of Obstetricians and Gynecologists, No. 84–495, decided June 11, 1986, 10, 23.

49. Transcript provided by Justice Department, 8, 9, 11.

50. Ibid., 5.

51. Op. cit., Thornburgh decision, White opinion, 2, 3, 29.

52. Op. cit., Thornburgh decision, Stevens opinion, 2, 5, 10.

53. Stuart Taylor, Jr., "Tasting the Salty Air of Politics and Criticism," *The New York Times*, A–8, July 18, 1986. Also, Al Kamen, "A Series of High Court Rebuffs for Reagan," Washington *Post*, A–7, July 7, 1986. Also, CIs with Justices.

54. Lyng v. Payne, No. 84–1948, decided June 17, 1986.

55. Ibid., Stevens dissent, 3. The case dealt with a claim by some Florida farmers that the government had failed to tell them about a program of emergency loans for disaster relief that could have helped the farmers recover from torrential rains that caused major losses of crops and property. By an eight-to-one margin, the Justices held that the Secretary of Agriculture had given the farmers sufficient notice about the program. But the Justices took the SG to task for misusing the doctrine of equitable estoppel. The classic example of the doctrine occurs when a government official conceals an important fact from a potential recipient of federal aid and, relying on the official's word, the applicant fails to qualify for help. Since the government misled the citizen, a court will hold that the government is "equitably estopped" from arguing that the citizen should have known better. Courts now frown on the doctrine and allow individuals to use it only when a misrepresentation is grave. In any event, in the Florida case equitable estoppel was not obviously relevant. The Secretary of Agriculture had not advertised the government's relief program, but in no instance had a farmer been misled. The heart of the farmers' case, which was the basis for the ruling in their favor in the lower courts, was that the government had failed to follow basic rules of administrative law and give the farmers proper notice about the existence of the relief program. Nonetheless, on appeal to the Supreme Court, the SG's office framed the farmers' case as one that rested on the outmoded doctrine of equitable estoppel, and argued that the farmers should lose. The Court unanimously criticized the SG for this mischaracterization. Writing for the majority, Justice O'Connor rejected the idea that any claim that was like an equitable estoppel could be thrown out as the SG had advised. If the Justices accepted that notion, she said, they would take from the courts a power that Congress had specifically given in order to let judges correct obvious government wrongs. In case the Solicitor General missed the reprimand, Justice Stevens made the comment quoted in the text above.

56. Op. cit., Stuart Taylor, Jr., "Tasting the Salty Air of Politics."

57. Docket Management Section, SG's office.

58. CIs. Also op. cit., interview with Charles Fried on July 1, 1986; and news accounts.

59. Op. cit., transcript of MacNeil/Lehrer News Hour, 3, July 2, 1986.

60. Local 28 v. EEOC, No. 84–1656, decided July 2, 1986, Brennan opinion, 57.

61. When Justice Brennan handed down his opinion for the Court in Local 28 of the Sheet Metal Workers' International Association v. Equal Employment Opportunity Council, he took pains to explain why a majority agreed, even though he wrote only for a plurality.

62. " 'Hardly ever?' " asked a onetime chairman of the U.S. Equal Employment Opportunity Commission, Eleanor Holmes Norton, at a symposium in Manhattan to celebrate the centennial of the Statue of Liberty, not long after the New York affirmative-action case came down. "Hardly ever," the SG repeated, according to the Philadelphia *Inquirer,* though he observed that while the Justices were "paid to make things a little clearer," they hadn't in the New York case. He said, "Who knows what these clowns mean?" Carlin Romano, Philadelphia *Inquirer,* July 7, 1986.

63. Bowers v. Hardwick, No. 85–140, decided June 30, 1986.

64. Op. cit., Stuart Taylor, Jr.

65. CIs.

66. Justice White's dissent in Roe v. Wade often comes to mind when scholars discuss this.

67. CIs.

68. John Jenkins, "Mr. Power: Attorney General Edwin Meese," *The New York Times Magazine,* 18, 92 (October, 12, 1986).

69. Edward H. Levi, *An Introduction to Legal Reasoning* (University of Chicago Press, 1949, 104 pp.).

70. Op. cit., interview with Charles Fried on June 28, 1986; Meritor Savings v. Vinson, No. 84–1979, October Term, 1985, decided June 19, 1986.

71. Ibid., Rehnquist opinion, 14.

72. Op. cit., Rehnquist opinion, 14.

73. SG's Meritor brief, 26: "If the employer has an expressed policy against sexual harassment and has implemented a procedure specifically designed to resolve sexual harassment claims, and if the victim does not take advantage of that procedure, the employer should be shielded from liability absent actual knowledge of the sexually hostile environment (obtained, e.g., by the filing of a charge with the EEOC"—that is, the government's Equal Employment Opportunity Commission—"or a comparable state agency)."

74. Interview with Charles Fried on June 28, 1986.

75. Op. cit., UAW v. Brock, Marshall opinion, 15.

CHAPTER XV

THE VIEW FROM THE COURT

1. CI.

2. The Federalist Society for Law and Public Policy was founded in 1982 by law students, law professors, and judges to challenge "the orthodox liberal ideology which advocates a centralized and uniform society." According to

the society's brochure, "In working to achieve these goals the Society has created a conservative intellectual network that extends to all levels of the legal community."

3. Interview with Paul Cassell, a law clerk to Chief Justice Warren Burger, on June 23, 1986.

4. Unless otherwise indicated, the quotations and facts in this paragraph are from CIs.

5. The quotations in this paragraph are from CIs.

6. Docket Management Section of the SG's office.

7. Figures provided by Virginia Bolling, in the Docket Management Section of the SG's office.

8. CIs.

9. CI.

10. CI.

11. CI.

12. Op. cit., interview with Charles Fried on June 28, 1986.

13. Op. cit., interview with Francis Lorson; *Legal Times*, 3, August 18, 1986; op. cit., Bethel v. Fraser.

14. CIs.

15. Letter from Charles Fried to Joseph F. Spaniol, Jr., about DiNapoli v. Northeast Regional Parole Commission, No. 85–335, October 29, 1985.

16. CI.

17. Letter from Charles Haydon to Joseph F. Spaniol, Jr., October 31, 1985, used with permission of Haydon and the Supreme Court.

18. Letter from Joseph F. Spaniol, Jr., to Charles Haydon, November 12, 1985.

19. Op. cit., interview with Justice Thurgood Marshall.

20. Unless otherwise indicated, the quotations and facts in this paragraph come from CIs.

21. Op. cit., Stuart Taylor, Jr.

22. *The New York Times*, A–1, July 11, 1986.

23. CBS TV, "Nightwatch," July 15, 1986.

24. CI.

25. Bowen v. City of New York, No. 84–1923, decided June 2, 1986, 9, 19.

26. Op. cit., interview with Charles Fried on June 28, 1986.

27. Maine v. Moulton, No. 84–786, decided December 10, 1985, 15.

28. Riverside v. Rivera, No. 85–224, decided June 27, 1986, 16, note 10.

29. CIs.

30. Op. cit., interview with Charles Fried on June 28, 1986.

31. Interview with Donald Ayer on September 10, 1986; CIs.

32. Confidential letter to the author.

33. Unless otherwise indicated, the quotations and facts in this paragraph are from CIs.

34. CIs.

35. U.S. v. Mendoza, op. cit., 573, and DeMarco v. U.S., op. cit. Also, CIs.

36. CIs.

37. CI.
38. CI.
39. CI.

CHAPTER XVI
THE RULE OF LAW

1. Interview with Johnny Killian, of the Congressional Research Service, Library of Congress, on September 10, 1986.
2. In 37 of 151 cases.
3. Op. cit., interview with Johnny Killian.
4. Vincent Blasi, *The Burger Court: The Counter-Revolution That Wasn't* (Yale University Press, 1983, 326 pp.), 6.
5. Op. cit., Bowers v. Hardwick.
6. Ibid., White opinion, 8, 9.
7. Al Kamen, Washington *Post*, A–1, July 13, 1986.
8. "The respondent had not been tried or convicted, and we had no occasion to consider possible defenses, such as one based on the Eighth Amendment, to an actual prosecution," the Justice explained at an American Bar Association conference. Address to the ABA Litigation Section, August 12, 1986.
9. Remarks of Justice Harry Blackmun to the Eighth Circuit.
10. Roy A. Schotland, "Elective Judges' Campaign Financing: Are State Judges' Robes the Emperor's Clothes of America Democracy?," 2 *Journal of Law and Politics* 57 (1985).
11. *The New York Times*, E–2, December 22, 1985.
12. NBC Nightly News, August 10, 1986.
13. Annual reports in the Washington *Post* on January 23, the day after the anniversary, from 1982 through 1987; Los Angeles *Times*, 1–3, October 7, 1985; Los Angeles *Times* interview on June 23, 1986; addresses on the State of the Union in 1985 and 1986.
14. Los Angeles *Times*, 1–17, June 2, 1986.
15. Op. cit., Richard Posner, *The Federal Courts*, 218, 219, and note on 219, where he reports that Georgetown University Law Center professor Mark Tushnet claims that judges should rule on the basis of whether a result will advance the cause of socialism, and that University of Texas law professor Lino Graglia claims that constitutional review should be abolished, taking away a principal function of federal courts.
16. CIs.
17. See Roberto Mangabeira Unger, *The Critical Legal Studies Movement* (Harvard University Press, 1986, 128 pp.). Also, *The New York Times Book Review*, 1, February 16, 1986.
18. Daniel Boorstin, "The Perils of Indwelling Law," in Robert Paul Wolff, ed., *The Rule of Law* (Simon & Schuster, 1971, 254 pp.), 75.

19. CIs.

20. Washington *Post*, A–1, October 7, 1986.

21. CIs.

22. U.S. v. Paradise, No. 85–999, decided February 25, 1987; Johnson v. Transportation Agency, Santa Clara, California, No. 85–1129, decided March 25, 1987; School Board of Nassau County, Florida v. Arline, No. 85–1277, decided March 3, 1987; Immigration & Naturalization Service v. Cardoza-Fonseca, No. 85–782, decided March 9, 1987.

23. Oversight Hearing on the Solicitor General's Office, U.S. House of Representatives, Committee on the Judiciary, Subcommittee on Monopolies and Commercial Law, March 19, 1987.

24. Op. cit., Carlin Romano, Philadelphia *Inquirer,* July 7, 1986.

25. *The New York Times,* A–1, March 28, 1987. Also, interview with Charles Fried, July 6, 1987.

26. Lecture by William Bradford Reynolds, "Securing Liberty in an Egalitarian Age," September 12, 1986.

27. Op. cit., Brennan Georgetown symposium speech.

28. Remarks by Edwin Meese and by William Bradford Reynolds at the Reynolds dinner on November 6, 1985. Also, op. cit., interviews with William Bradford Reynolds and Terry Eastland. Also, op. cit., Jenkins profile of Meese in *The New York Times Magazine.*

Acknowledgments

Many people helped me during the two and a half years I researched and wrote this book, and I want to thank them.

Nathan Lewin, a Washington lawyer and a onetime assistant to the Solicitor General, suggested that I write about the SG's office and got me started on my reporting.

At the SG's office, Virginia Bolling, Elizabeth Werling, and others in the Docket Management Section were regularly helpful in answering my requests for legal papers filed by the SG's staff. In the Public Information office of the Justice Department, Mark Sheehan, who was responsible for answering questions about the SG's office while I did my reporting, was similarly cooperative. Frank Lindh, who worked as a researcher at the SG's office, gathered speeches by past SGs, bar-journal articles about the office, and other relevant materials as part of his own work, and made copies for me. Quinlan J. Shea, Jr., who runs the Library at the Justice Department, shared with me his knowledge of the Library's resources and helped me learn how to use them.

At the Supreme Court, Toni House and her staff at the Public Information office, including Kathleen Arberg, Susan Coss, and Sheryl Farmer, were also regular sources of assistance. Elsewhere at the Court, Clare Bailey on the Technical Services staff, Francis Lorson in the Clerk's office, Linda McElroy in the Curator's office, and Sara Sonet on the Library staff, among others who answered my questions, gave especially useful help. Secretaries to a number of Justices were patient in helping me arrange or request interviews.

Many other people also eased my research or provided me with material, and I would like to thank several in particular: Nancy Broff, at the Judicial Selection Project; Erika Chadbourn, when she was Curator of Manuscripts at the Harvard Law School Library; Florence Coman, of the National Gallery of Art; Eddie Correia, Mark Gitenstein, Chip Reid, Phil Shipman, and Laurie Westley, on the staff of the Senate Judiciary Committee; Olive James, Abram Boni, and other staff members in the Loan Division of the Library of Congress; Johnny Killian, at the Congressional Research Service of the Library of Congress; Jeanne Smith at the Public Information office of the Library of Congress; Susan Liss, of People for the American Way; Benna Solomon, at the Academy for State and Local Government; and Joanne Zich, a librarian at American University's Washington College of Law. Staff members of the American Enterprise Institute, the Bureau of National Affairs, the *Congressional Quarterly,* the Heritage Foundation, the Los Angeles *Times, The New York Times,* and the Washington *Post* also responded quickly and courteously to my requests for information.

Others helped to improve my work by responding to my questions, suggesting material for reading, or otherwise acting as counselors. Some of these people are my friends, and others spoke with me because of their interest in the SG's office. They don't necessarily share my views about the SG's office or other topics in the law, but all made contributions for which I'm grateful: Stephens Broening, Paul Freund, Daniel Friedman, William Goodman, Jamie Gorelick, Philip Heymann, David Ignatius, Vicki Jackson, Bill McKibben, Daniel Meltzer, Ellen Semonoff, Robert Shapiro, William Shawn, and the late Charles Wyzanski. Raphael Sagalyn served as a first-rate agent for this project, and his assistants, Deborah Billig and Ann Sleeper, proved to be mine as well. At Knopf, Ashbel Green edited my manuscript and, with tact and intelligence, guided me to tell as well as I could the story I found in my reporting. Mildred Maynard and Melvin Rosenthal copy-edited the manuscript, and they skillfully improved the substance and presentation of this book. At *The New Yorker,* with verve and clarity, Robert Gottlieb helped me streamline the book into a two-part series of articles; Patrick Crow gave me excellent and welcome editorial counsel; and Richard Sacks carefully checked my assertions of fact and, very much a colleague, did much to ensure the book's accuracy.

There are several more people whom I'd like to include on this list, and to thank publicly for their help. But because of the nature of their current or past jobs, we've agreed that I should not mention them by name. I owe deep thanks to two in particular. They are both fine and insightful teachers, assiduously balanced in their judgments, and they exemplify in their work the commitment to the law represented by the SG's office at its best.

Finally, I want to thank my family. My parents, Lewis and Jane Caplan, encouraged me to make my way as a writer and to find the confidence to try a project as challenging as this. My sisters Joanna and Margi gave me strong and constant support. My brother-in-law Bob Blaemire guided my reading about some key questions of politics and law. My nephew Nicky was a wonderful companion on afternoons when the rest of the world seemed hard at work and I needed a break from mine. My cousin Dorothy Leavitt carefully read an earlier version of this book, and gave me valuable suggestions on how to improve it.

Most of all, my wife, Susan, to whom this book is dedicated, gave me help as a keen and patient editor, and spurred me on with faith and love.

L.C.

Index

Lincoln Caplan's first book was *The Insanity Defense and the Trial of John W. Hinckley, Jr.* As published in *The New Yorker*, it won in 1985 the American Bar Association's Silver Gavel Award, presented annually to works that make "an outstanding contribution to public understanding" of American law. Mr. Caplan was born in New Haven, Connecticut, in 1950, was graduated from Harvard College and Harvard Law School, and is a former White House Fellow. He is a frequent contributor to *The New Yorker* and has written for the Baltimore *Sun*, the Los Angeles *Times*, the *New York Times*, and the Washington *Post*, among other publications. He lives with his wife in Washington, D.C.

A NOTE ON THE TYPE

The text of this book was set in a digitized version of Janson,
a typeface long thought to have been made by the Dutchman
Anton Janson, who was a practicing type founder in Leipzig
during the years 1668–1687. However, it has been conclusively
demonstrated that these types are actually the work of
Nicholas Kis (1650–1702), a Hungarian, who most probably
learned his trade from the master Dutch type founder
Dirk Voskens. The type is an excellent example of the
influential and sturdy Dutch types that prevailed in
England up to the time William Caslon developed his own
incomparable designs from them.

Composed by The Haddon Craftsmen, Inc.,
Allentown, Pennsylvania
Printed and bound by R. R. Donnelley & Sons,
Harrisonburg, Virginia
DESIGNED BY PETER A. ANDERSEN